Working Americans
1898–2016

Volume XIV: African Americans

WORKING AMERICANS
1898–2016

Volume XIV: African Americans
First Edition

based on material from
Working Americans series by Scott Derks

A UNIVERSAL REFERENCE BOOK

Grey House
Publishing

PUBLISHER: Leslie Mackenzie
EDITORIAL DIRECTOR: Laura Mars
CONTRIBUTOR: Elaine Alibrandi
PRODUCTION MANAGER: Kristen Thatcher
MARKETING DIRECTOR: Jessica Moody
COMPOSITION: David Garoogian

Grey House Publishing, Inc.
4919 Route 22
Amenia, NY 12501
518.789.8700
FAX 845.373.6390
www.greyhouse.com
e-mail: books @greyhouse.com

Publisher's Cataloging-In-Publication Data
(Prepared by The Donohue Group, Inc.)

Names: Derks, Scott. | Smith, Tony (Charles Anthony), 1969–
Title: Working Americans ... / by Scott Derks.

Description: First edition. | Millerton, N.Y. : Grey House Publishing, [2000]- | Title varies. | "A universal reference book." | Additional author for Vol. 9: Tony Smith. | Some volumes contain material based on content published in prior volumes of the series. | Includes bibliographical references and indexes. | Contents: v. 1. The working class — v. 2. The middle class — v. 3. The upper class — v. 4. Their children — v. 5. At war — v. 6. Women at work — v. 7. Social movements — v. 8. Immigrants — v. 9. From the Revolutionary War to the Civil War — v. 10. Sports & recreation — v. 11. Inventors & entrepreneurs — v. 12. Our history through music — v. 13. Educators & education— v. 14. African Americans.

Identifiers: ISBN 1891482815 (v. 1) | ISBN 1891482726 (v. 2) | ISBN 193095638X (v. 3) | ISBN 1930956355 (v. 4) | ISBN 1592370241 (v. 5) | ISBN 1592370632 (v. 6) | ISBN 9781592371013 (v. 7) | ISBN 9781592371976 (v. 8) | ISBN 9781592373710 (v. 9) | ISBN 9781592374410 (v. 10) | 9781592375653 (v. 11) | 9781592371013 (v. 12) | 9781592378777 (v. 13) | 9781682171066 (v. 14)

Subjects: LCSH: Working class—United States—History. | Labor—United States—History. | Occupations—United States—History. | Social classes—United States—History. | United States—Economic conditions.

Classification: LCC HD8066 .D47 2000 | DDC 305.5/0973/0904—dc23

Table of Contents

1960-1979

1980-1999

Introduction

This first edition of *Working Americans: African Americans 1898-2016* is the 14th volume in the *Working Americans* series. Its 30 profiles of African Americans span 118 years. Like the other volumes in this series, this work observes the lives of working Americans—African Americans in this case—decade by decade. It covers all ages, a wide range of geographical and social backgrounds, and a vast variety of professions, some of which focus on fortune, some on fame, some on a regular paycheck, and some on no paycheck at all. But all profiles, each supported by dozens of images, demonstrate the challenges faced by African Americans, from musicians to athletes to civil rights advocates to members of the military.

Each 12-15 page profile starts with a brief introduction and photograph of the subject, then moves to three bulleted sections: **Life at Home** details what life was like in the home of those individuals profiled, with spouses, children, or parents. It might include what their house looked like, what kind of food they ate, what their daily routine was, and how they dressed. **Life at Work** details typical workday activities, from office to factory, from performance stage to teacher's desk. It includes work environments, attitudes, and relationships with co-workers. **Life in the Community** offers insight into the individual's community, or neighborhood. This section often includes some geographical and social history, as well as a sense of the area's economy and recreational opportunities.

Following these sections, **Historical Snapshots** are interesting collections of firsts and significant events that happened in the year profiled. Then, **Selected Prices** offers a number of everyday items, from violin to hotel room, and what they cost. This is followed by **Primary Sources**—magazine and newspaper articles, speeches, letters and diary entries. These original reprints help put the life of the profiled individual into historical context.

Following the 30 profiles, the back matter of *Working Americans: African Americans* includes:
- Census Brief statistics of the Black Population—24 pages of facts, figures, maps and charts;
- Snapshot of 2016 African Americans statistics in several major categories—jobs, business, education, income, health insurance, income, families, and more;

- Further Reading section;
- Detailed Index.

Like the other volumes in this series, *African Americans* is a compilation of original research—personal diaries, school files, family histories—combined with government statistics, commercial advertisements and news features. The text is presented in easy-to-read bulleted format, and supported by hundreds of graphics, from personal photographs to national campaign advertisements.

This volume celebrates the contributions of African Americans, chronicling both the progress they have made and the roadblocks they have faced. In a detailed fashion, this content helps the reader reflect on civil liberties, the civil rights movement, and the day-to-day lives of African Americans over the last 118 years.

The study of history offers all of us the opportunity to view change over time. The actions and contributions of one generation are rarely lost on the next. *Working Americans: African Americans* presents an engaging way to study the progress of African Americans in today's society.

1898: African American Wood Turner

George Patterson made a living creating handsome and durable plow handles in Farmville, Virginia, where his wife and oldest daughter, Sarah, worked as stemmers in a tobacco factory.

Life at Home

- The Pattersons rented a two-room home; the living room was on the first floor and the kitchen on the second. The staircase was open. The monthly rent was $3.00.
- George and Anna hoped to buy a lot near their home for $50.00 and build a three-room house, which would cost $300.00 to $500.00, depending upon how much work the family was able to do itself.
- George had applied to a building association in Farmville comprising white and black shareholders for assistance with financing the home; George had an excellent employment record, and so the association had agreed to help.
- George maintained a large vegetable garden to supplement the family diet and bring in a little extra cash during the summertime, when he was able to sell some of the produce.
- The foundry where George worked operated only when there were orders waiting; usually George worked 32 weeks a year.
- The other 20 weeks each year, while laid off, he fished, hunted, and tended the garden.
- The family kept chickens for eggs and meat; the children had the responsibility of caring for the chickens.
- Anna's mother had died when Anna was only two years old, so her father had raised her. As she recalled, "I had to work."
- "I learnt how to cook when I wasn't big enough to reach the stove. When I was little, my father used to carry me to the field with him and put me in a basket and sit me under a tree while he worked."
- The Patterson children, like all children in the community, had grown up working with their

George Patterson made plow handles in Virginia.

1

parents or else on a neighboring farm, where they were especially needed at planting time and at the harvest.

- The surveyor of Farmville found that many residents, including the Pattersons, could not answer the question "age at nearest birthday," because few vital records had been kept.
- The children attended school for approximately 109 days a year.
- None of the Patterson children-all of whom were under the age of 16, although Sarah was close-had yet married, breaking a pattern of early marriages or cohabitation set during slavery days and among the first generation of freedmen.
- In the Farmville community, about 42 percent of the people could read and write, 17.5 percent could read but not write, and 40 percent were "wholly illiterate." The literacy status of a small segment of the community was unknown.
- The Pattersons enjoyed reading *Demorest's Family Magazine*; Anna removed many of the color prints from the magazine and mounted them on the walls of their home.

The Pattersons enjoyed magazines and their colorful prints.

- She also liked *The Ladies' Home Journal,* which was very popular in the community because of its sewing and fashion tips.
- Black dolls for children had been manufactured in Germany since the early 1890s; they were widely available through advertisements in *Youth's Companion Magazine.*

Life at Work

- The woodworking foundry where George was employed was chiefly concerned with the turning of plow handles.
- The plow handles were turned on a mechanical lathe that required George to stand all day.
- The foundry employed ten black and four white mechanics, paying them from $0.75 to $1.00 a day "without discrimination."
- Anna worked as a stemmer in the tobacco sheds, where Sarah had recently joined her after leaving school.
- The manufacture of tobacco strips required separating the dry tobacco leaf from its woody stem.
- Loose tobacco was taken to the factory and placed on the floor according to grade, style, and quality.
- Once enough of a certain grade or style had been gathered into a "hogshead of strips," it was taken to another room and sprinkled and steamed, a little at a time.
- The bundles were stemmed once the leaves became supple and pliant.

- Women and young men drew out the stems, and children then tied the strips of tobacco into uniform bundles.
- These bundles were weighed, stretched on sticks, and hung up in the drying room for eight to ten hours.
- When thoroughly dried and cooled, the tobacco was again steamed as it hung and then cooled for two days. Finally, it was steamed a third time, in a steam box; straightened; and packed into a container known as a hogshead.
- Women who stemmed the tobacco were paid $0.50 for every hundred pounds of stemmed tobacco; with the aid of children, they could stem from 100 to 300 pounds a day.
- Anna made $6.00 a week for stemming about 200 pounds per day over a six-day week; Sarah, being relatively new to the task, was not yet as deft as her mother.
- Other women laborers received $0.35 to $0.40 a day.
- Children were often kept out of school for all or part of the harvest time to help with the factory work.
- Men who steamed and "prized" tobacco (packed the tobacco into hogsheads) received from $0.75 to $1.00 a day.

Life in the Community: Farmville, Virginia

- Farmville, Virginia, was located within Prince Edward County, near the center of Virginia. It produced seven-eighths of the tobacco crop of the state.
- Farmville, the county seat, was a market town of 2,500 inhabitants on the upper waters of the Appomattox.

- Agriculture dominated the economy of the county, tobacco being the leading crop, followed by corn, wheat, oats, and potatoes.
- More than 70 percent of the farms in the county were cultivated by their owners; 31 percent of the farms were fewer than 50 acres in size.
- The county's population in 1890 was more than 14,000; of that total, more than 9,000 were black and 5,000 white. At the time of the Civil War, the slave property of the county was valued at $2.5 million.
- The town was three-fifths African American; that fraction had been growing since 1850.
- An emerging African American middle class played a key economic role in the life of the community.
- After 1890, however, the black population had begun to decline because of the "Great Migration" of African Americans to the cities-principally Richmond, Norfolk, Baltimore, and New York.
- As a result of this emigration, Farmville's population included fewer persons aged 20 to 30 than might have been expected.
- The town's public buildings included an opera house, a normal school (teachers' college) for white girls, a courthouse and a jail, a bank, and a depot.
- The only school for black children was a large frame building with five rooms. The school term extended to six months, from September 15 to April 1.
- A teacher's salary averaged $30.00 a month, which restricted the competition for this job to residents of the town.
- Between the ages of 5 and 15 years, boys and girls attended school in the same proportions. After that, however, the boys generally dropped out to go to work.
- Of the 205 children who attended the school in 1896-1897, only 52 percent attended the full term of six months. Thirty-three percent attended half the term. Eleven percent stayed in school for less than three months.
- The Farmville area was described as having "good" air and an "abundance of lithia and sulphur waters, which now and then attract visitors."
- Farmville was the trading center for six counties; on Saturday, the regular market day, the town population swelled to nearly twice its normal size, "from the influx of county people-mostly Negroes-some in carriages, wagons, and ox carts, and some on foot."

A former slave owned the area's brickmaking business.

- Of the 459 African American working men in Farmville, 128 worked in the tobacco factory, 58 were laborers, 17 were porters, 14 worked for the canning factory, 10 worked in wood turning, 6 were coopers (barrel makers), five were barbers, and three peddled candy.
- The women were largely confined to jobs as domestic servants, teachers, day laborers, or tobacco and canning factory employees.
- Domestic servants ordinarily received $4.00 per month; a cook made $5.00 per month.
- Farmville's African Americans conducted some business enterprises entirely on their own, including a brickyard, groceries, barbershops, restaurants, a lumberyard, a whipmaking shop, a steam laundry, a hotel, and farms.
- The brickmaking business of Farmville was owned by a former slave who bought his own and his family's freedom, purchased his former master's estate, and eventually hired his former master to work for him. He owned a thousand acres of land in the county and a considerable number of buildings.

Anna Patterson worked as a stemmer in a tobacco factory.

- In his brickyard this very successful African American entrepreneur employed about 15 hands, mostly boys from 16 to 20 years of age. The brickyard ran five or six months a year, making 200,000 to 300,000 bricks. The employees received $12.00 a month and extra pay for extra work.
- More than half of the brick homes in the area were made with bricks from this establishment, and this entrepreneur repeatedly drove white competitors out of business.
- The next-wealthiest African American in the town was a barber who reportedly was worth about ten thousand dollars. There were five barbershops in the community-three for whites and two for blacks-and all were run by African Americans.
- In the years after Emancipation, many former slaves who had been house servants turned to barbering and restaurant management.
- The income of a barber varied from $5.00 to $15.00 a week.
- The position of preacher was the most influential of all positions in the community; of the two leading preachers in town, one was paid $480.00 a year plus house rent; the other made $600.00 a year.
- The economic importance of Farmville's African American population had brought many white men to call the preachers and teachers "mister" and to raise their hats to their wives.
- The African American town jailer was also a wood merchant, a whipmaker, and a farmer. His younger daughters were being educated at the Virginia Seminary in Lynchburg, a coeducational Baptist school for African American students.

- Many in the Farmville community were sharecroppers. Sharecropping, which grew out of conditions in the post-Civil War period, made it possible for planters to obtain labor without paying wages and for landless farmers to get soil without buying it or paying rent in cash.
- The lack of capital still impacted growth in Farmville, as well as elsewhere throughout the South.
- Only 47 national banks existed in the ten "cotton states" of the South, and many counties in Virginia had no banking facilities at all.
- The highly risky business of agriculture entailed competing for what little money was available.
- The unique credit institution that emerged to fill the gap was the country store: the country store merchant performed the functions of the banker for large and small farm owners.
- Sharecroppers' landlords had to furnish teams, tools, food, clothing, and shelter; the tenants produced the crops.
- The landowner seldom had sufficient cash on hand to cover these costs; cash was provided by the merchant, normally using the planter's share of the crop as a security pledge.
- Merchants often demanded that the sharecroppers grow "cash crops" such as cotton or tobacco-not vegetables-to improve their chances of being repaid.

HISTORICAL SNAPSHOT
1898-1899

- The "grandfather" clause marched across the South, restricting most Blacks from voting, and ushering in discriminatory "Jim Crow" laws

- Union Carbide Company was founded

- Motorcar production reached 1,000 per year

- Goodyear Tire and Rubber Company was founded

- The *New York Times* dropped its price from $0.03 to $0.01; circulation tripled

- Pepsi-Cola was introduced by a New Bern, North Carolina, pharmacist

- Uneeda Biscuits was created

- J.P. Stevens & Company was founded in New York

- The trolley replaced horse cars in Boston

- Wesson Oil was developed

- United Mine Workers of America was founded

- The boll weevil began spreading across cotton-growing Southern states

- Virginia continued to experience an influx of Scots-Irish farmers

1898 ECONOMIC PROFILE

Income, Standard Jobs

Bricklayers .... $3.41/day/48 hrs.
per week

Engineers .... $3.17/day/60 hrs.
per week

Glassblowers .... $3.97/day/54 hrs.
per week

Hod Carriers .... $1.97/day/48 hrs.
per week

Marble Cutters .... $4.22/day/48 hrs.
per week

Painters .... $2.47/day/50 hrs.
per week

Plumbers .... $3.74/day/48 hrs.
per week

Stonemasons .... $3.67/day/48 hrs.
per week

Selected Prices

Ayers Cherry Pectoral, for Coughs....... $1.00

Boy's Knee Pants $0.50

Bucklen's Arivica Salve for All Skin
    Eruptions $0.25

Canfield Baby Diaper $0.65

Cleveland Baking Powder............. $0.15

Cookie and Biscuit Cutter $0.15

Crackers, Baby Educator, Six in a Box.... $0.20

Dongola Button Shoes for Women....... $1.50

Gossamer Powder.................... $0.25

Insecticide, Tough on Flies, per Quart $1.00

Madonna Yarn, 25-Gram Ball $0.15

Man's Keep's Collar, Four-Ply Linen $0.15

Modene Hair Remover, for Face,
    Neck, Arms...................... $1.00

Paper Dolls, Set of Three, Two Girls,
    One Boy $0.15

Perfection Flour, Half Barrel $2.50

Salada Ceylon Tea, per Pound $0.50

Sewing Needles, Package of Four....... $0.25

Shingles, per Thousand................ $2.00

Stereoscopic Pictures, See the World,
    One Dozen...................... $1.50

Vegetable Seeds, Six Varieties.......... $0.25

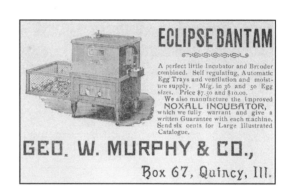

"Rural Free Delivery," by Max Bennet Thrasher:

"The reasons given for the opposition (to rural free delivery of mail) were generally that small local offices at a distance from the railroads would be discontinued, and the patrons did not believe they would be so satisfactorily served by the new arrangement. I think this feeling arose in the main from the rather common distrust of any innovation, especially when it has to do with an institution so old and respected as the post office. Moreover, the local office is usually located in a country store. The merchant, fearing that the doing away with the office will injure this trade, argues that it ought to be retained, and arrays on his side all those who are attached to him by friendship or by accounts of more or less longstanding on the store's ledger."

Insurance through the Trade Unions:

"Insurance, an important part of a worker's life and expenditures, was often provided by associates or craft guilds. The International Wood Carvers' Association of North America, for example, was organized in 1883 and boasted a membership of 1,800 on April 30, 1898. A benefit of $50 is paid on the death of a member. The total death benefits paid from January 1, 1897, to January 11, 1898, amounted to $1,850. Tool insurance, not to exceed $30.00 was also provided for. Only a national convention vote of all the locals can authorize the spending of the funds of the national body for strikes. The strike benefit is $6 a week for single men and $8.00 a week for married men. The union numbered only 700 members in 1897. In a similar fashion, the Sailors' Union of the Pacific was founded March 6, 1885. The membership on January 1, 1898, was 1,471. In 1897, $750 was spent for shipwreck benefit and $310.45 for the relief of the sick and burial of the dead."

1913: Young Singer of Spirituals

Sarah Washington grew up surrounded by the sounds of her mother singing "the old songs"—spirituals employing new words for old tunes that bridged the past and present.

Life at Home

- Sarah Washington was born into a desperately impoverished area of Denmark, South Carolina, in 1897.
- Yet she only learned she was poor at age nine, when she visited her rich cousins in Sumter, South Carolina.
- Sarah was astonished that one cousin owned three dresses and two pairs of shoes and could draw water from a pump inside the kitchen.
- While on the same trip, she saw a building that actually had electricity and would light up at night.
- More important, she became aware of the good things in her own life.
- Sarah quickly decided that her own church in Denmark was much more fun than her cousins' in Sumter.
- The people in Sumter were too dignified to sing and clap and dance; in Denmark, Sarah loved nothing more than being swept away by the magical singing of a praise meeting.
- Sarah decided right then she liked best a God who permitted his worshipers to make a loud, joyful noise.
- Besides, there was no reason that the devil should have all the best tunes.
- She didn't care that her cousins looked down on spirituals, seeing them as associated with "slave ways"; spiritual singing was meant to be fun.
- At home Sarah's mother daily breathed fresh life into the old spirituals.
- If the water turned sour, that dilemma joined the song being sung; when the rain arrived in sheets, that, too, was added; and if the cotton crop was excellent, her mother's jubilation came alive in song.
- In this way a spiritual tune was always under construction in Sarah's house.

Sarah Washington

- As one of 11 children, Sarah didn't have to be told when the crops were poor and money tight.
- Between planting season, deer season, sicknesses of her younger brothers and sisters, and demands that she help at home, Sarah rarely attended school more than 60 days a year.
- Sarah learned all the standard spirituals from the neighborhood ladies: "Deep River," Nobody Knows the Trouble I've Seen," "Little David Play Yo' Harp," and "Shout All Over God's Heab'n."
- Then she created her own spiritual songs—most dwelling on the woes she encountered herself—using the familiar biblical allusions, carefully crafted during the days of slavery.
- "Then Moses said to Israel/When they stood upon the shore/'Your enemy you see today/You will never see no more'/Old Pharoah and his host/Got lost in the Red Sea."
- Now that she was turning 16 and was ready to leave school, Sarah knew that her future included marriage, babies, and more farm work.
- But she wanted to sing spirituals.

Sarah didn't realize how poor she was until she visited a city.

Life at Work

- Spirituals and spiritual singing arrived in North America with the first African slaves, who were snatched from their homelands and deposited—with all their customs, habits, and aspirations—on the isolated plantations of the South.
- Over time, African rhythms blended with English words, and songs evolved—drenched in pain, expressing a yearning for freedom, and filled with double meanings.

City life was astounding for Sarah.

- Many spirituals were used to communicate escape plans or safe routes, or simply to convey resentment against the slave owner.
- Historically spirituals constituted a living folk art, with no authors, composers, or lyricists; nothing was written down, and spirituals had no fixed or authoritative text.
- Spirituals belonged to the community.
- Writer W. E. B. Du Bois called spirituals "sorrow songs," "the music of an unhappy people, of the children of disappointment; they tell of death and suffering and unvoiced longing toward a truer world."

- Spirituals were improvisational.
- Usually a lead singer sang one line and the others would repeat it or reply with a familiar chorus in an antiphony.
- Anyone could add new verses, and the best of those survived through a kind of musical natural selection.
- When singing spirituals, there was no separation between artist and audience, no distinction between creator and performer.
- The religious music of African-Americans also included the ring shout, the song sermon, the Jubilee, and the Gospel song.
- The ring shout survived because it did not violate the Protestant prohibitions against dancing and drumming, yet a ring shout is "danced" with the whole body, including hands, feet, and hips.
- The most common spirituals employed the call-and-response pattern, which Sarah's mother had perfected.

Sarah's schoolmates

- The songs most familiar to white audiences—"Nobody Knows the Trouble I've Seen," "Go Down Moses," and "Swing Low, Sweet Chariot"—represented a mixture of European and African music.
- Many of the songs had strong biblical allusions, especially to popular Old Testament stories that included conquest and personal achievement.
- "He delivered David from de lion's den/Jonah from de belly of de whale/And de Hebrew children from de fiery furnace/Why not everything, man?"
- An early custom of the rural African American church was "lining out" the song, whereby the preacher read the words before the congregation sang them.
- Over time, in the churches where hymn books were few and literacy low, the congregation learned the words by heart.
- Musically, this folk style of singing allowed everyone to sing the tune in unison without concern for harmony.
- Spirituals came to the attention of the non-African American public in the 1860s after they were described in popular publications such as the *Atlantic Monthly*, and in 1867 they were collected into a book, *Slave Songs for the United States*.
- In 1871 the Fisk Jubilee Singers, of Fisk College in Nashville, Tennessee, began to spread the message of spirituals through their nationwide tours, establishing spirituals in the national consciousness.
- In addition to raising enough funds to keep the college open, the Fisk Jubilee Singers popularized the "Negro spiritual" as a genre and made it part of American popular culture.
- Thanks to the presence in Denmark of a school for African Americans called Voorhees, Sarah saw an opportunity to avoid the trap of a too-early marriage and a plan to realize her desire to sing spirituals.
- The financially struggling Voorhees, created in the image of Booker T. Washington's famed Tuskegee Institute, was founded on the principle of self-help.

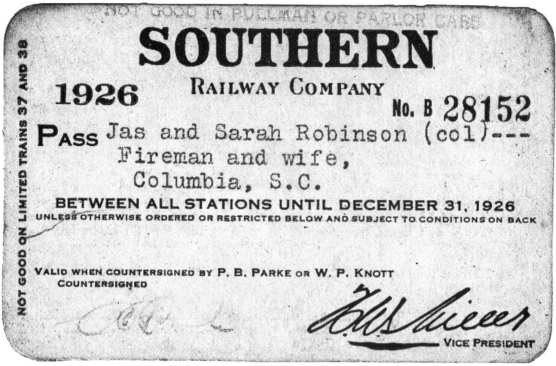

A train pass for an African American couple

- What if, Sarah asked herself, she could form a touring spiritual singing group similar to the Fisk Jubilee Singers that would support the college and herself?
- Already she had organized the youth choir of her church and an all-girl choir school, and she spent most of her days dreaming up new words for old songs.
- Why not, indeed?
- Voorhees was envisioned and created by Elizabeth Evelyn Wright, who was 23 when she came to Bamberg County.
- A native of Georgia, Wright had found her inspiration while studying at Tuskegee Institute.
- Tuskegee gave her a mission in life: being "the same type of woman as Mr. Washington was of a man."
- Knowing the importance of education, Wright moved to South Carolina with the intention of establishing schools for African Americans in the rural areas.
- She survived repeated threats, attacks, and arson.
- In April 1893 Wright's first attempt at creating a school for blacks—in McNeill, South Carolina, where she had gone at the invitation of Mrs. Almira Steele, a white trustee at Tuskegee—ended in a blazing fire.
- Wright's second attempt in McNeill ended when an arsonist, opposed to secondary education for African Americans, burned all the lumber purchased for a new building.
- Then, when she negotiated the purchase of a property in McNeill with existing buildings, all the buildings on the land were torched.
- Convinced that education was the path to black prosperity, Wright moved her vision to Denmark, eight miles from the new county seat of Bamberg.
- There, with the aid of Stanwix G. Mayfield, a leading white state senator, and a recommendation letter from Booker T. Washington, Wright founded the Denmark Industrial School in 1897—the year Sarah was born.

- Operating on the second floor of a general store building in the Sato district of Denmark, the school was modeled on Tuskegee.
- Only 14 students enrolled the first year, but in 1898 the school had 270 students.
- New Jersey philanthropist Ralph Voorhees and his wife donated $5,000 to buy the land and construct the first building of the school's permanent home; the school opened there in 1902.
- It was the only high school and industrial school for blacks in the area and soon was named Voorhees Industrial School to honor its primary benefactors.
- Wright, who had suffered from ill health during her time in Tuskegee, died at John Harvey Kellogg's Battle Creek, Michigan, sanitarium in December 1906, at age 34.
- About the same time Vorhees was founded, black urban intellectuals were beginning to bemoan the potential loss of spiritual singing, predicting that, as the literacy increased throughout the South, the old ways would be lost.
- Yet the crushing oppression of Jim Crow laws, designed to strip African Americans of most of their rights, was having an opposite impact: rural blacks, suffering more, were singing more, not less.
- By 1913 the notorious "black codes" of Jim Crow—state and local laws and regulations intended to oppress African Americans and keep them in a condition little better than slavery—had strengthened the African American church, especially the rural African American church.
- The African American church was the one institution white society couldn't touch.
- There black preachers, black deacons, and black women in huge hats held uncontested sway at least one day a week.
- Sarah understood that the singing of spirituals and gospel songs, rooted in the churches, was essential to African Americans' celebration of life.
- Sarah proposed to the leaders of Voorhees that a touring choir be formed from among its students and faculty.
- Her plan was for the first gathering of the Voorhees Jubilee Voices to take place in Columbia, South Carolina, the state capital, where a large paying audience was available.
- Her goal was to earn $100 for Vorhees, enough to prove her ability.
- Within days, the college was buzzing about the young girl who wanted to duplicate the success of the Fisk Jubilee Singers; many people, however, were discomfited that one so young had gained the initiative.
- Within a week Sarah had talked her uncle into driving her the 45 miles to Columbia in his horse and buggy.
- Three Baptist preachers in Columbia agreed to help launch the Voorhees Jubilee Voices—provided their choir could sing, also.
- Two more choirs were added later in the week, and suddenly Sarah was in charge of the biggest songfest—it would feature 120 singers—in years.
- Several attempts to push her aside were made by the more experienced men, but Sarah refused to budge.
- Instead she focused on building a still-bigger network and leading the newly created Voorhees Jubilee Voices.
- One of the more challenging aspects of her task was to get everyone to agree on a repertoire in which words would actually be sung.
- A former teacher got her a travel pass that allowed her to ride the train to Columbia; it carried the teacher's name, address, and racial designation: "col," for "colored."
- Three weeks before the event, Sarah actually persuaded the state newspaper to write a story about the coming "Negro spiritual gathering"—a feat the black Baptist ministers had declared to be impossible.

- Three days before the event, Sarah took her uncle's horse and buggy to Columbia, along with her supplies, convinced she would need the time to decorate the church.
- But two days were consumed simply in getting there; rain washed out roads and frightened her horse.
- Sarah slept in the buggy one night in the pouring rain, since no other accommodations were available, and she knew no one.
- Wet, cold, and insecure, Sarah arrived in Columbia on the morning of the big event to find the ministers energized, the choirs prepared, and more than 500 tickets sold at $0.25 each.
- First, she broke into tears—and then she broke into song.
- And the entire gathering joined in "Go Down, Moses."
- The event itself was a dream; the choirs and choir leaders meshed well, the audience was engaged, and the music was, Sarah thought, heavenly.
- Scheduled to last two hours, the concert lasted three.
- No one wanted the music to stop.

Life in the Community: Denmark, South Carolina

- In 1913 Denmark, South Carolina, was a farming community of approximately 750 people, evenly divided between whites and blacks.
- The town was originally known as Graham; it was named after the Z. G. Graham family, which sold 17 acres to the Charleston-Hamburg Railroad in 1837 for a rail siding named Graham's Turnout.
- By 1913 three railway companies crisscrossed the town, the name of which had been changed to Denmark, after a major railway promoter.

Denmark, South Carolina

Three railroads operated in the town.

- Cotton dominated the fields of South Carolina in 1913; cotton's value was greater than that of all other South Carolina agricultural products combined.
- Cotton production in the Palmetto State rose from 224,000 bales in 1870 to nearly one million in 1913.
- At the same time, rice production fell dramatically in the coastal regions of the state, as mechanized farming in the Southwestern states proved to give them a competitive advantage.
- "Bright leaf" tobacco—a gold-leafed variety, less vigorous than the commonly used darker variety, that thrived on poor soils and was flue-cured—was introduced into the state in the 1890s and transformed agriculture in the region, thanks to a boom in tobacco usage accompanying the introduction of machine-made cigarettes.
- But after the Civil War and into the 1900s, farmers' lives were most affected by the expansion of South Carolina railroad system.
- Nearly every town in the state was connected to others by rail.
- The time and energy required to get supplies in, and crops out, was dramatically decreased.
- Road improvements began in 1895, after the state legislature permitted counties to use convict labor to do the work.
- By 1913 the state had more than 20,000 automobiles.
- Overall the biggest economic change was the growth of textile manufacturing, which employed cheap white labor drawn from a pool of poor rural farmers eager to escape the vagaries and isolation of agricultural life.
- Public education, for blacks and whites, remained a low priority; in the rural areas, the typical school operated for only a few months a year.
- In 1907 the legislature allocated $8.00 per white enrollee annually and $1.57 per black pupil.
- In the same year, state-supported high schools for whites were created; no high schools were funded for African Americans.
- In 1911 the state's first rural elementary school superintendent reported, "The Negro schoolhouses are miserable beyond description…most of the teachers are absolutely untrained."

HISTORICAL SNAPSHOT
1913

- Delta Sigma Theta Sorority was founded on the campus of Howard University
- A rebuilt Grand Central Terminal in New York City opened as the world's largest train station
- The Sixteenth Amendment to the Constitution was ratified, authorizing the federal government to impose and collect income taxes
- The Armory Show opened in New York City, featuring cutting-edge artwork that both excited and repelled critics
- Woodrow Wilson succeeded William Howard Taft to become the 28th President of the United States
- The U.S. Department of Commerce and U.S. Department of Labor were established by splitting the duties of the 10-year-old Department of Commerce and Labor
- The first U.S. law regulating the shooting of migratory birds was passed
- In the First Battle of Bud Dajo, American troops decisively defeated Moro rebels in the Philippines
- The Seventeenth Amendment to the Constitution was passed, providing for the direct election of senators
- The Woolworth Building opened in New York City
- Mary Phagan was raped and strangled on the premises of the National Pencil Factory in Atlanta; Jewish supervisor Leo Frank was tried and convicted for the highly sensationalized crime
- Swedish engineer Gideon Sundback of Hoboken patented an all-purpose zipper
- The Paul Émile Chabas painting *September Morn* created a national sensation concerning nudity and censorship
- New York Governor William Sulzer approved the charter for the Rockefeller Foundation, which began operations with a $100 million donation from John D. Rockefeller
- The Arab Congress of 1913 opened, during which Arab nationalists met to discuss desired reforms under the Ottoman Empire
- The fiftieth anniversary commemoration of the Battle of Gettysburg drew thousands of Civil War veterans and their families to Gettysburg, Pennsylvania
- Stainless steel was invented by Harry Brearley in Sheffield, England
- President Woodrow Wilson triggered the explosion of the Gamboa Dike, ending construction on the Panama Canal
- The Lincoln Highway, the first automobile road across the United States, was dedicated
- Ford Motor Company introduced the first moving assembly line, reducing chassis assembly time from 12 and a half hours to two hours, 40 minutes
- The first crossword puzzle was published in the *New York World*
- The Federal Reserve was created
- The Anti-Defamation League was founded
- The Camel cigarette brand was introduced by R. J. Reynolds in the United States, the first packaged cigarette

Selected Prices

Baby Walker...$2.75
Cake Turner $0.02
Egg Incubator and Brooder.....................................$10.00
Inlaid Linoleum, per Yard.......................................$2.35
Phonograph Record $0.65
Piano, Steinway Baby Grand.............................$2,000.00
Toilet Paper, Six Rolls $0.27
Trunk...$16.95
Tuition, Harvard University, per Year $150.00
Umbrella $2.74

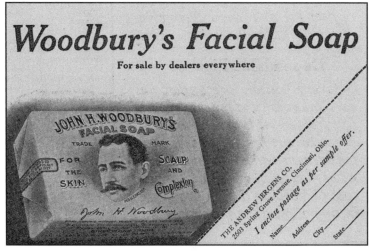

Booker T. Washington Quotations:

The plantation songs known as "spirituals" are the spontaneous outburst of intense religious fervor.... They breathe a childlike faith in a personal Father, and glow with the hope that the children of bondage will ultimately pass out of the wilderness of slavery into the land of freedom. In singing of a deliverance which they believed would surely come, with bodies swaying, with the enthusiasm born of a common experience and of a common hope, they lost sight for the moment of the auction block, of the separation of mother and child, of sister and brother. There is in the plantation songs the pathos and the beauty that appeals to a wide range of tastes, and their harmony makes abiding impressions upon persons of the highest culture. The music of these songs goes to the heart because it comes from the heart.

No race can prosper till it learns that there is as much dignity in tilling a field as in writing a poem.

Nothing ever comes to one that is worth having except as a result of hard work.

One man cannot hold another man down in the ditch without remaining down in the ditch with him.

Success in life is founded upon attention to the small things rather than to the large things, to the everyday things nearest to us rather than to the things that are remote and uncommon.

Success is to be measured not so much by the position that one has reached in life as by the obstacles which he has overcome.

The individual who can do something that the world wants done will, in the end, make his way regardless of his race.

There are two ways of exerting one's strength: one is pushing down, the other is pulling up.

Spiritual: "Going to Set Down and Rest Awhile"

Going to set down and rest awhile
When my good Lord calls me.

Sister Mary went to heaven
And she went there to stay
And she didn't go to come back no more.

She sang a song that the angels couldn't sing
"Hosanna, carry on."

Little children, don't you moan,
When my good Lord calls me.
O, Zion!
When my good Lord calls me.

Spiritual: "Changed My Name"

I tol' Jesus it would be all right
If He changed mah name

Jesus tol' me I would have to live humble
If He changed mah name

Jesus tol' me that the world would be 'gainst me
If He changed mah name

But I tol' Jesus it would be all right
If He changed mah name

Imagery in Plantation-Based Spirituals:

Satan = slave owner
King Jesus = slave benefactor
Babylon = winter
Hell = traveling farther south
Jordan (River) = first steps to freedom
Israelites = enslaved African-Americans
Egyptians = slaveholders
Canaan = land of freedom
Heaven = Canada or points north
Home = Africa

1916: African American U.S. Army Major

Major Rudy West was called upon to lead his men into Mexico and capture bandit and political leader Pancho Villa, whose men had killed 19 Americans during a raid in New Mexico.

Life at Home

- Rudy West grew up on the Illinois side of the Mississippi River, near St. Louis, in the community of Belleville.
- He was the youngest son of a minister and blacksmith and his seamstress wife; they had been born slaves but learned to read, and they valued God, hard work, education, and a little savings under the mattress.
- They taught their youngest child to love learning, sports, and music.
- Rudy spent many happy hours playing the battered keyboard of an upright piano at his father's church.
- Although Rudy was an excellent student, few opportunities were available to him beyond his community school.
- Then he learned about West Point.
- While working as a clerk in an insurance company, he read that his congressman was holding competitive exams for an appointment to the United States Military Academy at West Point.
- Few blacks had ever attended the academy, and fewer still had graduated.
- Relatives warned him about racism—being ostracized and even hated and cursed.
- During the midst of a community prayer meeting, the call came from the Lord, Rudy believed, to take the exam.
- After a tense day of test-taking in a drafty hall with a dozen white candidates, Rudy learned his score was the highest—the appointment was his!
- Passing the academy's entrance exam was all that lay ahead.
- His family and members of the congregation pooled their money for the trip to West Point and to hire a tutor to prepare him for the test.
- Instead of offering hostility and harassment, the other prospective cadets simply ignored him.

Major Rudy West

Rudy was sent to the Southwest in 1916.

- After only a few weeks in New York, isolated and homesick, Rudy wanted to return home; only because so many had sacrificed so much to send him there did he stay.
- He passed the test with room to spare and entered West Point in 1885.
- Rudy endured four years of abusive hazing, convinced it would make him both a better man and a better soldier.
- He was only the third black student to achieve a diploma.
- His assignments were limited to the military's black units—the 9th and 10th Cavalry and the 24th and 25th Infantry.
- By 1903 the U.S. Army was responsible for a number of national parks created by President Theodore Roosevelt; Rudy was made superintendent of two of the parks, located in California.
- His following three-year assignment was in Port-au-Prince, Haiti, as military attaché to gather intelligence and construct maps of the island terrain.
- Then a placement came in the newly formed Intelligence Office at Army Headquarters in Washington, District of Columbia; it was a dream assignment.
- Within the growing black middle class of the nation's capital, Rudy found friendship, comfort, and a place to be himself.

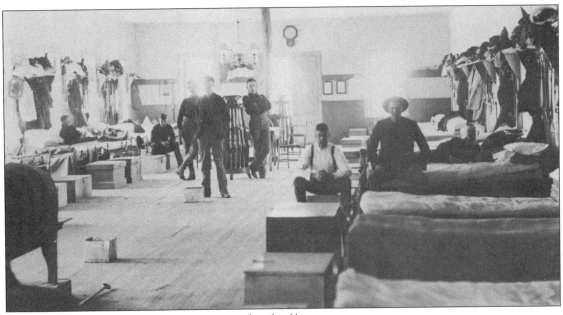

The barracks in Fort Huachuca, Arizona, were spacious and comfortable.

Rudy and his men were responsible for two national parks in California.

- An accomplished linguist capable of speaking Greek, French, Spanish, and German, he attracted a wide circle of friends.
- It was at a Washington party that he met his wife.
- Unfortunately, soon after the formerly confirmed bachelor walked down the aisle with his new bride, he was shipped to the Philippines, forced to leave behind his home in the capital, his friends, and his now-pregnant wife.
- In the Philippines he watched the slow, agonizing process of forming a democracy; in 1907 under U.S. rule, the Philippines became the first Asian state to establish a national legislature.
- Rudy learned about exotic diseases and the songs they inspired: "I've the dobie itch and Moro stitch/The jim-jams and the fever/The burning fart and the Samar dart/And maybe a kris in my liver!"
- He discovered that Manila's San Miguel beer was excellent, but three drinks of Filipino wine were dangerous.
- On his next assignment, as attaché in Monrovia, Liberia, his wife was allowed to accompany him.
- They were finding great joy living in a nation of former slaves when new orders arrived.
- In 1916 Rudy was assigned to Fort Huachuca, Arizona; his wife, and their three sons could remain with him.
- He was put in command of a squadron of the 10th Cavalry.
- Just as he was anticipating the chance to hunt mule deer, word arrived that American civilians had come under attack from Mexico.

Life at Work

- Information was sketchy, but on March 9, the Mexican political leader and bandit Francisco "Pancho" Villa had led a force of men across the United States border and attacked the community of Columbus, New Mexico.

Pancho Villa was ordered captured or killed by President Wilson.

- Buildings were burned, stores and homes looted, women raped, and 19 soldiers and civilians killed.
- President Woodrow Wilson, long troubled by uneasy relations with Mexico, immediately ordered a punitive expedition into Mexico to capture or kill Villa.
- Six regiments, including four cavalry and two infantry, all under the command of Brigadier General John Pershing, were ordered out.
- Rudy West and the 10th, who were only 250 miles away from Columbus, immediately saddled up, taking care to order two wagons loaded with rations, ammunition, and a double supply of horseshoes.
- In accordance with a tradition dating to the Indian Wars of 30 years before, the band played while the troops filed off the post.
- Both the 7th and 10th Cavalry first gathered at Colbertson's Ranch before crossing the border into the Mexican state of Chihuahua on March 16.
- In all, 1,500 men were made available to General Pershing; few expected the expedition to last a year.
- Under Rudy's command—he was an excellent horseman with a love of the outdoors—the 10th Cavalry was able to move faster than its supply line and subsisted on what they brought or could buy from the locals.
- After travelling 252 miles—30 miles a day—from Huachuca, the 10th was ordered to board a Mexican train to speed their journey south.
- One lieutenant described the trip as less than pleasant: "Our troubles in patching and nailing up the cars, getting materials for camps, collecting wood for the wood-burning engine and getting started late in the afternoon with the animals inside the freight cars and officers and men on top in truly Mexican style, were exceeded, if possible, only by the troubles in keeping the engine going by having the men get off and chop mesquite to burn in it, only to find the wood must be used to send the engine someplace for water, and so on ad infinitum."

- On the morning of April 1, the 10th encountered a force of Villa's men.
- Rudy felt invigorated by the brief engagement; when the Mexicans broke and ran, his troop pursued the invaders for two hours before trapping them in a ravine.
- There the soldier in him wanted to attack, but as an officer, he knew he must wait for the remainder of the regiment to improve their position.
- When the assault occurred, the infantry controlled the rim of the canyon so they could fire down.
- A machine gun covered the ground, and the 10th was free to charge into the ravine.
- Excited by the prospect of being part of the first cavalry charge since the Spanish-American War, Rudy relished the chance to draw his .45 and yell at the top of his lungs.
- The Mexicans fled.
- None of his men was hit; their horses, though, did not enjoy the skirmish.
- One horse was wounded, one dropped from exhaustion, and a third died the next night.
- During the next few days, with rumors rampant that Villa was dead or wounded, the expedition continued.
- Chasing Villa's men required treks through mountains and high deserts at altitudes of up to ten thousand feet.
- There the 10th Cavalry was assaulted by stinging snow and sleet, laced with sand; with freezing nights and days filled with dust, they quickly discovered why the region was called the "windiest place in the world."
- A dust storm could last 24 hours, making cooking impossible and sleep unlikely.
- The men were equipped with .30-caliber Springfield rifles, which weighed slightly more than eight pounds and took ammunition in five-round clips. The men believed the Springfield was far easier to load than the old Krag-Jorgensen rifles, the first U.S. military weapon to use smokeless powder.

Rudy and the 10th Cavalry travelled in brutal conditions, searching for Villa and his men.

- Other equipment changes, many instituted since 1910, were designed to put as much of the soldier's load as possible onto his back and remove bags that might bang against the legs.
- Reconnaissance for General Pershing was provided by four aircraft flying between the cavalry units and enemy lines, with Pershing himself delivering information.
- Mostly, though, the planes were of little use.
- Rudy and his men found themselves faced with an unstable and dangerous foe—angry Mexican citizens inflamed by the American invasion.
- The problems began on April 12 in Parral, Villa's hometown.
- Major Frank Tompkins entered the small community; it was filled with Mexican government troops who were officially allied with the Americans in pursuit of Villa and his men.
- When Tompkins attempted to secure supplies, trouble broke out.
- The seething resentment against the American invasion erupted in gunfire.
- The American troops were trapped by engaged Mexican townspeople and Mexican military.
- Only a few miles away when trouble started, the 10th Cavalry immediately mounted their horses and rode into the fray, dispersing the violence without losing a man.
- When Rudy returned to camp, he was greeted with a letter from the quartermaster general, demanding to know why the hides of slaughtered animals were not sold as called for by Army regulations.

The 10th Cavalry were exhausted as they entered Villa's hometown.

Life in the Community: Mexico

- As foreign investment in Mexico grew and the foreigners became wealthy using Mexican resources, native Mexicans began complaining that "Mexico was the mother of foreigners, and only a stepmother to Mexicans."
- Over half the nation's population—Indians and mestizos—were sharecroppers, with little hope of climbing out of debt.
- The Mexican Revolution against foreign influence started shortly after Porfirio Díaz became president of Mexico for the eighth time on October 4, 1910.
- By 1912 the country had become a battlefield of warring factions; the foreign oil companies, among many outsiders, were outraged.
- By 1913, when strongman Victoriano Huerta swept into power, the German, British, and Spanish governments quickly recognized his rule, but the United States was more cautious.
- The Zapatistas, an army of peasants who occasionally took time away to look after their corn and chili patches, combined with revolutionary armies led by Pancho Villa and Venustiano Carranza under the slogan, "Death to Huerta, down with the foreigners, Mexico for the Mexicans."
- By April 1914 the revolutionary armies controlled all of Mexico except the capital and a small area on the oil-rich coast.
- When the rebels took Tampico, the United States ordered the U.S Navy fleet into Veracruz, Mexico, to seize the port and occupy the city.
- Hatred of foreigners erupted in riots everywhere; American flags were torn and stamped upon in gutters, and businesses were stoned.
- Despite this American soldiers stayed, often working in the community to improve conditions.
- In Veracruz, when Army General Frederick Funston cleaned up the water supply, improved sewage, and imported 2,500 garbage cans from the United States, the death rate among city residents plummeted.

- In July, after President Huerta had fled the country and Carranza was installed as the new president, Villa and Zapata refused to demobilized their troops or accept Carranza as their leader.
- By 1916 Mexico was again a battleground, Mexican money was worthless, and citizens were often on the move to avoid the warring factions.
- With most jobs paying in devalued currency, many men attached themselves to whatever troops were sweeping through the area.

Mexican Invasion Calendar,
The Outlook, July 5, 1916

- March 9, 1916: Nineteen Americans were killed and about 20 wounded in a raid on Columbus, New Mexico, by Mexican bandits, supposedly led by General Villa.

- March 15: An American column under General Pershing crossed the border in pursuit of raiders. It was generally understood by the American public that this incursion was made with the consent of the Carranza government, that the Mexican de facto government would cooperate with the United States in the bandit hunt, and that American troops would be withdrawn as soon as the marauders who had attacked Columbus were killed or captured.

- April 19: General Pershing's expedition reached its "farthest south" by the arrival of two troops of the 13th Cavalry at Parral, about 400 miles from the border, where they were ambushed by Carranzista soldiers and townsmen and forced to retreat, with the loss of two killed and seven wounded. This virtually ended the pursuit of Villa by the Americans, and led to the dispatch of heavy reinforcements to General Pershing and a general contraction of his lines.

- April 29: Conferences began at Juarez, Mexico, and El Paso, Texas, between Alvaro Obregon representing Carranza, and Generals Scott and Funston representing the United States.

- May 15: Mexicans raided the "Big Bend" district of Texas, killing seven Americans.

- May 11: The conferences at Juarez and El Paso were discontinued, with no substantial agreement reached. About the same time, American cavalrymen captured 14 Mexicans alleged to have taken part in the raid on Glen Springs in the "Big Bend," and a little later other cavalrymen killed a number of the companions of these captured bandits.

- May 31: The American government received a note from the Carranza government stating that the Pershing expedition had gone into Mexico without the consent of Carranza, and asking for "the immediate withdrawal of American troops which are now in Mexican territory."

- June 11: Mexicans raided an American ranch near Laredo, Texas, with the result that 1,600 American regulars were drawn from the Engineer Corps of the Coast Artillery to further reinforce the defenses of the U.S. border.

- June 14-21: Texas soil was twice again raided by Mexicans. President Wilson's summons to the militia of all states, except the three border states already called, resulted on June 18. Sixteen warships were sent to watch Mexican ports.

- June 20: The president's reply to Carranza's demand for the withdrawal of U.S. troops was issued. The American government refused and, while admitting that "American troops had crossed the international boundary in hot pursuit of the Columbus raiders, and without notice to or the consent of your government," served notice that any attempt by the de facto government to expel the American soldiers by force would be followed by "the gravest consequences."

"Riding Mexican Trains through Chihuahua, Mexico, in Search of Pancho Villa," by Captain Rodney

It was a train by courtesy, nothing else. Six cattle cars were hitched to a wood-burning engine for which there was no fuel. Our first job was to rebuild the train, for great holes had been burned in the floors. Most of the cars had no doors, and every time the engine moved, the sides of the cars opened out just as the sticks in a fan separate. When we finally got the horses loaded, we placed bales of hay along the tops of the cars so the men would not fall off when asleep; then we set to work with camp hatchets to cut a supply of fuel for the engine. In this way, we finally got started, after demolishing a set of loading pens for fuel for which the government later had to pay $1,900. Then, we started, but it was only a start. From time to time a man would roll off the roof, or sparks from the engine would set fire to the hay bales; then the engine would stop for water and we had to cut down telegraph poles for fuel, and when we got the fuel, the water was gone. It took us 24 hours to run 25 miles, and we finally reached our destination about three hours after we would have reached it had we marched. At a little wood station called Rucio, we finally got the horses off the train. As there was no ramp for unloading, the train was stopped in a railway cut and we got the horses out by the simple process of pushing them out of the open car doors. Then, we started on our cross-country march to San Miguel rancho, where rumor said Villa had been hiding.

Selected Prices

Automobile, Seven-Passenger............................$1,395.00

Blouse, Woman's Silk Embroidered.......................$5.50

Bookcase, Oak...$8.00

Comb..$0.02

Hair Color, Makes One Pint..............................$0.25

Oil, per Bottle...$0.25

Pants, Man's Work Pants.................................$1.50

Raincoat, Woman's......................................$10.95

Room, Chicago, Illinois, per Week.......................$4.00

Tablespoons, Silver Plate, Set of Six...................$4.40

Telephone..$11.28

Tobacco, per Package....................................$0.15

Toilet Paper, Large Roll................................$0.09

Vacuum Cleaner, Electric...............................$24.50

Wooden Blocks, Set of 20................................$0.79

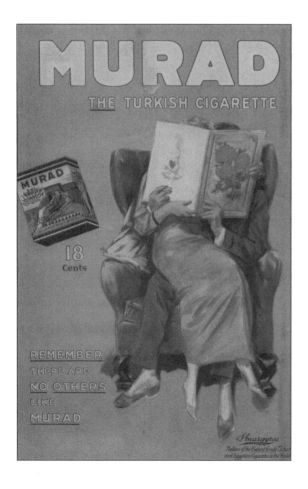

HISTORICAL SNAPSHOT
1916

- Man Ray painted *The Rope Dancer Accompanies Herself with Her Shadows*
- On the first day of the Battle of the Somme, 20,000 soldiers from Great Britain were killed, making it the bloodiest day in the British army's long history
- Joseph Goldberger showed that pellagra was a deficiency disease, not an infection
- Blood was refrigerated for safe storage for the first time
- The Piggly-Wiggly grocery store, Orange Crush, Nathan's hotdogs, Lincoln Logs, mechanical windshield wipers and the agitator washing machine all made their first appearance
- America boasted 21,000 movie theaters, with an average cost of $0.05
- Over 5,000 American Jews became British subjects in order to join the British war effort—ahead of American entry into the war—and assist in the liberation of Palestine from Turkish rule
- A polio epidemic struck 28,000 people, 6,000 of whom died
- President Woodrow Wilson continued unsuccessfully to mediate the European War
- A new mechanized home refrigerator was priced at $900, more than the cost of a car
- The United States bought the Virgin Islands from Denmark for $25 million
- Railway workers gained the right to an eight-hour day, preventing a nationwide strike
- Ring Lardner published *You Know Me Al: A Busher's Letters,* John Dewey wrote *Democracy and Education* and Carl Sandburg's *Chicago Poems* was released
- The Federal Land Bank System was created to aid farmers in acquiring loans
- Popular songs of the day included, "Ireland Must Be Heaven for My Mother Came from There" and "There's a Little Bit of Bad in Every Good Little Girl"
- Henry Ford chartered a "Peace Ship" to stop the war in Europe, caused, he said, by international Jews and Wall Street
- Margaret Sanger opened the first birth control clinic in the country and distributed information in English, Italian and Yiddish; she was arrested and charged with maintaining a "public nuisance"
- The Mercury dime and Liberty fifty-cent piece went into circulation
- High school dropout Norman Rockwell published his first illustration in *The Saturday Evening Post*
- Actor Charlie Chaplin signed with Mutual for a record salary of $675,000
- Multimillionaire businessman Rodman Wanamaker organized the Professional Golfers Association of America
- South Carolina raised the minimum working age of children from 12 to 14
- Lucky Strike cigarettes were introduced; a pack of 20 sold for $0.10

"The Man Hunted in Mexico," by Gregory Mason, *The Outlook*, April 19, 1916:

"There's more rivers an' less water, more cows an' less milk, an' you can see further an' see less here than in any country where I've ever been."

So an ebony trooper in one of the Negro cavalry regiments described, in the terms of a common Texan story, the barren northern Chihuahua country through which the American "Punitive Expedition" is pursuing the meager trail of Pancho Villa.

Right here, let it be said that the great bandit's name is not pronounced in English as it is spelled, nor is it pronounced *Vilya*, as it would be in Spain. In Mexico and on the border, they call it *Vee-yah*.

The event which the border army has impatiently awaited for three years, the entrance into Mexico, has not been so pleasant in the realization as it was in the anticipation. Armies are made to fight, and when they fight they like to fight like men. But the first three weeks of the Mexican jaunt of our expedition brought forth only two small, running skirmishes, which were more like rabbit drives than battles. And the tawny upland desert of northwestern Chihuahua is not the course one would choose for a hare-and-hound chase such as the pursuit of Villa has been in its first stages.

The greater scarcity of water in the rivers, which are unaided through their twisting channels by man, and the greater scarcity of milk in the cows, which are left to graze on the innutritious desert uncared for, is indeed the principal difference between the part of old Mexico, where eight regiments of our army are now sweating through the sand, and the border regions of New Mexico, Arizona, and Texas, where most of the men in those regiments had spent many days prior to that crimson dawn when Villa ran amuck at Columbus. For many miles on both sides of the border, the landscape is made up of broad ribbons of yellow sand spattered with blotches of savage, thorny vegetation in buffs and browns and grays uncoiling between walls of jagged and grotesquely shaped mountains of a cool, deep blue from a distance, which melts into an arid tan on approach. But through the clear air on the American side, the eye may rest on frequent flashing windmills surrounded by fair green cottonwoods and willows, while it is true that through the eye-smarting clarity of vistas south of the line, one can see farther and yet see much less that is worth the seeing.

We Americans have conquered the frontier within our own country, and the only zone within shot of our eyes where man is still mainly bested by nature lies over the Mexican border. Columbus, New Mexico, is a typical frontier town. Half a hundred one-storied shacks of brown or white adobe, with half a dozen two-storied frames of wood, are scattered about the town's center, marked by the ashes of four of the principal buildings which Villa's rum-crazed children of nature burned.

"The Dough-Boy and the Truck," by Gregory Mason, *The Outlook*, May 31, 1916:

"The cal-vreeman rides a big black horse
That car-ries him to fame,
The dough-boy has no horse at all,
But gets there just the same
What?
Yes, gets there just the same, boys,
He gets there just the same,
The dough-boy, he ain't got no horse,
But gets there just the same."

It was a limpid night, except for this bellowed refrain, as dead still as an Arctic tundra after a blizzard. In fact, although the scene was on a plateau in Chihuahua, farther south than Galveston or Los Angeles, and the time April, the big massed flakes of the afternoon's snow flurry were just melting around the grass roots, and the mountain peaks on every side were whitewashed pyramids. The sparks and smoke of the great bonfire of mesquite and cottonwood rose in a still column, only to break and quiver five feet above the ground from the explosive exhalations that came from the close-packed circle of mouths every three seconds, as the soldiers who stood six deep around the blaze barked hard on the second syllable of each line of this marching song of the infantry:

"The cal-vreeman rides a big black horse
That car-ries him to fame;
The dough-boy has no horse at all,
But gets there just the same."

At each detonation that came with "cal," "car," "dough," and "gets," the smoke pillar would crumble, then regather, only to writhe again before the next blare of vocal trumpets. But at the crescendo bellow of "who-wat?" shouted in all the dissonance of untrained voices roughened by night air and overuse, the cylinder of smoke was flattened into the fire and the whole plain reverberated.

These bronzed foot-soldiers who were chorusing their own praises around a campfire at General Pershing's headquarters near Colonia Dublan were part of a detachment that had "dug in" at this point to guard the sand-swept premises. They had been resting several days after the first feverish hike into Mexico, else they would not have had breath to spare in wrecking the peace of this upland evening. Little singing is done by our soldiers on the march, and after a day of tramping, the only vocal music heard at eve is of the unconscious, slumberous kind. This particular occasion was a "Vaudeville Evening" arranged by the five chaplains of the expedition.

The night before, these same chaplains, who, unlike the other men in the expedition, had not forgotten the calendar, had observed the Sabbath with services in the same temple with the sky for roof and the stars for candles. With great good sense, the chaplains had observed the day, cheering these men in a foreign country from which each knew he might never return, but not playing Billy Sunday with the men's emotions, not once lifting the lash of fear as a goad to conventional virtue.

To the audience of Baptists, Catholics, Lutherans, Methodists,

"The Dough-Boy . . ."*(continued)*

and Jews, each chaplain spoke briefly, packing his talk with common sense and salting it well with jokes. Father Joyce, for instance, known as the "Fighting Padre" of the Fourth Artillery, took a dig at his regiment which everyone appreciated when he said, "The only way to get an artilleryman into heaven is to convert him and then shoot him quick."

After these "sermons," so refreshingly different from what the correspondents at the service expected to hear, the meeting turned into an old-fashioned Sunday night "sing," such as still flourishes in odd corners of New England. First selected were hymns like "Shall We Gather at the River?" which were thrown across the Rio Casas Grandes, twisting through the plain in silvery curves, with an excellent enthusiasm and a melodic quality not to be despised by any college glee club. But the pious atmosphere of the gathering, never too dominant, wore off by degrees, and gradually the singing drifted to "The Girl I Left Behind Me" and "The River Shannon," with the quintet of chaplains warbling as bravely as anyone. Only the clear-bugled "Taps" stopped the flow of the song. But, as one of the "sky-pilots" said, "We've all got a lot of music in our systems yet." And so the Army Vaudeville was arranged for the following night.

There were all sorts of faces in that circle around the fire, for it was a characteristic army group. There were the buff, blond faces of Scandinavian and Teutonic countries, the black, flat, grinning faces of Africa, the dark, passionate faces of Italy and Greece, the sensitive faces of Russia and Poland, the alert, self-confident face of the Jew, and the also alert but more pugnacious face of Ireland. Yes, and there were some faces that seemed to belong to Maine, Georgia, Dakota, and California.

This variety of countenance which the firelight showed moved a chaplain to comment:

"I see we've got a little of everything here tonight. The army isn't what it used to be. When I joined it, the army was all Dutch and Irish. The two elements were continually fighting, and always, after these fights, the Dutchmen would go to the hospital and the Irishmen to the guardhouse."

The roar that followed showed that the army still holds a few of Erin's sons.

"Villa's Invasion," *The Literary Digest*, March 18, 1916:

Villa's descent of March 9 upon American soil was a surprise to readers of American newspapers, yet there has been presented evidence that it had been planned some time in advance. United States Army officers in command along the Mexican border were, of course, prepared for the worst, although in Columbus itself there had been no trouble during the past three years. An interesting story of Villa's preliminary movements, and of the ways of the man who ventured to go to war with the United States on his own account, was given in the story of an American woman who was his prisoner for several days preceding the Columbus battle. Mrs. Maud Hawk Wright, wife of an American ranch owner in Mexico, was visited on March 1 by a Villista officer Servantes. Their supplies and horses were taken, and Mr. Wright and the baby were sent away. The Villistas took Mrs. Wright prisoner, joined the main body, and compelled her to accompany them on a nine days' forced march. From the first, says Mrs. Wright:

"I knew that Villa intended to attack Columbus. It was freely discussed by the men and the officers. Some of the latter told me that Villa intended to kill every American he could find, but they pointed to me as an example of their decision not to harm women. Later, as we approached the border from Boca Grande, these same officers told me that Villa—his rage growing as he neared the boundary—would make torches of every woman and child, as well as of every man, in Columbus.

"'He intended,' they said, 'to kill everybody in the United States, and would be helped by Japan and Germany.' At Boca Grande I saw evidence of their determination. I did not see the three American cowboys named McKinney, Corbett, and O'Neill slain, but I saw officers wearing their clothing. That was after Villa had sent out 20 men to break up the Palomas cattle roundup and supply the hungry column with meat. . . .

"We left Boca Grande yesterday and crossed the border west of Columbus before four o'clock.

"As we entered the ditch leading past the American army camp below Columbus, the captain of my company told me that he and the 20 officers had crossed the border yesterday as spies, and found that only a few American soldiers were in the camp, that the others were farther west.

"I was in the line Villa threw along the railroad tracks after his troops swept eastward through the United States cavalry. A bullet hit the saddle of my horse as I stood dismounted behind it. Villa sent his men across the tracks into the town. Soon I saw buildings on fire. Then, the American troops apparently got into action, and in a little while the Mexicans came back. . . . I went back with the retreating forces until I reached a point near the house where Mr. Moore was killed and his wife wounded. Here Villa came upon me. Again I asked him to set me free.

"'You go; you are at liberty,' he said. I went to the Moores' house and found Mr. Moore lying facing down on the steps, dead; his wife was in a nearby field, wounded. She had seen her husband shot, but did not know he was dead."

1917: Civil Rights Advocate

Twenty-two-year-old Etta Graham had never been south of Coney Island, New York, but heard stories all of her life about how poorly colored people were treated down South, and she wanted to make a difference.

Life at Home

- Etta Graham, who was born and raised in Harlem, was used to hearing about the injustices suffered by colored people in the South.
- Relatives and neighbors who had escaped the oppression of the South often told stories about beatings and lynchings and humiliations.
- Some had left their homes in Marion, South Carolina, or Tupelo, Mississippi, with little more than the clothes on their backs.
- Etta was proud to live in Harlem, New York, where Negroes had a future.
- For more than a decade, her father had operated a successful store, selling groceries, carriage supplies, and hardware.
- Etta grew up in a spacious five-room apartment above the store and learned early that it took hard work to get ahead.
- Although she had sometimes objected to the discipline of work, she respected her parents and the life they had built.
- But life in Harlem was changing.
- Every day, Southern blacks with little education and less money were arriving in the city and looking for work.
- Most arrived knowing someone who would put them up, but poor people could only care for poorer people for so long.
- Twice, cousins from Mississippi had come to Harlem seeking work, and twice her father had faced the painful task of putting them out when the stay lasted too long.
- Work was plentiful to the skilled, but elusive to those with a third-grade education and experience only in row farming.
- They deserved better, Etta knew, but felt helpless until the idea of protesting the humiliating conditions of the South was announced at church.
- Everyone was already talking about the riots in East St. Louis, Illinois, where 40 Negroes were killed in mob

Etta Graham worked to improve the civil rights of colored people in the South.

violence and 6,000 black families were driven from their homes.

- The conflict was over jobs; hungry Negroes eager for any job were willing to work for lower wages than whites, igniting a race riot.
- In Etta's mind, a race riot was the same as an individual lynching; both involved white people taking the law into their own hands.
- Maybe that was why she was so captivated by the minister's call for a mass demonstration.
- The plan was brilliant in its simplicity: a silent protest parade of Negroes through the heart of Manhattan to condemn the injustice of racism, Jim Crow laws, and most of all, lynching.
- No shouting, no fighting, no words—only protest signs.
- Etta was intrigued by the boldness of the plan even as she fretted over how white New York might react.
- Would white troublemakers try to disrupt the silent protest? Could Harlem's Negroes contain themselves and not say a word? Would anybody have the courage to show up on a Saturday afternoon after working all morning?
- Fear troubled Etta's sleep all week.

Life at Work

- Marching on a Saturday meant that she would have to ask permission from her father, but even that was worth the risk.
- The National Association for the Advancement of Colored People had organized the event through New York's black churches in response to the riots in East St. Louis, Illinois.
- They envisioned it as the nation's largest organized demonstration by black Americans in U.S. history.
- By 1 p.m. on a warm Saturday in July, everyone had assembled at Fifty-ninth and Fifth.
- The ministers had decided that the 800 assembled children would lead the parade.
- They were followed by several thousand Negro women, who created a sea of white with their finest Sunday outfits.
- The third section of the silent march was composed of men.
- Along the parade route, another 20,000 Negroes stood in solidarity.
- The silence was profound.
- Before the march of 8,000 people was on the move, Etta's heart was pounding; what if the police attacked the parade? What if riots broke out?
- Marching for her race was frightening and exciting at the same time.
- Banners were everywhere.
- One woman displayed a banner showing a Negro woman kneeling before President Woodrow Wilson, appealing for him to bring democracy to America before carrying it to Europe.
- Etta thought it spoke volumes to a nation at war, but the police quickly declared it objectionable and organizers were forced to withdraw it.

"Great Results from Hard Beginnings"

BOARD OF NATIONAL MISSIONS
Of the Presbyterian Church in the U. S. A.
DIVISION OF MISSIONS FOR COLORED PEOPLE
507-511 Bessemer Building
Pittsburgh, Pa.

National Negro Health Week
Sixteenth Annual Observance [1930]
Sunday, March 30, to Sunday, April 6

"The photograph forms the concrete visualization that the line is bent that line's inclined."

Objective for the year 1930
More Regular Use of Existing Health Services

Issued by THE UNITED STATES PUBLIC HEALTH SERVICE, WASHINGTON, D. C.

- At the head of the march, a banner read, "Your Hands Are Full of Blood," referring to the racial violence in East St. Louis.
- Etta was proud to hold one end of a sign reading, "We Are Maligned as Lazy, and Murdered When We Work," which also referred to the cause of the East St. Louis riots: white resentment over black employment.
- In her heart, she knew that she would not be there but for the urging of her pastor, Rev. Charles D. Martin.
- Rev. Martin, like black preachers across New York, had called upon congregations to fight against lynching with a silent protest march up Fifth Avenue, a place Etta had only been once before.
- In all, more than 100 ministers, black civic clubs, and fraternal organizations called upon their members to join the protest.
- Rev. Martin talked about the hundreds of lynchings in the South, and the Jim Crow laws that prevented blacks from voting and using parks, libraries, and public transportation.
- But most of all, he discussed the daily humiliations suffered by every Southern Negro, and then asserted, "We must march because we deem it to be a *crime to be silent* in the face of such barbaric acts."
- She knew from talking to her Southern cousins that she could not change the South, but she could add her voice, even a silent one, to protest injustice.
- Suddenly, just before the march began, her whole body grew calm; only after her fear began to dissipate did she begin to realize that she was not marching as a member of a church, but as the representative of a whole race of people.
- So in silence she marched until she reached Twenty-third Street and the parade dispersed, when some of the protestors permitted themselves a few cheers.

Life in the Community: Harlem, New York

- The settlement of Harlem dated to 1658 and the founding of New York as a Dutch Colony.
- Initially, the land was populated by farmers.
- By the 1830s, the role of farming was diminishing when a railroad line was built linking Harlem with Manhattan's Park Avenue, spurring development.
- As New York City's population grew in the 1880s and transportation became more efficient, the development of Harlem became inevitable.
- Speculators built quality row houses for upper and middle class purchasers.
- In the 1890s, most of the buyers in Harlem were American-born white Protestants with first-generation immigrant servants from Ireland, Germany, and Sweden.
- The building boom abated in 1893 during the national recession, but resumed at a torrid pace by 1897.

With improved transportation, the development of Harlem was inevitable.

- The development of Harlem into a predominately black community began in the early days of the twentieth century when an oversupply of housing stock led landlords to begin advertising for African American tenants.
- A typical sign read, "Apartments to Let. 3 or 4 Rooms with Improvements For Respectable Colored Families Only."
- By 1914, 50,000 blacks lived in Harlem.
- Many of the newcomers arrived from the South where Jim Crow laws, the sharecropper system, and lynching made life unbearable.
- Many found greater tolerance in Harlem, but little opportunity for economic advancement, which was one of the reasons the National Association for the Advancement of Colored People (NAACP) thought that a silent Negro protest against lynching would be a success.
- During the late 1800s, the lynching of black people in the Southern and border states became an institutionalized way to terrorize.
- Lynching was conceived and carried out more or less spontaneously by a mob who publicly murdered individuals suspected of a crime.
- Most of the lynchings were by hanging or shooting, or both.
- Many involved burning at the stake, maiming, dismemberment, castration, and other brutal methods of physical torture.
- White southerners publicly declared that Negroes could only be controlled by fear.
- *The Chicago Tribune* first began to take systematic account of lynching in 1892.
- That same year, the Tuskegee Institute began to collect and tabulate lynching statistics.
- Beginning in 1912, the NAACP kept an independent record of lynching.
- Lynching peaked in 1892, when 230 persons were lynched; 161 were black and 69 were whites.
- The Southern states accounted for nine-tenths of the lynching.
- Mississippi had the highest incidence of lynching in the nation.
- Most black men were lynched for the crimes of raping white women and murder.

The Queensboro Bridge, completed in 1909, connected the borough of Queens to Manhattan.

- The racist myth of Negroes' uncontrollable desire to rape white women acquired a strategic position in the defense of the lynching practice.
- Lynching occurred most commonly in the smaller towns and isolated rural communities of the South where people were poor, often illiterate, and lacked power in the community.
- The people who comprised lynch mobs were usually small land holders, tenant farmers, and common laborers whose economic status was very similar to that of the blacks.

- Many Southern politicians and officials supported "lynch-law," and came to power on a platform of race prejudice.
- Because of the tight hold on the courts by local public opinion, lynchers were rarely indicted by a grand jury or sentenced.
- A study of 100 lynchings found that at least one-half were carried out with police officers participating.
- W. E. B. DuBois summed up white motivation, saying "The white South feared—more than Negro dishonesty, ignorance, and incompetency—Negro honesty, knowledge, and efficiency."
- The NAACP was instrumental in awakening the nation to the urgency of stopping lynching.

The public library on 5th Avenue in Manhattan.

HISTORICAL SNAPSHOT
1917

- As part of America's entrance into World War I, the United States Army opened its first all-black school for officer training in Des Moines, Iowa

- Clarence Birdseye discovered how to quick-freeze food to retain its freshness

- T. S. Eliot published *Prufrock and Other Observations*, Sinclair Lewis wrote *The Innocents*, and Irving Bacheller's book *The Light in the Clearing* achieved bestseller status

- Congress authorized the sale of War Certificates and liberty loans to support World War I

- C. G. Jung published *Psychology of the Unconscious;* Freud published *Introduction to Psychoanalysis*

- Oscar Micheaux produced and directed the silent film, *The Homesteader,* the first film to be produced and directed by an African American

- Courses in the German language were outlawed as part of the war effort

- Electric voting machines, a Jewish navy chaplain, electric food mixers, and *The Grumps* cartoon all made their first appearance

- Thomas Gainsborough's painting *Blue Boy* sold for $38,800

- The United States Supreme Court ruled that a Louisville, Kentucky law forbidding blacks and whites from living in the same neighborhood was unconstitutional

- A vaccine against Rocky Mountain spotted fever was developed

- Hit songs included, "Go Down Moses," "Goodbye Broadway, Hello France," "Nobody Knows de Trouble I've Seen," and "Hail, Hail, the Gang's All Here"

- The New York Philharmonic celebrated its seventy-fifth anniversary

- Six hundred blacks were commissioned as officers as America entered World War I

- Race riots broke out in East St. Louis, Illinois, stemming from white resentment over the employment of blacks in a local factory; at least 40 blacks were killed during the riots.

- A conflict erupted between black soldiers and white civilians in Houston, Texas; two blacks and 17 whites were killed in the violence

- Emmett J. Scott was made special assistant to the Secretary of War, where he worked for nondiscrimination in the Selective Service Act

- Silent movie premieres included *The Woman God Forgot* directed by Cecil B. DeMille; *Easy Street* and *The Immigrant,* both starring Charlie Chaplin; and *Les Misérables,* directed by Frank Lloyd

45

Selected Prices, 1917

Bloomers, Woman's $0.90
Coat, Man's Camel Hair and Wool $4.85
Deodorant Cream $0.25
Ice Cream Maker $3.00
Phonograph $6.95
Rum, Bacardi, Fifth $3.20
Telephone Call, Three Minutes, New York to San Francisco $20.70
Telephone, with Batteries $11.25
Toilet Paper, Large Roll $0.07
Vacuum Cleaner $24.50

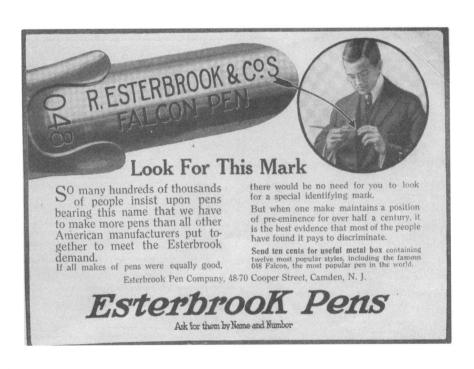

"Open your mouth and shut your eyes,
And I'll give you something to make you wise."

Painted by Edward V. Brewer for Cream of Wheat Co.   Copyright 1917 by Cream of Wheat Co.

Lynching Timeline

1900

Congressman George White of Pennsylvania, the sole remaining African American in Congress, introduced a bill making lynching a federal crime; "To cheapen Negro life is to cheapen all life. The first murder paves the way for the second until crime ceases to be abhorrent."

Congressman George White's bill was defeated soundly by a majority in Congress.

Three days of racial violence rampaged through New York City's theater district.

1901

African American Congressman George H. White gave up his seat in the U.S. House of Representatives; no blacks were elected to Congress for the next 28 years.

President Theodore Roosevelt invited Booker T. Washington to dine with him at the White House, making Washington the first black American to receive such an invitation.

One hundred and five black Americans were lynched.

1902

Eighty-five black Americans were lynched.

1903

W. E. B. DuBois' book, *The Souls of Black Folk,* was published, which called for action on behalf of the rights of blacks.

Eighty-four black Americans were lynched.

1904

Educator Mary McCleod Bethune founded a college in Daytona Beach, Florida, known today as Bethune-Cookman College.

Seventy-six black Americans were known to have been lynched.

1905

African American intellectuals and activists, led by W. E. B. DuBois and William Monroe Trotter, began the Niagara Movement, which renounced Booker T. Washington's accommodation policies set forth in his "Atlanta Compromise" speech 10 years earlier.

Fifty-seven black Americans were known to have been lynched.

1906

Black troops in Brownsville, Texas, rioted against segregation; President Theodore Roosevelt discharged three companies of black soldiers involved in the riot.

During a race riot in Atlanta, Georgia, 10 blacks and two whites were killed.

Sixty-two black Americans were lynched.

1908

An unrecorded number of men and women were killed and wounded in a race riot in Springfield, Illinois.

William Howard Taft was elected president.

Eighty-nine black Americans were lynched.

continued

Timeline . . . *(continued)*

1909

The National Association for the Advancement of Colored People (NAACP) was formed on February 12, the centennial of the birth of Lincoln, to promote use of the courts to restore the legal rights of black Americans.

Sixty-nine black Americans were lynched.

1910

The Census of 1910 showed a national population of 93,402,151, of which 9,827,763, or 10.7 percent, were black.

The first issue appeared of *Crisis*, a publication sponsored by the NAACP and edited by W. E. B. DuBois.

Baltimore approved the first city ordinance designating the boundaries of black and white neighborhoods.

Sixty-seven black Americans were lynched.

1911

The National Urban League was organized to help African Americans secure equal employment.

Sixty black Americans were known to have been lynched.

1912

Woodrow Wilson was elected president.

James Weldon Johnson published *The Autobiography of an Ex-Colored Man*.

Sixty-one black Americans were known to have been lynched.

1913

The fiftieth anniversary of the Emancipation Proclamation was celebrated.

Former slave, abolitionist, and freedom fighter Harriet Tubman died.

The Wilson administration began government-wide segregation of work places, rest rooms, and lunch rooms.

Fifty-one black Americans were lynched.

1914

World War I began in Europe.

Fifty-one black Americans were lynched.

1915

Renowned African American spokesman Booker T. Washington died.

Fifty-six black Americans were lynched.

1916

The NAACP launched an anti-lynching crusade.

Fifty black Americans were lynched.

1917

America entered World War I; 370,000 African Americans served in military service.

A bloody race riot erupted in East St. Louis, Illinois, resulting in the deaths of 40 people; 6,000 others were driven from their homes.

Thousands of African Americans marched down Manhattan's Fifth Avenue on July 28 to protest lynching, race riots, and the denial of rights.

continued

Timeline . . . *(continued)*

1917

Riots erupted in Houston, Texas, between black soldiers and white citizens; two blacks and 11 whites were killed; 18 black soldiers were hanged for participation in the riot.

Three thousand men, women, and children camped out overnight in a field to witness an announced lynching in Memphis, Tennessee.

The U.S. Supreme Court struck down the Louisville, Kentucky ordinance mandating segregated neighborhoods, voiding segregation laws in Baltimore, Maryland; Dallas, Texas; Greensboro, North Carolina; Louisville, Kentucky; Norfolk, Virginia; Oklahoma City, Oklahoma; Richmond, Virginia; Roanoke, Virginia; and St. Louis, Missouri.

Thirty-six black Americans were lynched.

"Why Do We March?" Leaflet distributed by black Boy Scouts during the Silent March, July 28, 1917:

We march because by the Grace of God and the force of truth, the dangerous, hampering walls of prejudice and inhuman injustice must fall.

We march because we want to make impossible a repetition of Waco, Memphis, and East St. Louis the conscience of the country, and to bring the murderers of our brothers, sisters, and innocent children to justice.

We march because we deem it a crime to be silent in the face of such barbaric acts.

We march because we are thoroughly opposed to Jim-Crow Cars, Segregation, Discrimination, disenfranchisement, LYNCHING, and the host of evils that are forced on us. It is time that the spirit of Christ should be manifested in the making and execution of laws.

We march because we want our children to live in a better land and enjoy fairer conditions than fallen to our lot.

We march in memory of our butchered dead, the massacre of honest toilers who were removing the reproach of laziness and thriftlessness hurled at the entire race. They died to prove our worthiness to live. They live in spite of death shadowing us and ours. We prosper in the face of the most unwarranted and illegal oppression.

We march because the growing consciousness and solidarity of race, coupled with sorrow and discrimination, have made us one; a union that may never be dissolved in spite of shallow-brained agitators, scheming pundits, and political tricksters who secure a fleeting popularity and uncertain financial support by promoting the disunion of a people who ought to consider themselves one.

**Signs carried during the
Silent March up Fifth Avenue:**

MOTHER, DO LYNCHERS GO TO HEAVEN?

MAKE AMERICA SAFE FOR DEMOCRACY

INDIA IS ABOLISHING CASTE, IS AMERICA ADOPTING IT?

**"Fair Play for the Negro," Letter to the Editor by James E. Shepard,
President, National Training School, *The New York Times*, July 7, 1917:**

To the Editor of *The New York Times*:

The increasing lynchings of a helpless people both North and South, in many instances for trivial things, are having depressing effects on people who love their country and who are loyal and true to the flag. The courts of the land are in control of the whites, so there is never an excuse for a lynching. All crimes should be justly and severely punished and there need be no fear that any a Negro criminal or supposed criminal will ever escape.

The Negro is asking for a right to live and to hope. I appeal to the righteous sense of the Anglo-Saxon and ask the aid of your great paper to stir up sentiment against lynching, the murder of helpless women and children, and the burning of human beings. The spirit of the Anglo-Saxon is for fair play and that the strong do not unnecessarily oppress the weak. Please arouse this dormant spirit and cause America to awaken so that we work side by side to help make the world a better place in which people can live.

**"Federal Agents Assert They Have Evidence of Plot to Incite Negroes,"
The New York Times, April 7, 1917:**

BIRMINGHAM, Ala.—With the arrest of a white man and a Negro here late yesterday, federal agents, who have the two men in custody, have announced they have evidence of a movement by German agents to incite Negroes in the South. These agents, the federal authorities say, have worked particularly in Alabama, Louisiana, Georgia, the Carolinas, and Mississippi. Posing as Bible salesmen and ministers of the gospel, federal agents declare, they have urged the Negroes to migrate to Mexico, telling them that special trains will carry them there April 15.

A Negro arrested by federal authorities yesterday at the Birmingham railway station is accused of having made speeches to fellow members of his race, in which he urged them to denounce this government and turn their efforts in behalf of Germany.

"$100,000 for Negro Babies," *The New York Times*, March 20, 1917:

A number of men who had luncheon yesterday at Delmonico's at the invitation of George Foster Peabody, Jacob C. Klinck, Clinton L. Rossiter, Lawrence Smith Butler, and L. Hollingsworth Wood started a campaign to raise $100,000 for equipping the Howard Orphanage at Kings Park., L.I., to care for the dependent children of Negro families who have emigrated from the South in the last year. The meeting was occasioned by the conditions among the Negroes now in this part of the country who answered the call of high wages and came North unprepared for cold weather and incapable of meeting the requirements of living conditions here despite the wages they received.

William J. Doherty, Deputy Commissioner of Charities, said that 150,000 Negroes left the South and came North in 1916, and that suffering was widespread among them. He predicted that 250,000 would come in 1917 if the present wages continued, and pointed out that private agencies were needed to care for the Negroes because the laws prevented public institutions of the city and state from taking charge of persons who had lived in New York for a year.

The New York Age, July 29, 1917:

They marched without uttering one word or making a single gesticulation and protested in respectful silence against the reign of mob law, segregation, "Jim Crowism," and many other indignities to which the race is unnecessarily subjected in the United States.

"The South Blamed for Negro Exodus, Lynching a Big Factor," *The New York Times*, July 2, 1917:

A mass meeting of New York Negroes to discuss the problems created by the wholesale migration from the South in the last year, held yesterday afternoon in the Abyssinian Baptist Church, 240 West 40th Street, showed plainly that Northern Negroes are watching the exodus of their people with deep interest and approval, and that they believe the reason for it is not higher wages in the North, but treatment in the South to which they object. The church was packed to the doors, and the speakers were freely applauded.

Several of the speakers alluded to the extent of Negro migration from the South in the past year. Mr. Powell estimated that 350,000 Negroes had left Georgia, Alabama, Florida, and other Southern states within 10 months, and he placed the economic loss to that region, due to their departure, at $200 million.

In Ocala, Fla., he said, the Rev. A. L. James, a Negro clergyman, found his flock so depleted that he gave up his parish and came to New York. Arriving in Harlem, within two days, he found 12

continued

1919: Female African American Entrepreneur

Madam C. J. Walker learned at a young age how to survive tough situations, and used her skills to found her own successful hair care business.

Life at Home

- Sarah Breedlove McWilliams Walker was 37 years old before she launched the hair care business that made her one of the richest African American women in America.
- She was born on the Burney plantation in Delta, Louisiana, on December 23, 1867, to Owen and Minerva Breedlove, former slaves who worked as sharecroppers on the cotton plantation.
- Sarah was the first in her family to be born outside of slavery.
- The shack in which the family lived had no windows, no water, no toilet, one door, and a dirt floor.
- Built from cottonwood logs gathered on the plantation, the cabin had a fireplace used for cooking and warmth that dominated one wall of the one-room structure.
- The shanty's other prominent feature was the bedstead, topped with a homespun mattress sack stuffed with Spanish moss, gathered from trees in the area.
- Though now sharecroppers and no longer slaves, the Breedlove family still lived in a dangerous and hostile environment.
- Venomous snakes and mosquitoes, the latter of which caused diseases such as malaria and yellow fever, were always lurking in the sweltering, swampy climate of the Delta.
- From the day she was born, Sarah Breedlove spent nearly every moment with her parents.
- As a baby, she was strapped to her mother's back while Minerva worked in the fields.
- At the age of four, Sarah had learned to work alongside her parents, drilling holes in the field where she carefully dropped cotton seeds.
- Each year she received material from the plantation owner for her one sackcloth dress.
- Sarah had no time to attend school even if one had existed; instead, she learned to pick cotton and pick it well.
- An orphan at age seven, she had few options, and she was moved across the Mississippi River to Vicksburg, Mississippi, with her sister

Sarah Walker, a.k.a. "Madam C.J. Walker"

Being a laundress was physically demanding, and Sarah couldn't compete with washing machines.

Louvenia and her sister's abusive husband, Jesse Powell, in 1876.
- Life in Vicksburg was hard for the Breedlove sisters; work was scarce and the shanty in which they lived was crowded.
- After the birth of Louvenia's son Willie, her husband became increasingly hostile; there was never enough money or food to sustain the growing family.
- To escape the volatile situation in her sister's home, Sarah became a live-in domestic worker for a white family who provided her with meals, lodging, and a small salary.
- Too young to cook, she laid fires, dusted, mopped, washed dishes, scoured pots and pans, changed bed linens, polished boots, and took in washing and ironing.
- In 1882, at age 14, she married Moses McWilliams and left her domestic position to work as a laundress.
- "I married at the age of 14 in order to get a home of my own," Sarah explained years later.
- In the 1880s machines were taking over the laundry business even in Vicksburg, where a new Chinese laundry advertised the newest vacuum-type washing machines.
- Sarah realized she could not compete with the steam laundries on the grounds of speed and productivity; instead she kept her customers by offering reliability and professionalism.
- Sarah Breedlove McWilliams gave birth to a daughter she named Lelia on June 6, 1885; just two years later she found herself a widow and a single parent.
- After the sudden death of her husband, who was rumored to be one of 95 black men lynched nationwide in 1888, she left Vicksburg for St. Louis, Missouri, where her brother Alexander was a barber.

- The steamboat trip up the Mississippi River consumed a week and cost $4.00 for a mother and child.
- St. Louis was a city filled with black entrepreneurs, including nearly 300 black barbers who shaved their white customers daily.
- Within a decade the barbering business would dramatically change when King Gillette introduced the easy-to-use safety razor, designed for home use.
- Alexander lived in the mostly black Mill Creek Valley section of the city.
- The two-story tenement apartment in which Sarah lived with her brother and her young daughter was a one-room affair which served as a kitchen and sleeping room.
- Sarah soon took a job in a steam laundry.
- A survey by the St. Louis public schools showed that of 5,076 black parents, 22.6 percent worked as laundresses and 42.6 percent were laborers.
- White steam-laundry owners considered blacks particularly suited to the task, given their legendary tolerance for heat and sweltering conditions.

Sarah was married at the age of 14.

- The work required Sarah to stand over hot tubs of boiling water all day, stirring the laundry with a long stick, a task demanding great strength and stamina.
- She was married again, briefly, in 1894.
- At age 35, when she began her new career in hair care products, Sarah was making $1.50 a day.
- She was living on $468 a year; after deducting $8.00 a month for rent and $3.00 a week for food, she was left with $216 a year for fuel, medicine, transportation, clothing, church donations, and all other expenses.

Life at Work

- Sarah Breedlove McWilliams was on the edge of becoming entirely bald when she was introduced to Annie Turnbo hair care products for black women.
- Annie Turnbo's agents sold her brand of hair straightener door-to-door.
- For years, like many African-American women, Sarah had shampooed her hair only monthly—less often in the wintertime—and she suffered from acute dandruff, lice, eczema, and psoriasis.
- In addition, she had used harsh lye soaps, goose fat, and meat drippings to straighten her hair; the lye and sulfur had burned her skin and destroyed her hair follicles, resulting in hair loss.
- To hide her condition, Sarah often wore a scarf in the fashion she had learned on the farm.
- Even within the black community, long, straight hair denoted prosperity and beauty, while poor hair care marked a woman as coming from the country; rural women were presumed to be unsophisticated and uneducated.
- Eager to cure her baldness, Sarah had tried a variety of concoctions, including several that promised to simultaneously grow and straighten her hair.
- Most failed miserably.
- But after using the Pope-Turnbo Wonderful Hair Grower made by Annie Turnbo and experiencing miraculous results, Sarah joined the army of women selling Pope-Turnbo products door-to-door.

- As part of her front-porch sales pitch, Sarah told the story of how the Wonderful Hair Grower had changed her life.
- She quickly became their leading saleswoman.
- The Pope-Turnbo promotional literature made the connection between beautiful hair and prosperity very clear.
- "Clean scalps mean clean bodies. Better appearance means greater business opportunities, higher social standing, cleaner living and beautiful homes," the brochure said.
- Turnbo's competitors hawked hair straighteners and shampoos with names such as Kinkilla, Kink-No-More, and Straightine.
- The Boston-based Ozono promised in its advertisements to take the "Kinks out of Knotty, Kinky, Harsh, Curly, Refractory, Troublesome Hair."
- Some products were so patently dangerous—or useless—that black-owned newspapers refused to carry their advertising.
- Most black intellectuals, including Booker T. Washington, disdained the hair-straightening products sold to Negro women.
- But that had little impact on Sarah's success in St. Louis or Denver, when she took her sales operation farther west.
- In July 1905, with $1.50 in savings, 37-year-old Sarah moved to Denver, where she worked as a cook for druggist E. L. Scholtz and moonlighted selling Turnbo's products.
- Even though the State of Colorado's entire population of 540,000 was smaller than that of the city of St. Louis, Sarah sensed opportunity in the mining town.
- She used $0.25 of her $1.50 savings to buy business cards advertising Pope-Turnbo Wonderful Hair Grower, now available in Denver; as orders arrived, Sarah reinvested the profits in more advertising.

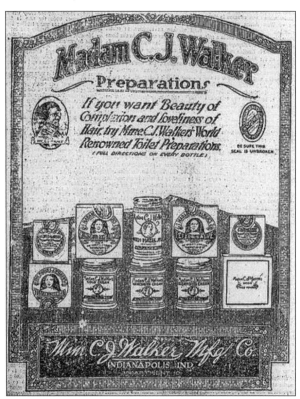

Druggist E.L. Scholtz helped Sarah devise her hair care product.

- She found the city welcoming: women could vote, and there was less racial animosity toward African Americans than she had encountered elsewhere (although Denver's Chinese population was increasing dramatically, and the Chinese were despised).
- Then Scholtz suggested that she provide him with a sample of the Wonderful Hair Grower so that he could analyze it and help her devise a formula of her own.
- Consequently a new company was launched, featuring a wide variety of hair care products.
- Later Sarah would say that the magical concoction came to her in a series of dreams brought by a man with very specific instructions; competitor Annie Turnbo thought otherwise.
- Turnbo, however, had not trademarked her product; she did so in 1906, under the name Poro—a West African word denoting a discipline promoting physical and spiritual enhancement.
- In 1906 Sarah married Charles Joseph Walker, a salesman, and developed her own

line of hair care products under the name Madam C. J. Walker; that year she tripled her income, to $3,652.

- For the next 18 months, Sarah and her husband demonstrated and sold their products throughout the South, systematically canvassing the region where 90 percent of the nation's African Americans still lived.

- In each city they would contact the Baptist or African Methodist Episcopal (AME) Church, rent the best house they could afford, introduce themselves to the local black fraternal organizations, arrange a demonstration at the church or lodge, hold classes to train agents, and take orders for Madam C. J. Walker's Wonderful Hair Grower.

- Then they would travel on to their next stop.

- "All the people who know me are just wild about my hair," Sarah was told by one customer; "I have to take it down and let them see and feel it for themselves. I tell you, I am quite an advertisement here for your goods."

Sarah pledged $1,000 to help build a YMCA for the black youth in Indianapolis.

- In the summer of 1907, the volume of orders had become so great Sarah decided to relocate the business to Pittsburgh, where 16 rail lines offered convenient shipping nationwide—a critical component of her mail-order business.

- In 1908 Madam Walker earned $6,672, nearly twice the previous year's earnings; one year later she took home $8,782.

- She attracted the attention of the Pennsylvanian Negro Business Directory, which called her "one of the most successful businesswomen of the race in this community."

- When women saw her photo and heard her life story, they clamored to take her course and sit for treatments; for thousands of maids and laundresses, Sarah symbolized the progress possible even for black women without a formal education.

- After two and a half years in Pittsburgh, the peripatetic Madam Walker was ready to relocate again, this time to Indianapolis, where a small article in the *Indianapolis Recorder* described her as "the noted Hair Culturist."

- "Hair culturist" was Sarah's preferred description for her work.

- Advertisements placed by Sarah advised women "calling for treatments will kindly bring comb, brush and two towels"; consultations were free, while scalp treatments cost $1.00 and tins of her Wonderful Hair Grower sold for $0.50 each.

- There she built a manufacturing facility, employed three dozen women and constructed a beautiful six-bedroom house for herself; her income exceeded $10,000.

- Indianapolis was the nation's largest inland manufacturing center, with banks willing to finance startup companies.

- The city's central location gave Sarah access to Chicago and Cincinnati as well as to her markets in the South and East.

- Press notices preceded her arrival in Indianapolis as she toured the city in her chauffeur-driven $1,500 Pope-Waverly electric runabout.
- Following the opening of her factory, her sales soared to $250,000 annually, and Sarah could legitimately claim to have the largest black-owned company in the United States.
- And still she hustled for more business, attending dozens of black-sponsored conventions and gatherings to lecture on hair care.
- Constantly searching for new customers, the restless Madam Walker was always adding to her commissioned workforce of 950 saleswomen.
- She personally trained agents throughout the South and designed their own advertising.
- Meanwhile her marriage to C. J. Walker was disintegrating; it ended in 1912.
- Sarah discovered the power and pleasure of philanthropy.
- In 1911, when the concept of building YMCAs for black youth was in its infancy, Sarah stepped forward to accept the challenge laid down by Sears, Roebuck executive Julius Rosenwald to build a YMCA in Indianapolis.
- Sarah made a pledge of $1,000—setting the standard for others, especially in the white community, to match.
- The *Indianapolis Freeman* declared her to be the "First Colored Woman in the United States to Give $1,000 to Colored YMCA Building" and featured her in an article that was read throughout the nation.
- Next, Sarah became involved with the National Association of Colored Women, through which she met and helped support Mary McLeod Bethune, a proponent of education of black girls.
- Sarah's $5,000 donation to the NAACP Anti-Lynching Campaign was the largest in the campaign's history.
- She also joined a delegation that traveled to Washington to protest the blight of lynching and President Woodrow Wilson's silence on the matter.
- Moved by men and women willing to better themselves, Sarah promoted a Valentine's Day charity benefit for Indianapolis's only black harpist—a 15-year-old girl who had lost her mother at the age of nine.
- She also supported family members, including her daughter, who worked in the business; a sister-in-law; four nieces; and her elder sister.
- Nevertheless, despite her continuing business success and philanthropic donations, African American leader Booker T. Washington continued to ignore her and her company—largely because of his disdain for hair straightening products.
- As a diversion from business, Sarah often attended movies to watch silent romances, Westerns, and comedies featuring entrepreneurs who had found success.
- The movie theaters also propelled her to leave Indianapolis for New York; after the owner of the Isis Theatre arbitrarily increased ticket prices from $0.10 to a quarter "for colored people," Sarah vowed to move.
- During 1914 and 1915, she traveled extensively, especially in the West, giving lectures on hair care and making donations, particularly scholarships for worthy students.
- Often, especially in California, Sarah had more invitations for speaking engagements than she could fulfill; everywhere she went, she trained new agents, sold Wonderful Hair Grower, and laid the groundwork for new business.
- By the time Sarah moved her operation to Harlem, in New York City, she employed ten thousand commissioned agents, making her the largest employer of black women in America.
- The agents were organized into Walker Clubs that rewarded their members based on contributions raised for charities well as on total sales.
- By 1916 Sarah had real estate investments in Indiana, Michigan and Oklahoma and in the city of Los Angeles; according to her federal tax returns, her business and real estate interests gave her a net worth of $600,000.

Harlem, New York

- Sarah moved into a beautifully renovated brownstone on West 136th Street and Lenox Avenue, but she saw a flood of poor, undereducated women in need of her services throughout Harlem.
- For women seeking something other than domestic or factory work, Madam C. J. Walker offered an alternative: selling Walker's Scientific Scalp Treatment for the chance to earn between $15 and $40 per week.
- And for working women, making the most money they had made in their lives, Sarah offered an urban, modern look for $1.75 per tin.
- Her goal, she said repeatedly, was to grow hair and confidence.
- Potential agents were tempted by written testimonials: "It is a Godsend to unfortunate women who are walking in the rank-and-file that I had walked. It's helped me financially since 1910. We have to been able to purchase a home and overmeet our obligations."
- Despite the luxury she had created for herself in New York City, Sarah spent the last three years of her life traveling for the war effort, seeking to encourage the patriotic service of Negro men.
- She also took the opportunity to train additional agents.
- On several occasions her travels were halted by nervous exhaustion and her failing health.
- For her final crusade, Sarah returned to the issue of lynching, armed with a report that said 3,200 people had been lynched in the United States between 1889 and 1918; the vast majority were black men, and almost all the lynchings took place in the South.
- In 1918 alone, 63 African-Americans, including five women, as well as four white men, had been lynched.
- To that cause alone Sarah pledged $5,000, one of many charitable gifts she made "to help my race."

Life in the Community: Harlem, New York
- Until the early 1870s, Harlem had been a distant rural village of mostly poor farmers in the northern end of Manhattan Island.
- But at the end of that decade, with the launching of the city's first elevated train, Harlem became the city's first suburb.
- Soon thereafter, contractors built opulent brownstones, and Harlem became known for its many mansions.
- An expansion of the Interborough Rapid Transit Line brought a second wave of growth, principally fueled by Irish and Jewish families.
- But when the overheated real estate market collapsed in 1905, West Harlem was saturated with vacant apartments, which became the home of middle-class blacks eager to escape the tenements of the Tenderloin and the San Juan Hill districts.

Many African Americans worked in factories.

- In 1911 the prosperous St. Philip's Episcopal Church, an all-black congregation, engineered a million-dollar real estate transaction in Harlem that became the symbolic beachhead for the black presence.
- Three years later, when Sarah gave her first serious thoughts to a New York move, Harlem was home to 50,000 African Americans.
- A National Urban League report said, "Negroes as a whole are...better housed in Harlem than any other part of the country."
- At the same time, large numbers of African Americans were being pushed from the South by the floods of 1915 and the boll weevil infestations of 1916.
- Many were pulled to Northern cities, including New York City, where they found employment at factory jobs left vacant when the two-decade-long flood of European immigrants was halted by the beginning of World War I.
- Many African Americans found they could make as much as $8.00 a day in a Northern city after a lifetime of making only $0.40 a day farming in the South.
- Black churches, newspapers, YMCAs, and advocacy groups such as the National League on Urban Conditions sprang up.
- Manhattan's population topped two million.
- Manhattan could claim the world's tallest buildings, from the 60-story terra-cotta Woolworth Building on Broadway and Park to the 50-story Metropolitan Life Insurance Building farther uptown on Madison Avenue near 23rd Street.

HISTORICAL SNAPSHOT
1919

- The Eighteenth Amendment to the United States Constitution, authorizing Prohibition, went into effect despite a presidential veto
- The World War I peace conference opened in Versailles, France
- Bentley Motors was founded in England
- The League of Nations was founded in Paris
- The Seattle General Strike involving over 65,000 workers ended when federal troops were summoned by the State of Washington's Attorney General
- Oregon placed a $0.01 per gallon tax on gasoline, becoming the first state to levy a gasoline tax
- Congress established most of the Grand Canyon as a National Park
- The American Legion was formed in Paris
- Eugene V. Debs entered the Atlanta Federal Penitentiary in Georgia for speaking out against the draft during World War I
- Edsel Ford succeeded his father as head of the Ford Motor Company
- The University of California opened its second campus in Los Angeles, initially called the Southern Branch of the University of California (SBUC); it was eventually renamed the University of California, Los Angeles (UCLA)
- Albert Einstein's theory of general relativity was tested and confirmed by Arthur Eddington's observation of a total solar eclipse in Principe, and by Andrew Crommelin in Sobral, Ceará, Brazil
- Congress approved the Nineteenth Amendment to the United States Constitution, which would guarantee suffrage to women
- The U.S. Army sent an expedition across the continental United States to assess the condition of the Interstate Highway System
- Race riots occurred in 26 cities
- The first NFL team for Wisconsin—the Green Bay Packers—was founded by Curly Lambeau
- Hit songs included "Swanee," "Baby, Won't You Please Come Home?" and "When the Moon Shines on the Moonshine"
- President Woodrow Wilson suffered a massive stroke, leaving him partially paralyzed
- Robert Goddard proposed using rockets to send a vehicle to the moon
- Conrad Hilton spent his $5,000 life savings on the Mobley Hotel in Frisco, Texas
- The first Palmer Raids were conducted on the second anniversary of the Russian Revolution; over 10,000 suspected communists and anarchists were arrested in 23 U.S. cities

Selected Prices

Dress Pattern $0.10

Farmland, per Acre $20.00

Gin, Fifth.. $2.15

Hair Color... $0.25

Hair Curlers.. $0.25

Hair Pins $0.05

Phonograph Record.. $0.65

Radium Water, 50 24-Ounce Bottles.......................................$25.00

Shampoo $0.33

Travelers' Checks $0.50

**BEAUTY IS AN ASSET
CULTIVATE IT**

Advertisement, "Asbestos—the only rock on which plants thrive,"
***Leslie's Weekly*, November 15, 1919:**

Industry thrives most where waste is least. And since the development of Asbestos has gone hand in hand with the saving of heat, power and friction, this mineral of wonderful qualities has played an important part in Industrial Conservation.

It is the base of all efficient heat insulation—the necessary *other* 15% in 85% magnesia.

It is, as well, the basic material in the most efficient of friction reducing packings.

As roofings it has qualities of durability and fire-resistance that no other material can approach.

And in innumerable other forms it works miracles of industrial economy that a decade ago would have seemed impossible.

For more than half a century the Johns-Manville Company has steadily grown with the growth of industrial demand for Asbestos.

The Johns-Manville asbestos mines are the largest in the world. In the Johns-Manville plants every Asbestos product is produced under super advantages both of experience and equipment. The Johns-Manville sales-organization, operating through branches in all large cities, is an engineering organization as well, carrying a helpful practical Service, that varies to meet each new requirement but always has for its object—Conservation.

"Wealthiest Negress Dead. Mrs. C.J. Walker, Real Estate Operator, Made Fortune in Few Years," *The New York Times*, May 26, 1919:

Mrs. C.J. Walker, known as New York's wealthiest negress, having accumulated a fortune from the sale of so-called anti-kink hair tonic and from real estate investments in the last 14 years, died yesterday morning at her country estate at Irvington-on-Hudson. She was proprietor of the Madam Walker hair dressing parlors at 108 West 136th Street and other places in the city. Her death recalled the unusual story of how she rose in 12 years from a washerwoman making only $1.50 a day to a position of wealth and influence among members of her race.

Estimates of Mrs. Walker's fortune have run up to $1,000,000. She said herself two years ago that she was not yet a millionaire, but hoped to be some time, not that she wanted the money for herself, but for the good she could do with it. She spent $10,000 every year for the education of young negro men and women in Southern colleges and sent six youths to Tuskegee Institute every year. She recently gave $5,000 to the National Conference on Lynching.

Born 51 years ago, she was married at 14, and was left a widow at 20 with a little girl to support. She worked as a cook, washerwoman, and the like until she had reached the age of about 37. One morning while bending over her wash she suddenly realized that there was no prospect on her meager wage of laying away anything for old age.

She had often said that one night shortly afterward she had a dream and something told her to start a hair tonic business, which she did, in Denver, Col., on a capital of $1.25.

In a few years she had accumulated a large sum, and invested in real estate in the West and South and in New York State, nearly all the property greatly increasing in value. She then owned a $50,000 home in the northern part of this city, which some years ago she gave to her daughter, Mrs. Lelia Walker Robinson, associated with her in business.

In 1917 Madam Walker completed at Irvington, on the banks of the Hudson, a mansion which cost $250,000, and since then had made her home there. The house, which is one of the showplaces in the vicinity, is three stories high and consists of 30 or more rooms. She had installed in this home an $8,000 organ with furnishings, including bronze and marble statuary, cut glass candelabra, tapestries, and paintings, said to be of intrinsic beauty and value.

"$25 for 'Gouging' Soldier. Barber Fined for Charging $4.60 for a Haircut and Shave," *The New York Times*, May 15, 1919:

It cost Arthur Stading, a barber employed in a shop at 138 West 34th Street, $25 yesterday for the various operations he performed on the unsuspecting head of Cecil Bell, a former member of the Third Anti-Aircraft Machine Gun Battalion, who has just returned from overseas.

Bell entered the barber shop last Monday morning for a haircut, shave "and trimmings." When the barber got through he got a check for $4.60. Bell paid it without a murmur, being unfamiliar with the ways of metropolitan barbers, but his comrades told him that he had been overcharged, so he obtained a summons and Stading was arraigned in Jefferson Market Court before Magistrate Corrigan yesterday morning.

Stading protested that he was only carrying out the instructions of the proprietor, and showed an itemized bill, which included $2 for a "peroxide steaming" and $1 for "mange treatment."

"Have you got the mange?" inquired Magistrate Corrigan of Bell.

"No," replied the soldier. "I didn't ask for the treatment. I didn't know what they were putting on my head."

"This is an outrage," said the court. "That mange cure can be bought for 20 cents a gallon. We have frequent complaints of overcharging from the barber shops and it appears that they have one price for civilians and another for soldiers. If I had the proprietor here I would fine him $100. As it is, I will fine you only $25. That shave and haircut and a lot of superfluous treatment will cost you just $20.40."

Thereupon the magistrate complimented Bell on his initiative in having the barber brought to court.

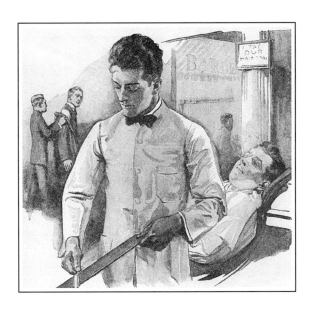

"Art in Eyebrows," *The New York Times*, May 11, 1919:

Lovers in these days might well write sonnets to their ladies' eyebrows—supposing sonnets were a twentieth-century form of love-making—the eyebrows of the girl of today are works of art. The delicately arched eyebrow, which physiognomists might consider to stand for delicacy of character, means nothing now, for its owner may be naturally a beetled-browed damsel. The round-eyed expression of innocence it gives her is not the work of nature but of her hairdresser.

For the last five or six years there has been more or less experimentation with the eyebrows, but it has not been until this year that the practice of toning down eyebrows that are too heavy or giving the girl who wishes it an eyebrow which appears delicately penciled has become comparatively general. A shampoo, a hair wave and treatment of the eyebrows are now all in a single day's work. Shaving is sometimes practiced, but that is not considered as desirable as the use of a pair of tweezers. A little cold cream is put on before the operation and a simple astringent after it and it can be classed as a minor operation. Where the eyebrows are heavy and scattering, trimming up in this way gives a trim, clean look to the face without altering the expression. The delicately arched eyebrow, where it does not belong, turns the wearer into a different person. There may be a general doubt as to its being an improvement, but there are enough people who like it to make it a regular business for the hairdresser. It does not require doing very frequently; the time differs with different people. Ordinarily, eyebrows pulled with tweezers make their appearance again in about two months.

1927: Blues Singer Florence Mills

The "bell-like voice with bird-like qualities" of blues singer Florence Mills helped make her one of the most prominent entertainers of the 1920s.

Life at Home

- Known as the "Queen of Happiness," Florence Mills, born Florence Winfrey, captivated the public with her enchanting song "I'm a Little Blackbird Looking for a Bluebird" and with her stage performances.
- The youngest of three daughters of John and Nellie Winfrey, Florence was born into extreme poverty on January 25, 1895, probably in Washington, D.C., or in the vicinity of the city.
- Both her parents were born in slavery in Amherst County, Virginia, and worked in the tobacco industry.
- When tobacco farming tanked, the family moved from Lynchburg, Virginia, to Washington, D.C., where her father worked as a day laborer and her mother took in laundry.
- Both parents were illiterate.
- Florence grew up in the streets of Goat Alley, Washington, DC's infamous slum, where she first demonstrated the natural gifts as a singer and dancer that would bring her to the attention of an international audience.
- At age five, Florence won prizes for cakewalking and buck dancing, and she was awarded a bracelet by the wife of the British ambassador for entertaining her international guests from the diplomatic corps.
- The family moved to Harlem, in upper Manhattan, in 1903.
- By age seven, Florence was a regular performer in theaters and private homes, and she rapidly developed a name for herself on the vaudeville and burlesque circuits.
- Some of her earliest roles were as a "pickaninny," or "pick," in white vaudeville, and she performed as part of a sister act on the black popular entertainment circuit.
- It was a tough life for a young girl, playing small venues all over the country, putting in endless hours rehearsing and traveling.

Florence Mills

- The high point of her childhood was her appearance in the road company production of Bert Williams and George Walker's *Sons of Ham*, in which she sang "Miss Hannah from Savannah."
- As a result, the traveling white vaudeville team of Bonita and Hearn hired her.
- By age 14 Florence had organized a traveling song-and dance act with her sisters known as the Mills Sisters.
- From then on, Florence Mills was the name she used, instead of Florence Winfrey.
- Florence was innovative: skilled in all varieties of jazz and tap dance, she was especially renowned for her "acrobatic" and "eccentric" dancing.

Tobacco farm

- Her lessons in tap came from her close personal friend Bill "Bojangles" Robinson when she was living in Chicago in 1916-1917.
- Florence also learned much from her husband, Ulysses S. "Slow Kid" Thompson, the originator of "slow motion dancing" and one of the earliest practitioners of "Russian dancing," or "legomania."
- Thompson was a fine dancer, and he conducted the orchestra for a traveling act called the Tennessee Ten, which Florence was invited to join in 1915.
- In 1917 the vaudeville star Nora Bayes brought the Tennessee Ten to New York to perform with her in a new show.
- After the United States entered World War I, however, Thompson was drafted; he was given military training and was sent to France in 1918.
- After his return in 1919, Slow Kid and Florence performed with the Tennessee Ten in *Folly Town*, a very successful burlesque revue with an integrated cast that starred the white vaudevillian Bert Lahr.
- Florence's big break came soon afterward in *Shuffle Along,* which had music and lyrics by black songwriters Noble Sissle and Eubie Blake.
- By the time *Shuffle Along* opened in 1921, Florence and Slow Kid had married.

Life at Work

- *Shuffle Along* was the off-Broadway hit show that introduced syncopated song and dance to white America.

Alberta Hunter on the Black Swan record label

- When the show opened in New York, it was an immediate hit. The star originally was Gertrude Saunders, but when Saunders departed, Florence replaced her.
- Writer Langston Hughes believed *Shuffle Along* initiated the Harlem Renaissance and inaugurated the decade when the "Negro was in vogue."
- Florence's uninhibited singing and dancing stunned the audiences.
- She was paid $125 per week.
- "We were afraid people would think it was a freak show and it wouldn't appeal to white people," said Eubie Blake. "Others thought that if it was a colored show, it might be dirty."

- Sissle and Blake had first joined forces as members of the World War I "Hell Fighters" Jazz Band of the 369th Infantry, led by James Reese Europe.
- They transformed an old sketch named "The Mayor of Jimtown" into a lively musical featuring hit songs such as "I'm Just Wild about Harry" and "Love Will Find a Way," combined with energetic dancing.
- After a while, concurrently with *Shuffle Along*, Florence appeared after theater hours at the Plantation Room, a club on the

Florence Mills and Johnny Hudgins rehearsing Blackbirds on a London rooftop, 1926

rooftop of the Winter Garden Theater, in an act that also featured a wide range of black talent, including visiting performers such as Paul Robeson.
- Florence was convinced to do the show by Lew Leslie, a white promoter, who built the show around her.
- The show—which charged $3 admission—entranced white audiences with the ebullient, fast-paced rhythms of black music.
- Edith Wilson and the Jazz Hounds served as Florence's house orchestra.
- Florence was paid $200 per week.
- In 1922 the nightclub act was converted into a Broadway show called *The Plantation Revue;* Slow Kid Thompson joined Florence in the cast.
- Florence was positioned to become one of the first black female performers to break into the racially restricted show business establishment.
- She was paid $500 per week, for no fewer than 35 weeks a year.
- Civil rights crusader Bert Williams, of the Bert Williams-George Walker duo, believed that Florence would accomplish more than he had: "This is once where the pint is better than the quart."
- Florence did it all: she sang blues, "hot jazz" and ballads, plus she danced, acted, and was an accomplished comedian and mime.
- Luminaries such as Jelly Roll Morton, James P. Johnson, and Willie "The Lion" Smith helped dub her the "Queen of Jazz."
- Composer Irving Berlin said that if he could find a white woman who could sing like Florence, he would be inspired to write a hit a week.
- Writer James Weldon Johnson wrote, "The upper range of her voice was full of bubbling, bell-like, bird-like tones.
- "It was a rather magical thing Florence Mills used to do with that small voice in her favorite song, 'I'm a Little Blackbird Looking for a Bluebird,' and she did it with such exquisite poignancy as always to raise a lump in your throat."
- But that did not change the fact that the set where she performed was fashioned like a pre-Civil War southern plantation featuring a large watermelon slice, whose seeds were electric lights, and a bandanna-coifed black woman flipping pancakes.
- Nonetheless, Florence brought the house down with the naughty song, "I've Got What It Takes But It Breaks My Heart to Give It Away"; Edith Wilson performed her showstopper in the same revue: "He May Be Your Man, But He Comes to See Me Sometimes."

- Florence was reported to be the "highest-salaried colored actress on the American stage."
- The Great White Way was not solely white anymore.
- On opening night for the second, 1922-1923 season, the audience included Charlie Chaplin, Irving Berlin and Irene Bordoni.
- One of the new songs added to the second season, "Aggravatin' Pappa," became a radio hit—by Sophie Tucker; by the end of the year, a dozen female singers had recorded Florence's new song.
- When Sir Charles B. Cochran began looking for attractions for

King and Carter Jazzing Orchestra, 1921 (Robert Runyon Photograph Collection)

the London stage, he invited the Plantation Company to the Pavilion in the spring of 1923, despite a newspaper headline reading, "Nigger Problem Brought to London."
- The show that Cochran devised was called *Dover Street to Dixie*; it was staged with an all-English cast in the first half and featured Florence and the Plantation cast in the second half.
- It proved so successful that issues of race were soon forgotten.
- The Prince of Wales was said to have seen the show numerous times; Florence became so popular that she was to London what Josephine Baker was to Paris.
- Composer Duke Ellington wrote a musical portrait for Florence called "Black Beauty"; she was featured in *Vogue* and *Vanity Fair* and photographed by Bassano and Edward Steichen.
- In 1923, on her return to New York, Florence received an invitation to appear in the Greenwich Village Follies annual production—the first time a black woman was offered a part in the major white production.
- She was also offered a contract to join the Ziegfeld Follies, but she turned it down.
- She elected to stay with Lew Leslie to create a rival show with an all-black cast.
- Florence felt she could best serve her race by providing a venue for an entire company of actors and singers; "If in any way I have done anything to lift the profession, I am unconscious of it, and

Mamie Smith on the Okeh record label

it was done only for love of my art and for my people."
- Florence enjoyed a triumphant return.
- Her popularity knew no bounds—she was now an international star.
- Florence and her husband bought a new house—a five-story brownstone in the middle of Harlem—and furnished it with carpets imported from China and a music box that played records without rewinding.
- *Dover Street to Dixie*, which had thrilled in London, became *Dixie to Broadway* when it opened in New York on October 29, 1924, with a brand-new slate of songs.

- Advertisements proclaimed Florence to be the "World's Greatest Colored Entertainer: The Sensation of Two Continents."
- One critic said, "The vital force of the revue proceeds from the personality of Miss Mills."
- In 1926, when Leslie produced *Blackbirds*, Florence achieved her goal of creating a major all-black revue with the opening of this show at the Alhambra Theatre in Harlem.
- The show moved in September to London's Pavilion Theatre and enjoyed 276 performances.
- Exhausted from so many successive performances, Florence went to Germany to rest, but her condition did not improve.
- In 1927 she returned to New York to a royal welcome.
- Finally compelled to deal with her health problems, she was diagnosed with "pelvic tuberculosis," and it was decided that she needed surgery.

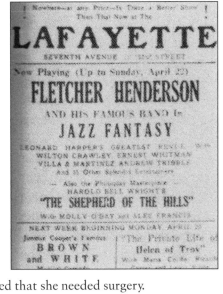

- On October 24, 1927, she entered the hospital.
- One week later, on November 1, 1927, after two operations, Florence Mills died, at age 31.
- Some 3,000 people attended her funeral at the Mother AME Zion Church; kings sent flowers, Americans—black and white—mourned.
- Harlem came to a standstill as 150,000 people—the largest such gathering in Harlem's history—lined the streets during the funeral procession.

Life in the Community: Harlem, New York City, New York

- Harlem's history was defined by a series of boom-and-bust cycles, with significant ethnic shifts accompanying each one.
- A housing boom in the 1890s produced an overabundance of houses, and by 1903, builders had opened their doors to tenants of all colors and races.
- Entrepreneur Philip Payton and his Afro-American Realty Company actively recruited black families already living in the city, almost single-handedly igniting the migration of blacks from their previous New York neighborhoods, the Tenderloin, San Juan Hill and Hell's Kitchen.

A view of Harlem north of Columbia University

- The move by black residents to northern Manhattan was partially driven by fears of anti-black riots, which occurred in the Tenderloin in 1900 and in San Juan Hill in 1905.
- New black residents began to arrive from elsewhere en masse in 1904, the year of the beginning of the Great Migration by Southern blacks fleeing poverty, lack of opportunity, and aggressive enforcement of discriminatory Jim Crow laws.
- By 1910 Harlem had a population of approximately 500,000, of whom 50,000 were African-American and 75,000 were native-born whites; the rest

were immigrants from Ireland, Germany, Hungary, Russia, England, Italy and Scandinavia.

- In the 1920s the district was the setting of the "Harlem Renaissance," an unprecedented outpouring of artistic and professional work by African Americans.
- By this time new opportunities were developing for the black artistic community, which had long been subject to humiliating discrimination and Jim Crow laws.
- White promoter Otto Heinemann and his company OKeh Records were struggling to get established; Heinemann was willing to try anything when he asked Cincinnati's young black singer Mamie Smith to cut a record.
- For the premiere recording, Smith sang "That Thing Called Love" and "You Can't Keep a Good Man Down," backed by the house orchestra—to keep the record from sounding "too colored."
- This was quickly followed by the recording of "Crazy Blues" and "It's Right Here for You (If You Don't Come Get It, 'Taint No Fault of Mine)," this time accompanied by a five-piece black band known as the Jazz Hounds.
- The result was impressive and possibly the first actual blues recording by a black artist with black accompaniment.
- Within a month, 75,000 copies of "Crazy Blues" had been sold in Harlem record shops; in only seven months, national sales topped one million copies.
- Mamie Smith and her band were pure gold; everything they recorded sold immediately.
- Smith made more than $100,000 in recording royalties alone; in addition, she was making between $1,000 and $1,500 a week in the large theaters of New York and Chicago.
- As a result, record companies scrambled to sign new blues singers; Columbia Records even bragged that it had "more colored artists under exclusive contract than any company today."
- Black Swan Records, produced for Pace Phonograph Company of New York, advertised itself as the "only genuine colored record. Others are only passing for colored."
- In this period Harlem earned a reputation as the Mecca for jazz and blues.
- Venues such as the Cotton Club and the Apollo Theater made stars out of many entertainers, including Fletcher Henderson and Duke Ellington.
- During World War I, expanding industries recruited black laborers to fill new jobs.
- By 1920 central Harlem was 32.43 percent black; between 1920 and 1930, according to census figures, 118,792 white people left the neighborhood and 87,417 blacks arrived.

School band in Harlem

HISTORICAL SNAPSHOT
1927

- The first transatlantic telephone call was made from New York City to London
- The U.S. Federal Radio Commission began to regulate the use of radio frequencies
- In New York City, the Roxy Theater was opened by Samuel Roxy Rothafel
- The first armored car robbery was committed by the Flatheads Gang near Pittsburgh, Pennsylvania
- The Great Mississippi Flood of 1927 affected 700,000 people in the greatest natural disaster in U.S. history
- Philo Farnsworth transmitted the first experimental electronic television pictures
- *To The Lighthouse* was completed by Virginia Woolf
- The Academy of Motion Picture Arts and Sciences was founded
- Saudi Arabia became independent of the United Kingdom under the Treaty of Jedda

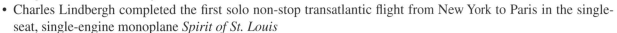

- Charles Lindbergh completed the first solo non-stop transatlantic flight from New York to Paris in the single-seat, single-engine monoplane *Spirit of St. Louis*
- Mount Rushmore was dedicated with promises of national funding for the carving
- The Columbia Phonographic Broadcasting System, later known as CBS, was formed and went on the air with 47 radio stations
- A treaty signed at the League of Nations Slavery Convention abolished all types of slavery
- *The Jazz Singer*, a movie with sound, ushered in "talkies" in the United States
- Leon Trotsky was expelled from the Soviet Communist Party, leaving Joseph Stalin with undisputed control of the Soviet Union
- The Holland Tunnel opened to traffic as the first Hudson River vehicular tunnel linking New Jersey to New York City
- After 19 years of Ford Model T production, the Ford Motor Company unveiled the Ford Model A, available in four colors, with a self-starter
- The musical play *Show Boat*, based on Edna Ferber's novel, opened on Broadway—one of 268 plays on Broadway
- Harold Stephen Black invented the feedback amplifier
- Sears, Roebuck and Co. distributed 15 million catalogues to American homes
- Arthur H. Compton won the Nobel prize in physics for his discovery of wavelength change in diffused x-rays
- The Voluntary Committee of Lawyers was founded to bring about the repeal of Prohibition in the U.S.
- Hit songs included "Ol' Man River," "Can't Help Loving Dat Man," "I'm Looking Over a Four Leaf Clover," "The Best Things In Life Are Free" and "Me And My Shadow"
- The world population reached two billion

Selected Prices

Bath Salts, Jar	$1.50
Bathtub	$29.95
Cigarette Case	$11.72
Dress, Crepe	$49.50
House Paint, Gallon	$2.15
Incense and Burner	$1.00
Iron	$4.45
Oil Heater	$4.95
Refrigerator, Ice Capacity 100 Pounds	$56.95
Toilet	$6.95

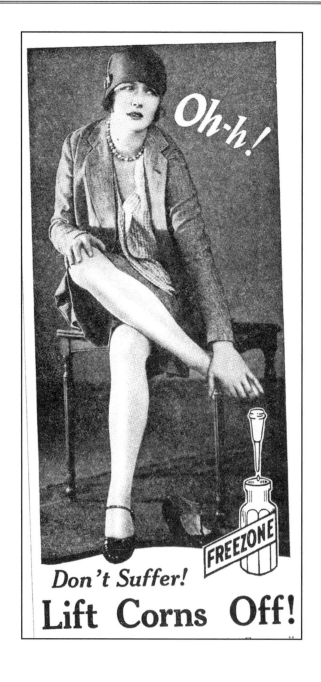

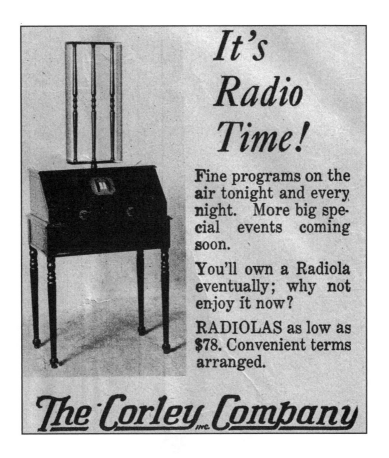

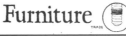

The creation of jazz by black artists gave this country a language that it was searching for, and gave it a rhythmic identity, and so it makes perfect sense that the composers would use this inventive language and rhythm for the theater.

—George C. Wolfe, director

"The Turn of the Tide, What's Going On in the World," *McCall's*, April 1928:

Under the masterly direction of Prince Otto von Bismarck and Count Helmuth von Moltke, the greatest military machine ever devised by man sprang into being during the '60s and '70s of the last century. In order to make this machine yet more potent, a doctrine of "blood and iron" was proclaimed. The State—social, political, and industrial—was molded into a compact organization for its successful enlargement by means of war, and Denmark, Austria and France successively succumbed to its irresistible force.

Bismarck, in his wisdom, halted to allow his Fatherland to consolidate and become accustomed to the sudden change from a kingdom to an empire. What might have happened had Bismarck lived and held his power no man may say, but the direction of German affairs fell into less capable hands and disaster came. The deed was done and the consequences were to follow.

While in Germany war had become glorified, the balance of Europe was terrified by this new menace to peace. Fear led the Great Powers, in self-protection, to form an iron circle around the dreaded borders of this great military state.

Through the bitterness of defeat in the Great War came salvation, not alone for the German people, but, perhaps, for Europe as well. Today, the tide has turned in the nation formerly the protagonist of ruthless and relentless war, and has become an earnest advocate of disarmament and peace. Germany has gone so far as to announce her intention to accept the optional clause in the World Court making obligatory peaceful settlements of international disputes of judicial character. In Geneva, the voice of Germany constantly is raised on behalf of every measure having for its purpose conciliation as opposed to war. The terms of reproach heretofore leveled at her by opponents are now used against other nations less yielding in the cause of disarmament and compulsory arbitration.

It may be of interest for Americans to know that the wartime ambassador from Germany to the United States—Count von Bernstorff—is one of the foremost leaders in the movement for general disarmament and the abolition of war. Together with the German Minister for Foreign Affairs—Gustafson Stressemann—he has represented Germany at the League of Nations' conferences and has gone further than almost any delegate in his demands for measures to secure the peace of Europe.

Those, from long habit, still critical of Germany see in her a sinister purpose. It is said that she is restrained by the Versailles Treaty from having a large army and navy, and that she is actuated not so much by a change of heart as by a change in circumstance. But it may well be that the German people are awakened to the truth that peace has more possibilities for their welfare than war, and if they lead as fervently in the direction of peace as they formerly did for war, the ultimate result will not alone be of advantage to Germany, but to all of Europe as well.

There is a tremendous urge among the small nations of Europe against war. This feeling has never been so strong as now. The fear of another catastrophe like that of 1914-1918 hangs over them. This dread is one of the most marked results of the Great War. It is a shadow that can never be wholly lifted during the lives of this generation.

While the forebears of the American people came almost wholly from Europe, it is difficult for us to think in terms of Europeans. From the dawn of history until now, the fear of aggressive wars has haunted them. From the tribal raids of the misty past all through the ages, we find the same story. Civilization has hewn its way with the sword. The cost, the misery, and the mental anguish are beyond computation. And in our day of supposed enlightenment came the greatest holocaust of all. The madness of it is just beginning to make an impression sufficiently strong to give the world hope.

1935: African American Couple Emigrate from Rural South to Urban North

This couple migrated from the Deep South to Harlem, New York, where they were able to build a future together, due to the husband's secure job as a railroad porter.

Life at Home

- Sam and Edna Whitley, like thousands of other Southern Blacks, moved to Harlem, New York from rural South Carolina to escape the poverty of the sharecropper system.
- Sam found work as a Pullman Porter and Edna worked as a domestic, when employment is available; they had no children.
- Living as sharecroppers in South Carolina, they lost hope of ever being free from constant debt to buy their own land.
- When the Whitleys first arrived in New York, they refused government relief; Sam had too much pride to consider taking charity from the government.
- They were each 18 when they married eight years ago.
- Sam had little formal education though his mother taught him the rudiments of reading and writing using the family Bible.
- He dropped out of school in the third grade to support his mother; he does not remember ever meeting his father.
- Edna was a preacher's daughter; she could both read and write.
- She left school after the sixth grade, when she was forced to work in the cotton fields full-time.
- The couple wanted children, but were uncertain about their jobs.
- They lived in a three-room tenement house that included one bedroom, high ceilings and faulty plumbing and wiring, and no refrigerator.
- Their landlord was unresponsive, but the Whitleys could not find a better living situation because the demand for housing in Harlem was so great.
- Sam and Edna decided to improve the looks of their home a bit by buying a new bedspread from Montgomery Ward for $1.94.

Sam Whitley worked as a Pullman Porter on the railroad.

Life at Work: The Pullman Company

- Sam worked as a Pullman Porter, serving the first class passengers who travelled with a sleeper.
- He often made the long trip from New York to Miami working up to 18 hours at a stretch.
- When he got the job, Sam went through a short training program, then worked for six months on probation before being hired.
- He was taught to be courteous, efficient, and to do whatever it took to make their first class travelers comfortable.
- Sam also made up berths, kept the cars in order, handled luggage, and saw that the washrooms were clean and adequately supplied with towels.
- In addition to coping with the long hours of being on call—to meet every whim of the passenger—Sam was often subjected to the abuse of passengers with very little recourse.
- Sam had seen other Pullman Porters fired for slight infractions, including drinking on the job—even when the porter in question didn't drink.
- He eventually had enough experience to bid for a "port-in-charge" position, but did not have the reading and writing skills to complete the paperwork and keep appropriate records.
- Sam worried about rumors that the declining first class traffic will reduce the number of weeks he could work.
- A large percentage of Sam's income was from customers' tips, and his base salary was not adequate.
- Sam knew that for the Pullman Company saw African Americans as perfect employees for its sleeping cars, first because of their skills as former slaves and second because they were happy with much less money than their White counterparts.
- Many Americans still preserved their antebellum attitudes toward the former slaves, and gave Pullman a ready market for their services; even the common man, for the price of a Pullman ticket, was waited upon in all the comfort of a Southern gentleman.

Life in the Community: Harlem, New York

- Harlem was known as a slum, and real estate was dominated by Whites, so even though people in Harlem paid higher rent, very few repairs were made.
- Rent parties were a common sight among residents of Harlem. As the name suggests, they were primarily used to raise enough money to pay the rent. The typical entrance fee was $0.25, and inside one finds live music and the opportunity to buy refreshments (including liquor much of the time), dance, etc.
- Bandleader Count Basie was creating a revolution in jazz; the Basie piano style de-emphasizes the left hand while promoting the use of the high-hat cymbal and the relaxed style of the saxophone.
- The density of people in Harlem was 336 per acre, while the density of people in Manhattan was 223 per acre; many Black families take in borders to supplement their incomes.
- The Afro-American Realty Company told clients that it doesn't matter how many people lived in the house as long as the rent was paid up.
- Unemployment was 20.3 percent.
- As jobs grew scarce and African-American migration increased, many workers in Harlem were grossly over-qualified for the positions they held; a doctor of medicine might be a janitor in a hospital or a man with a master's in business might work in a factory with no hope of ever being promoted to management.
- The passage of the National Labor Relations Act, also known as the Wagner Act, established a mandate for industry to bargain with unions—the first time in American history the national government had placed its weight behind the principle of unionism.
- Harlem was in an uproar over the riots, started when a young African-American boy was caught stealing and word spread that the boy had been beaten and killed by the shop owner; the Young Liberators and the Young Communist League fanned the flames of the riot with fliers that alleged brutality.
- Following the riots, New York Mayor La Guardia created a committee to investigate conditions in Harlem that led to the riot, including housing, playgrounds, discrimination in employment, education, and relief agencies.
- A nationwide government study of working class families showed some improvement in living conditions.
- Basic food needs were met more fully, milk consumption had increased, housing was more comfortable, with plumbing and electricity the norm rather than the exception.
- In addition, radios were commonplace, most working class homes switch from cooking with coal or wood to gas and use of machines was common.

The Sharecropper System

- By moving to New York, the couple broke the cycle of poverty inherent in the sharecropper system.
- In general, the tenant farmer borrowed everything he needed to work with-seed, plow, mule, etc.-from the landowner, who was paid back with a portion of the crops.
- This system came into play after the Civil War, according to some "so that plantation owners could pretend that the Emancipation Proclamation had never occurred."
- This system normally imprisoned the tenant farmer; rarely could enough "good years" equal the cost of the goods "borrowed" so the sharecropper could purchase land.
- Their decision was reinforced by the boll weevil invasion of 1923, which wiped out entire cotton fields, and caused a general depression in the South. They moved North to see if what they had heard about freedom was true.
- They were not alone; in 1920, 85 percent of all Blacks lived south of the Mason-Dixon line compared with 92 percent at the time of the Civil War; by 1940 the percentage would drop to 76 percent.

- The couple did not engage in any practices such as illegal liquor distilling to supplement their income, despite the temptation; they needed the money but after a neighbor was taken to jail for manipulating the gas meter, the husband decided that it was better for him not to engage in those activities.

Poverty was a constant companion under the sharecropper system.

৵৵৵৵৵৵৵৵

Those Pullman Blues, quoting Malcolm X, speaking of his days as a food seller on the coaches for New Haven

"We were in that world between Black train employees and White passengers: We were in that world of Negroes who are both servants and psychologists, aware that White people are so obsessed with their own importance that they will pay liberally, even dearly, for the impression of being catered to and entertained."

Those Pullman Blues, quoting Norman Bookman

"One time a man was riding with us on the Lark. He was talking and they were discussing politics, and they were saying, 'Well, there's so many niggers in San Francisco and so many niggers in L.A.,' and so on. The woman with him looked up at me-I didn't say anything till the next morning. [The train] came in, and she was with him. They were not together. And I said, 'Pardon me, I'd like to ask a question if I may. What did I do wrong last night? I've been up all night wondering what was done wrong. I thought I was giving fair service.'

Then he started apologizing for having made the mistake in saying those words, and he wanted to give me a little piece of change for it. I said, 'Oh, no, you don't owe me nothing.' But now, you see, I could have put it another way or jumped in that night. They're all drinking, and it could have been an embarrassing thing, or he could have gotten angry, or maybe I got angry and cussed him out, or something else. So you learn how to handle these things this way."

Historical Snapshot
1935–1936

- The Social Security Act passed Congress

- The Emergency Relief Appropriation Act gave $5 billion to create jobs

- Fort Knox became the United States Repository of gold bullion

- One-tenth of one percent of U.S. corporations made 50 percent of earnings

- Sulfa-drug chemotherapy was introduced to relieve veneral disease sufferers everywhere

- Nylon was developed by Du Pont

- Beer cans were introduced

- One-third of farmers received U.S. treasury allotment checks for not growing food or crops

- New York State law allowed women to serve as jurors

- Polystyrene became commercially available in the United States for use in products such as kitchen utensils and toys

- An eight-hour day was passed in Illinois

- Seven million women paid more than $2 billion for 35 million permanents

- Margaret Mitchell's *Gone with the Wind* sold a record one million copies in six months

- A *Fortune* poll indicated that 67 percent favored birth control

- Trailer sales peaked; tourist camps for vacationing motorists gained popularity

1935 Economic Profile

Income, Standard Jobs

Average of All Industries,
    Including Farm Labor $1,115.00
Bituminous Coal Mining. $957.00
Building Trades. $1,027.00
Domestics $485.00
Farm Labor $324.00
Federal Civilian $1,759.00
Federal Military $1,154.00
Gas and Electricity Workers. $1,589.00
Manufacturing, Durable Goods. $1,264.00
Manufacturing, Nondurable Goods $1,178.00
Medical/Health Services Workers $829.00
Motion Picture Services $1,892.00
Passenger Transportation Workers $1,361.00
Personal Services $915.00
Public School Teachers. $1,293.00
Radio Broadcasting $2,089.00
Railroads $1,645.00
State and Local Government Workers. $1,361.00
Telephone and Telegraph Workers. $1,378.00
Wholesale and Retail Trade Workers $1,279.00

Selected Prices

Baby Seat, Loom Woven Lined
    with Cotton $12.98
Birdbath, Sandstone $50.00
Broiler Pan, Oval Aluminum. $0.75
Charcoal Grill $1.95
China Cabinet, Pine, Extra Width $32.50
Dinnerware, Semi-Porcelain, for Six. $4.98
Fishing Reel $8.25
Flashlight $1.39
Garden Tractor, Handiman,
    Four Hp Motor $242.00
Gun Case, Custom Made with
    Lambskin. $3.00
Jergens Lotion $0.69
Olive Oil $0.39
Paper Pattern for Dress $0.15
Pocket Radio $2.90
Pressure Cooker, Eight-Quart $7.45
Razor Blade $1.00
Shotgun, Double Barrel. $30.00
Sportman's Encyclopedia. $1.00
Tire, Goodyear All Weather $15.55
Waterhose, 25' Green ⅝" $3.00

1939: Female Pianist and Musical Arranger

Pianist and musical arranger Mary Lou Williams wrote and arranged countless hits for Benny Goodman and Tommy Dorsey, and played to packed houses with the band Clouds of Joy.

Life at Home

- Born Mary Elfreida Scruggs, Mary Lou was one of 11 children, and moved to Pittsburgh when she was five or six years old.
- Her mother played the organ, and Mary Lou began playing the piano for money when she was seven, sometimes earning $20 to $30 a day.
- When Mary Lou was 10, the Mellon family paid her $100 to play piano for a party and brought her to the event in a chauffeur-driven limousine.
- When she was 11, Mary was asked to substitute for the regular pianist on a touring show of the Earl Hines Band, *Hits and Bits,* and all the coaching she needed was a cast member simply humming the tunes for her on the day of the performance.
- For the next two summers, she traveled with the show, which brought her into contact with popular groups like McKinney's Cotton Pickers and Duke Ellington's Washingtonians.
- By the time she turned 13, she was a veteran musician with fans all along the East Coast.
- One of those fans was future husband and saxophonist John Williams, whose combo played with *Hits and Bit.*
- When Seymour and Jeanette, a top vaudeville team on the Orpheum circuit, proposed that John Williams could join their circuit, he insisted on taking Mary Lou along.
- "Cut her hair and put pants on her!" shouted Seymour in response. "We cannot have a girl in the outfit."
- After hearing her play the piano, however, Seymour changed his mind and she stayed with the act until it broke up a year later.
- When she was 15, and jamming with McKinney's Cotton Pickers at Harlem's Rhythm Club at 3 am, Louis Armstrong entered the room, paused to listen, then "Louis picked me up and kissed me."
- After they were married, John Williams and Mary Lou toured the South with her own small band until John joined *Clouds of Joy.*
- Soon after they moved to Kansas City, Missouri for a job at the Pla-Mor, one the

Mary Lou Williams was a jazz pianist with fans all along the East Coast–including Louis Armstrong–by the time she was 13 years old.

city's top ballrooms, and worked in Kansas City for seven years.

- "Kaycee was really jumping," Mary Lou said. "So many great bands have sprung up there or moved in from over the river. It attracted musicians from all over the South and Southwest."

Life at Work

- Kansas City was a wide-open town, firmly under the control of political boss Tom Pendergast, who ignored the national Prohibition against alcohol sales, while promoting gambling and other vice in the city.
- "Naturally, work was plentiful for musicians," Mary Lou Williams said.
- Talented musicians flocked to the town-where the music never went to bed-to play in after-hours jam sessions with established musicians like Herschel Evans, Coleman Hawkins and Lester ("Prez") Young.
- "We didn't have closing hours in those spots," Mary Lou said. "We'd play all morning and half through the day if we wished, and, in fact, we often did. The music was so good we seldom got to bed before midday."
- Kansas City jazz was recognized as a unique sound with its preference for a 4/4 beat that made it more relaxed and fluid.
- New York had developed its own swinging jazz sound, Chicago was recognized as a center for its own jazz style, and the crossroads community of Kansas City owned its own distinctive sound.
- Extended soloing fueled by a culture whose goal was to "say something" with one's instrument also marked Kansas City jazz as distinctive.
- At times, one "song" could be performed for several hours, with the best musicians often soloing for dozens of choruses at a time.
- Constructed around a 12-bar blues structure, rather than the eight-bar jazz standard, the style left room for elaborate riffing by individuals or pairs.

Louis Armstrong at the piano.

Clouds of Joy's success was a direct result of the songs that Mary Lou wrote and arranged for them.

- Since the big bands in Kansas City also played by memory, composing collectively rather than sight-reading, the KC style was often looser and more spontaneous.
- It was a sound that suited Mary Lou's musical skills.
- Critics wrote of Mary Lou, "If you shut your eyes, you would bet she was a man."
- *Time* magazine said she played "the solid, unpretentious, flesh-&-bone kind of jazz piano that is expected from such vigorous Negro masters as James P. Johnson."
- For a decade, Andy Kirk's *Clouds of Joy* and Mary Lou were inseparable.
- She wrote most of its arrangements, and many, such as "Roll 'Em" and "Froggy Bottom" quickly became classics among jazz players.
- Writing up to 15 scores a week, she provided the *Clouds of Joy* with 200 arrangements, including "Walkin' and Swingin'," "Twinklin'," "Cloudy'," and "Little Joe from Chicago."
- During a recording trip to Chicago, Mary Lou recorded "Drag 'Em" and "Night Life" as piano solos.
- The records sold briskly, lifting Mary Lou to national prominence.
- She also began playing solo gigs and working as a freelance arranger for Earl Hines, Benny Goodman, and Tommy Dorsey.
- Mary Lou and the *Clouds of Joy* also scored another hit with "Until The Real Thing Comes Along," and suddenly, their sound was coming from every bar; when they played live to packed houses, and from the newly developed jukebox.
- Some nights they performed "Real Thing" half a dozen times because the demand was so great, despite the fact that its gloomy sound was a departure from KC swing.
- When she wrote *In the Groove* with Dick Wilson, Benny Goodman asked Mary Lou to write a blues number for his band.
- The result was "Roll 'Em," a boogie-woogie piece based on the blues, which followed her successful "Camel Hop," Goodman's theme song for his radio show sponsored by Camel cigarettes.

- Goodman wanted Mary Lou to write for him exclusively, but she refused, preferring to freelance and make her own path.

Life in the Community: Kansas City, Missouri

- Kansas City, Missouri straddles the border between Missouri and Kansas at the confluence of the Kansas and Missouri rivers.
- Incorporated in 1850 as Town of Kansas with a population of 1,500, it quickly became known for its famous Kansas City streak, and the Pendergast Era (1840-1940), when Democrat city bosses James Pendergast and Tom Pendergast, ushered in a colorful and influential era for the city.
- The Pendergasts declared that national Prohibition was meaningless in Kansas City, and developed the Kansas City boulevard and park system.

The Chester?eld Club was one of many popular jazz clubs in Kansas City.

- American aviator Charles Lindbergh helped convince the new Transcontinental & Western Airline (later TWA) to locate its corporate headquarters in Kansas City because of its central location, making Kansas City a hub of national aviation.
- Kansas City was also often a national crossroads of cultures as transcontinental flights and train journeys most times required a stop in the city.
- Jazz musicians associated with the style were born in other places but got caught up in the friendly musical competition among performers that could keep a single song being performed in variations for an entire night.
- Members of the Big Bands would perform at regular venues earlier in the evening, and go to the jazz clubs later to jam for the rest of the night.
- Clubs were scattered throughout the city, but the most fertile area was the inner city neighborhood of 18th Street and Vine.
- Among the clubs were the Amos 'n' Andy, Boulevard Lounge, Cherry Blossom, Chesterfield Club, Chocolate Bar, Dante's Inferno, Elk's Rest, Hawaiian Gardens, Hell's Kitchen, the Hi Hat, the Hey Hey, Lone Star, Old Kentucky Bar-B-Que, Paseo Ballroom, Pla-Mor Ballroom, Reno Club, Spinning Wheel, Street's Blue Room, Subway and Sunset.

"Mary Lou Williams With Andy Kirk Band," *Cumberland Evening Times* **(Maryland), July 13, 1937:**

Mary Lou Williams is featured with Andy Kirk's Orchestra Thursday evening at Crystal Park. She is known as "America's Sweetheart of the ivories," and the most talked about "swing" pianist in the orchestral world. She's the girl that swings the band. She makes the piano speak in a language to which every dance responds...an unusual personality...she's America's foremost femme stylist of the piano.

Mary Lou Williams is the gal that makes all of Benny Goodman, Lou Armstrong, and Bob Crosby's special swing numbers.

HISTORICAL SNAPSHOT
1939

- The Hewlett-Packard Company was founded
- Amelia Earhart was officially declared dead two years after her disappearance while attempting to fly around the world
- *Naturwissenschaften* published evidence that nuclear fission had been achieved by Otto Hahn
- Adolf Hitler ordered Plan Z, a five-year naval expansion effort intended to create a huge German fleet capable of crushing the Royal Navy by 1944
- Hitler prophesied that if "Jewish financers" started a war against Germany, the result would be the "annihilation of the Jewish race in Europe"
- The Golden Gate International Exposition opened in San Francisco, and the 1939 World's Fair opened in New York City
- Sit-down strikes were outlawed by the Supreme Court
- In Bombay, Mohandas Gandhi began a fast protesting against British rule in India
- Students at Harvard University demonstrated the new tradition of swallowing goldfish to reporters
- British Prime Minister Neville Chamberlain gave a speech in Birmingham, stating that Britain will oppose any effort at world domination on the part of Germany
- African-American singer Marian Anderson performed before 75,000 people at the Lincoln Memorial in Washington, DC, after having been denied the use of both Constitution Hall by the Daughters of the American Revolution, and of a public high school by the federally controlled District of Columbia
- John Steinbeck's novel *The Grapes of Wrath* was published
- Billie Holiday recorded "Strange Fruit," the first anti-lynching song
- *Batman*, created by Bob Kane, made his first comic book appearance
- Major League Baseball's Lou Gehrig ended his 2,130 consecutive games played streak after developing amyotrophic lateral sclerosis (ALS)
- Pan-American Airways begins transatlantic mail service with the inaugural flight of its *Yankee Clipper* from Port Washington, New York
- The *St. Louis*, a ship carrying 907 Jewish refugees, was denied permission to land in Florida after already having been turned away from Cuba, and was forced to return to Europe, where many of its passengers later died in Nazi death camps during the Holocaust
- The National Baseball Hall of Fame and Museum was officially dedicated in Cooperstown, New York
- The 1st World Science Fiction Convention opened in New York City
- The sculpture of Theodore Roosevelt's head was dedicated at Mount Rushmore
- Albert Einstein wrote to President Franklin Roosevelt about developing the atomic bomb using uranium, leading to the creation of the Manhattan Project
- MGM's classic musical film *The Wizard of Oz*, based on L. Frank Baum's novel, and starring Judy Garland as Dorothy, premiered
- As World War II began in Europe with Germany's attack on Poland, the United States declared its neutrality

- Gerald J. Cox, speaking at an American Water Works Association meeting, publicly proposed the fluoridation of public water supplies in the U.S.
- Nylon stockings went on sale for the first time
- *Hedda Hopper's Hollywood* premiered on radio with Hollywood gossip columnist Hedda Hopper as host
- La Guardia Airport opened for business in New York City
- General Motors introduced the Hydra-Matic drive, the first mass-produced, fully automatic transmission, as an option in 1940 model year Oldsmobiles

Selected Prices

Camera, Kodak	$20.00
Coca-Cola	$0.25
Home Movie, 16 mm	$8.75
Movie Camera	$49.50
Movie Ticket	$0.25
Nylons	$1.95
Pocket Telescope	$1.00
Seat Covers, Sedan	$5.85
Toothpaste	$0.25
Wall Clock	$6.98

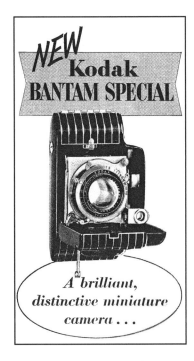

> **"The New York World's Fair Music Festival," Olin Downes,**
> *Etude Music Magazine*, **May 1939:**
>
> A visitor from Cape Town, South Africa, who was taken for a preview through the New York World's Fair grounds, was heard to exclaim in a kind of neo-Mayfair accent, "My word, one couldn't begin to see all this in a lifetime." The reason for this, doubtless, is that highly experienced and energetic men behind the huge project realized that Canadians who will visit the World's Fair would be presented with an enormous variety of appeals—high-brow, low-brow, broad-brow and narrow-brow—something representative of everything under the sun, for everyone under the sun.
>
> One might say that the same dimensions and characteristics apply to the music programs arranged and still being arranged for the World's Fair. In fact, these dimensions are so extensive that, even though I have been surrounded with them since the beginning, I'm still bewildered by their size. They've long since left the boundaries of the Fair itself.
>
> This reminds me of the story of a colored man named Esau, who worked upon the campus of a little Southern college in a town invisible upon the map. At the time of the Chicago Fair, he was enraptured by the posters in the railroad station so as to take his savings to venture upon the long trip. Practically none of the colored folks had ever been more than three miles from town. When he left, every worker from the neighboring plantations was at the station to see him off. He was gone a month. Colored picture postcards of the Fair thrilled his friends. When he came back, an anxious and excited crowd was on hand to greet him. The president of the college asked the traveler what he liked best at the Fair. Esau scratched his head, meditated, and then said, "Well, Massa Boss, you see when I got to Chicago I just got so busy I never did get time to get to the fairgrounds."
>
> As a matter of fact, the plans for the music of the Fair, as now outlined, will very properly be devoted to concerts and operas in New York City itself. About one-half of the celebrations will be upon Manhattan Island and one-half at the fairgrounds. As projected, the first six months of the fair season (May 1 to November 1) will include so many important occasions that one can confidently predict that it will be the most significant musical festival the world has ever known....
>
> We have given a suggestion as to the participation of some foreign governments. It may be interesting to know that several countries overseas recognize the importance of music as a glorified expression of national ideals, and therefore these countries have arranged to engage great American symphony orchestras to play the music of their famous composers at a distinguished series of concerts given under the auspices of these countries. The plans are so far-reaching that I can give here only a sketch. Two performances of the New York Philharmonic Symphony Orchestra are certain, and six to 10 are possible. Poland has engaged this great orchestra for a Polish program Monday third; and Roumania has engaged it for May 5. Roumania has also engaged the Philadelphia Orchestra from May 14 to 16, to be conducted by the eminent Roumanian composer George Enesco. Czechoslovakia, Brazil, Switzerland, Finland, Argentina, and other nations are now negotiating for similar engagements with American orchestras. Practically all of the leading American orchestras have been invited to come to the Fair, and many have accepted.

There was usually something worth hearing in town in those days, even if Pittsburgh was not one of the jazz centers. One Saturday night I went to the theater on Frenchtown Avenue where all the Negro shows were booked. But I hardly noticed any part of the show; my attention was focused on a lady pianist who worked there. She sat cross-legged on the piano, cigarette in her mouth, writing music with her right hand while accompanying the show with a swinging left! Impressed, I told myself, "Mary, you'll do that one day." And I did, traveling with Andy Kirk's band in the 1930s on one-nighters.

—Mary Lou Williams

Recorded Popular Songs: 1939

- "Over the Rainbow"
  (Judy Garland)

- "God Bless America"
  (Kate Smith)

- "Three Little Fishies"
  (Kay Kyser)

- "When the Saints Go Marching In"
  (Louis Armstrong)

- "Moonlight Serenade"
  (Glenn Miller)

- "Beer Barrel Polka"
  (Will Glahe)

- "Sunrise Serenade"
  (Glenn Miller)

- "Says My Heart"
  (Red Norvo)

- "Little Brown Jug"
  (Glenn Miller)

- "South of the Border (Down Mexico

  Way)" (Shep Fields)

- "Jeepers Creepers"
  (Al Donohue)

- "If I Didn't Care"
  (Ink Spots)

- "Wishing (Will Make It So)"
  (Glenn Miller)

- "And the Angels Sing"
  (Benny Goodman)

- "Deep Purple"
  (Larry Clinton)

- "Heaven Can Wait"
  (Glen Gray)

- "They Say"
  (Artie Shaw)

- "Stairway to the Stars"
  (Glenn Miller)

- "Scatter-Brain"
  (Frankie Masters)

- "At the Woodchopper's Ball"
  (Woody Herman)

1942: Guitarist with Transformative Technique

As bebop and cool jazz continued to develop, guitarist Charlie Christian perfected the single-string technique, which brought the instrument out of the rhythm section and onto center stage.

Life at Home

- The man who transformed the role of the guitar, Charlie Christian, grew up surrounded by music and musical instruments; as a pre-teen he danced and played in a quartet with his father and brothers
- Born on July 29, 1916, in Bonham, Texas, Charles Henry Christian was the son of Clarence James and Willie Mae Booker Christian
- Charlie's father played a wide variety of instruments and enjoyed a diverse musical palette; his mother was a musician and singer who played background music at the local silent movie houses
- They taught their three sons to play a variety of instruments and popular songs of the day
- When Charlie was a baby, his father would place small stringed instruments next to the child and let him explore the sonority
- In the fall of 1918, when Charlie was two, his father was struck blind from fever and moved the family to Oklahoma City to find work
- As the child grew, so would the size of the instruments; he sampled the trumpet and the tenor saxophone, and played stringed instruments he made from a cigar box
- Charlie attended Douglass Elementary School at Oklahoma City, where the music instructor, Miss Zelia Breaux, taught the children music appreciation, including the classics, and offered personal instruction
- By the time Charlie was a teenager, he was already proficient on the guitar, and used those skills as a street performer, or busker, playing music with his brothers for cash or clothing in the better neighborhoods of Oklahoma City
- In 1936, Christian played shows in Dallas during the Texas Centennial and purchased his first electric guitar, a Gibson, in 1937 when he was 20

Charlie Christian's technique brought the guitar out of the rhythm section and into the spotlight.

- Beginning in the late 1800s, Orville Gibson built mandolins and guitars with a carved top design before he incorporated Gibson Mandolin and Guitar Co., Ltd in Kalamazoo, Michigan, in 1902
- After years of success as a mandolin and "F Hole" archtop guitar manufacturer, in 1937 Gibson Guitars introduced their first electric guitar, the ES-150
- Charlie's skills would transform how the guitar was viewed at the same time Louis Armstrong was demonstrating to young blacks that they could achieve financial, if not racial, equality through jazz.
- Duke Ellington was making his mark on a national radio broadcast originating from New York City; jazz was beginning to break down some racial barriers
- Charlie also learned from his father the passion of baseball life, when the Negro Leagues offered a chance at financial freedom and racial pride
- But it was local trumpeter James Simpson and guitarist Ralph "Bigfoot Chuck" Hamilton who boosted Charlie's career when they secretly taught him three popular songs: "Rose Room," "Tea For Two," and "Sweet Georgia Brown."

Charlie learned to love baseball from his father.

- When he was ready, Charlie wrangled an invitation to one of the many after-hours jam sessions along "Deep Deuce," Northeast Second Street in Oklahoma City, where his older brother Edward was already a regular
- "Let Charles play one," they told Edward
- Edward was reluctant, but when Charlie played all three new songs on the guitar that resulted in two encores, Deep Deuce was in an uproar
- Charlie then coolly dismissed himself from the jam session; his mother knew about his success before he got home
- From then on the young guitarist immersed himself in jazz, marijuana, and wearing fine clothes, like his hero Louis Armstrong

Life at Work

- By the time he turned 21, Charlie Christian and his guitar established a regional following in Oklahoma City
- Heralded for his unique single-note soloing style, he jammed with many of the big-name performers traveling through Oklahoma City, including Teddy Wilson and Art Tatum, and toured with Alphonso Trent and his orchestra
- It was Mary Lou Williams, pianist for Andy Kirk and His Clouds of Joy, who told New York record producer John Hammond about Charlie
- She pronounced him the "greatest electric-guitar player" she'd ever heard and was instrumental in persuading Hammond to give Charlie an audition
- Hammond was so blown away by what he heard, he orchestrated a surprise audition of Charlie with bandleader Benny Goodman, one of the biggest names in the business

- Goodman was one of the few white bandleaders willing to hire black musicians for his live band presentations
- Goodman had already made a musical statement when he hired Teddy Wilson on piano in 1935, and Lionel Hampton on vibraphone in 1936.
- At the time as the audition, Goodman was trying to buy out Floyd Smith's contract from Andy Kirk, but hired Charlie instead
- Initially, the meeting between the young, shy Charlie and the famous bandleader did not go well, so Hammond arranged for Charlie to sit in with the Goodman band that night without consulting Goodman
- Displeased at the surprise, Goodman called for "Rose Room," a tune he assumed that Christian would be unfamiliar with
- Charlie had been reared on the tune, and when he came in with his solo, it was unlike anything Goodman had heard before
- That version of "Rose Room" that night lasted 40 minutes-including some 20 distinctive solos from Charlie
- As a member of the Goodman sextet, Charlie went from making $2.50 a night to making $150 a week, and joined talents as renowned as Lionel Hampton, Fletcher Henderson, Artie Bernstein, and Nick Fatool
- In December 1939, *Downbeat Magazine* headlined the story "Guitar Men, Wake Up and Pluck! Wired for Sound, Let Them Hear You Play."
- Charlie was determined that the guitar would be a frontline band instrument like a saxophone or trumpet; in February 1940, Charlie Christian dominated the jazz and swing guitar polls and was elected to the Metronome All-Stars
- By the spring of 1940, Goodman had reorganized his band to bring together Charlie Christian, Count Basie, Duke Ellington, Cootie Williams, Georgie Auld, and later, drummer Dave Tough
- This all-star band reigned over the jazz polls in 1941, and brought another election for Christian to the Metronome All-Stars
- Charlie's distinctive solos, which helped move the electric guitar into the forefront, were heavily influenced by horn players such as Lester Young and Herschel Evans, whose sounds had been influencing the frontline of jazz
- In addition, after his electric guitar was featured on recordings from 1939 to 1941, country and western music moved quickly to elevate the role of the guitar

Benny Goodman was one of the few white bandleaders willing to hire black musicians.

The guitar was becoming a popular addition to many musical groups.

- Charlie wanted his guitar to sound like a tenor saxophone and helped to usher in a style later known as "bop" or "bebop."
- His use of tension and release, a technique present on "Stompin' at the Savoy," and his use of eighth-note passages, triplets and arpeggio all made a contribution to the sounds of early 1942
- Many of these sounds were shared, cultivated and matured as a regular in the early- morning jam sessions at Minton's Playhouse in Harlem with Charlie Parker, Thelonious Monk, Dizzy Gillespie, and Kenny Clarke
- Unfortunately, Charlie's brilliant career was cut short by tuberculosis
- Following several short hospital stays, Charlie was admitted to Seaview, a sanitarium on Staten Island in New York City
- He was reported to be making progress, and *Downbeat Magazine* reported in February 1942 that he and Cootie Williams were starting a band
- Charlie died March 2, 1942, at 25 years old
- "Solo Flight," the Goodman hit featuring Charlie Christian, made the top of Billboard's Harlem Hit Parade in 1943

Life in the Community: Oklahoma City, Oklahoma

- Oklahoma was born amidst the Native American relocation to the Oklahoma Territory in the 1820s, when the United States Government forced the Five Civilized Tribes to endure a difficult resettlement into the lands of Oklahoma
- Much of the western lands of Oklahoma, were part of the "Unassigned Lands," including what is now Oklahoma City

Oklahoma City skyline

- These areas were settled by a variety of white pioneers in the late 1800s
- Often settling on the land without permission, these pioneers were referred to as "Boomers," and eventually created enough pressure that the U.S. Government opted to hold a series of land runs for settlers to claim the land
- On April 22, 1889, an estimated 50,000 settlers gathered at the boundaries; some, called "Sooners," snuck across early to claim some of the prime spots of land
- Oklahoma City was immediately popular to the settlers as an estimated 10,000 people claimed land there
- By 1900, the population in the Oklahoma City area had more than doubled, and out of those early tent cities, a metropolis was being born
- Oklahoma became the forty-sixth state of the Union on November 16, 1907
- As a result of oil speculation, Oklahoma grew exponentially in its early years, and by 1910 the capital of Oklahoma was moved to Oklahoma City as its population surpassed 60,000
- Oklahoma City's various oil fields not only brought people to the city, but they also brought fresh ideas, giving rise to a vibrant music culture
- Oklahoma City became a meeting place of different people for the blending of the songs and dance music of the American Indians, Anglo-Celtic ballads from the upland South, country blues from the Mississippi Delta, black and white spirituals from the lowland South, European immigrant music from Italy, Germany, and Czechoslovakia, polka music from the upper Midwest, and Mexican mariachi from the Rio Grande Valley
- This cultural confluence of different genres of American music encouraged cross-cultural innovation and became the perfect breeding ground for the formulation of jazz styles
- Deep Deuce, or Northeast Second Street, was the core for Oklahoma City jazz, harboring institutions such as the Aldridge Theater, Ruby's Grill, Richardson's Shoe Shine Parlor, and Rushing's Café-all of which catered to jazz musicians and enthusiasts

- Uptown ballrooms, such as the Ritz, were also important outlets
- In addition, in the 1920s and 1930s, numerous bands including the Jolly Harmony Boys, Pails of Rhythm, and Ideal Jazz Orchestra worked out of Oklahoma City
- This musical gumbo city produced many notable jazz artists, including Jimmy Rushing, Henry Bridges, Charlie Christian, and Don Cherry
- Appropriately, jazz has been called "America's classical music," and was nurtured in many sections of the United States
- Originally inspired by ragtime and folk songs, early jazz artists drew their musical inspiration from country dances, field hollers, work songs, and the blues
- Oklahoma musicians were instrumental in the creation of the so-called "Kansas City" style of jazz, a bluesy dance music contrasting with the Dixieland ragtime of New Orleans, or the sounds dominating Chicago or New York

Oklahoma City became a meeting place for people from various cultures.

HISTORICAL SNAPSHOT

1942

- The United States and The Philippines fought the Battle of Bataan as Manila was captured by Japanese forces and General Douglas MacArthur was forced to flee
- A German air-raid on Liverpool, England, destroyed the home of William Patrick Hitler, Adolf Hitler's nephew, who emigrated to the U.S. and joined the navy to fight against his uncle
- Japan declared war on The Netherlands and invaded The Netherlands East Indies
- The Americans made *Sikorsky R-4*, the first mass-produced helicopter during World War II
- Actress Carole Lombard and her mother were among those killed in a plane crash near Las Vegas, Nevada, while returning from a tour to promote the sale of War Bonds
- Nazis at the Wannsee conference in Berlin decided that the "final solution to the Jewish problem" was relocation and extermination

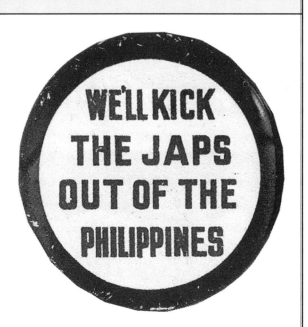

- President Franklin Delano Roosevelt signed an Executive Order directing the internment of Japanese-Americans and the seizure of their property
- Daylight saving time went into effect in the U.S.
- *The Voice of America* began broadcasting
- *How Green Was My Valley* won best picture at the 14th Academy Awards ceremony
- The Nazi German extermination camp Bełżec opened in occupied Poland; between March and December 1942, at least 434,508 people were killed
- The FCC required TV stations to cut airplay from 15 hours to four hours a week during the war
- Tokyo was bombed by B-25 Mitchells commanded by Lieutenant Colonel James Doolittle
- The Battle of the Coral Sea, which ended in an Allied victory, was the first battle in naval history in which two enemy fleets fought without seeing each other
- Aaron Copland's *Lincoln Portrait* was performed for the first time by the Cincinnati Symphony Orchestra
- The first African-American seamen were taken into the U.S. Navy
- At the Battle of Midway, the Japanese naval advance in the Pacific was slowed
- On her thirteenth birthday, Anne Frank made the first entry in her new diary
- Walt Disney's animated film *Bambi* premiered
- Mohandas Gandhi was arrested in Bombay by British forces
- A Japanese floatplane dropped incendiary devices at Mount Emily, near Brookings, Oregon, in the first of two "Lookout Air Raids," the first bombing of the continental United States
- Award-winning composer and Hollywood songwriter Ralph Rainger ("Thanks for the Memory") was among 12 people killed in the midair collision between an American Airlines DC-3 airliner and a U.S. Army bomber
- In the naval Battle of Guadalcanal, the U.S. Navy suffered heavy losses, but retained control of Guadalcanal
- The movie *Casablanca* premiered at the Hollywood Theater in New York City
- Gasoline rationing began in the U.S.
- DDT was first used as a pesticide

Selected Prices

Ashtray	$8.50
Automobile, De Soto	$2,200.00
Barbell	$8.95
Electric Food Liquidizer	$35.00
Guitar	$8.45
Home Permanent Kit	$1.40
Mattress	$54.50
Radio Phonograph	$199.95
Record Cabinet	$13.50
Trombone	$12.50

"Dave Rose Arranged His Way to Film, Radio Fame," Robert Bagar,
Movie-Radio Guide, October 10, 1942:

Dave Rose was tinkling away at a piano for all he was worth with a band in Chicago some years ago. A saxophone player, during an intermission, complained that he had lost his part. The musicians all looked high and low, but it was no use; it was gone.

The leader of the outfit asked Rose to try to fill in the missing lines for the despairing saxophonist. He did. And so well that from that moment he became the band's arranger. He got a reputation for the unusual color effects of his orchestrations, and soon his work was much in demand.

He went with Ted Fio-Rito's Orchestra as pianist and arranger, remaining with the group for a year. After that he became a staff pianist at NBC's Chicago station. It was Roy Shield who shifted him to the position of staff arranger.

In 1938, Rose gave up his Chicago job to accept what he thought was an offer to write and arrange music for Hollywood films. However, when he got to the film capital, he discovered that he had been the victim of a hoax. There was no job. Making the best of a bad bargain, he decided to remain in Hollywood and look around for something to do. But in practically no time at all, as his fortune decreed, he was making arrangements for the well-known singing stars of filmland Dorothy Lamour, Jeanette McDonald, Martha Raye, Don Ameche and others.

Subsequently, he was appointed music director of the Los Angeles radio station, a post that provided him with complete artistic freedom, and that was the real beginning of his batonistic career, which is currently being sustained through his directorship of the Ginny Simms-Philip Morris *Johnny Presents* show over NBC Tuesday.

Rose was born in London, but he came to this country with his parents when he was four. He spent his early years in and around Chicago and obtained his musical education at the Chicago Musical College. While a student there, he composed three tone-poems, "Ensenada Escapade," "Shadows," and "Swing Etude," all three of which were premiered by the Chicago Symphony Orchestra.

Dave Rose is a teacher of student pilots for the U.S. Army, a job that takes four days each week, being an exceptional flyer. He composes, arranges until all hours of the morning. He hopes to write the great American symphony someday.

1945: Female Trombonist in Traveling Band

Trombonist Helen Elizabeth Jones was a diminutive star in the all-girl traveling band, The International Sweethearts of Rhythm, which was formed to raise money for her impoverished Mississippi school.

Life at Home

- Helen Elizabeth Jones was born in Meridian, Mississippi, in 1923 and initially placed in a white orphanage
- She was removed when it became obvious that Helen was of mixed racial parentage and was no longer eligible to be in a white institution in the Jim Crow South.
- At three, she was adopted by Lawrence Clifton Jones, the founder of the Piney Wood Country Life School, and his wife Grace Morris Allen Jones
- From then on her history became deeply entwined in the development of the school and the activities her adoptive father, Lawrence Jones
- The oldest of four children, Lawrence Jones was born in St. Joseph, Missouri, in 1882, and was 44 when he rescued Helen
- His father was a hotel porter and his mother an industrious and practical homemaker and seamstress
- Spurred by his parents' dreams of self-improvement, Lawrence Jones became the first Negro graduate from the University of Iowa in 1907
- His wife, Grace Morris Allen Jones, grew up in Burlington, Iowa, and studied at the Chicago Conservatory of Music
- The couple met at a missionary society function during Jones's junior year, and they married in 1912
- Piney Woods Country Life School had begun three years earlier with Jones teaching one student sitting on a log underneath a cedar tree
- Formerly occupied by sheep, snakes and weeds, the school was fully operational by New Year's Day 1910
- A prominent local African American farmer donated the shed, 40 acres of land, and added $50 in cash at a time when a hammer cost $0.66
- Students cleared the grounds and made the necessary repairs and improvements to the building

Helen Jones played trombone in The International Sweethearts of Rhythm.

Most young children discovered music in school.

- By the close of the first full school year, Jones had secured the services of five teachers, enrolled 85 students, and laid the foundation for the first school building
- For the school year 1912-1913, the Piney Woods' income was $3,269 against expenses of $3,617, leaving the school $348 in debt
- At that time, the average annual income for black teachers was $311 per year
- The State of Mississippi paid an average of $10.60 per year to educate each white child, while paying $2.26 per black child.
- In 1913, Piney Woods Country Life School officially received its charter from the State of Mississippi
- Its mission, according to the charter of incorporation, was to establish, develop and maintain a country life school in which to train "the head, heart and hands of boys and girls for a life of Christianity, character and service."
- To meet the needs of all families, Piney Woods School allowed children with no financial means to work at the school to earn the $12 monthly tuition
- Everyone enrolled at Piney Woods worked to support the institution through home economics endeavors or industrial arts, farming or forestry
- Jones agreed with Booker T. Washington's decree that "no race can prosper until it learns there is as much dignity in tilling a field as in writing a poem."
- After the sudden death of her adoptive mother in 1929, six-year-old Helen became part of the general student population of the school
- Since the 1920s, Dr. Jones had been sending choral groups on tour following a model established by Fisk University to bring in money and give the musicians a wider view of the world
- Helen got her first exposure to the music world in the mid 1930s when she toured with the school's Cotton Blossom Sisters, performing plantation songs like "Old Black Joe" and "Carry Me Back to Old Virginny."

- To increase the school's fundraising, in 1937 Dr. Jones decided to form an all-girl swing band composed of students; the Swing Era had pulled big band jazz into the forefront of American music again
- The best female musicians were chosen from the concert and marching bands to perform for the International Sweethearts of Rhythm
- Dr. Jones chose to use "international" because many of the girls were of mixed parentage, and he thought it reflected a global vision; the students included American blacks, Native Americans, Mexicans, Chinese and Puerto Ricans
- The 15-piece band took to the road during the 1938-1939 school year, first touring their home state to attract other musically inclined students to Piney Woods

Lawrence Jones adopted Helen when she was three years old.

- Most of the students who traditionally entered the school had never played a musical instrument, could not read music, had never seen an orchestra or performed in public
- Seventeen-year-old Helen played the trombone and traveled extensively through Tennessee, Alabama, Louisiana, Arkansas and Texas in a specially designed semi-trailer equipped with Pullman beds, laboratory facilities, a kitchenette, and closets for each performer
- In the segregated South, where few black motels existed, such facilities were essential to the survival of the troupe
- The International Sweethearts of Rhythm shows were so successful that professional musicians asked to join the band

Life at Work

- Helen Jones and the International Sweethearts of Rhythm were originally led by Consuela Carter, who graduated from Piney Woods in 1927 and remained with the institution for 15 years
- Under Carter's direction, Helen and the other girls, all between the ages of 14 and 19, began to climb toward national recognition
- The dance music combined African rhythms, Indian war dancing and the charm of the Orient
- Indicative of the band's rise in popularity, in September 1940 they played nine engagements in 11 days, including dates in Alexandria, Emporia, Petersburg and Martinsville, Virginia
- By December 1940, they were ranked 11th in the Number One Fan poll held by the black-owned *Chicago Defender* newspaper
- On and off the bandstand, chaperone Rae Lee Jones demanded that the girls exude professionalism and refinement; contact with the audience was limited to protect their reputations and virtue.
- Renowned trumpet player Jean Starr was the first of many established performers to express an interest in joining the Sweethearts
- In early 1941, negotiations were underway for Helen and the International Sweethearts of Rhythm to film two movie shorts in Hollywood
- Daniel Gary, a Washington, DC, agent with business savvy and vision, was hired to handle bookings
- Rated as one of the nation's best draws by January 1941, the Sweethearts had broken box office records at both Cincinnati's Cotton Club and DC's Howard Theatre

The International Sweethearts of Rhythm early in their career.

- The original Sweethearts had proven that they could survive the arduous touring, and working together without bickering, petty jealousies and hostilities against one another
- The young women who had entered Piney Woods with the simple aspiration to acquire a basic education and the skills for just bookkeeping or stenography were competing with Count Basie and Duke Ellington in the popularity polls
- But trouble was brewing
- In the beginning, it was proposed that the Sweethearts would tour only during the summer months, returning to classes in the fall
- However, as their popularity grew, they were soon touring year round and traveling extensively without the benefit of school
- Helen and each of the Sweethearts were allotted only $2.00 a week in wages and $0.50 a day for traveling expenses, while they earned thousands of dollars for the school's coffers
- Then, when several seniors were told they would not receive their high school diplomas because they had missed too many classes, the girls began to openly question the motives of the administration concerning their personal academic development
- Also, strong disagreement between chaperone Rae Lee Jones and founder Dr. Lawrence Jones over operational procedures bubbled to the surface
- In April 1941, the 17 attractive and talented young women, including the school founder's adopted daughter Helen Jones, broke their affiliation with the Piney Woods Country Life School
- The school attempted to have the orchestra arrested for stealing the school bus, but failed
- The group fled to Washington, DC, where booking agent Daniel Gary secured the option on a house at 908 S Quinn Street in Arlington, Virginia, as their headquarters
- After three months of grueling rehearsals under new music director Eddie Durham, the Sweethearts made their professional debut at the Howard Theatre in Washington, DC, in late August 1941

- Two weeks later, they headlined an all-female review at New York's famous Apollo Theater, where they received rave reviews
- By 1944, the Sweethearts were ranked by *DownBeat Magazine* as the number one all-girl orchestra in the nation
- When World War II ended a year later, the State Department was bombarded by requests for the Sweethearts by GIs who remained in Germany with the U.S. occupation forces.
- So on July 15, 1945, Helen Jones and the band, attired in their USO uniforms, sailed for Europe to entertain the troops; during the previous four years, 4,500 entertainers had participated in USO Camp Shows scattered across the war fronts of the world
- The Sweethearts' tour lasted six months, entertaining primarily the third Army and the seventh Army, where they performed their unique sound in venues large and small and on radio
- And they always left the men dancing in the aisles

By 1944, the group ranked as the number one all-girl orchestra in the nation.

Wartime Entertainers

- The United States entered World War II only months after the International Sweethearts of Rhythm broke with the Piney Woods Country Life School and turned professional
- Despite being well established, touring was difficult
- The creation of all-female ensembles was seen by some detractors as novelty acts to be admired more for their looks than for their musical ability
- At the same time, male musicians defined jazz as essentially a male activity and thought that girl bands like the International Sweethearts of Rhythm lacked the power and drive to blow hot jazz
- Plus, hotel accommodations for racially diverse groups such as the Sweethearts were virtually out of the question in most of the nation
- On one occasion in El Paso, Texas, Jewish saxophone player Roz Cron was arrested and held overnight in jail for being a member of a racially integrated group
- On such occasions, the white girls pretended to be racially mixed, claiming that their fathers were white and their mothers were black, as this arrangement would seem more acceptable.
- White trumpeter and bassist Toby Butler related that these experiences helped her mature emotionally, providing her with a greater understanding of the black experience
- Responding to the needs of a nation at war, in September 1942, 38-year-old Glenn Miller disbanded his popular and successful swing orchestra to enlist in the Army
- Miller, like nearly every other patriotic American, felt obliged to lend as much support to the war effort as possible

Many male jazz musicians did not take female bands seriously.

- He would turn his music toward a wartime ideal that would affect millions of young people nationwide
- However, not all musicians shared Miller's zeal to serve America in its hour of need
- Some sought to avoid the draft by hatching schemes which ranged from drug use to professing homosexuality, often with mixed results
- In 1943, just as young Frank Sinatra's star was ascending, he was declared ineligible for military service and the activities of his fervent female fans were scandalizing the nation
- The swooning young women displayed their passion for Sinatra by tossing their undergarments onto the stage when Frank performed
- Labeled a 4-F slacker by enlisted men, Sinatra was hated by GIs irate with his draft status
- At the New York Paramount Theater, where Sinatra was performing, sailors yelled from the audience, "Hey, wop, why aren't you in uniform?"
- In response to his own personal experiences with intolerance, Sinatra became an early crusader for racial equality, often speaking and performing at high schools where racial incidents had occurred

Female musicians often worked harder than their male counterparts.

HISTORICAL SNAPSHOT
1945

- The evacuation of Auschwitz concentration camp opened the eyes of the world to the Holocaust
- Franklin D. Roosevelt was inaugurated to an unprecedented fourth term as president of the United States
- Eddie Slovik was executed by firing squad for desertion, the first American soldier since the American Civil War to be executed for this offense
- President Roosevelt and British Prime Minister Winston Churchill met with Soviet leader Joseph Stalin at the Yalta Conference
- About 30,000 U.S. Marines landed on Iwo Jima where a group of Marines were photographed raising the American flag by Joe Rosenthal
- Jewish Dutch diarist Anne Frank died of typhus in the Bergen-Belsen concentration camp
- American B-29 bombers attacked Tokyo, Japan, with incendiary bombs, killing 100,000 citizens
- The 17th Academy Awards ceremony was broadcast via radio for the first time; Best Picture was awarded to *Going My Way*
- Cartoon character Sylvester the cat debuted in *Life with Feathers*
- Adolf Hitler, along with his new wife Eva Braun, committed suicide
- Hamburg Radio announced that Hitler had died in battle, "fighting up to his last breath against Bolshevism"
- President Roosevelt died suddenly at Warm Springs, Georgia; Vice President Harry S. Truman became the 33rd President, serving until 1953
- Rodgers and Hammerstein's *Carousel*, a musical play based on Ferenc Molnár's *Liliom*, opened on Broadway and became their second long-running stage classic
- The Western Allies rejected any offer of surrender by Germany other than unconditional on all fronts
- Ezra Pound, poet and author, was arrested by American soldiers in Italy for treason
- A Japanese balloon bomb killed five children and a woman near Bly, Oregon, when it exploded as they dragged it from the woods; they were the only people killed by an enemy attack on the American mainland during World War II
- Trinity Test, the first of an atomic bomb, required about six kilograms of plutonium, succeeded in unleashing an explosion equivalent to that of 19 kilotons of TNT
- Winston Churchill resigned as the United Kingdom's Prime Minister after his Conservative Party was soundly defeated by the Labour Party in the 1945 general election
- A United States B-29 Superfortress, the *Enola Gay*, dropped an atomic bomb, codenamed "Little Boy," on Hiroshima, Japan
- The Zionist World Congress approached the British Government to discuss the founding of the country of Israel
- Arthur C. Clarke promoted the idea of a communications satellite in a *Wireless World* magazine article
- At Gimbels Department Store in New York City, the first ballpoint pens went on sale at $12.50 each
- John H. Johnson published the first issue of the magazine *Ebony*
- The Nag Hammadi scriptures were discovered
- The Berklee College of Music was founded in Boston, Massachusetts
- At the Mayo Clinic, streptomycin was first used to treat tuberculosis
- Percy Spencer accidentally discovered that microwaves can heat food, leading to the invention of the microwave oven
- The herbicide 2,4-D was introduced

Selected Prices

Deep Freezer	$225.00
Fountain Pen	$15.00
Harmonica	$1.79
Hotel Chesterfield, New York, per Day	$2.50
Ouija Board	$2.00
Pressure Cooker	$10.50
Records, Four 12"	$4.72
Silk Stockings	$0.98
Trumpet	$135.00
Whiskey, Seagram's, Fifth	$2.70

On our troopship bound for Europe in April 1945, the only place where I and a few other guys could play our "hillbilly" music was the latrine. The toilet was a long trough through which sea water was pumped. Crude wooden seats were fastened to the top. So while we sat on those seats pickin' and grinnin', water trickled between us like a babbling brook.

—David Massey, Raleigh, North Carolina

"Here Comes the Band!" *The Etude*, August 1945:

The days when troops went into combat with the roll of guns and the blare of trumpets are gone. They do not advertise their approach with music, now. Every bandsman must undergo basic military field training. When the steel begins to fly, the bandsmen are called into action just as any other G.I. Joes….

Music is a powerful morale factor in the life of G.I. Joe at the fighting front. Realizing this, the Army trains its bands to follow the troops to the combat zone, so that battle-weary men may be entertained by music which runs the gamut from boogie-woogie to symphonic concerts.

The first duty of the bandsman is to be a good soldier, and at Camp Lee's Army Service Forces Training Center, the 326th and in 328 ASF bands receive battle conditioning training no less rugged than Quartermaster troops who drive trucks, work in laundry units, or in any of the other specialized Quartermaster fields.

The obstacle courses, hiking, rifle marksmanship, and long hours of drilling are no strangers to Camp Lee bandsmen. But in addition to these basic duties, they play for retreat parades and other army functions, maintain a regular schedule of concerts, and are called upon for such diversified tasks as presenting their talent to boost the sale of War Bonds.

Recently, the band spent two weeks in A.P. Hill Military Reservation, near Fredericksburg, Virginia, where they learned to operate in the field under simulated battle conditions. They took forced marches, learned how to solve compass and combat problems, lived in "pup" tents, ate from mess gear, wore gas masks, steel helmets, and carried automatic pistols at all times. The regular schedule was supplemented by two open-air Sunday concerts for the trainees, and two concerts for soldiers confined at the Reservation's Station Hospital.

1946: African American Newspaper Reporter

Meredith Dempsey, after years of reporting on WW II for the country's largest Black newspaper, the Pittsburgh Courier, *was unsure about his future in the newspaper business.*

Life at Home

- The Dempseys are enjoying the birth of their first child, but are shocked by the cost of everything from baby food to diapers
- Their baby was born in a hospital, the first child on either side of the family not to be born at home; the Urban League has played a key role in linking improved medical care to new arrivals
- Until she got pregnant, Jeanine worked as a nurse's aid in the same hospital where her baby was born
- To hold down inflation but allow prices to rise to competitive levels, the government has been gradually lifting the wartime controls; recently, because the Office of Price Administration approved a two percent increase in the price of cotton fabrics and yarns, Jeanine knows the price of cloth diapers is bound to go up

- According to the newspapers, the average price of goods has risen 18.5 percent in a year; her budget tells her the government's report is low
- The retail price of chocolate bars, cooking chocolate, and cocoa recently jumped 27 percent
- Until recently, she was thinking about supplying a local market with baked goods to supplement their income, but now she is unsure if she can turn a profit
- Before the baby arrived, she had grown tired of the long hours Meredith devoted to his job; now she wants him to leave the newspaper business and find a job with more regular hours
- He loves being a reporter so much she is afraid to tell him her thoughts

Meredith Dempsey had a reputation for tough, insightful writing.

The Pittsburgh Courier *was often passed from one apartment to the next and emerged as the national voice of blacks during WW II.*

Life at Work

- When covering a story, Meredith is expected to defend the Negro position, and to seek civil rights at every turn
- Although the *Chicago Defender* defined the role of the Black press during World War I and the Black great migration period of the 1920s and 1930s, his paper, the *Pittsburgh Courier*, is emerging as the national voice of blacks during World War II
- The Pittsburgh Courier is the largest Black newspaper in the country; its circulation ex ceeds 280,000
- Because the *Courier* is often passed from apartment to apartment, many believe its influence is four times greater than its circulation numbers
- One of its readers is the FBI; several times, agents have come to visit the newspaper following the publication of an article
- The FBI is concerned that the newspaper is "holding America up to ridicule"; they also want to know whether any outside forces are trying to influence the paper
- In the past, the army has stated publicly that the Japanese and communists are using the Negro press to influence Americans
- The Courier replied to the charges of disloyalty, saying, "The Japanese, Germans, Italians, and their Axis stooges know that it is futile to seek spies, saboteurs, or Fifth Columnists among American Negroes. Every attempt in that direction has been a miserable failure."
- Meredith knows several of his contacts are linked to the Communist party; they will occasionally call him to write a story that will help a family whose father has been lynched or simply is in desperate need
- He believes the Courier has given a voice to African Americans

- He is especially proud that the *Courier* launched the famous Double V campaign, thanks to a letter to the editor from a factory worker in Kansas
- The Double V campaign calls for victory abroad and victory at home, meaning an end to Jim Crow, and has become a national symbol for blacks
- Some of his stories recently dealt with a rising tide of anger now that the war has ended; he believes the paper serves as a safety valve within the community, and that without the Black press there would be more riots, not fewer
- His stories are frank and clear, just what his editors demand; writing politely is for the White press, he has been told repeatedly
- Since labor disputes are rampant now that the war has ended, he has spent much of the year covering strikes
- Strikes in Pittsburgh alone have involved bellhops, waitresses, the Independent Union of Duquesne Light Company, steelworkers, state and county workers, and textile workers
- A recent story he wrote focused on who was to blame for an act of sabotage during the strike against Duquesne Light Company; a rope thrown over a 22,000-volt line caused it to burn out and pitch the city into darkness for 15 minutes
- The strike at the power company has also forced more than 100 large steel-fabricating factories to close; their output ranges from straight pins to steel for houses, autos, refrigerators and multi-ton heavy machinery
- In sympathy, the city's 2,700 streetcar motormen have also staged a work stoppage, virtually closing the city down
- The pressure for a settlement is intense and tempers are short
- Covering strikes can be exhausting since neither side trusts a reporter, and management will rarely even meet with a reporter from the Black press, especially the *Pittsburgh Courier*
- In an attempt to keep up with breaking events, Meredith has a cot set up near the presses at the newspaper office; some days he does not go home
- The paper now has 10 regular columnists, and although he has enjoyed reporting, he thinks he now wants to leave "beat" work and write a column
- Many of the columns are written by professors, businessmen, and labor leaders; columnists for the *Courier* currently include two non-blacks: a Chinese man and an Indian woman

The Double V campaign was demonstrated in a variety of ways.

The war led to aggressive campaigns to end segregation in America.

- He is also desperate for money and thinks a columnist job will both pay better and allow him to make money on the side
- *The Courier* began in 1907 when Edwin Nathaniel Harleston, a security guard at the H.J. Heinz food packing plant, decided to put his love for poetry to use and started a newspaper, *A Toiler's Life*; sales were slow
- By January 15, 1910, the four-page newspaper had a new name, the *Courier*, new partners, and a press run of 500
- Within five years, the paper was a social force for neighborhood issues and was calling for Southern blacks to "come North."
- To meet the demand of the newly arrived rural blacks from the South, the Courier wrote extensively about the need for housing, health, and education reform
- During World War I, the paper advised blacks who had gained employment to "save your money and prepare for the day when white soldiers return from war and reclaim their old jobs."
- In 1925, the *Courier* sent George Schuyler on a nine-month tour of the South, during which he visited every city with more than 5,000 African Americans
- Also in 1925, Florida was given the "pennant in the Lynching League of America" because eight blacks were lynched in the Sunshine state that year; seven were lynched in Texas, four in Mississippi, three in South Carolina, two in Arkansas, and one person each was lynched in Georgia, Kansas, New Mexico, and Tennessee
- Emboldened by its successes, the paper then battled White government, complacent Black churches, Marcus Garvey's *Back to Africa Movement*, and the "do-nothing" NAACP
- By 1936, the *Courier* boasted a circulation of 174,000
- *The Courier*, like most Black newspapers, attracts few regular advertisers, while the few that do appear are for skin creams and lucky charms; most of its income results from subscriptions

- By the start of the war, the Courier was calling for mass meetings and rallies to protest the exclusion of blacks from the military and the industrial defense program

Life in the Community: Pittsburgh, Pennsylvania

- Since the start of the war, Pittsburgh's steel industry had been working around the clock to supply tools and weapons to defeat the enemy
- Since Pearl Harbor Day, Pittsburgh has produced 95 million tons of ingot steel, and is proud of its contribution to the war effort
- Unfortunately, Pittsburgh's long association with steel has given it the nickname, "The Smoky City," even though industry has made strides to reduce pollution
- For decades, the city has accepted smog so heavy it turns day into night
- The battle to control smoke in the 1940s has been led by Edward T. Leech, editor of the *Pittsburgh Press*, and several other prominent citizens
- The impact on the city has been dramatic; buildings once thought to be black have been scrubbed white
- Beginning in 1916, the Black population of Pittsburgh began to swell as part of the great migration of blacks from the South
- They moved North between 1910 and 1930 for the same reason that eastern European immigrants came to America in the preceding decades, jobs in the iron and steel mills
- Between 1910 and 1930, the Black population of Pittsburgh grew 115 percent from 25,623 to 54,983; the number of black iron and steel workers in Pittsburgh jumped 326 percent from 786 to 2,853
- In 1917, a survey of black immigrants showed that half were in their prime work years-18 to 30, most resided in boardinghouses for unmarried men, and more than two-thirds had been in the city for less than six months.

Buildings once thought to be black due to the constant smog were scrubbed white.

- In 1920, the average black family, including two wage earners brought home $3.60 per day; rents were generally $10 per month
- The migration continued in the 1920s; the ravages of the boll weevil drove many black families off the Southern farms, while restrictive immigration policies designed to close the door to eastern Europeans created new job opportunities
- During World War II, some jobs opened to black workers in Pennsylvania, thanks to the Committee on Fair Employment Practices
- President Franklin D. Roosevelt created the committee to investigate complaints of job discrimination, while an order was issued to prevent black leader A. Philip Randolph from leading a march on Washington

Pittsburgh's steel industry worked around the clock to supply tools and weapons for the war.

- Several labor strikes have taken place because black workers were added to the work force
- As labor shortages grew during the war, many blacks were hired to platform jobs at the Pittsburgh Railroad, or as welders at the Sun Shipbuilding Company

The Black Press
- When Franklin D. Roosevelt entered Office in 1933, there were 150 Black newspapers with a combined circulation of 600,000, but by 1943, the Black press had more than doubled its weekly circulation to 1.6 million; in 1946, the combined total was 1.8 million copies weekly
- Only five newspapers had a circulation of more than 50,000; nationwide, the 1940 cen sus showed a Black population of 13 million
- The Black, or Negro, press became known as a "fighting press" or "crusading press"; it always kept its eyes on the United States Government and its policy toward blacks
- To create a more united front on confronting racial issues, the National Negro Publishing Association was created in 1940
- The issues included the U.S. Navy's recruitment policy that virtually excluded blacks, the rampant use of employment discrimination, concerns over possible governmental charges of sedition and disloyalty during the war, and the need to balance the timidity of advertisers with the desire for militancy
- The Black press and the traditional federal government did not always see eye to eye
- When the Black press began pushing in 1939 for more Negroes in the army, particularly the officer corps, the White House declared "the policy of the War Department is not to intermingle colored and white enlisted personnel in the same regimental organizations."
- When 13 Negro seamen aboard the U.S.S. Philadelphia wrote to the *Pittsburgh Courier* to voice their discontent with the navy's racial policy, the sailors were jailed and scheduled to be court-martialed
- The editorial work of the *Courier* resulted in the soldiers' release without trial or court-martial; the sailors were sent back to the United States and released with bad conduct discharges
- Later in 1941, during the attack on Pearl Harbor, the Courier made the world aware of a black navy mess attendant, Dorie Miller, who dragged his captain to safety, then manned a machine gun

until it ran out of ammunition; although the paper called for the Congressional Medal of Honor, Miller received the Navy Cross

- Taking the lead of the *Pittsburgh Courier*, Black newspapers nationwide began promoting the Double V: "victories over totalitarian forces overseas and those at home who are denying equality to Negroes."
- Nationwide, the Double V campaign improved circulation for all papers; the Courier boosted circulation to 270,000, The Afro-American in Baltimore reached 229,000, followed by the *Chicago Defender* with 161,000, and the *Journal and Guide* in Norfolk, Virginia
- The increased circulation allowed the Negro press to become more aggressive
- The government wanted the Black press to give up its demands for full black rights until the end of the war, having made the same demand during World War I

Racial policies and prejudice extended to the military during WW II.

"The Negro in the United States," by Franklin Frazier

"The Negro reporter is a fighting partisan. The people who read his newspaper expect him to put up a good fight for them. They don't like him tame. They want him to have an arsenal well-stocked with atomic adjectives and nouns. They expect him to invent similes and metaphors that lay open the foe's weaknesses and to employ cutting irony, sarcasm, and ridicule to confound and embarrass our opponents. The Negro reader is often a spectator at a fight. The reporter is attacking the reader's enemy and the reader has a vicarious relish for a fight well fought."

᷍᷍᷍᷍᷍᷍᷍

"Editorial," by Perival Prattis, Editor, *Pittsburgh Courier*, 1942, following a meeting with the Federal Office of Facts and Figures

"The hysteria of Washington officialdom over Negro morale is at once an astonishing, amusing, and shameful spectacle.

It is astonishing to find supposedly informed persons in high positions so unfamiliar with the thought and feeling of one-tenth of the population. One would imagine they had been on another planet, and yet every last one of them insists that he 'knows the Negro.' It is amusing to see these people so panicky over a situation which they have caused and which governmental policies maintain.

It is shameful that the only 'remedy' they are now able to put forward is Jim Crowism on a larger scale and the suppression of the Negro newspapers, i.e., further departure from the principles of democracy.

If the Washington gentry are eager to see Negro morale take an up turn, they have only to abolish Jim Crowism and lower the color bar in every field and phase of American life

Squelching the Negro newspapers will not make the Negro masses love insult, discrimination, exploitation, and ostracism. It will only further depress their morale."

HISTORICAL SNAPSHOT
1946

- United Airlines announced it had ordered jet planes for commercial purposes
- Dr. Benjamin Spock's *The Common Sense Book of Baby and Child Care* was published, written while he was in the Navy Medical Corps in charge of severe disciplinary cases
- The auction of FDR's stamp collection brought $211,000
- Automobile innovation included wide windows on the Studebaker and combined the wood station wagon and passenger car with the Chrysler Town and Country
- With more men returning from war, the birth rate increased 20 percent over 1945 to 3.4 million
- Albert Einstein and other distinguished nuclear scientists from the Emergency Committee of Atomic Science promoted the peaceful use of atomic energy
- Within a year after the end of the war, the size of the military went from 11 million to one million soldiers
- As wages and prices increased, the cost of living went up 33 percent over 1941
- With sugar rationing over, ice cream consumption soared
- Electric blankets, Tide detergent, the FDR dime, mobile telephone service, Fulbright awards, Timex watches, and automatic clothes dryers all made their first appearances
- Strikes aided 4.6 million workers with a loss of 116 million man-days, the worst stoppage since 1919
- The National Broadcasting Company and Philco Corporation established a two-way television relay service between New York and Philadelphia
- The Dow Jones Industrial Average peaked at a post-1929 high of 212.50
- U.S. college enrollments reached an all-time high of more than two million
- Ektachrome color film was introduced by Kodak Company
- Hunt Foods established "price at time of shipment" contracts to cope with inflationary pressures
- Blacks voted for the first time in the Mississippi Democratic primary
- Oklahoma City offered the first rapid public treatment of venereal diseases
- Former Secretary of State Henry Wallace became editor of the *New Republic*
- *The New Yorker* published John Hersey's *Hiroshima*
- John D. Rockefeller, Jr., donated $8.5 million for the construction of the United Nations building along the East River in New York City
- *Family Circle, Scientific American,* and *Holiday* all began publication

1946 ECONOMIC PROFILE

Income, Standard Jobs

Average of All Industries,
    Excluding Farm Labor $2,529
Average of All Industries,
    Including Farm Labor $2,473
Bituminous Coal Mining. $2,724
Building Trades $2,537
Domestics $1,411
Farm Labor $1,394
Federal Civilian $2,904
Federal Employees, Executive
    Departments $2,490
Federal Military. $2,279
Finance, Insurance, and Real Estate $2,570
Gas and Electricity Workers $2,697
Manufacturing, Durable Goods $2,615
Manufacturing, Nondurable Goods. . . . $2,404
Medical/Health Services Workers $1,605
Miscellaneous Manufacturing $2,442
Motion Picture Services. $2,978
Nonprofit Organization Workers $2,070
Passenger Transportation Workers,
    Local and Highway $2,886
Personal Services $1,881
Public School Teachers $2,025
Radio Broadcasting and
    Television Workers $3,972
Railroad Workers $3,055
State and Local Government
    Workers $2,093
Telephone and Telegraph
    Workers $2,413
Wholesale and Retail Trade
    Workers $2,378

Selected Prices

Dixie Belle Gin per Fifth $3.12
Ouija Board Game $1.59
Silvertone Commentator Radio $11.75
Steel-Frame Baby Swing $1.85
Biltwell Baby Shoes $1.79
Illinois Clothing Manufacturing Suit . . . $27.00
Kerrybrooke Purse. $4.69
Harmony House Box Springs $21.98

Craftsman Broad Hatchet. $1.69
Rose Bushes. $1.15
Craftsman Hammer $1.39
Harmony House Mirror $5.31
Tablevogue by Rosemary
    Tablecloth, 54" x 54" $1.69
Walgreen's Mineral Oil, per Pint. $0.05
Brewer's Yeast Tablets. $0.27
Allstate Seat Covers. $3.33
Silvertone Harmonica $1.79
Toni Home Permanent Kit $2.00
Flower Grower Magazine
    Subscription for Two Years. $4.00

Thousands of Southern blacks migrate to the tenement housing of Pittsburgh, seeking jobs.

"Pittsburgh Help Quits 8 Hotels, Bellhops, Waitresses, Maids Strike in Wage Dispute after Voting 4 to 1," October 1, 1946:

"Employees of eight major hotels in Pittsburgh went on strike at 12:01 a.m. today after voting a few hours earlier for a work stoppage in a wage dispute. . . . The union is asking for a 40-hour week at the same wages as for the present 48 hours, with time and a half for the additional eight hours. The hotels say they have offered an increase of $15.25 a month for women and $16.64 a month for men who do not receive tips, and half that for those who receive tips."

"Race Bias Charged in Hospitals Here," *New York Times*, October 1, 1946:

"While 'whole sections of hospitals' are being closed because of the serious nursing shortages, 'discriminatory polices still reign even in our municipal hospitals as to the number of Negro doctors and nurses that gain employment in these tax-supported institutions,' it was declared last night at the first fall meeting of the Physicians Forum at the New York Academy of Medicine, by Dr. Ernest P. Boas, chairman of the Forum."

Labor strikes following the war are the worst since 1919.

1946: African American Sailor and Desegregation Advocate

John William Gibson, frustrated by the racial discrimination in the U.S. Navy, met with the battalion commander and aired the grievances of the Black troops.

Life at Home

- As war and rumors of war grew more pronounced in 1940, most African Americans were deeply skeptical of American participation
- John William Gibson was an exception to the rule
- He had grown up hearing tales of World War I told by his uncle, Pink Beam, who had been stationed in France
- Uncle Pink had served in one of the few Black units to actually see combat, so his stories included tales of both glorious battles and widespread acceptance of the Black doughboys in France
- Uncle Pink had shared drinks with French civilians, earned the respect of White soldiers who would never have spoken to him in America, and shared the appreciation of the French people as they showered praise on Black and White soldiers without discrimination
- "The military may be the ticket to helping the White man and the colored man live together, but not in my lifetime," Uncle Pink told J.W., as John William was known. "Maybe in your lifetime, but not in mine."
- After a few drinks and out of J.W.'s earshot, Uncle Pink would describe the mistreatment, violence and intolerance committed against the colored troops after they returned home from the Great War
- "It wears a man out to fight for his life in France, only to fight again at home."
- J.W. followed the campaign for the desegregation of the military through articles in the Pittsburgh Courier, the most widely circulated Black newspaper in the country
- Since 1937 the Courier had been running a campaign to end segregation in the armed forces
- This effort became more focused in 1941, when Labor leader A. Philip Randolph organized a Negro march on Washington to demand equal participation in the military

John William Gibson was frustrated by the racial discrimination in the Navy.

- President Franklin D. Roosevelt resented the tactic of a staged protest in front of the White House
- Randolph was summoned to the White House and asked to call off the march
- In the absence of a firm commitment from Roosevelt to end job discrimination in the defense industries and the military, Randolph refused to stop the march, which would include thousands of Blacks
- Days before the scheduled protest, Roosevelt signed order 8802, decreeing "there shall be no discrimination in the employment of workers in the defense industries or in government because of race, creed, color or national origin."
- Even though the order did not mention the desegregation of the military, Randolph called off the protest march, for which he was widely criticized
- After the attack on Pearl Harbor in December 1941, the Pittsburgh Courier stepped up its efforts for desegregation by launching the "Double V for Victory" campaign
- One "V" signified victory over fascism in Europe and Asia, and the other "V" was for victory over Jim Crow in America

John's parents in North Carolina

- The Courier also provided J.W. with news of race riots at Ft. Oswego, fighting at Camp Davis, discrimination at Fort Devens; Jim Crow conditions at Camps Blanding and Lee; stabbings at Fort Huachuca, killings at Fort Bragg, and an edict "not to shake a nigger hand" at Camp Upton
- Undeterred and thoroughly convinced that Uncle Pink was right about the potential of the military to end discrimination, J.W. decided in 1942 to enlist in the Navy Seabees, a recently formed construction arm of the navy, one of the segregated branches in the military
- J.W. was especially qualified; since he was 10 years old, he had worked alongside his father, a carpenter and mason
- After graduation from high school, J.W. attended the North Carolina Agricultural and Technical Institute in Greensboro for two years, majoring in construction management
- And he was eager to make an impact on the all-encompassing war effort
- The need for a militarized naval construction force was paramount after the Japanese attack on Pearl Harbor and the U.S. entry into the war
- Judge William H. Hastie was appointed civilian aide to the Secretary of War to help integrate Blacks into the defense program
- It was a difficult assignment; the military was wrestling with the festering wound of Black discrimination while also preparing for war
- Rear Admiral Ben Moreell requested authorization to activate, organize and man navy construction units on December 28, 1941, just three weeks after the Japanese attack
- Admiral Moreell looked first for men already trained in construction

- In July, 1942, 24-year-old John William received orders to report to Camp Allen in Norfolk, Virginia, to begin boot camp training
- There, J.W. completed the three-week Seabee training course that emphasized military discipline and the use of light arms
- Most of the first Seabee recruits were experienced in construction; nearly all were volunteers, not draftees
- The average age of the early recruits was 37
- These were men who had helped to build Boulder Dam, the national highways and New York's skyscrapers
- Most were able to quickly adopt the civilian construction skills to military needs
- All were ready to do their patriotic duty by building a new naval base in Puerto Rico; the new base had been planned on so large a scale it was nicknamed "The Pearl Harbor of the Caribbean."

John's Uncle Pink served in one of the few Black units to see combat.

Life at Work

- After boot camp, John William Gibson of Eden, North Carolina, was assigned to Roosevelt Roads, Puerto Rico, which was slated for a massive expansion by the navy
- Initial reports indicated that the base would rival the size and scope of the badly damaged facility at Pearl Harbor, Hawaii
- There, the construction battalion, the fundamental unit of the Seabee organization, comprised four companies that included the necessary construction skills required for any job, plus a headquarters company composed of medical and dental professionals, administrative personnel, storekeepers, cooks and other specialty personnel
- The standard battalion complement was 32 officers and 1,073 men
- Construction man Gibson was assigned to Charlie Company, Third Platoon, First Squad.
- Most of the other Black soldiers also were assigned to "C" Company, which was composed of builders and steelworkers
- Most of C Company's assignments, however, involved painting and general labor such as mixing mortar or staging materials
- J.W. became especially frustrated that the colored troops always got the low-skilled, dirty jobs, while less experienced White sailors got the plum assignments
- He became aware that Company C Blacks were not given the opportunity to rate as equipment operators, construction mechanics, construction electricians, utilities men or engineering aides jobs for which J.W.'s experience and education qualified him

John was assigned to Charlie "C" Company in the military, where his assignments included painting and mixing mortar.

- Also, when his leadership skills were needed, the task always involved labor details, concrete pours or painting details
- Nevertheless, J.W. decided that he and his peers would be the best labor force available and make themselves indispensable
- Excellence, not complaining, would most impress the White officers who looked down on Negro soldiers
- In Puerto Rico, J.W. found it difficult to follow the experiences of other Black soldiers after the military declared newspapers such as the Pittsburgh Courier contraband, so J.W. and his fellow Seabees relied on stateside relatives to secretly send the Courier via care packages
- Race mixing in military camps resulted in fights and other types of violence during the war

John became frustrated that colored troops always got low-skilled jobs while less experienced white sailors were rewarded with better assignments.

- The alleged beating of the wife of a Black soldier by a White military policeman sparked a race riot at Camp Stewart, Georgia, in which one White MP was killed and four others wounded
- False rumors of race riots resulted in the death of one Negro soldier, and one White soldier was critically wounded when fights between Black and White soldiers erupted en route from Fort Bliss to El Paso, Texas
- Sparking even deeper resentment was the treatment accorded German prisoners of war incarcerated in the South
- Much to the exasperation of Black soldiers, German prisoners were allowed to dine with the White civilian population on trains while Black soldiers were told to eat behind a Jim Crow curtain
- The NAACP issued posters attacking the Red Cross' segregated blood drives, citing scientific evidence that the composition of Black and White plasma was the same
- But the nature of segregation came home to J.W. when he convinced his fellow Seabees that Jim Crow must go in Puerto Rico

Most of the black soldiers were assigned to "C" Company, composed of builders and steelworkers.

- To ease racial tensions, the military began calling for the elimination of Jim Crow discrimination on military bases to include the desegregation of transportation and recreational facilities
- All these issues came to a head one afternoon, when two dozen Black soldiers became furious after a fight broke out resulting from a mix-up in segregated scheduled ball field practice time
- For the Black soldiers of C Company, it was the last straw
- First J.W. listened to their anger, mixed with years of earned bitterness
- He allowed the men to scream and rage themselves into exhaustion
- Only after every man had taken the time to tell the others how segregation had held him back did J.W. explain his plan

- First they would list all their grievances on a single piece of paper
- Any man could put a complaint on the list; only a unanimous vote could take it off the list
- The list of concerns would be held to 12 items that a delegation could present to the battalion commander
- The Seabees worked hard on the list, arguing, demanding and cajoling to get their personal grievances included in it
- The complaints involved equal opportunity in military promotions, construction projects and the post exchange; the list also called for equal treatment on liberty buses and the removal of restrictions on which beaches that Black soldiers could use and when
- Only when the list was complete did J.W. meet with the battalion commander to obtain an appointment, which was granted two days hence
- The in-person meeting was designed to be off the record and respectful

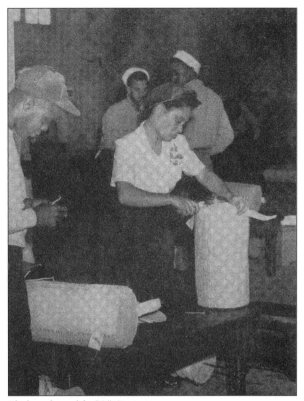

Black workers of the "C" Company.

- In all, 16 men agreed to meet with the commander; J.W. was designated as their leader
- Then, on the day of the meeting, an emergency arose; J.W. was ordered to stand the watch of a shipmate who had broken his arm in an accident.
- The group voted to go without him
- As disciplined soldiers who had thought through the issues, they went to meet the battalion commander
- Two military police stood on each side of the commander as the 15 members of C Company made the presentation that J.W. had prepared
- They began with the concept that the military could lead the nation in fighting Jim Crow traditions by awarding Negro soldiers the dignity they deserved
- Then they respectfully listed their requests
- The men were nervous
- The commander sat in stony silence, as usual, until the end
- All of the Negro soldiers believed that speaking off the record to the commander was the proper path
- They were wrong
- When the last man had spoken, the commander rose to his feet and barked, "How dare you bring a mob to demand anything? Being a Seabee is not enough, so now you expect to be treated White. Lock these men up. I will not have race riots on my watch."
- All 15 men were escorted from the commander's office, arrested for insubordination and court-martialed
- They were all dishonorably discharged and sent back to the states
- When his fellow soldiers were disciplined, J.W. stepped forward to receive his punishment, but was told to return to duty

- One miserable year later, 34-year-old J.W. was honorably discharged, more than ready to rejoin civilian life
- His dream was to marry Volia Wilkerson, an elementary school teacher who had faithfully written him letters during the war years
- By 1946, he was one of 1.2 million African Americans who had served their country, battling for freedom across the globe
- He was disillusioned and angry
- But J.W. quickly discovered that returning Black soldiers were more defiant and less willing to accept Jim Crow thinking from civilians who had not gone to war
- On February 12, 1946, Sgt. Isaac Woodward, a decorated Pacific veteran, was blinded in a struggle after being arrested for sitting with a White soldier on a bus returning the men home from Camp Gordon, Georgia
- Woodward's offense was demanding that the bus driver "talk to me like a man."
- Black veteran John Jones was beaten to death by a group of White men in Louisiana; a dispute over a radio in Columbia, Tennessee, between a White army veteran and a Black navy veteran resulted in the mobilization of 500 National Guardsmen to calm the race riot

Life in the Community: Roosevelt Roads Naval Station, Puerto Rico

- Roosevelt Roads Naval Station was located in the eastern part of Puerto Rico in the town of Ceiba, about 50 miles from San Juan
- It was named for then assistant secretary of the Navy Franklin D. Roosevelt, who conceived the idea in 1919 on a surveying trip
- He envisioned it as one of the largest naval facilities in the world
- The station was first commissioned as a U.S. naval operations base in 1943, designed to become the keystone of the Caribbean Defense System with a well-protected anchorage, a major air station and an industrial establishment capable of supporting 60 percent of the Atlantic fleet under wartime conditions
- There was even talk that if the British Empire ever fell to Axis powers, Roosevelt Roads would become the new operating base for the British fleet
- But by 1943, it was clear that with Allied operations focusing on Europe and the Pacific, a major defense hub on the island would be unnecessary
- Construction on the base was halted in 1944 and Naval Operating Base Roosevelt Roads was put in a maintenance status with a public works officer, a detachment of Seabees and a large civilian workforce

Letters to the Editor, *Yank*, 1944

Dear *Yank*:

Here is a question each Negro soldier is asking. What is the Negro soldier fighting for? On whose team are we playing? Myself and eight other soldiers were on our way from Camp Claiborne, Louisiana, to the hospital here at Fort Huachuca. We had to lay over until the next day for our train. On the next day we could not purchase a cup of coffee at any of the lunchrooms around here. As you know, Old Man Jim Crow rules. The only place where we could be served was at the lunchroom at the railroad station but, of course, we had to go into the kitchen. But that's not all; 11:30 a.m. about two dozen German prisoners of war, with two American guards, came to the station. They entered the lunchroom, sat at the tables, had their meals served, talked, smoked, in fact had quite a swell time. I stood on the outside looking in, and I could not help but ask myself these questions: Are these men sworn enemies of this country? Are they not taught to hate and destroy all democratic governments? Are we not American soldiers, sworn to fight for and die if need be for this our country? Then why are they treated better than we are? Why are we pushed around like cattle? If we are fighting for the same thing, if we are to die for our country, then why does the government allow such things to go on? Some of the boys are saying you will not print this letter. I'm saying that you will.

-Cpl. Rupert Trimmingham, Fort Huachuca, Arizona, April 28, 1944

———————

Dear *Yank:*

Just read Cpl. Rupert Trimmingham's letter titled "Democracy" in a May edition of *Yank*. We are White soldiers in the Burma jungles, and there are many Negro units working with us. They are doing more than their part to win this war. We are proud of the colored men here. When we are away from camp working in the jungles, we can go to any colored camp and be treated like one of their own. I think it is a disgrace that, while we are away from home doing our part to help win the war, some people back home are knocking down everything we are fighting for.

We are among many Allied nations' soldiers that are fighting here, and they marvel at how the American army, which is composed of so many nationalities and different races, gets along so well. We are ashamed to read that the German soldier, who is the sworn enemy of our country, is treated better than the soldier of our country, because of race.

Cpl. Trimmingham asked: What is a Negro fighting for? If this sort of thing continues, we the White soldiers will begin to wonder: What are we fighting for?

-Pvt. Joseph Poscucci (Italian), Burma, June 1944

HISTORICAL SNAPSHOT
1946

- Weight Watchers was formed
- Popular music of the day included: "Oh, What It Seemed to Be" by the Frankie Carle Orchestra with Marjorie Hughes; "Personality" by Johnny Mercer; "Day by Day" by Frank Sinatra; and "Guitar Polka" by Al Dexter
- In Japan, 28 former leaders were indicted in Tokyo as war criminals
- The first packages from the relief agency CARE (Cooperative for American Remittances to Europe) arrived in Europe, at Le Havre, France
- The musical *Annie Get Your Gun* opened on Broadway starring Ethel Merman
- A patent was filed for the hydrogen bomb
- The United States Supreme Court struck down Virginia's segregation statute on interstate buses
- The United States exploded a 20-kiloton atomic bomb near Bikini Atoll in the Marshall Islands in the Pacific Ocean
- The Philippines, which had officially become a territory of the United States in 1902, gained its independence on July 4
- The bikini bathing suit made its debut during a fashion show in Paris
- In Japan, Emperor Hirohito publicly rejected the notion that the emperor was a living god and that the Japanese were superior to other races
- The first General Assembly of the United Nations convened in London
- The United Mine Workers rejoined the American Federation of Labor
- The Electronic Numerical Integrator and Calculator (ENIAC), was unveiled at the University of Pennsylvania; the machine took up an entire room, weighed 30 tons and used more than 18,000 vacuum tubes to perform functions such as counting to 5,000 in one second
- The Republican Party took control of the Senate and the House in mid-term elections
- Walt Disney's *Song of the South* was released
- The first artificial snow was produced from a natural cloud at Mt. Greylock, Massachusetts
- Lillian Hellman's play *Another Part of the Forest* premiered in New York City
- The Supreme Court granted Oregon Indians land payment rights from the U.S. government
- President Harry Truman created the Committee on Civil Rights by Executive Order
- The United Nations International Children's Emergency Fund (UNICEF) was established
- The United Nations General Assembly voted to establish the U.N. headquarters in New York City
- The film *It's a Wonderful Life,* starring James Stewart and Donna Reed, premiered

Selected Prices, 1946

Automobile, Mercury Convertible $2,209.00
Girdle $6.95
Hair Dryer $9.95
Handkerchiefs $0.69
House, Five-Room, North Carolina $5,700.00
Movie Ticket $1.00
Night Cream, Noxema $0.59
Pepsi-Cola, Bottle $0.05
Television, General Electric $189.95
Whiskey, Fifth $3.98

African American Military Timeline

1917

The United States entered World War I and declared war on Germany.

After Congress passed the Selective Service Act, about 700,000 Black men volunteered for the draft on the first day; over two million ultimately registered.

The Central Committee of Negro College Men organized at Howard University furnished over 1,500 names in response to an army requirement for 200 college-educated Blacks to be trained as officers.

Army senior leaders publicly expressed doubts about enlisting large numbers of Blacks because they believed Blacks could not fight and were concerned about possible subversion by an "oppressed minority."

Congress authorized 14 training camps for White officer candidates but none for African Americans; after Black protests the U.S. Army established the first all-Black officer training school at Fort Des Moines, Iowa.

The first American troop ship dispatched to France included over 400 Black stevedores and longshoremen; by the end of the war 50,000 African Americans in the U.S. Army were employed as laborers in French ports.

Racial tension involving U.S. servicemen flared into a major riot in Texas where Black troops were assigned to Camp Logan to guard the construction of a training facility, resulting in the death of 16 Whites, including five policemen.

1918

Racial violence was sparked in Manhattanville, Kansas, by a local theater's refusal to admit a Black sergeant, a type of discrimination prohibited by state law.

The all-Black Ninety-second ("Buffalo") Division arrived in France, then moved to the front; despite individual acts of heroism, army leaders maintained that the division did not perform well under combat conditions.

An editorial in the National Association for the Advancement of Colored People (NAACP) publication, *Crisis*, urged Black Americans to put the war effort before their own needs by "closing ranks" with White Americans in support of the fighting in France.

The French liaison to the American Expeditionary Force (AEF) headquarters advised French officers to keep their distance from any Black officers, to give only moderate praise to Black troops, and to keep Black troops and White French women apart.

German propaganda leaflets dropped on African American troops encouraged desertion: "To carry a gun in this service is not an honor but a shame. Throw it away and come over to the German lines. You will find friends who will help you."

Over 367,000 African American soldiers served in this conflict, 1,400 of whom were commissioned officers.

Most Blacks were placed in noncombat services of supply units which provided labor.

Approximately 100,000 African Americans went to France during World War I; despite the American restriction on the use of Blacks in combat units, about 40,000 African Americans fought in the war.

The 369th (or "Harlem Hellfighters") was the first Allied regiment to reach the Rhine River during the final offensive against Germany.

Members of the 370th Infantry Regiment won 21 American Distinguished Service Crosses and 68 French Croix de Guerre during WWI.

The Army Nurses Corps accepted 18 Black nurses on an experimental basis following the influenza epidemic.

The White 369th Infantry Regiment was honored in a grand parade down New York City's Fifth Avenue, while most Black units were ignored.

In St. Joseph, Missouri, Black veterans refused to march at the back of a victory parade.

continued

Timeline . . . *(continued)*

1919

During the summer following the Armistice of November 1918, racial violence spawned serious riots in Texas, Nebraska, Illinois, and Washington, DC.

Ten veterans were among the 75 African Americans lynched by White mobs.

The American Legion, a veterans' organization, allowed Black veterans to join, but only in segregated posts.

1925

An Army War College study reported that African Americans would never be fit to serve as military pilots.

1932

The U.S. Navy allowed African Americans to enlist, lifting the restriction in place since the end of WWI that excluded Blacks from serving in the navy.

1936

Black cadet Benjamin O. Davis, Jr., graduated from West Point, after enduring four years of "silencing."

1939

The Committee for the Participation of Negroes in National Defense was formed and successfully helped to get nondiscrimination clauses inserted into the Selective Service Act passed in September 1940.

Congress passed the Civilian Pilot Training Act to create a pool of trained aviators in the event of war; seven different institutions enrolled Blacks for flight training, but the Army Air Corps continued to exclude African American pilots.

Britain and France declared war after Germany invaded Poland, while President Franklin D. Roosevelt announced American neutrality in a fireside chat.

1940

President Roosevelt signed the Selective Training and Service Act, the first peacetime draft in U.S. history; the act contained an anti-discrimination clause and established a 10 percent quota system to ensure integration.

Segregation of troops remained official U.S. Army policy throughout World War II.

Black leaders met with the Secretary of the Navy to present a seven-point program for the mobilization of African Americans that included demands for flight training, the admission of Black women into military nursing units, and desegregation of the armed forces.

The War Department established a quota for enlisting Blacks based on a percentage of their numbers in the general population.

Judge William H. Hastie, dean of the Howard University Law School, assumed the position of civilian aide to the Secretary of War in Matters of Black Rights.

1941

The U.S. Army activated the 366th Infantry Regiment, the first all-Black Regular Army unit officered by African Americans only.

continued

Timeline . . . *(continued)*

1941

Labor and civil rights leader A. Philip Randolph, president of the Brotherhood of Sleeping Car Porters, proposed a massive March on Washington in July 1941 to protest unfair labor practices in the defense industry and the military's discrimination against African Americans.

Secretary of War Henry L. Stimson formally approved the establishment of the flight training program at Tuskegee Institute.

The U.S. Army established the 78th Tank Battalion, the first Black armor unit.

President Roosevelt issued Executive Order 8802, which reiterated the federal government's previously stated policy of nondiscrimination in war industry employment in keeping with a promise made to A. Philip Randolph if he would call off his planned "March on Washington."

The Army opened its integrated officers' candidate schools, although Black officers were not allowed to command White troops.

The U.S. Army Air Corps began training African American pilots at the Tuskegee Institute in Alabama.

Black leaders launched the "Double V" campaign, and urged African Americans to support the war effort as a way to fight racism abroad.

The U.S. Army activated the 93rd Infantry at Fort Huachuca, Arizona, the first Black division formed during World War II.

Black newspapers that ran articles strongly criticizing segregation and discrimination in the armed forces had trouble obtaining newsprint until they softened their stance; the U.S. Justice Department threatened to charge 20 editors with sedition.

1942

Approximately 1,800 Blacks sat on draft boards in the United States.

President Roosevelt ordered the U.S. Navy and U.S. Marine Corps to enlist African Americans into their regular military units.

The U.S. Coast Guard recruited its first 150 Black volunteers.

The 761st Tank Battalion was activated at Camp Claiborne, Louisiana, with six White officers, 30 Black officers, and 676 enlisted men.

The U.S. Navy began accepting Black inductees from the Selective Service Board for the first time.

About 167,000 Blacks served in the U.S. Navy in WWII; 123,000 of these men served overseas, and almost 12,500 African Americans served in the Seabees, as the navy's construction battalions were called.

The U.S. Marine Corps began admitting African American recruits for the first time in 167 years; of the 19,168 Blacks who served in the Marine Corps during the war, 12,738 served overseas.

1943

The First Marine Depot was the first Black USMC unit to be sent overseas in World War II.

Judge William H. Hastie resigned his position as civilian aide to the Secretary of War because of continuing discrimination and segregation in the armed forces.

The Women's Marine Corps was created, the only WWII-era women's auxiliary that did not admit any African Americans.

The federal government barred all war contractors from discriminating on the basis of race.

continued

Timeline . . . *(continued)*

1943

African Americans reported White hostility to their presence in war plants, including a race riot in Detroit, Michigan, in which 25 African Americans and nine Whites were killed.

1944

The percentage of African Americans employed in war production rose from less than 3 percent in 1942 to over 8 percent.

The War Department prohibited racial discrimination in recreational and transportation facilities on all U.S. Army posts.

American film director Frank Capra produced *The Negro Soldier,* the first U.S. Army training film to favorably depict African American servicemen.

The percentage of Black soldiers in the U.S. Army peaked at 8.74 percent.

The U.S. Army's racial policies became an important issue during this year's presidential campaign; Black leaders continued to criticize the army's restricted use of Black troops in combat.

The U.S. Navy commissioned 13 African Americans as its first Black officers.

The U.S. Army Air Corps' all-Black 332nd Fighter Group, also known as the Tuskegee Airmen, first saw combat.

The *USS Mason,* a destroyer escort, was the first naval warship with a predominantly Black crew and at least one Black officer.

The first African American Marines to be decorated by the Second Marine Division—Staff Sergeant Timerlate Kirven and Corporal Samuel J. Love, Sr.—won purple hearts for wounds received in the assault on Saipan.

Army Lieutenant John Roosevelt Robinson, one of the 761st "Black Panther" Tank Battalion's few Black officers, refused orders to sit in the back of a military bus at Fort Hood, Texas; he was court-martialed, but acquitted because the order was a violation of war.

During fighting along the Gothic line in Italy, the 92nd Infantry Division lost momentum and was forced into a disorderly retreat; the division commander and his staff used racist remarks to explain the division's initial combat failure.

The WAVES accepted its first 72 Black women, two of whom became officers.

The U.S. Army integrated Black volunteers with White troops to fight during the "Battle of the Bulge," the Germans' last desperate counteroffensive to break through in the Ardennes forest in Belgium; it was the first and only example of an integrated army fighting force in WWII.

1945
The U.S. Navy eliminated all of its segregated stations and schools.

continued

Timeline . . . *(continued)*

1945

Colonel Benjamin O. Davis, Jr., taking command of the 477th Composite Group of Godman Field, Kentucky, was the first African American to command a military base in the United States and the first to command a U.S. Army Air Force installation.

The National Association of Colored Nurses forced the U.S. Army Nurse Corps to drop its racial restrictions on qualified nurses.

The first and only Black WACs assigned to overseas duty were the 800 women of the 6888th Central Postal Directory Battalion.

The "Black Panthers" helped to breach the Siegfried Line in Germany.

Members of the "Tuskegee Airmen" from the 477th Bombadier Squadron "mutinied" in protest against a discriminatory policy; a group of 104 African American Army Air Corps officers was arrested after entering the officers' club at Freemen Field, Indiana, which was closed to non-Whites.

Wesley A. Brown received an appointment to the U.S. Naval Academy at Annapolis, Maryland, and became the first African American to graduate and earn his commission from the academy four years later.

At the end of WWII, 695,000 African Americans were in the U.S. Army.

MEN WANTED: UNCLE SAM ISSUES CALL FOR EXPERTS

The Army needs men skilled in almost every profession, business, and trade. Whatever your job is, if you are extra good at it, you may be wanted. Here are some of the posts now being filled:

PROFESSIONS	WHERE SERVICES ARE REQUIRED
ENGINEERS AND PRODUCTION MEN	Electrical engineers in Signal Corps and other branches (urgent). Mechanical engineers in Ordnance Department and other branches. Metallurgists and metallurgical engineers in several branches. Some sanitation and public-utility engineers. Probably some draftsmen, inspectors, supervisors, foremen, and other skilled men for production, especially metal fabrication, and maintenance work.
CHEMISTS	Chemical engineers and chemists in Chemical Warfare Service and other branches.
COMMUNICATIONS MEN	Radio, telephone, and telegraph engineers, and others in Signal Corps and other technical branches. Radio maintenance men and telephone and telegraph operators (heavy demand).
TRANSPORTATION MEN	Railroad traffic and operating executives and other experts in various branches (urgent). Air-transport executives and other air experts in Air Corps and other branches (urgent). Experienced truck-fleet operation and maintenance men in Quartermaster Corps (urgent). Some water-borne transportation men.
BUSINESS MEN, BANKERS, AND LAWYERS	Personnel, office, and finance executives, and clerical supervisors in administrative posts in ground and air forces. Some economists, foreign and domestic-trade specialists, and lawyers. Wholesale and retail executives, especially with food, textile, and clothing experience, in Quartermaster Corps. Men with retail and chain-store experience as post-exchange officers.
ACCOUNTANTS	Accountants, auditors, and statisticians in several branches.
WAREHOUSEMEN	Experienced men for Army depots.
MISCELLANEOUS	Many men for censorship work—those speaking a foreign language especially valuable.

ARMY SPECIALIST CORPS PAY RATES

OFFICERS		ENLISTED SPECIALISTS	
Colonel	$6,500	Specialist, 1st Class (master sergeant)	$2,900
Lieutenant Colonel	5,600	Specialist, 2nd Class (technical sergeant)	2,600
Major	4,600	Specialist, 3rd Class (staff sergeant)	2,300
Captain	3,500-3,800	Specialist, 4th Class (sergeant)	2,000
First Lieutenant	3,200	Specialist, 5th Class (corporal)	1,800
Second Lieutenant	2,600-2,900		

"Report on the Negro Soldier," by Major Robert F. Cocklin, *Infantry Journal,* December 1946:

The relationship of White and colored people in America is too complex for discussion here, and of course, it carried over when the Negro became a soldier. Lifelong prejudices survived the expansion of the army, although the pressure of work, training and war tended to force them somewhat into the background.

The Doolittle Committee and its subsequent report have clearly indicted the reluctance of the civilian in general to accept the more disciplined life of the soldier. In this, the colored soldier in no way differed from his White countryman. But unfortunately, the rigors of military discipline were all too frequently tagged "discrimination" when they concerned the Negro soldier. In this regard, I firmly believe that a large part of the Negro press did a disservice to the members of their race. Since they provided the chief source of news about their race, Negro publications were read with avid interest by every colored soldier who could lay his hands on one. Often, these papers were handed around until they were almost worn out.

Much of the Negro press, with its sensational news stories, continually screamed that the colored soldier was being discriminated against at every turn. Obvious distortions of facts were often evident. Journalism of this type may have been good for circulation but it was definitely poor for the morale of the troops and served only to stir up unrest. . . .

Perhaps the biggest problem confronting the officers who trained the Ninety-third Division was the general inability of the colored soldier to assimilate instruction. The Army General Classification Test scores of by far the greater part of the soldiers assigned to the Ninety-third fell in the lower two of the five classified categories. This was, of course, far below the average on which the War Department had based its training plans and periods. In consequence, we simply had to slow our training programs down and simplify it as much as possible. We went through the basic training cycle three times.

1948: U.S. Delegate and Postwar Architect

Successful New York architect Bartholomew Holmes was part of a U.S. delegation sent to England to assist with postwar restoration, where one of his children joined him to tour Britain's most damaged cities.

Life at Home

- Bartholomew Holmes is currently touring England with a team of 25 Americans, giving advice, inspecting buildings and working with the British government to solve its housing shortage.
- An architect by training, he has spent the past few years redeveloping sections of New York, including the launching of many projects in which he and his father were direct investors
- He is being paid $1 a year plus expenses for his work in England, and is one of two African Americans on the trip who both gained encouragement from former First Lady Eleanor Roosevelt to take a visible role in the mission
- He was shocked when he arrived in London to find block after block of flattened rubble created by consistent German bombing of the nation's cities
- In Kent, southeast of London and within the flyway of the German attack planes, he met with a farmer whose land contained 93 bomb holes
- In general, the British economy is in shambles; since August 1945, Britain has wrestled with the task of reallocating resources, rebuilding industrial potential and restoring exports
- Throughout the country, government officials are terrified of repeating the mistakes of World War I, which resulted in high inflation and massive unemployment
- He is unsure that the new Labour government, which replaced Winston Churchill's Conservatives in July 1945, is experienced enough for the job of restoring the economy; its pledge in 1945 to build four million houses over a 10 year period is already way behind schedule
- He believes that the United Kingdom is more interested in preserving tradition than in solving the housing shortage
- Bartholomew's family traces its roots and wealth to Chicago, where his Civil War era grandfather established a lucrative business transporting hogs; Chicago's strategic position as a transportation hub gave him an opportunity to profit from the hogs, and later beef, flowing through the city's slaughterhouses
- Later his two sons, using the profits of the business, went into the printing business just as the African American

Bartholomew Holmes assisted in the restoration of Britain.

mi gration to northern cities began;
the brothers did extremely well
supplying news, advertising and print
jobs to Chicago's growing middle class
- Bartholomew's father, sensing a rising
tide of racism in Chicago, sold the
printing business to white investors
after the First World War and moved
to New York City
- His son has spent his entire adult life
in New York, except for his
undergraduate years at Harvard
- Along with his father, Bartholomew
bought depressed properties in New
York and created new housing
develop ments; the quality of their
work attracted the attention of city
and federal officials, helping father
and son easily at tr act investment
capital for bigger and bigger projects
- Recently, his 17-year-old daughter
Joyce joined the group during her
summer break, and has been amazed,
not only by the destruction, but also
by the dreariness of English fashion
- She resents the stereotype harbored by
British boys that American Negro girls
are loose, so she sticks close to her
father's touring group whenever
possible.

The ancient stained glass of Britain's cathedral was removed and stored during the war.

Life at Work

- When the American delegation arrived in England, an early stop was St. Paul's Cathedral, which stands by the Thames River in London
- Although German planes throughout the Second World War had flown along the river at night and bombed London, the ancient cathedral, designed by Sir Christopher Wren in the 1600s, miraculously survived
- St. Paul's Fire Watch was restarted in 1939 with more than 300 people from around the world who volunteered to protect the church from incendiary bombs dropped by the German war planes
- Up to 40 people would sleep in the cathedral at night; known as "kickers," they would literally kick bombs off the roof and grounds of the cathedral to keep it safe, an enormous task because of the many complex angles on the roof and hundreds of corners and crannies where an incendiary bomb could lodge and start a fire
- Over time, St. Paul's Cathedral stood as a visible symbol of hope for many Londoners; if they could see the dome of St. Paul's the morning after an air raid, it fueled their courage to fight on
- After London, Holmes is touring Exeter, Bath, Norwich, York and Canterbury, all traditional spots before the war

The dome of St. Paul's Cathedral served as a symbol of hope during the dark days of the blitz.

- The German air raids of these cities were nicknamed the "Baedeker raids" from the assumption that the popular Baedeker tourist guidebooks had been consulted when the list of German targets was drawn up
- In other parts of England, fourteenth-century abbeys and churches are covered in scaffolding to replace elegant stained-glass windows, many of which were taken out during the early days of the war and stored in the buildings' crypts
- Despite the enthusiasm for new ideas and different ways to develop the countryside, Britain has little money for the programs Holmes would like to undertake
- Privately, he hopes he can duplicate his success in New York while allowing the government to take a substantial level of risk
- Unfortunately, British wartime expenditures on troops and munitions were paid for through the transfer of British securities to creditors rather than in cash payments, creating ongoing obligations
- To repay these obligations and finance the necessary imports for recovery, exports must be increased quickly
- The abrupt termination of the Lend-Lease arrangements with the United States now requires that future supplies be paid in American dollars, further pinching Britain's resources and forcing the Labour government to juggle its internal and external priorities
- To increase domestic demand too quickly would threaten the export drive and absorb greater imports, putting the balance of payments at risk; thus, much of the nation's consumer goods such as clothing, food and coal are still restricted, years after rationing has been lifted in the United States
- In fact, the number of consumer expenditures subject to rationing in Britain has actually risen since 1946

- In June 1946, the British armed forces stood at more than two million people; today only 810,000 are still in the armed services, with more returning every day, while approximately 1.3 million women have left war-generated factory jobs
- Yet, the coal shortage of 1947 that threatened the very stability of the new Labour government was caused largely by a shortage of labor in the mines; returning war veterans were unwilling to return to the pits, preferring jobs above ground
- Holmes believes that the much discussed aid from the United States under the Marshall Plan will give the country the capital injection it needs to consider new proposals like his
- This is particularly important since the country is now moving in what he believes is a dangerous direction—nationalization—under which industry is brought into public ownership to be run and controlled by the government
- The goal is to ensure that industry works in the interest of the country as a whole rather than for the profit of individuals
- Bartholomew is surprised that the Conservative Party has not taken a more aggressive stance against what he considers a socialist action
- Currently, more than 1.5 million workers, employed by the Bank of England, the National Coal Board, Cable and Wireless, British Transport Commission and British Electrical Authority, are all nationalized

Life in the Community: London, England
- The Second World War was the least unexpected war in history
- Britain began to prepare in 1935 when it became clear that Hitler was leading the German people toward the attempted mastery of Europe; in 1937, the Air-Raid Precaution Act made preparations compulsory
- As the outbreak of war drew nearer, important buildings throughout Britain were pro tected from bomb blasts by being faced with sandbags
- The film "Wuthering Heights," starring Merle Oberon and Laurence Olivier, was on at the Regal Cinema and a Shirley Temple film, "The Little Princess," was showing at the Arts Theater in the city of Cambridge when Hitler's troops invaded Poland in September 1939
- On September 7, 1940, the first night of the blitz in London, nearly 2,000 people were killed or wounded.
- At the height of the blitz, approximately 177,000 people slept in the underground tube stations of the city; nightly bombings were so frequent Londoners began wearing a lapel badge reading, "Don't tell me, I've got a bomb story, too."
- Shops and offices closed early to allow their workers time to get home before the air-raid warning sirens sounded

- Much of the damage to Britain's major cities came in the last years of the war, thanks to the German's V-1 revenge weapon, a mechanically guided, pilotless aircraft launched by a 180-foot catapult, first used in 1944 one week after D-Day in Europe
- By 1943, 90 percent of single women and 80 percent of married women were engaged in war work
- England has been changed by the war effort and the passage of more than 1.5 million GIs (Government Issue) through Britain
- In all, more than 80,000 GIs took home British brides
- American GIs were better paid than British soldiers and had access to the base PX, where Lucky Strike Cigarettes, razor blades of prewar quality, and chocolate were available
- To escape the claustrophobic atmosphere at home, people went to the movies in droves, lining up for hours to attend movies; 25 to 30 million tickets were sold each week
- Though the most popular were the adventure films, espe cially Westerns and musicals from the United States, Gone with the Wind played in London's West End nonstop from the spring of 1940 to the spring of 1944

Britain during the War

- As war loomed in 1938, the government distributed 38 million gas masks house to house to British families
- Gas masks became a regular feature of children's wear; they carried them to school, hauled them to the bomb shelters and, when adults were not around, they blew air into the masks so the side would flap and produce rude sounds
- To show solidarity, the Queen has created a "limiting mark" on her bathtub to indicate the approved level of water permissible
- To provide protection from the bombing, millions of residents erected "Anderson Shelters," which served as bunkers against the raids and were designed to accommodate six people
- To support the war effort, household aluminum pots were collected from homes throughout the United Kingdom and melted to make Spitfire fighter planes, while ornamental railings were stripped from the nation's parks to make ships and tanks
- Starting in 1941 and lasting throughout the war, the countryside of Britain was populated with German and Italian prisoners of war, who were used to work the fields
- To meet coal shortages within the country, more than 15,000 young boys were assigned by the national service to work in the mines instead of in the army
- At Christmastime, British carol singers were told not to ring bells in case they were confused with air-raid signals; in many cities, traditional midnight Christmas mass was cancelled because of the difficulty of blacking out the huge church windows during the service

British solidarity remained fortified despite the catastrophic damage to major cities during the war.

- The war effort required widespread rationing, including bans on automobile and bike tires, hot-water bottles, beach balls and rubber floor mats
- Kleenex was virtually unobtainable, and toilet paper was perennially scarce; in 1943, shoes were rationed, with civilians eligible for two pairs a year
- To deal with the increased pressure to move soldiers and war materials rapidly, the railroads finally made the switch from steam-powered locomotives to diesel engines
- The BBC broadcast its programming in 24 languages to support the resistance movements in countries such as France, Norway and Denmark, even broadcasting coded messages, such as "Barbara's dog will have three pups," to inform resistance workers of the arrival of three refugees.

Marriage ceremonies were held despite the bombing and destruction.

HISTORICAL SNAPSHOT
1948

- A Gallup poll reported that 94 percent of Americans believed in God
- Inflation drove nearly all costs up; clothing expenses rose 93 percent from 1939 to 1948, while a house priced at $4,440 in 1939 had risen to $9,060
- Both Baskin-Robbins and McDonald's began operations
- Nationwide, 50 cities banned comic books dealing with crime or sex; psychiatrist Fredric Wertham charged that heavy comic-book reading contributed to juvenile delinquency
- President Harry Truman ordered racial equality in the armed forces
- Jack Benny sold his NBC radio program to CBS for a reported $2 to $3 million; the IRS then claimed 75 percent for personal income taxes
- New York began a fluoridation program for 50,000 children
- A transistor developed by Bell Telephone Laboratories permitted miniaturization of electronic devices such as computers, radios and television
- Gerber Products Company sold two million cans and jars of baby food weekly
- Dial soap was introduced as the first deodorant soap
- One million homes had television sets
- Garbage disposals, heat-conducting windshields, Nestlé's Quick, Michelin radial tires and Scrabble all made their first appearance
- The Nikon camera was introduced to compete with the Leica
- 360,000 soft-coal workers went on strike, demanding $100 per month in retirement benefits at age 62
- Dwight D. Eisenhower requested a move by the Democratic Party to draft him as a candidate for president of the United States
- Peter Goldmark of CBS invented a high-fidelity, long-playing record containing up to 45 minutes of music
- Ben Hogan won the U.S. Open and was the top PGA money winner with $36,000
- A new liquid hydrogen fuel was created that was touted as having the potential to send men to the moon
- The Dow-Jones Industrial Average hit a high of 193
- The United Nations passed the Palestine Partition Plan, creating the State of Israel
- Mahatma Gandhi was assassinated by a Hindu extremist

1948 ECONOMIC PROFILE

Annual Income, Standard Jobs

Average of all Industries,
    Excluding Farm Labor $2,999.00
Average of all Industries,
    Including Farm Labor $2,933.00
Bituminous Coal Mining $3,388.00
Building Trades, Union Workers $3,125.00
Domestics $1,500.00
Farm Labor $1,541.00
Federal Civilian $3,256.00
Federal Employees,
    Executive Departments $2,949.00
Federal Military $2,676.00
Finance, Insurance and
    Real Estate $2,954.00
Gas and Electricity Workers $3,223.00
Manufacturing, Durable Goods $3,163.00
Manufacturing, Nondurable
    Goods $2,892.00
Medical/Health Services Workers . . . $1,918.00
Miscellaneous Manufacturing $2,808.00
Motion Picture Services $2,964.00

Nonprofit Organization Workers . . . $2,334.00
Passenger Transportation
    Workers, Local and Highway $3,101.00
Personal Services $2,120.00
Public School Teachers $2,538.00
Radio Broadcasting and
    Television Workers $4,234.00
Railroad Workers $3,611.00
State and Local Government
    Workers $2,593.00
Telephone and Telegraph
    Workers $2,776.00
Wholesale and Retail Trade
    Workers $2,832.00

Selected Prices

Bacon, One Pound	$0.59
Bedspread, Chenille	$3.99
China, Haviland, 100 Pieces	$250.00
Chinese Checkers	$0.95
Corn Remover, Freezone	$0.16
Dye, Rit	$0.25
Flying Lessons	$2.00
Harmonica	$1.79
Hat, Man's Stetson	$12.50
Magazine, *Jack and Jill*, 10 Months	$1.98
Manicure Set	$15.00
Mink Coat	$1,650.00
Playpen	$11.98
Radio, Silvertone	$11.75
Record Cabinet	$13.50
Soap, Woodbury's	$0.23
Television, GE 16	$189.95
Tricycle	$5.98
Washing Machine, Kenmore	$119.95
Water Heater, Presto	$4.98

The Legacy of War, Keeping Left, Labour's First Five Years and the Problems Ahead, by a group of members of Parliament, 1948:

We need not here do more than list the problems which arose from the war itself.

i) War damage, including shipping losses and obsolescence, had depreciated our capital assets by £3,000 millions. We had sold overseas investments to the tune of over £1,000 millions, and we had mortgaged the bulk of the remainder against external debts (sterling balances), which had increased by well over £3,000 millions.

ii) On the other hand, the average standard of living, thanks to the artificial stimulus of Lend-Lease, had only dropped about 15 percent, and this had been offset for most people by wartime fair shares. The man in the street, with high wages, subsidised prices and no unemployment, felt secure, well-off and entitled, by the role Britain had played in defeating the Nazis, to a 'good time' as soon as the war was over. He did not realise that, for the first time since the Industrial Revolution, Britain was a nation without anything in the kitty.

iii) The U.S.A. came out of the war with a 50-percent increase in its industrial potential and a 16-percent increase in its standard of living. Moreover, as the 'arsenal of democracy,' she had built cargo ships and transport planes, while we, nearer the front line, built destroyers and fighters. This made the disparity still more grave. America was not only 10 times more powerful, but could also turn over more quickly to peacetime production.

iv) Our recovery was possible only if world trade revived. But our exports had sunk by two thirds. War had paralysed our European markets and sources of supply, and the Far East was in a ferment. The cold war was still further aggravated by this problem. Politically and economically, we were linked with the U.S.A. But economic interests demanded that we should also trade with the Eastern bloc, since it needed our capital goods and could provide us with some part of our needs in foodstuffs and raw materials.

These postwar problems, however, were merely the immediate expression of a long process of world revolution. By 1945, Europe had finally ceased to be the centre of world politics and become one of the objects of dispute between two non-European powers. Simultaneously, the centre of world finance had shifted to Washington. London was still the capital of the single biggest trading area in the world; but the sterling area could not recover out of its own resources. This is one of the many reasons why, however much we dislike it, we had in the end to take sides in the Cold War."

"Meals on Wheels," by Margaret Cooper, *Worcestershire Countryside Magazine*, July-September 1948:

"Four days a week in wintertime and well on into the spring, the Women's Volunteer Society in Worcester takes hot dinners to old-age pensioners. In Stourbridge there is a similar system three days a week, and at Malvern, a notoriously scattered series of communities, the hot food is delivered to local centres whence the old people or their more robust relatives fetch on a cash-and-carry basis.

If you are around eighty it stands to reason that to queue for a meal is out of the question, and if you live alone in an almshouse, one person's rations do not go very far. On the other hand, hot food at British Restaurant prices is very welcome.

It happened to be a bitterly cold spring morning when the pictures were taken, and it was clear enough what a blessing this voluntary service is.

At the kitchen in St. Martin's Gate, which supplies the British Restaurants of Worcester, three W.V.S. workers loaded a small van with containers of hot meat pie, potatoes, greens, gravy, and milk pudding, and then bestowed themselves inside as well.

Away went the van to Berkeley's Almshouses, where one of the 'crew' walked briskly along the two rows of houses knocking on doors and calling out 'dinners.' Doors opened, heads and shoulders wrapped in shawls came out, trembling old hands knotted with age and rheumatism held out clean plates and pie dishes. One dear old man collected his nearest neighbor's dishes and trotted off to the van outside the gates, where the remainder of the crew busied themselves serving out the food, ladling the gravy carefully over the vegetables, and noting in a book the payments of the customers."

Meals on Wheels, supported by the British Restaurant, are providing much needed meals to the elderly and persons living in almshouses.

Teas on the Cathedral lawn are once again a feature of life in Worcester.

"Friends of Worcester Royal Infirmary," *Worcestershire Countryside Magazine*, October–December 1948:

"Nothing rouses more fury in the average open-air citizen of Britain than the discovery that his favorite footpath has suddenly been closed. In wartime he will patriotically suppress his indignation, and leave the barbwire entanglements alone, but as soon as the emergency is past, he (and his children, and his dog) will take strong measures to open up that path, possibly during the night since no one ever seems to see the actual tearing-down of rails, cutting of wires, and destruction of notice boards. Landowners generally are more particular about respecting the rights of way over routes sanctified by long tradition and usage, but now and then someone takes an unfair advantage, or decides that it is in the public interest to stop a footpath and grow some vulnerable crop where strollers used to enjoy themselves; and then the baffled and bewildered pedestrian writes a caustic letter to the county council.

It is well to know that the Worcestershire County Council intends to protect public rights in this direction, and that its members are especially asked to inspect footpaths in their area, consult with parish councils, and report to the county council on any obstructed footpath which they may find, and should it prove that a real wrong has been done, the county council can and will take legal action."

1951: Former Slave and Proud Matriarch

Born as a slave on a plantation in South Carolina, Ida Davis was the proud matriarch or four generations, living for over 70 years in the same cabin that she and her husband built when they were married.

Life at Home

- Ida Davis was old, but not exactly sure of her age, so she told her friends she was 88.
- Born as a slave on the Davis Plantation in Pine Tree Bluff, South Carolina, Ida lived on the same property, in only two houses, her entire life.
- The first was the wood cabin in which she was born. She lived there until she was 16, when she married Columbus Davis, known as Boy-Boy.
- They built a cabin together on the Davis Plantation, where she lived ever since.
- Neither house had running water or an indoor bathroom.
- Electricity arrived in 1940, thanks to the rural electrical cooperatives that brought service to the farm regions of the state.
- Ida and Boy-Boy had 14 children, 10 of whom lived to adulthood.
- Over time, eight of their children moved away—one to New York, three to Baltimore, two to Columbia, SC and two to Sumter, SC.
- One child moved to the nearby town of Summerton, while the oldest child, known as Junior, sharecropped with his daddy in Pine Tree Bluff.
- Today, Ida has 56 grandchildren and more great- and great-great-grand children than nearly anyone can count, except for Ida.
- She meticulously created a set of scrapbooks, dedicating a page or two for each great grandchild using pictures, locks of hair and other memorabilia to honor every birth.
- Her favorite leisure activity, after churchgoing, is to look at her "sweet memory" books, or listen while her children read her letters or the newspaper clippings stored in the books.
- Born during the Civil War, Ida never learned to read or write; times were hard and schools few for the former slave children of the Reconstruction South, when Ida was a girl.
- Following a lifelong habit, Ida listened hard and remembered well when the Bible, letters and articles were read aloud.

Ida Davis was the matriarch of several generations.

- Ida placed great stock in the belief that education is the key to lifting the Negro out of poverty.
- She was proud that all of her children stayed in school until at least the eighth grade; two even graduated high school, as have many of the grandchildren.
- Many of the grandchildren, who were raised in the North, returned to Summerton to raise their children and live near the family matriarch.
- Ida was particularly focused on the progress of the great-grandchildren who were drafted into the newly racially integrated army to fight in Korea.
- She was almost beside herself with joy that one of the great-grands was accepted at the new law school for Negroes in nearby Orangeburg, SC.

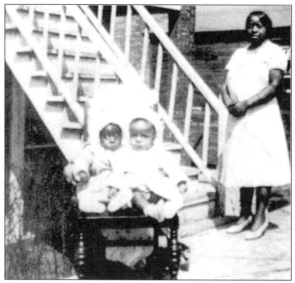

Ida's family visited her often.

- Having one of the family on the verge of becoming a lawyer ranked alongside the moment her grandson Zebulon became a minister, or when the first of several granddaughters became teachers.
- Most of the family up North had jobs in industry, a couple worked as domestics, two sons in Baltimore owned a grocery together, and one son was a porter on the railroad.
- Though she never considered herself an activist, Ida was always been keenly interested in seeing that the members of her community had opportunity and education.

Life at Work: Midwife

- Ida Davis was trained by her aunt as a midwife, and for more than 60 years she cared for most of the black babies and many of the white ones born in her part of the county.
- Her family insisted she "retire" on her eightieth birthday.
- The family offered to build her a brick home with electricity, running water and a septic system, but she figured that the little unpainted frame house where she spent the last 72 years had too many happy memories to move away from.
- The house started out with a large main room and a small bedroom, and two other bedrooms were added over time, one for the boys and one for the girls.
- The living room was neatly wallpapered with the covers of *Life* magazine, a project of many years in which Boy-Boy took great pride.
- One of the former bedrooms was where she made quilts, and was filled with cloth scraps that family members brought whenever they visited.
- All the descendants came to expect a Mama Ida quilt on their sixteenth birthday.
- She said that she was too old to sew anymore and will stop soon, but her family knew that when she stopped, her last breath would be near.
- She went to the Mt. Hebron Methodist Church where her grandboy Zeb preached.
- He often complained, only half in jest, that she knew the Bible better than he did, even though she couldn't read.
- Years of careful listening made an impression.
- When Ida was in her forties, she was so active in the church, the congregation asked her to represent them at a church convention in Little Rock, Arkansas.

- She traveled by train and was quite proud of going, but never accepted another call by the church to travel that far again.
- The unfamiliar places and names were just too hard to comprehend without knowing how to read.
- Her illiteracy also prevented her from voting, although she knew of many neighbors who could read, but were prevented from voting by draconian "literacy" and poll taxes.
- In her part of the state, it cost $2.00 to vote in a local or national election.
- Just a couple of years before, South Carolina's governor, Strom Thurmond, ran for president on the States' Rights ticket, promising to preserve segregation.
- Still, things were are better now than they were earlier in the century when the Ku Klux Klan ran rampant.
- During those days, one of her sons-in-law was lynched. The newspaper ran a picture of the lynch mob with his body and the photographer tried to sell prints of the lynching for $2.00 plus postage.
- No one was ever punished, and no trial ever held.
- Over the years, many of her family members were threatened and harassed by the Klan and less formal groups.
- By and large, however, white people treated Ida well over the years, especially the women whose babies she delivered.
- Five years ago, after her husband Boy-Boy died, the Davises, the white family still in possession of the plantation, paid his medical bills.
- She kept a garden beside her house, although the grandchildren and great grandchildren did most of the work.
- Depending on the season, she grew corn, okra, tomatoes, cucumbers, collards, mustard and turnip greens, lima beans, field peas and peanuts.
- When peanuts were in season, Ida had a kettle of them boiling in the yard whenever large numbers of young guests were expected.
- Ida was known countywide for her boiled peanuts.
- Until electricity came to the area, vegetables had to be used quickly.
- Since electricity, they were stored in the refrigerators and freezers of nearby relatives in the area, which helped feed the family in winter, when food was scarce.
- Fall was Ida's favorite time of year.

Ida and Boy Boy liked pretending to drive Mr. Davis's car.

- During September, October and often November, she sat in a chair Boy-Boy made for her, located just outside the door of her home, and smoked her hand-carved pipe.
- It made her feel close to Boy-Boy and the life they had together.
- She liked to sit and look at pictures, and her favorite was of her and Boy-Boy pretending to drive Mr. Davis's car.
- The porch chair was also a great place to watch for the old Ford truck that belonged to her grandgirl Lucasta's husband Tom.

- They regularly brought Ida a meal that included steaming greens and cornbread, along with a mess of children who demanded Ida's loving attention.

Life in the Community: Summerton, South Carolina

- The Summerton community was in an uproar when the school district refused to buy a school bus to transport black kids to their school.
- Every school morning, the whites' school bus rolled past black children walking several miles to the colored, segregated school.
- Nationally, a movement was started to integrate the schools, Ida's children told her.
- The National Association for the Advancement of Colored People (NAACP) was determined to fight the issue in the courts.
- Ida was not sure how she felt about this.
- She knew she wanted her family to receive the best education, but she also believed that the Lord made the races different for a reason.
- When school integration talk started, one local gas station and store posted signs reading, "No Nigger or Negro allowed inside building."
- Another sign read, "Negros not wanted in the North or South. Send them back to Africa where God Almighty put them to begin with. That is their home."
- With the backing of the NAACP, 20 parents of black schoolchildren filed a lawsuit on May 16, 1950—*Briggs v. Elliott*—challenging the unequal treatment of their children.

Talk of school integration encouraged racism.

HISTORICAL SNAPSHOT
1951

- World War II inflation continue to drive up prices

- The Korean conflict was underway

- After 16 years, *Time* discontinued the "March of Time" newsreels shown in movie theaters

- Metropolitan Life Insurance Company reported obesity as a cause of early death

- Television advertising companies discovered that dressing actors as doctors to peddle health products dramatically improved sales volumes

- The top television shows included *Arthur Godfrey's Talent Scouts¸ I Love Lucy, The Red Skelton Show, The Roy Rogers Show* and *Superman*

- Sugarless chewing gum, Dacron suits, the telephone company answering service, and power steering in cars all made their first appearance

- Monogram Pictures cancelled a movie about Henry Wadsworth Longfellow because of their concern that Hiawatha, an Indian peacemaker, might be viewed as a communist sympathizer

- *An American in Paris* received the Academy Award for Best Picture, beating out *The African Queen, Detective Story* and *A Streetcar Named Desire*

- An estimated three million people turned out for a New York City parade honoring General Douglas MacArthur

- African American baseball star Willie Mays was the National League Rookie of the Year

- Avis Rent-a-Car charged $6 a day and eight cents a mile

- Scientists led by Edward Teller set off the first thermonuclear reaction

- *The Grass Harp* by Truman Capote, *Requiem for a Nun* by William Faulkner, *The Ballad of the Sad Café* by Carson McCullers, *The Strange Children* by Caroline Gordon and *Betty Crocker's Picture Cook Book* were all published.

- The U.S. Census Bureau purchased Remington Rand's UNIVAC, the first commercially produced, large-scale computer

- Hit songs for the year included "Cold, Cold Heart," "Mockin' Bird Hill," "Tell Me Why," "In the Cool, Cool of the Evening" and "Unforgettable"

- Glenn T. Seaborg won the Nobel Prize in chemistry for the discovery of plutonium

- The five-cent phone call rose to 10 cents in New York and other large cities

- Hiroshima A-bomb survivor Shigeki Tanaha, 19, won the Patriots Day Marathon in Boston

Selected Prices

Dress, Linen, Sleeveless $30.00
Girdle $6.95
Refrigerator, Frigidaire $199.75
Record Album $4.85
Cake Mix, Betty Crocker $0.35
Blanket, Fieldcrest $9.95
Blender, Waring $44.50
Vaporizer $5.95
Lip Balm, Chapstick $0.25
Automobile, 1951 Buick Riviera $1,995.00
Wallet, Leather $3.50
Set of Old Spice After-Shave and Cream $1.65

1952: Olympic Gold Medal Hurdler

Harrison Dillard , who won four Olympic gold medals, had much in common with his hero Jesse Owens: both were African American, grew up in Cleveland, went to the same high school, and were coached by the same man.

Life at Home

- At age 13, Harrison Dillard gathered with his family around the radio to listen to the 1936 Summer Olympic Games broadcast from Berlin.
- He was most interested in track and field and the African American superstar, Jesse Owens, especially since he and Owens attended the same high school, East Tech.
- Owens was a local hero in Harrison's hometown of Cleveland, Ohio, and adored in the black community for his amazing achievements in sports.
- As Owens wowed the Berlin audience and the world press, he shattered the ideal promoted by Adolph Hitler in Germany, which was that the Germans would dominate and that African Americans were inferior.
- Owens spoiled this plan by winning four gold medals: 100 meter sprint; long jump; 200 meter sprint; and 4X100 meter relay.
- After he attended a parade in Cleveland honoring Jesse Owens, Harrison vowed to work harder at becoming faster and stronger.
- Summers meant more to Harrison than fun, ice cream and fireworks.
- In baseball, he showed his speed and athleticism by constantly stealing bases.
- In track, Harrison got serious about hurdling, a skill he began practicing at 8 years old using springs from car seats taken from abandoned vehicles.
- Rising at five am, Harrison ran through the quiet streets of his poor Cleveland neighborhood, encouraged by knowing that Jesse Owens had overcome this tough environment.
- He knew that black athletes—even the great Jesse Owens—had to work harder to succeed.
- Jim Crow, state and local racial segregation laws enacted between 1876 and 1965, was still alive and well in many parts of America.
- After a post-Olympic New York ticker-tape parade in his honor, Jesse Owens had to ride the freight elevator to attend his own reception at the Waldorf-Astoria.
- Harrison felt blessed to work with Charles Riley, Jesse's old coach.

Harrison Dillard emulated his hero, Jesse Owens.

- In high school, hurdles became his specialty, and he won 82 consecutive events.
- He started Baldwin-Wallace College in Beretha, Ohio, and was drafted two years later, serving in the military until 1946.
- In 1948, despite not qualifying for the hurdles in the Olympics, he was chosen as a member of the 1948 USA Olympic relay team, which captured a gold.
- Harrison kept training, hoping to quality for the hurdle event in the 1952 games in Helsinki, Finland.
- At 5'10" and 152 pounds, he was considered frail for the Olympics, and was nick named "Bones."

Harrison and Jesse Owens ran in the same Cleveland neighborhood.

Life at Work: Olympic Athlete

- As the 1952 Olympics in Helsinki approached, Harrison Dillard was determined to erase the memory of failing to qualify for the hurdles in the 1948 Olympics.
- His hard work paid off, and he qualified for the hurdle event.
- Helsinki beat out Los Angeles, Philadelphia, Detroit, Minneapolis, Amsterdam and Chicago for the opportunity to host the games.
- The Finns were very hospitable, and lived up to their motto, "You First."
- Some thought so highly of Finland that there was support to make Helsinki the Olympic destination for all time.
- In all, 5,678 athletes, representing 69 nations, were on hand to participate in 43 events in 19 sports.
- Quivering with anticipation, Harrison lined up, waiting for the starter pistol to fire.
- At the sound of the shot, he came up out of his position and raced down the track.
- He leaped over the hurdles ahead of everyone and managed the 110 meters of the race with grace and fortitude.

Harrison felt a rush when he closed in for the gold.

- Bones crossed the finish line to win the gold, with vociferous cries from the Helsinki crowd.
- The race was a sweep for the U.S., with Jack Davis and Arthur Barnard winning the silver and the bronze, respectively.
- The usually reserved Harrison leaped with joy and exclaimed, "Good things come to those who wait!"
- His Olympics were not over, for he still had the 4X100 meter relay.
- The Soviet team was considered a fierce competitor, but Harrison was confident, having been a part of the 1948 gold medal winning team.
- Harrison was running the second leg of the relay, and took the baton in his left hand from Dean Smith, who carried it in his right.

- Harrison was behind both USSR's Levan Kalyeyev and Hungary's Geza Varasdi.
- He overtook them easily, hearing only the quick, padded slap of his feet on the track and the beating of his heart within his chest.
- He breathed deeply as he rounded the track, made the transfer of the baton to Lindy Remigino's right hand, and watched his teammate run ahead of the crowd.
- As his teammate crossed the finish line to win the gold, white and black American athletes hugged and celebrated together.
- Harrison had become the first man ever to win Olympic gold medals in both the sprints and the high hurdles.

Life in Olympic Community: Helsinki, Finland

- Helsinki, Finland, was originally awarded the 1940 Olympic Games, but due to World War II, the games were canceled and Helsinki was awarded the 1952 games.
- Germany and Japan, both denied participation in the 1948 games as aggressor nations, were permitted to compete in 1952.
- Much controversy revolved around the USSR, which emerged after World War II as an American foe in the Cold War.
- The media and politicians were obsessed with the potential controversy, wondering what the reaction of the athletes might be in this atmosphere.
- Harrison wasn't worried.
- Having participated in the 1948 games, he knew athletes were not about politics or even ethnicity.
- As an African American athlete, Harrison learned in 1948 that most of the athletes put aside race and worked as a team and a community.
- Athletes from the USSR invited other Olympians to a pre-games party, serving caviar and other fine foods.
- Harrison and his fellow Americans were not interested in Capitalists versus Communists, just being the best athletes they could be.
- The new Russian team felt the same.
- The games brought out goodwill and sportsmanship among the athletes, and Harrison was glad to rise above the political intrigue.
- Not only did Germany, Japan, and the USSR create headlines, but also, for the first time ever, Israel was represented.

ॐॐॐॐॐॐॐॐ

HISTORICAL SNAPSHOT
1952

- The Federal Reserve Board voted to dissolve the A.P. Giannini banking empire, headed by Transamerica Corporation, which controlled the nation's largest bank, Bank of America
- Popular movies included *High Noon, The Greatest Show on Earth,* and *The African Queen*
- The Metropolitan Opera in New York began charging $8.00 for an evening performance and $30 per seat on opening night
- Books published included *Invisible Man, East of Eden, The Natural, The Old Man and the Sea,* and *Charlotte's Web*
- Vice Presidential candidate Richard M. Nixon declared he was not a quitter in his famous "Checkers" speech
- Jonah Salk at the University of Pennsylvania began testing a vaccine against polio
- W. F. Libby of the University of Chicago dated Stonehenge in England to about 1842 BC

- Reports circulated that the U.S. had exploded a hydrogen bomb
- The transistor radio was introduced by Sony
- Songs included "Walking My Baby Back Home," "Wheel of Fortune," and "Glow Worm"
- Nationwide, 55,000 people were stricken with polio, an all-time high
- The New Revised Standard Version of the Holy Bible was published
- The U.S. Air Force reported 60 UFO sightings in two weeks
- President Harry Truman ordered the seizure of the nation's $7 billion steel industry to prevent a walkout of 650,000 workers; the Supreme Court ruled the move unconstitutional
- *The Today Show* premiered on NBC-TV

- Edward Mills Purcell and Felix Bloch won the Nobel prize in physics for work in the measurement of magnetic fields in atomic nuclei
- The average house cost $9,050
- *Mad Magazine* was introduced, with a circulation of 195,000; 55 percent of college students and 43 percent of high school students voted it their favorite periodical
- Products making their first appearance included the 16 mm home movie projector, two-way car radios, adjustable showerheads, bowling alleys with automatic pin boys and Kellogg's Sugar Frosted Flakes
- Fifty-two million automobiles were on the highways, up from 25 million in 1945
- Thirty-seven-year-old Jersey Joe Walcott knocked out Ezzard Charles to become the oldest heavyweight boxing champion at 37
- An all-white jury in North Carolina convicted a black man for assault, for leering at a white woman 75 feet away

Selected Prices

Automobile, Pontiac Club Coupe	.$2,195.00
Electric Shaver, Schick	.$17.50
Hope Chest	.$47.95
Lawn Mowe	.$88.00
LP Record	.$4.85
Magazine, *Woman's Day*, Monthly	.$0.05
Man's Belt, Leather	.$10.00
Scotch Whiskey, 4/5 Quart	.$4.59
Sleeping Bag	.$4.88
Steam Radiator	.$108.00

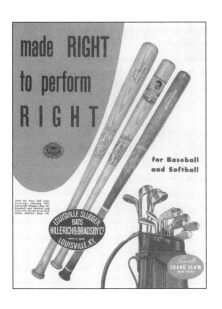

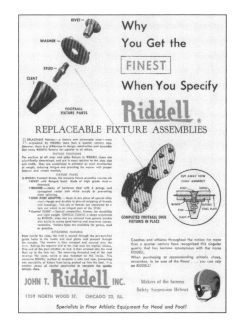

Olympics Timeline

1892

Baron Pierre de Fredi called for a rebirth of the Olympic Games, saying, "It is clear that the telegraph, the railways, the telephone, passionate scientific research, the congresses and exhibitions have done more for peace than any diplomatic convention. Well, I hope athleticism will do even more."

1896

The first games were held in Athens, Greece, with 14 nations participating in nine sports with 245 athletes (all male). Every winner received a silver medal and an olive branch.

1900

In Paris, women competed in four of the 20 sports, including lawn tennis, in which the ladies played wearing hats and long dresses.

1904

The Olympics were held outside of Europe, as St. Louis, Missouri, hosted the games; the low point came when an exposition was mounted to show the inferiority of African Americans and Native Americans.

For the first time, gold, silver, and bronze medals were awarded to the top three contestants.

1912

New technologies included electronic timing devices, photo finishes, and loudspeakers.

1916

No Olympic Games were held, as Berlin, the city awarded the site, was at war.

1920

The oldest medal winner in Olympic history was Sweden's 72-year-old Oscar Swahn, who won the gold in the double shot running deer event.

1924

The Olympic motto, "Citius, Altius, Fortius" (Swifter, Higher, Stronger), was introduced as France became the first nation to host the games twice.

1932

In order to finance their visit to Los Angeles, Brazilians traveled with a cargo of coffee that was sold along the way.

American Peter Mehringer won the gold medal in freestyle wrestling, having learned the sport through a correspondence course.

The Olympics made a profit for the first time, nearly $1 million.

1936

The Berlin Games, intended to be a showcase for Hitler's ideal man, were overshadowed by African American athletes led by Jesse Owens.

continued

Olympics Timeline . . . (continued)

1940, 1944
The games were suspended due to World War II.

1948
The Olympics were televised for the first time.

The first political defection occurred when Marie Provaznikova refused to return to Czechoslovakia.

1952
Bill Havens, who declined an Olympic invitation in 1924 for rowing because of his wife being pregnant with their first son, watched his son, Frank, win the gold medal in singles canoeing.

Records Held by Harrison Dillard
World Record: 120 yd. hurdles—13.60 (April 17, 1948-)
Olympic Record: 100 m—10.30 (July 31, 1948-)

Championships
1948 Olympics: 100 m—10.30 (First)
1948 Olympics: 400 m relay (First)
1952 Olympics: 110 m hurdles—13.70 (First)
1952 Olympics: 400 m relay (First)
1947 AAU: 60 yd. hurdles (First)
1948 AAU: 60 yd. hurdles (First)
1949 AAU: 60 yd. hurdles (First)
1950 AAU: 60 yd. hurdles (First)
1951 AAU: 60 yd. hurdles (First)
1952 AAU: 60 yd. hurdles (First)

"America's Speed Classic," H. Wieand Bowman, *Auto Sport Review*, April, 1952:

This year will mark the 36th running of the International Sweepstakes at Indianapolis. In an area 13 times as large as the famous Circus Maximus of Rome, 33 cars will try to make 200 circuits of the rectangle track surface at near peak speed. That probably no more than a dozen will complete the entire distance is a foregone conclusion.

Few of the 175,000 or more fans expected to attend this year's go will remember the first "500" run back in 1911 or the number 32 Marmon which carried ex-ribbon clerk Ray Harroun the distance at 74.59 mph average. Ray won a $14,250 b.t. purse for his efforts. And before taxes 14 grand plus with the best steak in town at four bits wasn't just so much mown grass.

Since 1911 a limited few racers have been paid altogether more than two and a half-million dollars in purse and lap monies for their attempts to win the big one. Even with taxes, that ain't hay.

Few spectators on Memorial Day, 1952, would know many of the makes of cars that were entered in the three-day race back on August 19, 1911, when the track was surfaced with oiled dirt. Bob Burman won that first main event, a 250-miler, in slightly more than four and a half hours. His winning car was a Buick pitted against a field comprising three Buicks, a Knox, two Nationals, a Jackson and two Stoddard-Daytons. But the first race ever run at the Speedway was a five-miler earlier that same day, and the winning car was a Stoddard-Dayton.

During the inaugural meet—curtailed after accidents had taken a death toll of a driver, two mechanics and two spectators—Barney Oldfield in a German Benz smashed world records for five-, 10-, 15-, 20-, and 25-mile distances and proved the circuit was fast, if unsafe.

The track was resurfaced with 3,200,000 pressed paving bricks and four more race meets were held before the first annual Memorial Day Classic was conducted in 1911.

In 1925 Peter DePaolo, with Norm Batten as relief driver, was the first race car racer to break the magical 100 mph average mark, winning with a 101.13 mph pace for the distance. DePaolo's mount was an eight cylinder Duesenberg of 121.5 c.i. piston displacement and equipped with a 5-1 ratio centrifugal blower. . . .

A radical increase in cubic inch allowance in 1930 brought in a tremendous array of equipment with representative engines of four, six, eight and 16 cylinders and a top piston displacement limit 366 c.i.s. imposed with superchargers barred on four cycle engines. The 100.448 mph mark of Billy Arnold in the front-drive Miller-Hartz still fell short of DePaolo's 1925 record. Miller's once again outshone the other designs with the first four spots going to Harry Miller's designing genius. . . .

The trend for '52 will be toward lighter chassis weight with increased use of dural and magnesium frame components. Fuel injection systems will largely replace conventional carbureton. Those in the know insist that the 140 mph qualifying mark will be topped and the current combination of the 138.122 mph record holding driver, Walt Faulkner and car owner J.C. Agajanian, may again be the record-shattering combination. It is generally thought that averages of under 132 mph won't make the 33-car starting field and the possibility of 128 mph mark plus average for the distance is high.

1959: Rock 'n' Roll Pioneer and Prisoner

Johnny Bragg, while in Tennessee State Prison for crimes he did not commit, formed the Prisonaires, a band that caught the attention of Governor Clement. When Johnny was paroled, he began a successful musical career.

Life at Home

- Singer-songwriter Johnny Bragg's mother Maybelle died in childbirth and the baby she left behind in 1926 was blind, black and poor in segregated Nashville, Tennessee, and needed constant care.
- It was not a propitious beginning for the rock and roll pioneer discovered while in prison serving 594 years for rapes he did not commit.
- Johnny's father, Wade, was a railway man who worked 12 hours a day, six days a week; he earned $6 weekly for his 72 hours of labor.
- Unable to care for the motherless flock, Wade Bragg farmed out Johnny and his three siblings to the children's grandmother and later their uncle, who was a minister and a lover of gospel music.
- At an early age Johnny learned to sing songs that reflected his life: "My Blue Heaven," and "What You Goin' to Do When the Rent Come 'Round?"
- The three boys, who saw their father only on Sundays, shared one room and one bed.
- At the age of six, Johnny inexplicably regained his sight, was able to enter school and immediately discovered he had no interest in an education.
- Johnny was a wild kid who relished fighting chickens for sport and when he was 14, served a month's confinement for riding in a stolen car.
- His life changed forever in 1943 when he caught his girlfriend, Jenny, having sex with his best friend.
- The girl angrily attacked Johnny and later, to explain her bruises, she accused Johnny of raping her.
- Her mother phoned the police, who beat Johnny until he signed a confession.
- While he was in his jail cell, the police paraded a dozen rape victims in front of Johnny, six of whom claimed that the 16-year-old had raped them.
- Even after Johnny's former girlfriend retracted her story and told the truth, Johnny was tried for the other crimes and given six 99-year sentences.

Johnny Bragg's musical talent was developed while he was in prison.

- He was sent to the notorious Tennessee State Penitentiary and, on his seventeenth birthday, Johnny Bragg began his 594-year sentence, assigned to making prison clothes.
- Prison was where he became reacquainted with the gospel music of his youth.
- When Bragg heard a group of prisoners singing spirituals, he quickly moved into the role of lead tenor and encouraged the singers to be as disciplined as the groups he heard in church.
- He began to write songs, even though he could barely read and write.
- "I'd pick up an old piece of paper off the ground. If the song had the word 'heart' in it,

Johnny formed the Prisonaires *with other prisoners.*

all I would put in it was maybe a T or an H. If there was a girl I'd put G. I wrote a lot of songs that way."
- He formed the *Prisonaires* vocal group with Ed Thurman, tenor (who had killed the man who had killed his dog), William Stewart, baritone (charged with bludgeoning a white man to death, even though someone else had confessed to the killing), Marcell Sanders, bass (who stabbed the man who stabbed his girlfriend), and John Drue Jr., tenor (serving time for car theft).
- Their first performances were serenading prisoners before their state-sponsored execution in the electric chair.
- After the singing and the disturbing sight of a man's death by electrocution, Johnny would stay behind to loosen the straps on the condemned and clean up the mess.
- At the beginning of the decade, Big Bands had dominated popular music, especially those led by Glenn Miller, Tommy Dorsey, Duke Ellington, and Benny Goodman.
- Bing Crosby's smooth voice made him extremely popular, vying with Frank Sinatra, Dinah Shore, Kate Smith, and Perry Como for the public's attention.
- By the end of the decade, bebop and rhythm and blues were merging with distinctly black sounds, epitomized by Charlie Parker, Dizzy Gillespie, while Thelonious Monk, Billie Holiday, Ella Fitzgerald, and Woody Herman forged new avenues in blues and jazz.
- Radio was the lifeline for Americans in the 1940s, providing news, music and entertainment; programming included soap operas, quiz shows, children's hours, mystery stories, fine drama, and sports.
- Within the Tennessee State Prison, the radios, all of which were owned or controlled by the guards, blared blues, gospel, country-western, and some pop music all day long.
- Nashville stars would sometimes perform at the prison and, when Johnny met Hank Williams, he asked, "Do you ever sing songs written by other people?" "Depends," said Williams, "Are you one of those other people?"
- Johnny sang Williams a song which Williams bought for $5.
- Johnny always insisted that the song eventually became "Your Cheatin' Heart," a country standard.

Life at Work: Prisoner and Musician

- Johnny Bragg's music career outside the walls of the Tennessee State Penitentiary began with the election of Frank Clement—a politician whose style was a cross between the Rev. Billy Graham and President "Give 'em Hell" Harry Truman.
- Interested in being Tennessee's governor since he was 16, Clement became the nation's youngest governor at age 32 in 1953.

- To please his wife, Clement transformed the Governor's mansion into a showcase for music makers and music lovers and to please himself, he tackled the thorny issues of Prison reform.
- Johnny Bragg and the *Prisonaires* were the benefactors of both.
- In an unprecedented move, the *Prisonaires* were allowed to perform under armed guard at churches and civic functions, and then on local radio.
- For their first performance at the Governor's mansion, a 1929 Georgian brick estate boasting 22 rooms, the prisoners were driven and escorted by the warden's petite wife when the assigned prison guard failed to show up on time.
- They wore suits fashioned by Johnny in the prison laundry, were allowed to enter through the front door of the Governor's mansion, were introduced personally by the governor by name, and then sang for an élite group of guests that included future president Texas Senator Lyndon Johnson and U.S. Senator Albert Gore of Tennessee.

Tennessee Governor Frank Clement.

- The evening was a grand success, and within weeks the *Prisonaires* became regulars on local white radio stations, at churches and services organizations.
- "The *Prisonaires* represent the hopes of tomorrow rather than the mistakes of yesterday," Governor Clement announced the same week the men performed briefly on radio Station WSM, home of the Grand Ole Opry, a musical institution since 1926.
- Their next big break came when Johnny was walking across the courtyard to his duties in the laundry with habitual housebreaker and thief, Robert Riley.
- As the rain beat down, Johnny said, "Here we are just walking in the rain and wondering what the girls are doing," Riley said. "That's a song."
- Within a few minutes, Johnny had composed two verses and was convinced it was a hit: "Just walkin' in the rain, gettin' soakin' wet, torturin' my heart, tryin' to forget."

The Prisonaires *wore prison-made suits when performing.*

- Unable to read and write, he asked Riley to write it down in exchange for a writing credit.
- When the group recorded their first record for Sam Phillips of Sun Records, "Just Walkin' in the Rain" was on the A side-the song most likely to become popular.
- Johnny heard his song for the first time on WSOK, one of two stations that gave them their start.
- "We was coming in from dinner. Some of the guys were already in their cells. I passed Ed's headbolter desk where a radio was playing. I get within earshot and I keep moving closer to a familiar sound. The radio's playing 'Just Walkin.' Ed, he walked in behind me and sat at his desk. I said, 'Ed you hear that? That's us,' and he said, 'Yeah, it is. Sounds all right.'"

- By that time, the cellblock came alive with voices yelling with excitement.
- "The guards, they were looking us up and down, but they let it go."
- Soon after its June 1953 release, "Just Walkin'," with its elegant but simple arrangement, made the nation's R&B Top 10 and quickly sold 50,000 copies.
- The record was produced by Sun Studios, the same studio where Elvis Presley, Johnny Cash, and Carl Perkins had their starts.
- According to Johnny, he and Elvis Presley often traded musical ideas.
- The *Prisonaires* then received national publicity when the country star Roy Acuff presented them with a Gibson guitar.

The Prisonaires *frequently entertained at the Governor's mansion.*

- Their privileges were such that when bass singer Marcell Sanders was offered parole, he refused, saying that he wanted to stay with the group.
- In August 1953, they recorded a raucous "Softly and Tenderly" with Ike Turner on piano; their third single, the plaintive "A Prisoner's Prayer," was printed with stripes on the label, and their next, "There Is Love in You," was recorded at the penitentiary itself.
- The whole prison caught the magic of performing and writing songs; producer Sam Phillips picked up two songs from white inmates, "Without You" and "Casual Love Affair," that he was to rehearse with Elvis Presley.
- Eventually, Sanders was told that he would have to leave the prison, and tenor John Drue was also given parole.
- Not eligible for parole, Bragg reconstituted the group even though the mood at the prison began to change.
- Other prisoners became resentful of Johnny's freedom to leave the prison to perform, fights were started, and four white inmates threatened to cut out his vocal cords.

To change their image, the Prisonaires *became the* Marigolds.

- Also, to meet the demands of the new rock 'n' roll era, the *Prisonaires* began recording more upbeat material and decided to change their name.
- They first chose the name *Sunbeams,* then switched to the *Marigolds* to record the song "Rocking Horse," which quickly topped the R&B chart; it was outsold by a cover version for the pop market by the *Fontane Sisters.*
- Songs originated by black groups but covered by white singers were becoming increasingly common.
- In 1956, Johnnie Ray's record producer, Mitch Miller, rediscovered "Just Walkin' in the Rain" and realized it was perfect for the popular singer nicknamed the "Cry Guy."

- Ray's performing style included rock 'n' roll theatrics, including beating up his piano, writhing on the floor and crying, earning the Oregon-born white singer the nicknames "Mr. Emotion," "The Nabob of Sob," and "The Prince of Wails."
- Ray's fully orchestrated and highly histrionic performance went to No. 2 in the U.S. and topped the U.K. chart.
- The No. 1 American song was Elvis's "Don't Be Cruel."
- Johnny Bragg's songwriting royalties topped $8,700 for the year—the most money he ever made—that was put into a trust fund for him.

Lunch counters were popular—and segregated—in Nashville.

- He was even invited to the Broadcast Music Inc. black tie banquet because of the level of radio play that "Just Walkin'" had received.
- The warden did not allow him to attend.
- When Governor Clement asked the *Marigolds* to perform at an event at the Governor's mansion honoring Elvis Presley, he told them to perform "Jailhouse Rock."
- Presley had a wonderful time harmonizing with the inmates and suggested that they record together, but his manager Colonel Parker did not consider this a good career move.
- In March 1956, the *Marigolds* went to Nashville to record "Foolish Me" and "Beyond the Clouds," while "Heartbreak Hotel" by Elvis Presley was enjoying an eight-week run at the top of the charts.
- Thanks to the efforts of the Governor, Johnny Bragg was released on parole in January 1959 as one the last acts of Governor Clements.
- He was 32 years old and had spent 15 years in prison for crimes he did not commit and he was ready to begin again.

Life in the Community: Nashville, Tennessee

- When Johnny Bragg was growing up, Nashville, Tennessee, was considered to be the "Athens of the South," even though a pattern of racial exclusiveness prevailed in Nashville's schools and public facilities.
- In 1958, local black leaders founded the Nashville Christian Leadership Conference (NCLC), an affiliate of Martin Luther King, Jr.'s Southern Christian Leadership Conference.
- Early in 1959, the NCLC began a movement to desegregate downtown Nashville.
- The policy of segregation was tested at Harvey's and Cain-Sloan's department stores, where the Reverends Smith and James M. Lawson, Jr.'s students John Lewis, Diane Nash, James Bevel, Marion Barry, and others bought goods and then attempted to desegregate the lunch counters.
- Before the end of 1959, students from Nashville's black colleges, including Fisk University, Tennessee A&I State University, Meharry Medical College, and American Baptist Theological Seminary, were being trained to participate in the non-violent protests.
- Opened in 1898, the Tennessee State Prison was located near downtown Nashville, Tennessee.
- The Tennessee Prison contained 800 small cells, each designed to house a single inmate.

- The prison's 800 cells were opened to receive prisoners on February 12, 1898, and that day admitted 1,403 prisoners, creating immediate overcrowding which persisted throughout the next century.
- It was the advent of the Grand Ole Opry in 1925, combined with an already thriving publishing industry, that positioned Nashville to become "Music City USA."
- Beginning in the mid-1950s, the Nashville sound turned country music into a multimillion-dollar industry.
- Under the direction of producers such as Chet Atkins, Owen Bradley, and later Billy Sherrill, the sound brought country music to a diverse audience and expanded its appeal.

Tennessee State Prison held 800 cells.

- The sound borrowed from 1950s pop stylings: a prominent and smooth vocal, backed by a string section and vocal chorus.
- Leading artists in this genre included Patsy Cline, Jim Reeves, and Eddy Arnold.
- The "slip note" piano style of session musician Floyd Cramer was an important component of this style.

Music Trivia

- Little Richard's song "Tutti Frutti" originally contained the lyrics "Tutti Frutti, good booty," but in 1955, Specialty Records had songwriter Dorothy LaBostrie tame it down to "Tutti Frutti, oh Rudy."
- Ray Charles's 1959 release "What'd I Say" was created on the spot when he ran out of songs during a marathon dance show in Pittsburgh; concerning the sexy vocal bridge that made the song famous, Charles said, "Hell, let's face it, everybody knows about the ummmmh, unnnh. That's how we all got here."
- The rock 'n' roll song "Johnny B. Goode" by Chuck Berry, which was released in 1958, originally contained the words "That little colored boy could play," but was changed to "country boy" so the record could get airtime on the radio.
- Elvis Presley's release of "Hound Dog" in 1956 went through 31 takes at the RCA studios in New York. "I don't care what you say," he told a reporter. "It ain't nasty."
- The title of the Buddy Holly and the Crickets song "That'll Be the Day" came from a recurring line in the John Wayne Western movie *The Searchers*.
- Fats Domino's biggest hit "Blueberry Hill," released in 1956, was originally recorded by Gene Autry in 1940.

HISTORICAL SNAPSHOT
1959

- CBS Radio eliminated four soap operas: *Backstage Wife, Our Gal Sunday, The Road of Life*, and *This is Nora Drake*
- Alaska was admitted as the forty-ninth U.S. state; Hawaii became the fiftieth
- The United States recognized the new Cuban government of Fidel Castro
- Motown Records was founded by Berry Gordy, Jr.
- Walt Disney released his sixteenth animated film, *Sleeping Beauty*— Disney's first animated film to be shown in 70 mm and modern six-track stereophonic sound
- A chartered plane transporting musicians Buddy Holly, Ritchie Valens, and The Big Bopper went down in foggy conditions near Clear Lake, Iowa, killing all four occupants on board, including pilot Roger Peterson
- At Cape Canaveral, Florida, the first successful test firing of a Titan intercontinental ballistic missile was accomplished
- The United States launched the *Vanguard II* weather satellite
- Racecar driver Lee Petty won the first Daytona 500
- Recording sessions for the album "Kind of Blue" by Miles Davis began at Columbia's 30th Street Studio in New York City
- The Marx Brothers made their last TV appearance in *The Incredible Jewel Robbery*
- The Barbie doll debuted
- Busch Gardens in Tampa, Florida, was dedicated and opened its gates
- The Dalai Lama fled Tibet and was granted asylum in India
- NASA selected seven military pilots to become the first U.S. astronauts
- The St. Lawrence Seaway linking the North American Great Lakes and the Atlantic Ocean officially opened to shipping
- The USS *George Washington* was launched as the first submarine to carry ballistic missiles
- Charles Ovnand and Dale R. Buis became the first Americans killed in action in Vietnam
- The first skull of *Australopithecus* was discovered by Mary Leakey in the Olduvai Gorge of Tanzania
- The Soviet rocket *Luna 2* became the first manmade object to crash on the moon, and *Luna 3* sent back the first-ever photos of the far side of the moon
- Rod Serling's classic anthology series *The Twilight Zone* premiered on CBS
- MGM's widescreen, multimillion-dollar, Technicolor version of *Ben-Hur*, starring Charlton Heston, was released and won a record 11 Academy Awards
- The Henney Kilowatt went on sale in the United States, becoming the first mass-produced electric car in almost three decades

Selected Prices

Clearasil	$0.59
Cornet	$99.50
Fruit Cocktail	$0.93
Guitar, Washburn	$27.50
Hamburger, Burger King Whopper	$0.37
Hotel Room, Ritz-Carlton, Boston	$9.00
Man's Shirt, Arrow	$5.00
Movie Projector	$89.95
Theatre Ticket, New York	$3.85
Vodka, Smirnoff, Fifth	$5.23

"No Longer Walkin' in the Rain," *Long Beach Independent*, **January 2, 1959:**

Johnny Bragg, who wrote "Walkin' in the Rain" in prison, walked into the sunshine of freedom Wednesday.

The Negro convict faced almost certain imprisonment for life when he was sentenced to six 99-year terms for rape when he was 17 years old. He spent 16 years in the Tennessee Penitentiary here.

Wednesday, he was paroled. Former Gov. Frank Clement, who had befriended and helped Bragg, commuted his sentence to life just before he left office earlier this month. With time served and good behavior, Bragg became eligible immediately for parole.

The Pardons and Parole Board said Bragg appeared to have been rehabilitated, and that he has a job in his uncle's barbershop in Nashville. He must report regularly to a parole officer for the rest of his life.

Bragg was the last of a prison singing group which he organized to be released. The group, "The Prisonaires," often entertained at parties given by Clement. Bragg wrote and collaborated on a number of popular tunes, but "Walkin' in the Rain" was his biggest hit.

Recorded Popular Songs: 1950s

1950
1. The Fat Man—Fats Domino
2. Please Send Me Someone to Love—Percy Mayfield
3. Teardrops From My Eyes—Ruth Brown
4. Mona Lisa—Nat "King" Cole
5. Tennessee Waltz—Patti Page
6. Long Gone Lonesome Blues—Hank Williams
7. Mardi Gras In New Orleans—Professor Longhair
8. I'm Movin' On—Hank Snow
9. Rollin' Stone—Muddy Waters
10. Double Crossing Blues—Johnny Otis (Little Esther & the Robins)

1951
1. Sixty Minute Man—Dominoes
2. Rocket 88—Jackie Brenston
3. Dust My Broom—Elmore James
4. Cry—Johnnie Ray
5. Too Young—Nat "King" Cole
6. Cold Cold Heart—Hank Williams
7. Glory of Love—Five Keys
8. Three O'Clock Blues—B.B. King
9. Hey Good Lookin'—Hank Williams
10. How High The Moon—Les Paul & Mary Ford

1952
1. Lawdy Miss Clawdy—Lloyd Price
2. Jambalaya (On The Bayou)—Hank Williams
3. Have Mercy Baby—Dominoes
4. One Mint Julep—Clovers
5. Night Train—Jimmy Forrest
6. My Song—Johnny Ace
7. Goin' Home—Fats Domino
8. Moody Mood For Love—King Pleasure
9. Juke—Little Walter
10. Baby, Don't Do It—"5" Royales

1953
1. Money Honey—Drifters featuring Clyde McPhatter
2. Your Cheatin' Heart—Hank Williams
3. Crying In The Chapel—Orioles
4. Gee—Crows
5. Shake a Hand—Faye Adams
6. Honey Hush—Joe Turner
7. Mama, He Treats Your Daughter Mean—Ruth Brown
8. Hound Dog—Willie Mae "Big Mama" Thornton
9. Kaw-Liga—Hank Williams
10. The Things That I Used To Do—Guitar Slim

1954
1. Rock Around The Clock—Bill Haley & His Comets
2. Shake, Rattle and Roll—Joe Turner/Bill Haley & His Comets
3. Earth Angel—Penguins
4. Sh-Boom—Chords
5. That's All Right—Elvis Presley with Scotty and Bill
6. Pledging My Love—Johnny Ace
7. Goodnite Sweetheart Goodnite—Spaniels
8. I've Got a Woman—Ray Charles
9. White Christmas—Drifters featuring Clyde McPhatter
10. Work With Me Annie—Royals/Midnighters

1955
1. Tutti Frutti—Little Richard
2. Maybellene—Chuck Berry
3. Bo Diddley—Bo Diddley
4. Why Do Fools Fall in Love?—Teenagers
5. The Great Pretender—Platters
6. Ain't That a Shame—Fats Domino
7. Folsom Prison Blues—Johnny Cash and the Tennessee Two
8. Speedo—Cadillacs
9. Story Untold—Nutmegs
10. My Babe—Little Walter

1956
1. Hound Dog—Elvis Presley
2. Long Tall Sally—Little Richard
3. Blue Suede Shoes—Carl Perkins/Elvis Presley
4. Don't Be Cruel—Elvis Presley
5. Be-Bop-a-Lula—Gene Vincent & the Bluecaps
6. Roll Over Beethoven—Chuck Berry
7. In the Still of the Night—Five Satins
8. Blueberry Hill—Fats Domino
9. Please, Please, Please—James Brown & the Famous Flames
10. I Walk The Line—Johnny Cash and the Tennessee Two

1957
1. Jailhouse Rock—Elvis Presley
2. Whole Lotta Shakin' Going On—Jerry Lee Lewis
3. That'll Be the Day—Crickets
4. Bye Bye Love—Everly Brothers
5. Great Balls of Fire—Jerry Lee Lewis
6. School Day—Chuck Berry
7. Rock and Roll Music—Chuck Berry
8. Peggy Sue—Buddy Holly
9. Lucille—Little Richard
10. Rocking Pneumonia & the Boogie Woogie Flu—Huey "Piano" Smith & the Clowns

1958
1. Johnny B. Goode—Chuck Berry
2. Summertime Blues—Eddie Cochran
3. Good Golly Miss Molly—Little Richard
4. For Your Precious Love—Jerry Butler & the Impressions
5. Sweet Little Sixteen—Chuck Berry
6. Yakety Yak—Coasters
7. La Bamba—Ritchie Valens
8. Since I Don't Have You—Skyliners
9. Rumble—Link Wray
10. Lonely Teardrops—Jackie Wilson

1959
1. What'd I Say—Ray Charles
2. I Only Have Eyes for You—Flamingos
3. Mack the Knife—Bobby Darin
4. There Goes My Baby—Drifters
5. Shout—Isley Brothers
6. Kansas City—Wilbert Harrison
7. Poison Ivy—Coasters
8. Money—Barrett Strong
9. Love Potion No. 9—Clovers
10. You're So Fine—Falcons

1960: Self-trained Olympic Weightlifter

Jim Bradford developed his own technique for success while training at his local YMCA basketball court in Washington, D.C. His first national event was the Junior Nationals in 1946, and in 1960 he competed in his last Olympics.

Life at Home

- Jim Bradford weighed 247 pounds on his fourteenth birthday.
- Until he discovered a copy of the weightlifting magazine *Strength and Health,* he was just an overweight black teen walking the streets of the nation's capital.
- Inspired by the pictures and the personal stories of weightlifters, Jim began working out at home.
- But after a dumbbell mishap in the second-floor bedroom of his home sent plaster crashing upon his family downstairs, Jim was dispatched to the 12th Street YMCA.
- There he began working out, largely training himself, relying heavily on strength, not technique.
- As a result he taught himself to lift with virtually no split of his legs on the way up, only bending his back as he lifted the bar over his head.
- This technique was developed, he later confessed, from fear of dropping the weights on the YMCA basketball court and getting barred from the court for having scarred the floor.
- After four years of training and competing on a local level, a very muscular Jim entered his first national event, the 1946 Junior Nationals.
- There he learned some of the lifting techniques of veteran weightlifters and made slow progress.
- Four years later, at age 22, he won the Junior Nationals and placed third in the Senior National Championship.
- In 1951 he placed second in the Senior Nationals and earned a spot on the 1951 World Championship team.
- Here Jim battled aging teammate John Henry Davis, the reigning "World's Strongest Man" and world champion since 1938.
- But John Davis was hurt, and Jim Bradford was young and hungry. At the conclusion of the snatch lift, John Davis was in terrific pain, his undefeated reign truly endangered.
- As the clean and jerk competition began, the arena was charged with energy. Everyone knew that history was about to be made.

Jim Bradford was a self-trained Olympic weightlifter.

- Jim made his first clean and jerk smoothly, and Davis did the same, through the pain.
- Jim answered with an easy second attempt, which was also matched by Davis, who was barely able to leave the stage after the lift.
- Jim knew that if he made his last lift at a still-higher weight, Davis would be forced to match him, risking permanent injury.
- A gold medal and the glory of winning the World Championship were in Jim's grasp-a lifetime dream come true.
- But winning meant defeating an injured legend and stripping a teammate of his undefeated status.
- Jim declined this last lift in the spirit of sportsmanship.
- John Davis retained his title as World's Strongest Man, and newspapers heralded Jim's decision as one of the greatest acts of sportsmanship in the history of athletics.
- Jim won a silver medal at the 1952 Olympics in Helsinki.
- He joined the Army, serving in the Korean War, and his weightlifting career was interrupted.
- In 1954 he was called upon to replace an injured member of the World Championship team.
- Jim jumped on an airplane without hesitation and placed second, winning valuable points for the United States.
- By the time the 1960 Olympics in Rome rolled around, he was ready for one more opportunity on the world stage.
- This time he wanted the gold.
- He was 32 years old; married, with three children; and earned $56 a week as a documents clerk in the Library of Congress.
- His monthly mortgage was $105—half his income.
- Since paid leave would have jeopardized his amateur status under Olympic rules, Jim took an unpaid leave from his clerk position, which he could barely afford.

Life at Work

- One of the oldest sports of the modern Games, weightlifting was one of the final events at the 18-day-long 1960 Olympics in Rome.
- At the opening parade of nations, African American Rafer Johnson marched at the head of the US delegation, causing a stir as the first black athlete to carry the American flag in the highly visible ceremony.
- The 305 US men looked sharp in the US Olympic team dress uniform: McGregor-Doniger olive-green sports coat, Haggar slacks and Van Heusen beige knit shirt.

The USA running team at the Olympics in Rome.

- After weeks of anticipation and the thrill of marching in the opening ceremony, Jim Bradford was brimming with energy.
- The US men's contingent was housed in large buildings in the middle of the Olympic Village, sharing 50 suites, each of which held 3 to 8 athletes.
- Americans had their own dining facility, open 22 hours a day, from 5 a.m. to 3 a.m.
- The dining room was operated by an Italian chef with 76 employees, who cooked mostly beef, to suit the tastes of the Americans.
- Jim loved to travel.
- While at a competition in Warsaw, Poland, the year before, he had made a point of meeting locals, attempting their language and eating indigenous foods.

- To the media, the weightlifting competition, comprising seven weight classes, was the perfect metaphor for the clash of the two superpowers—the United States and the Soviet Union—in a time of "Cold War."
- Americans had collected more gold medals during the two previous Olympics, in Helsinki and Melbourne, but current momentum favored the Soviet strongmen.
- Jim's American coaches believed that winning the weight contest in Rome "would be our best propaganda weapon" in the Cold War.
- The political tension that invaded the 1960 Olympics had begun two years earlier when a delegation of US track and field athletes became the first team to visit the USSR since the start of the Cold War.
- Russians, cheered on by the home crowd, scored a 172-170 victory, which was interpreted in the wider world as a victory for the Communist way of life.

The Cold War brought contention into the Olympic games.

- A lot more than a gold medal was on the line.
- When it was Jim's turn to compete, the Soviets had won four matches and the team title.
- Jim prepared by spending hours meditating in the Olympic Village, visualizing the handling of immense weights.
- In weightlifting the mental preparation was as critical as the physical.
- In the first round, Jim easily pressed 374.5 pounds.
- He made his 396.5-pound press with apparent ease.
- The Soviet opponent, Yuri Vlasov, made his lift, but the judges ruled Vlasov's lift was illegal, and the lead went to Jim.
- In the next round, the snatch, Vlasov was the clear winner, by 11 pounds.
- Jim's lead was precariously thin, and he was concerned.
- It appeared the gold medal would be decided by the clean and jerk.
- That's when the officials announced the initial ruling against Vlasov had been overturned on appeal.
- Jim protested vehemently, but Vlasov was given a comfortable lead going into the last event.
- Eventually, the Soviets claimed the gold.
- Rumors of drug use by the Soviet team didn't bother Jim.
- He came from the old school: excuses didn't count.
- But to lose because of the judges' ruling was too outrageous for words.
- Officials asked that he not create an international incident.
- Silence in the face of injustice was a terrible burden for Jim to carry.

The 1960 Olympics opening ceremony.

Life in the Community: The Olympic Village, Rome

- The Olympic ideal of pure athletic competition staged once every four years was designed to rise above the competing ideologies and international disputes raging around the world.
- In 1960 the increasingly hot rhetoric of the Cold War was only one of many intrusions of strife into the Games.
- One week before the opening ceremony, the American pilot Francis Gary Powers was convicted of espionage charges in a Moscow court after his U-2 reconnaissance plane was shot down over Russia.
- Just days before the closing ceremony, Soviet premier Nikita Khrushchev staged a dramatic appearance at the UN General Assembly in New York, railing against the United States and the West and pounding his delegate desk with his fists and then, allegedly, with one of his shoes.
- Questions were raised concerning which flag East Germany and West Germany would use in the competition; the unified German team marched under a neutral flag in the opening ceremony. A major uproar erupted when the athletes from Taiwan attempted to march as the delegation of China.

Olympic Stadium in Rome, 1960.

- At the same time, new nations—particularly in Africa—were lobbying for more participants in a wider variety of events, women wanted to run longer distances and civil rights activists in South Africa wanted the International Olympic Committee to live up to its Olympic Creed and expel the apartheid delegation from South Africa.
- Simultaneously conflict was raging over the definition of an "amateur athlete."
- Increasingly the rigid rules on "amateur" status were being challenged by athletes, who saw everyone but themselves making money from their efforts.
- Seventy-two-year-old Avery Brundage, president of the International Olympic Committee, was the personification of the Olympic movement—and the object of considerable ridicule.
- Endorsements, sponsorships and subsidized work programs were all strictly forbidden—although some athletes had begun quietly taking money to wear certain shoes.
- Rafer Johnson, a competitor in the decathlon, was told he would be ineligible for the Olympics if he appeared in *Spartacus*, an upcoming film about a slave revolt in ancient Rome.

The USA delegation included 305 athletes.

- The Olympic Committee ruled that Johnson had been hired not for his acting ability but because he was a famous athlete.
- Johnson declined the role.
- Champion hurdler Lee Calhoun lost his eligibility for a year because he and his wife got married on the *Bride and Groom* TV game show and accepted gifts and a honeymoon.
- All these issues were played out before a worldwide television audience.

- In the United States, CBS News paid $600,000 for the exclusive rights to broadcast the summer Olympics (and additional footage) for the first time.
- Under its contract, CBS could broadcast approximately 1 hour and 15 minutes per day, up to 20 hours of programming, from August 25 to September 11.
- The Italian broadcasting network RAI decided, largely without consultation, which events would be covered and provided the necessary camera work, which then required that CBS transcribe the Italian picture, cast at 625 lines per second, into the standard US picture of 525 lines per second.
- Ponderous TV cameras, each weighing more than 60 pounds, lumbered through the broadcast sites, tethered to cables the circumference of boa constrictors.
- Tapes of each event were flown by commercial aircraft to the United States, a 9.5-hour trip.
- Jim McKay, a former *Baltimore Sun* police reporter, would then edit the film, write the copy and provide the voiceover, all from a studio in New York City's Grand Central Station.
- *Encyclopedia Britannica* was a major source of background information for the broadcasts.

Olympic athletes ignored the international strife that was brewing outside the games.

Olympic Weightlifting Terms

Press: The barbell is lifted from floor to chest and then chest to overhead in two smooth movements with a slight bend but no shifting of the feet.

Snatch: The weight is lifted floor to overhead in one explosive movement; the lifter is allowed to shift his feet.

Clean and jerk: The weight is taken from floor to shoulder height, held there briefly, then lifted overhead with a squat and spring of the legs.

Historical Snapshot
1960

- The National Association of Broadcasters reacted to a payola scandal by threatening fines for any disc jockeys who accepted money for playing particular records

- Four students from North Carolina Agricultural and Technical State University in Greensboro, North Carolina, began a sit-in at a segregated Woolworth's lunch counter, which triggered similar nonviolent protests throughout the Southern United States

- Joanne Woodward received the first star on the Hollywood Walk of Fame

- Adolph Coors III, chairman of the board of the Coors Brewing Company, was kidnapped for $500,000 and later found dead

- The United States announced that 3,500 American soldiers would be sent to Vietnam

- Arthur Leonard Schawlow and Charles Hard Townes received the first patent for a laser

- The United States launched the first weather satellite, TIROS-1

- *Ben Hur* won the Oscar for Best Picture

- A Soviet missile shot down an American Lockheed U-2 spy plane; the pilot, Francis Gary Powers, was captured, tried, and released 21 months later in a spy swap with the U.S.

- President Dwight D. Eisenhower signed the Civil Rights Act of 1960 into law

- The U.S. Food and Drug Administration announced that it would approve birth control as an additional indication for Searle's Enovid, making it the world's first approved oral contraceptive pill

- The nuclear submarine *USS Triton* completed the first underwater circumnavigation of Earth

- In Buenos Aires, four Mossad agents abducted fugitive Nazi Adolf Eichmann, who was using the alias "Ricardo Klement"

- The Soviet Union beat Yugoslavia 2-1 to win the first European Football Championship

- Harper Lee released her critically acclaimed novel *To Kill a Mockingbird*

- The two leading U.S. presidential candidates, Richard M. Nixon and John F. Kennedy, participated in the first televised presidential debate

- Nikita Khrushchev pounded his shoe on a table at a United Nations General Assembly meeting to protest the discussion of Soviet Union policy toward Eastern Europe

- Entertainer Sammy Davis, Jr. married Swedish actress May Britt

- Basketball player Wilt Chamberlain grabbed 55 rebounds in a single game

- Production of the DeSoto automobile brand ceased

- President Eisenhower authorized the use of $1 million toward the resettlement of Cuban refugees, who were arriving in Florida at the rate of 1,000 a week

- The U.S. Supreme Court declared in *Boynton v. Virginia* that segregation on public transit was illegal

- The U.S. Census listed all people from Latin America as white, including blacks from the Dominican Republic, European whites from Argentina, and Mexicans who resembled Native Americans

- The world population was 3,021,475,000

Selected Prices

Board Game, Monopoly $3.33
Bologna, per Pound $0.39
Boy Scout Uniform $10.75
Dictaphone $161.00
Drive-in Movie, per Car $1.50
Driving Lessons $46.88
Fountain Pen $14.95
Microfilm, 100 feet, 16 mm $4.90
Tuition, Augusta Military Academy, Year $1,300
Whiskey, Canadian Club, Quart $7.85

"1,500 Will Cover Olympics," *Pacific Stars and Stripes,* July 31, 1960:

About 1,500 newsmen, photographers, and radio and television commentators will cover the Olympic Games in Rome from August 25 through September 11.

The Italian organizing committee issued 1,200 passes to newsmen from all over the world, and 300 photographers and radio and television men. . . .

Rome's telephone company also has put 2,500 telephones and 500 phone booths at the disposal of the press. The telephones are scattered in various sports arenas and in the main press center. . . .

The organizing committee made several separate accords with various television companies in Europe, the United States and Japan to telecast the games.

Seventy foreign radio organizations have asked the Italian Radio Company (RAI) for technical equipment for their services in connection with radio information in the games.

To meet such a great demand RAI set up a radio center at the Rome Music College near the Foro Italico, which will be the site of many Olympic events. . . .

Technical installations at the radio center include 58 special studios which will be placed at the disposal of various foreign countries for production of their radio programs.

RAI installed more than 800 circuits to ensure links between the radio center and the competition arenas, and to the international center of the Italian State Telephone Company. . . .

More than 250 operators and technicians, from various RAI stations throughout Italy, will be brought to Rome for the games and will be used exclusively for this radio service.

To handle the flood of news copy expected to amount to hundreds of thousands of words a day, special telegraph, cable and radio circuits are being opened between Rome and major cities on every continent.

"Former Carbondale Man on Olympic Team," *Southern Illinoisan*, July 10, 1960:

David Lurie, recently chosen member of the U.S. equestrian team, has long dreamed of becoming a star in this last aristocratic Olympic sport.

His father, George Lurie, an executive of Good Luck Glove Company, Carbondale, said his son "decided when he was still young that regular horseback riding was for girls" and that he had his sights set on the more rugged phases of the sport.

Lurie, 20, formerly of Carbondale and who now lives in St. Louis, was named to the Olympic equestrian team that will represent the U.S. in Rome in September after trials recently at Pebble Beach, California.

The phase of riding at which Lurie has excelled is far from being a sissy sport. His father said that the sport takes better conditioning on the part of the athlete than hockey and boxing and is more dangerous.

The three-day equestrian event is made up of three phases: dressage, an endurance test, and stadium jumping. Dressage is where the horse and rider go through intricate maneuvers. The endurance test is a type of steeplechase similar to the Grand National. It is, in effect, a combination of all phases of riding.

Only one horse is allowed to be used for all three phases of the event. The Olympic Committee furnishes the horses to be used but Lurie also owns his own jumper, Capal.

Most of the horses qualified for this event cost from $10,000-$15,000.

The danger that exists is underlined by an accident that kept him out of the Pan American Games in Chicago last year. In a Colorado Springs practice session in 1957, his horse hit a jump and landed on top of him and Lurie suffered a broken collarbone.

In the obstacle course on the endurance test lies the big danger. The course for the Olympic trials at Pebble Beach was specially built for the maximum degree of difficulty. Some of the jumps were 12 to 15 feet in length and about six feet high.

One shuddering jump, called "the coffin" by the horsemen, has a deep ditch behind the jump. The horse must jump both a wall and a ditch after sliding down a deep incline.

The senior Lurie has some fear for his son in the Olympics with reason. In the 1956 Olympics at Stockholm, 53 horses fell on one jump alone and some of the horses had to jump over ones lying injured atop a fence. In 33 obstacles over a five-mile stretch, there were 107 falls and 21 horses that did not make the finish line.

The horse never sees the jumps prior to the race, but the rider can walk around the course ahead of time.

Sample of Apparatus Needed for Olympics, Rome 1960, David Maraniss:

Here is but a small, random sample of what was needed: 12 pole vault uprights, 100 competition hurdles, 384 training hurdles, 40 competition discuses, 165 ash javelins, 40 competition hammers, 138 shots for putting, 96 starting blocks, 110 writing frames for judges, 100 wooden folding chairs, 130 relay batons, 3 mobile luminous indicator boards, 4 special starter pistols, 1,000 metallic torches to fuel the marathon course, 3,000 black competitor numbers on white background for men, 1,500 yellow competitor numbers on black background for women, 300 white competitor numbers on black background for marathon, 110 official basketballs, 60 training balls, six backboards, nine basketball nets, 570 boxing gloves, 580 elastic bandages, 27 speed balls, 47 jump ropes, four brass megaphones for rowing, 40 bicycle carrier frames, 318 plastic armlets, 2 horse slaughter pistols, 100 cockades for horses, 20 electrified blades for sabers, 150 mats for fencing, 480 field hockey balls, 100 sawdust pillows for shooting lines, 60,000 targets for small bore rifles, 50 water polo balls, 153 water polo caps, 262 weights, 39 steel bars for weights, 40 wrestling whistles, 60 protest flags for Finn Class yachting, 400 floating smoke signals, 340 baskets holding 7,200 pigeons, and a fleet of 288 Fiats, 142 buses, 76 Lambretta motor scooters, and 100 Vespas.

"New Grid League Has Troubles," *GRIT,* November 27, 1960:

Owners of clubs in the American Football League are discovering there are plenty of headaches connected with launching a new grid circuit, foremost of which is bucking the established National Football League to the box office. In the battle for the entertainment dollar, the NFL is way out in front.

Crowds of more than 50,000 are common in NFL games, whereas the AFL has few crowds of more than 25,000. On one Sunday alone, five NFL games featured cliffhanging action, out-rivaling any work of fiction. Less than one touchdown separated the rivals, and in just about every case the winning points were scored in the final minutes of play. That's tough competition for a new loop with few "name" players to attract fans.

Tune in to a broadcast of an NFL game and you hear the scores of other league games, but no scores of games in the rival loop. On an AFL broadcast, however, you get scores in both loops. It's a tipoff on which league has the clamp on the Pro football TV fans.

Commissioner Joe Foss, of the AFL, freely admits the new circuit will lose about $2 million this year. Other observers estimate losses will be even higher. And if it weren't for television, the league would lose close to $4 million in its first season. Under a five-year contract with the sponsors, each team in the AFL gets $225,000 yearly from TV. Without this fee, some of the teams might have folded already.

"Negro Singer to Wed White Actress Sunday,"
The Danville Virginia Bee, November 12, 1960:

The Sunday wedding of Sammy Davis, Jr., 34, and Swedish actress May Britt, 26, took on a formal note today with the following communiqué issued by the Negro performer's press representatives:

"Following a private family wedding ceremony, Mr. and Mrs. Sammy Davis, Jr., will go to the Nordic Room of the Beverly Hills Hotel, arriving there at 4 p.m.

"They will remain in the Nordic Room posing for photographs and answering questions from the press for approximately 30 minutes. They will then depart for a private wedding which, for the convenience of their guests, Mr. and Mrs. Davis have requested to be closed to the press."

Newspapers as far away as Stockholm, Miss Britt's hometown, have sent reporters here to cover the rites.

The ceremony will be held at Davis's home above Sunset Strip and will be performed by a rabbi. Frank Sinatra will be Davis's best man and Miss Britt's bridesmaids will include the wives of Davis's business manager and his pianists.

Both Davis and his bride-to-be converted to the Jewish faith.

"Boom in Organized Bowling Continues, No End in Sight,"
GRIT, October 23, 1960:

If you are bowling in one or more leagues this year, you are a member of the fastest-growing participant sport in the nation.

The boom in bowling is so swift that even those who are directing it have difficulty keeping pace with it today.

"Four years ago our membership showed a 10 percent gain," said Frank Baker, executive secretary of the American Bowling Congress. "The next year the gain went up about 12 percent. We look, then, for a leveling off. But for the last two years the surge reached 20 percent."

The progress, said Baker, has been almost incredible since the Second World War. ABC membership in 1946 was 880,000. Today it is 3,500,000 and still growing. It's estimated the total will reach 5,000,000 by 1965.

The interest in the tenpins sport is tremendous. Bowling shows on lanes have contributed to the rapid growth of the sport.

Professional bowlers compete on one TV show for king-size stakes. Six straight strikes are worth from $25,000 up. Frank Clause, of old Forge, Pa., won a $40,000 jackpot on one recent show.

There also is a marked increase in the number of youngsters participating. It is estimated 11,300,000 boys and girls will be firing at tenpins during the new bowling year, most of them taking part in the Junior bowling program of the ABC. This represents an increase of 4,000,000 young bowlers in the two-year period.

"Defending the Jump Shot," Jerry Grunska, coach, Highland Park, Illinois, High School, *Scholastic Coach Magazine,* October 1960:

As a basketball coach, I don't claim to have the antidote to the plague known as the jump shot. I doubt if there is one. If there is, it's certainly a well-kept secret. I know I've never seen anything on the defense of this lethal weapon.

Too many coaches are fatalistic on this score. They're inclined to throw up their hands and say, "What can you do against the good jump shooter?" Other coaches are content to tell the guards to stay close to the jump shooter, force him away from the choice shooting spots, and to nudge him off balance (with the chest) when he goes up for the shot.

Rather than adopt the fatalistic attitude or trust in divine providence (luck), I've attempted to develop a number of skills in blocking the jump shot. These individual techniques have been developed through trial and error by our squad members, observation of college and pro athletes, and analysis of the tactics employed by our opponents.

No question about it, the tremendous challenge of blocking a jump shot stems from the fact that the shooter knows when he is going to jump in the air, while the defense doesn't. Should the defender anticipate the move, he is likely to be faked off his feet. And if his reaction time isn't hair-trigger quick, he'll always be late in timing his leap.

He must respond to the stimuli of the shooter's movement. Admittedly, the simple laws of stimulus and response give the shooter the advantage of prior movement. The defender can hardly avoid being a trifle late in his timing no matter how hard he tries. The process of timing the defensive leap is so complex that I feel it's nearly unteachable. It must be an inherent factor in the athlete's make up, a sort of "sixth sense" in his reflexes.

Even when the timing is right, there's always the big danger of fouling that shooter. Jump shooters nearly always leap straight into the air. They hang at the height of their jump while they shoot and follow through, and usually descend almost straight downward.

The defender usually takes off from a point several feet from the shooter. To have any hope whatever of blocking the shot, he must leap toward the shooter. This will cause his downward progress to be forward as well, so that even if his upward movement hasn't caused contact, his downward flight is likely to.

The defender has one factor in his favor. Whereas the shooter must carry the ball above his head with two hands, the defender can achieve greater extension by using one hand to block the shot. This is his lone advantage. Since he doesn't have the ball and since he uses only one hand, his free arm gives him a chance to gain balance, even while in flight. His jump can be controlled. And it must be to be effective.

1961: Educator and Civil Rights Pioneer

Septima Clark taught school in South Carolina for 40 years before being fired for refusing to resign her membership in the NAACP, for which she had been Vice President of the Charleston chapter.

Life at Home

- Septima Poinsette was born on May 3, 1898, in Charleston, South Carolina.
- Her mother, Victoria Warren Anderson, was raised in Haiti and excelled in its challenging educational environment, which was modeled on that of Europe.
- As a young woman, Victoria came to live in the United States, where she met and married Septima's father, Peter Porcher Poinsette.
- Peter, a Muskhogean from the Sea Islands of Georgia, was born a slave on a coastal plantation.
- Freed at the end of the Civil War, he found work on a steamship that traveled between Charleston and New York.
- Once married, Victoria and Peter took up residence in Charleston.
- Septima was the second of their eight children.
- Septima's mother, having been reared outside of the American South, had never been a slave and did not allow the prevailing prejudice to inhibit her from demanding opportunities for her children.
- In the first grade, Septima went to a public school called the ABC Gallery, under less-than-perfect conditions.
- There were approximately a hundred other students in her class. The facility had outdoor bathrooms and bleachers for seating, and beatings were administered daily for disciplinary infractions.
- So Septima's mother sent her instead to a private school in the home of a woman and her niece.
- It was common at the time for black women to run small schools in their homes.
- The woman who ran this private school reserved admission for the children of "free issues"—African Americans who had never been slaves—since they were considered to be of higher social standing.
- The head teacher was very strict, because she believed that the children of free issues should be held to a higher standard of behavior.
- The school's rules extended beyond the classroom and the school day; children could be whipped for infractions in their spare time away from school.

Septima Poinsette Clark taught school in the South Carolina school system for 40 years.

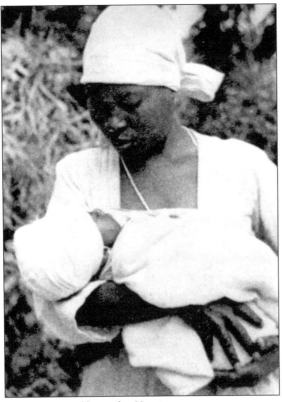

Infant Septima and her mother, Victoria.

- For instance, if the teacher saw a student outside a store eating candy from a paper bag, it was considered unacceptable behavior and grounds for a beating.
- When she was about eight years old, Septima returned to public school, attending Mary Street School for two years, followed by two years at Burke Industrial School, where she completed the seventh grade.
- Septima recalled, "I shall never forget those years. They were the most important for me, and I shall to the end of my days be grateful to my parents for them. They were hard years, years of struggle for both my father and my mother. There were eight children to feed and clothe, and always there was little money with which to provide even the bare necessities. But love made the household a home, and though constant toil from sunup until the late hours of the night was the year-round routine, it was a happy home. Despite the hardships, the children were able to trudge off each day to school after a hot breakfast and with a lunch, and there were hot meals when they returned from school. Some days there was even a penny with which to buy a piece of candy, for in our childhood days a penny would indeed buy a little treat."

- On completion of the seventh grade, Septima had earned a teaching certificate. The Charleston public schools, however, still were not hiring black teachers.
- Two circumstances—Septima's high scores on an exam, which would exempt her from having to complete the eighth grade, and her mother's insistence that she continue her schooling—led her to matriculate at Avery Normal Institute in the ninth grade.
- Avery was a coeducational school for African American students.
- The school was developed at the turn of the twentieth century by the American Missionary Association, and it was sponsored by the Congregational Church.
- Avery was staffed primarily by white teachers from the North, predominantly from New England.
- In order to pay her tuition at Avery, Septima worked for a couple who lived across the street from her parents, serving as a companion, housekeeper and babysitter for the woman while her husband was away on business.
- Septima and the woman were close in age and became good friends.
- The woman would make lovely dresses for Septima, and the two would go on outings together.
- At Avery Septima loved the library and astronomy.
- She loved the teachers for their dedication. They taught her how to cook and sew.
- When Septima was a junior at Avery, Benjamin F. Cox, a black man, became president of the institute.
- Cox brought many positive changes to Avery, improving the facilities and expanding the curriculum.
- With Cox came the appointment of black teachers to the faculty.
- Black teachers and white teachers living together in the faculty dormitories was unacceptable to the white establishment in Charleston, and the city outlawed this arrangement.

Septima worked on developing a curriculum for adult students.

- Thus Avery Normal Institute had to dismiss its white teachers.
- In her senior year at Avery, Septima passed another teaching exam, earning her a first-grade teaching certificate.
- Her teachers encouraged her to seek enrollment at Fisk College in Nashville, Tennessee, but at $18 per month, Fisk cost more than Septima's family could afford, and she began looking for work as a teacher.
- Charleston's public schools did not employ black teachers at the time, so in 1916 Septima found work at Promised Land School on Johns Island, off the coast of South Carolina.
- Septima met her future husband, Nerie Clark, in January 1919.
- He was a sailor aboard the USS *Umpqua*, which docked in Charleston Harbor.
- During a three-day leave in May 1919, Nerie returned to visit Septima.
- The two were married a year later.
- Septima's family did not approve of or consent to the relationship, because they did not think the two had had sufficient time to become acquainted.
- Septima and Nerie had a daughter, named Victoria after Septima's mother, but the baby died soon after birth.
- Nerie never met his daughter, because he was away at sea when she was born.
- Soon after Nerie's return, he and Septima moved to North Carolina to live with his family.
- There Septima became pregnant again.
- Nerie left the Navy, and the couple moved to Dayton, Ohio.
- Septima's second child, a son, was born in a Dayton hospital.
- The child was named Nerie, after his father.
- While Septima was still in the hospital following her son's birth, she found out that her husband had an ex-wife, of whom she had been unaware.
- Septima also learned of another woman in Dayton with whom her husband had practically been living.
- At this time Nerie Clark asked his wife to take their newborn child and move away from Dayton as soon as possible.
- Septima moved back to Hickory, North Carolina, to live with her in-laws.
- Ten months later, Nerie was dead from kidney failure.
- Septima transported Nerie's body back to his family home in the mountains of North Carolina, and she stayed there to teach for a year.
- Then she moved with her son back to Johns Island and resumed teaching at Promised Land School.
- But the island winters proved to be too harsh for her child, and the rigors of her schedule were too great for her to provide him with adequate care.
- Though it would bring her anguish, Septima entrusted her son to the care of his paternal grandparents.

Life at Work

- On Johns Island there were 14 schools for black students, staffed by one or two teachers each.
- For white students, there were three schools, each staffed with one teacher.

Racism was part of life for Septima.

- Septima was rated a principal, earning $30 per month from the State of South Carolina, with an additional $5 per month as a supplement from Charleston County.
- She shared the responsibility of teaching 132 students with one other teacher, a fellow graduate of Avery Normal Institute.
- The white teachers on Johns Island were responsible for as few as 3 and not more than 18 students; those with teaching certifications comparable to Septima's were paid $85 per month.
- The school itself was a log cabin-like building with an open fireplace for which the students had to collect their own firewood.
- The only materials provided for the school were an ax, a water bucket and dipper, a table and chair and some makeshift benches and chalkboards.
- Teachers had to provide their own chalk and erasers.
- Of greater concern was the wide range of children's skills and ages; individual instruction was a daily task.
- Moreover, those students old enough to work were contractually obligated to labor on the plantations on behalf of their families; attendance at school was erratic.
- In 1918 Septima accepted a job teaching sixth grade at Avery Normal Institute, and she moved back to Charleston.
- She was paid $30 per week.
- "The experience of teaching at Avery was one of the most important and formative experiences of my life. It was then that I first became actively concerned in an organized effort to improve the lot of my fellow Negroes. Sometimes I have the almost certain feeling that I was providentially sent to Avery that year."
- During the next decade, Septima held a series of teaching positions and began attending interracial meetings in Columbia, South Carolina.
- In the summer of 1930, Septima went to Columbia University in New York, studying math, curriculum building and astronomy.
- At Columbia she learned to incorporate the vernacular of her students into the reading lessons in order to improve their comprehension and teach them new words.
- She studied astronomy so she could include information about, and words pertaining to, the natural world in the lessons she taught.
- In the summer of 1937, Septima went to Georgia to study at Atlanta University; specifically, she wanted to learn more about working with rural populations.
- One of her professors was W. E. B. Du Bois, the intellectual leader of the National Association for the Advancement of Colored People (NAACP).

"JOIN THE FIGHT FOR FREEDOM"
CAMPAIGN of N.A.A.C.P.

.................................196........

Received from..
                          (Name)

....
                          (Address)

Paid $.............

Signed ....
                          Solicitor

Address ....

If you receive no acknowledgement from National Office, write Lucille Black, Membership Secretary, 20 West 40th Street, New York 18, N. Y.

Septima was fired for her association with the NAACP.

Anti-black protesters took their concerns to Washington D.C.

- Many of Septima's fellow students in Atlanta were from rural areas where work on plantations and on contract farms were common.
- Often these students found her attention to the racial inequalities and injustices of the day threatening and controversial.
- "But nevertheless, I went on, and I got to the place where I had to give my concerns regardless of where I was. The problem, I realized, was not only whites against blacks. It was men against women; it was old against young. You had all those things to fight all the time regardless, and it's still a constant fight."
- Working her way through college while teaching, Septima earned a Bachelor of Arts degree in 1942 from Benedict College in Columbia, South Carolina.
- Once she had completed her B.A., she wanted to pursue a Master's degree.
- In 1944 she began classes at Hampton Institute in Virginia.
- Over the course of three summers, she worked toward and earned her Master's.
- During the 18 years that Septima lived in Columbia, her teaching salary increased from $780 to $4,000 per year.
- In addition to earning two degrees during that time, she also helped to fight for and win equal pay for black teachers.
- Black teachers in Columbia had earned only around half of what white teachers with equivalent education and experience made.
- The NAACP took up the cause, sending Thurgood Marshall, then its chief legal counsel, to represent Septima and her colleagues.
- In 1945 Judge Julius Waties Waring ruled in federal court that teachers with comparable credentials must be compensated equally, regardless of race.
- School officials drafted the National Teacher's Exam for the purpose of evaluating teachers.
- Septima was one of 42 teachers to take the exam the first time it was administered.
- She scored an A, and with it, she earned a raise from $62.50 to $117 per month.
- In 1947 she moved back to Charleston to take care of her mother, who had suffered a stroke.
- She became involved with the Young Women's Christian Association (YWCA), serving as the chairperson of administration for the black YWCA.
- Through her work with the YWCA, she became close personal friends with Judge Waring and his wife Elizabeth.
- It was a friendship anchored by a shared belief in the justice of an integrated society and their mutual efforts toward building one.
- Judge Waring's court rulings and friendships caused controversy. Friends ceased to associate with him and his wife, they were refused service at local businesses, and they had to be accompanied by guards in public.
- Ultimately the Warings were forced to leave Charleston.

Black students had a difficult road to walk in the 60s.

A propaganda postcard, claiming the Highlander Falls School was a breeding ground for communism.

- Septima was criticized by her colleagues and her principal for her friendship with the Warings; her neighbors worried that she would bring trouble to the entire neighborhood.
- She was the target of obscene and threatening phone calls, and she had to live daily with the reality that her work and her associations made her a target for all those who would resort to violence in an effort to maintain a culture of white supremacy.
- In 1954 Septima went to the Highlander Folk School for the first time.
- The school, set on 200 acres on the Cumberland Plateau, in Monteagle, Tennessee, was the only place in the South at that time where interracial education and organization were taking place.
- At Highlander every aspect of life was communal and integrated; for many it was their first experience in this kind of environment.
- After her initial visit to Highlander, Septima became very active in the work of the school, transporting groups there from South Carolina, leading workshops, and drafting pamphlets.
- In 1954 she collaborated on two pamphlets: "A Guide to Action for Public School Desegregation" and "What Is a Workshop?"
- "At Highlander I found out that black people weren't the only ones discriminated against. I found out that whites were against whites. The low-income whites were considered dirt under the feet of the wealthy whites, just like blacks were. I had to go to Highlander to find out that there was so much prejudice in the minds of whites against whites. I didn't dream—I thought that everything white was right. But I found out differently. I found out that they had a lot of prejudice against each other."
- Septima continued to teach elementary school in Charleston and work with local civic organizations as the civil rights movement developed throughout the United States, particularly in the South.
- She also kept up her involvement at Highlander, returning in the summer of 1955, when she worked with and got to know Rosa Parks.
- Throughout the South the white establishment—including, in most cases, local government entities such as legislatures and law enforcement—was reacting to the changes being achieved through the coordinated efforts of civil rights organizations.
- Following the 1954 *Brown v. Board of Education* decision, in which the Supreme Court deemed segregated schools to be unconstitutional, the white power structure of the South sought to disable the NAACP, the driving force behind much of the legal action and resulting change.
- To this end the heads of state legislatures in the South called special sessions ruling that the NAACP must make public its membership lists.
- The NAACP refused to do so.
- The individual states reacted in different ways, some obtaining injunctions to stop the operation of the NAACP.
- In 1956 the South Carolina legislature passed a law banning all persons employed by either the city or the state from any membership in, or association with, civil rights organizations.

- Having been a long-time member of the NAACP, Septima became the vice president of the Charleston chapter in 1956.
- She refused to sever her ties with the organization despite the state's ruling.
- As a result she was fired from the teaching position she had held for 40 years and lost the pension she had earned along with it.
- She attempted to organize the teachers of South Carolina to fight the injustice of the new law, but there was little response to her letters and entreaties.
- The culture of intimidation was working, she saw; teachers feared for their lives and livelihoods and would not fight the new law.
- It was at this moment that Septima came to the realization that what she was asking of the people she was trying to mobilize was more than they were prepared to take on.
- She remembered thinking, "I'm going to have to get the people trained. We're going to have to show them the dangers or the pitfalls that they are in, before they will accept. And it took many years."
- Septima was offered a job at the Highlander Folk School as director of workshops, and she moved to Monteagle in June 1956.
- In her new role, she traveled widely, and she continued to be active in her Charleston community as well.
- While at Highlander Septima developed the "citizenship school" model, which she then implemented throughout the South.
- The objective of the citizenship schools was to teach black adults to read and write and also to teach them the information necessary to become registered voters.
- The first citizenship school was started on Johns Island, South Carolina.
- It was a collective effort by Septima, Highlander head Myles Horton and a man from Johns Island named Esau Jenkins.
- Jenkins wanted to run for election to the school board, but he couldn't get elected unless his supporters were allowed to cast ballots.
- Voters told him that if he could help them learn the requisite information to pass the voter registration tests, then they would vote for him.
- Jenkins had attended Highlander, and he worked with Horton and Septima to develop a curriculum for these adult students.
- When it came time to open the school on Johns Island, no church, school or civic organization was willing to assume the risk associated with such an undertaking.
- With financial support from Highlander, the Progressive Club, a voter education group started by Jenkins, bought a building in which to hold citizenship school classes, at a cost of $1,500.
- The site housed a cooperative store, which operated out of the front of the building, while the citizenship school classes took place in a windowless room in the back.
- This nonviolent, direct action—educating black voters so that they could claim their political voice—had to be concealed to prevent violence.
- The first citizenship school teacher was Septima's cousin Bernice Robinson.
- The method of teaching involved students telling stories about their daily activities.
- They would then record the stories and read them back to the class.
- Any challenging words would be used in the spelling lessons.

Septima and her colleagues created a positive environment for black and white students alike.

- Classes were organized with attention to civic participation and empowerment.
- Following the success of the Johns Island Citizenship School model, Highlander developed a program to train teachers to lead citizenship schools all over the South.
- Septima recalled, "Working through those states, I found I could say nothing to those people, and no teacher as a rule could speak with them. We had to let them talk to us and say to us whatever they wanted to say. When we got through listening to them, we let them know that they were right according to the kind of thing that they had in their mind, but according to living in this world, there were other things they needed to know. We wanted to know if they were willing then to listen to us, and they decided that they wanted to listen to us."
- Because of its integrated environment and its work in training and educating blacks and the rural poor to empower themselves, Highlander Folk School was accused of advocating communist ideals and activities, and it fell under the scrutiny of the FBI.
- "Anyone who was against segregation was considered a communist," Septima recalled.
- "White Southerners couldn't believe that a Southerner could have the idea of racial equality; they thought it had to come from somewhere else."
- In 1959, during Highlander's twenty-fifth anniversary celebration, the Rev. Dr. Martin Luther King Jr. was photographed sitting near a reporter for *The Daily Worker*, a communist newspaper.
- The reporter had not made her affiliation with the communist paper known when seeking admission to the celebration.
- Throughout the South, the photograph was used as propaganda to "prove" that Highlander was a communist training center.
- This prompted the authorities of the State of Tennessee to investigate the "subversive activities" taking place at the school.
- The state legislature met and solicited the district attorney to bring any suit against Highlander so that the school's charter might be revoked.
- Though it was integration on the Highlander campus that Tennessee authorities wanted to end, they couldn't bring that charge against the school with a reasonable expectation of winning because the Supreme Court had already ruled that segregated schools were unconstitutional.
- Ultimately the state felt most confident that it could successfully charge Highlander with the possession of alcohol and intent to sell it.
- On July 31, 1959, nearly 20 Tennessee police raided the Highlander Folk School.
- They detained Septima, and "finding" moonshine at the residence of Myles Horton, they arrested her and some of the students.
- In court Septima testified that the liquor found the night of the raid had at no time been in her possession.
- Despite incongruities in the statements of the prosecution's witnesses, the court upheld the possession charge.
- The initial consequence was an order that the administration building be temporarily padlocked.
- Subsequently, the Grundy County Circuit Court revoked the school's charter.
- "I wasn't going to let them scare me to death. I just wouldn't let them. But it wasn't an easy thing, because when you'd go home, you would keep thinking what they could do and what they might do, because they were very, very harassing and very mean, very much so."
- By early 1961, 82 teachers who had received training at Highlander were conducting citizenship classes in several Southern states.
- In the summer of 1961, the legal status of Highlander was so tenuous that the citizenship school program was relocated to the Dorchester Co-operative Community Center in McIntosh, Georgia.
- The project of the citizenship schools was taken up by the Southern Christian Leadership Conference (SCLC).
- Septima, for a time, was both employed by Highlander and working on behalf of the SCLC.
- She traveled widely in the South and throughout the country recruiting and fundraising for the citizenship school program.

Life in the Community: Charleston, South Carolina

- Charleston had a long colonial history and was the original capital of the Carolina Colony.
- It was established to serve as a major port city, an expectation it fulfilled.
- As such it was the primary location for the unloading and selling of humans captured in Africa and transported to be sold as slaves in the colonies (later, the United States).
- As a result of its role as a trade center, Charleston became the wealthiest city south of Philadelphia and the fourth-largest in the colonies by the mid-1700s.
- More than half of Charleston's population was made up of slaves.
- In the nineteenth century, black slaves and domestic servants continued to make up the majority of the city's population.
- South Carolina grew increasingly adamant that states' rights superseded the power of the federal government.
- In 1832 the state passed an ordinance whereby it could nullify the mandates of the federal government.
- Federal troops were, therefore, dispatched to Charleston's forts to collect tariffs. The state's history of conflict with and resistance to the federal government had begun.

The Civil War wreaked havoc on the city of Charleston.

- On December 20, 1860, following the election of Abraham Lincoln as president, South Carolina's General Assembly voted to secede from the Union.
- Thus began the Civil War.
- Charleston incurred heavy bombardment and severe damage during the war.
- In 1865 Union troops moved into Charleston and took control of much of the city.
- Following the Civil War, federal troops were dispatched to South Carolina to oversee Reconstruction.

Charleston was an important seaport.

- The war had devastated both Charleston's economy and its infrastructure.
- Freed slaves faced poverty, discrimination, intimidation and various abuses and other forms of disenfranchisement.
- Many former slave owners refused to free their slaves.
- South Carolina languished economically for the remainder of the nineteenth century.
- Once one of the nation's wealthiest states, South Carolina by 1890 was near the bottom in per capita income.
- Illiteracy impacted 45 percent of the population; public health was so poor that 44 percent of the state's military volunteers for the Spanish-American War were rejected.
- Cities began aggressively developing textile manufacturing as a sign of progress; the standard work week was 66 hours before a 1907 law reduced it to 60 hours.

- Charleston's public school system was one of the best in the state, but statewide, private education continued to play a major role. In 1916 one in eight high-school students was enrolled in a private school.
- The outbreak of World War I brought a handful of federal military training centers to the state and dramatically increased the activity in the Charleston Naval Yard.
- But agriculture, particularly the growing of cotton, continued to dominate the economy.
- In 1939 approximately 80 percent of the state's male high school and college graduates moved elsewhere in search of better opportunities.
- A survey in 1945 showed that 40 percent of those desiring a college education indicated they planned to go to school out of state.
- Following the World War II, industrial recruitment accelerated; within nine months, Charleston had attracted 19 new companies employing 812 people.
- There followed major investments of federal dollars as a large military presence in the region helped to shore up the city's economy.

Early Charleston, South Carolina.

HISTORICAL SNAPSHOT
1961

- At the National Reactor Testing Station near Idaho Falls, Idaho, atomic reactor SL-1 exploded, killing three military technicians
- In his farewell address, President Eisenhower warned Americans of the increasing power of a "military-industrial complex"
- Ham the Chimp was rocketed into space aboard *Mercury-Redstone 2* in a test of the Project Mercury capsule, designed to carry U.S. astronauts into space
- The U.S. launched its first test of the Minuteman I intercontinental ballistic missile
- The Beatles performed for the first time at the Cavern Club
- President John F. Kennedy established the Peace Corps
- Max Conrad circumnavigated the earth in eight days, 18 hours and 49 minutes, setting a new world record
- The first U.S. Polaris submarines arrived at Holy Loch
- The Twenty-third Amendment to the Constitution was ratified, allowing residents of Washington, DC, to vote in presidential elections
- Soviet cosmonaut Yuri Gagarin became the first human in space aboard *Vostok 1*
- The Bay of Pigs Invasion of Cuba failed to overthrow Fidel Castro
- Freedom Riders began interstate bus rides to test the new Supreme Court integration decision
- Alan Shepard became the first American in space aboard *Mercury-Redstone 3*
- A bus full of Civil Rights Freedom Riders was fire-bombed near Anniston, Alabama, and the Civil Rights protestors were beaten by an angry mob
- *Venera 1* became the first manmade object to fly by another planet—Venus—but failed to send back any data
- President Kennedy announced before a special joint session of Congress his goal to put a man on the moon before the end of the decade
- Peter Benenson's article "The Forgotten Prisoners" was published in several internationally read newspapers, leading to the founding of the human rights organization Amnesty International
- Russian ballet dancer Rudolf Nureyev requested asylum in France while in Paris with the Kirov Ballet
- President Kennedy delivered a widely watched TV speech on the Berlin crisis, and urged Americans to build fallout shelters
- The Walt Disney anthology television series, renamed Walt Disney's Wonderful World of Color, began telecasting its programs in color
- Baseball player Roger Maris of the New York Yankees hit his sixty-first home run in the last game of the season to break the 34-year-old record held by Babe Ruth
- The Soviet Union detonated a 58-megaton-yield hydrogen bomb, the largest ever manmade explosion
- The *Fantastic Four #1* comic debuted, launching the Marvel Universe
- *Catch-22* by Joseph Heller was first published
- President Kennedy sent 18,000 military advisors to South Vietnam
- Nazi Adolf Eichmann was pronounced guilty of crimes against humanity by a panel of three Israeli judges and sentenced to death for his role in the holocaust
- "Barbie" got a boyfriend when the "Ken" doll was introduced

Selected Prices

Bedroom Set, Walnut	$645.00
Coffee Maker, Percolator	$16.88
Lipstick, Cashmere Bouquet	$0.49
Mattress, Serta	$79.50
Nylons	$1.00
Paneling, 70 Panels	$47.00
Refrigerator	$259.00
Typewriter, Smith-Corona, Electric	$209.35
Vacuum Cleaner, Eureka	$69.95
Watch, Bulova	$59.50

"30 More Virginia Schools to Integrate This Week,"
The Martinsville Bulletin (Virginia), September 3, 1961:

Seventy-three Virginia schools will admit Negro pupils—30 of the schools for the first time—at opening sessions this week.

Negro enrollment in the commonly white schools is estimated at 537, more than double the Negro enrollment in the 1960-61 term.

Last year, 211 Negroes attended 43 white schools in 11 localities, while for the 1961-62 session, that figure has jumped to 73 schools in 19 localities.

Enrollment of Negro pupils in the predominately all-white classrooms is expected to proceed without incident and no special precautions are being taken anywhere in the state.

Heaviest concentration of integration in the state is in the Northern Virginia area across the Potomac River from Washington. These for localities—Alexandria, Falls Church, Arlington County and Fairfax County—account for more than half of the Negroes admitted.

The other localities are scattered from Virginia's Tidewater to the Blue Ridge Mountains.

Most of the Negro students were assigned to the schools by the state Pupil Placement Board, which only last week assigned seven more Negroes to white schools in five localities. Others were ordered admitted by federal judges.

Reverend Dr. Martin Luther King, Jr.'s Address to the
AFL-CIO Convention [excerpt], 1961:

"How can labor rise to the heights of its potential statesmanship and cement its bonds with Negroes to their mutual advantage?

First: Labor should accept the logic of its special position with respect to Negroes and the struggle for equality. Although organized labor has taken actions to eliminate discrimination in its ranks, the standard for the general community, your conduct should and can set an example for others, as you have done in other crusades for social justice. You should root out vigorously every manifestation of discrimination so that some international, central labor bodies or locals may not besmirch the positive accomplishments of labor. I am aware this is not easy or popular—but the eight-hour day was not popular nor easy to achieve. Nor was outlawing anti-labor injunctions. But you accomplished all of these with a massive will and determination. Out of such struggle for democratic rights you won both economic gains and the respect of the country, and you will win both again if you make Negro rights a great crusade.

Second: The political strength you are going to need to prevent automation from becoming a Moloch, consuming jobs and contract gains, can be multiplied if you tap the vast reservoir of Negro political power. Negroes given the vote will vote liberal and labor because they need the same liberal legislation labor needs....

If you would do these things now in this convention—resolve to deal effectively with discrimination and provide financial aid for our struggle in the South—this convention will have a glorious moral deed to add to an illustrious history."

"Desegregation Developments, Education," *The Americana Annual 1962,*
An Encyclopedia of the Events of 1961:

As the eighth school year after the U.S. Supreme Court's desegregation decision began, only three states—Alabama, Mississippi, and South Carolina—continue to have complete segregation at all levels of the public education system.

The number of Negroes attending classes with white children was still small. As of November 1961, according to the *Southern School News*, 7.3 percent of the 3,210,724 Negro children enrolled in schools of the 18 previously segregated states were attending biracial schools. However, of the 233,509 Negroes in mixed classes, 88,881 were in Washington, DC, 47,588 in Maryland, 20,636 in Kentucky, an estimated 35,000 in Missouri and 15,500 in West Virginia, 10,555 in Oklahoma and 8,448 in Delaware. In the rest of the previously segregated states, fewer than 7,000 Negroes were in mixed schools.

Continued

"Desegregation Developments, Education,"... *(Continued)*

The increase of 31 in the number of the segregated school districts in the fall of 1961 was extremely small, and led to the enrollment of only 392 additional Negroes in previously all-white schools. Nevertheless, the segregation steps taken were significant. Three of the largest cities in the south—Atlanta, Dallas, and Memphis—were desegregated, and all fall school openings were without violence....

Outside the South, efforts were being made in 1961 to eliminate what is called de facto segregation. Such moves were underway in Chicago, New York, Pasadena, Montclair, New Jersey, and New Rochelle, N.Y.

"Special Message to Congress on Urgent National Needs" [excerpt], President John F. Kennedy, May 25, 1961:

Finally, if we are to win the battle that is now going on around the world between freedom and tyranny, the dramatic achievements in space which occurred in recent weeks should have made clear to us all, as did *Sputnik* in 1957, the impact of this adventure on the minds of men everywhere, who are attempting to make a determination of which road they should take. Since early in my term, our efforts in space have been under review. With the advice of the Vice President, who is Chairman of the National Space Council, we have examined where we are strong and where we are not. Now it is time to take longer strides—time for a great new American enterprise—time for this nation to take a clearly leading role in space achievement, which in many ways may hold the key to our future on Earth....

I therefore ask the Congress, above and beyond the increases I have earlier requested for space activities, to provide the funds which are needed to meet the following national goals:

First, I believe that this nation should commit itself to achieving the goal, before this decade is out, of landing a man on the moon and returning him safely to the Earth. No single space project in this period will be more impressive to mankind, or more important for the long-range exploration of space, and none will be so difficult or expensive to accomplish. We propose to accelerate the development of the appropriate lunar space craft. We propose to develop alternate liquid and solid fuel boosters, much larger than any now being developed, until certain which is superior. We propose additional funds for other engine development and for unmanned explorations—explorations which are particularly important for one purpose which this nation will never overlook: the survival of the man who first makes this daring flight. But in a very real sense, it will not be one man going to the moon—if we make this judgment affirmatively, it will be an entire nation. For all of us must work to put him there.

1962: From Orphan to Self-made Golf Caddie

Raymond Walker was eight-years-old when his father killed his mother and himself. At 14, he left his aunt's public housing apartment, moved in with a friend, and began work as a caddy at Baltimore's country club, despite having never been on a golf course.

Life at Home

- Raymond Walker grew up in the Cherry Hill public housing project, which included a sprinkling of federally subsidized apartments and low-cost, privately owned homes.
- When Raymond was eight years old, his father killed Raymond's mother and then himself, leaving behind a suicide note that said he was worried about money and ashamed he would be unable to purchase any Christmas gifts for his children.
- Only two items were found with the note: a $25 money order made out to Raymond's grandmother for the care of the children and Raymond's newly printed package of school pictures, which he had proudly given to his mother before he went out to play.
- His parents died at 4:30 in the morning in his father's powder-blue 1950 Plymouth station wagon, which they had parked near the construction site of the new colored high school.
- *The Afro-American*, Baltimore's biweekly black newspaper, put the murder-suicide on its front page for two consecutive issues.
- Raymond's parents were buried separately, three days apart; Raymond refused to attend either funeral, even though he always believed he was his father's favorite child.
- The children's grandmother, already suffering from cancer, died a month later, so three aunts agreed to raise the children, each taking one child.
- Raymond moved to a public housing unit with his Aunt Etta, her husband and their six children.
- Nine people shared an apartment with only four rooms: a kitchen, a living room and two bedrooms, all with concrete floors.
- The apartment also had a single bathroom with a tub, but no shower, while the kitchen had two sinks: a shallow one for washing dishes and a deeper one for laundry, which was done using a washboard.
- Raymond's aunt and uncle slept in one of the two bedrooms, which they shared with their youngest daughter, who still slept in a crib. The two next-youngest children bedded down on the sleeper couch in the living room, while the four oldest boys shared the other bedroom, two in each twin bed.

Raymond Walker's parents died when he was young, and he lived with his aunt and cousins.

Raymond's aunt believed in education, and wouldn't let him think of quitting school.

- Meals often included fried salt pork, syrup and bread.
- On Fridays dinner was usually fried fish; Saturday's dinner was baked beans and hot dogs from the A&P. On Sundays the family ate fried chicken.
- When money ran low, supper consisted of a pot of navy beans or pancakes. Spam and potted ham were also staples.
- To make ends meet, Raymond's aunt often sent one of the children to shop at a grocery store where everything could be bought in individual units—one egg for the family that could not afford a dozen, or a few loose cigarettes instead of a pack.
- When Raymond got in trouble, his aunt would holler, "I'm going to give you some medicine you don't want to take!"
- The house was a football field away from the edge of the city dump, and some in the community made ends meet by picking through the mounds of garbage for something to eat— "shopping at the dump," the kids on the street called it.
- Because of its closeness to Baltimore's harbor, the trash dump got most of the fruits and vegetables that failed to clear customs, giving neighbors another reason to "go shopping."
- Sometimes, Raymond and his friends would go to the dump simply for sport—to kill rats by beating them with sticks as they ran for cover.
- When one of Raymond's friends got a BB gun, they formed hunting teams; one group of boys would beat the trash pile to make the rats run, while the others would take turns shooting the gun at the fleeing rodents.
- When times were good, Saturdays were spent at the lone neighborhood movie theater; Raymond's aunt would give him a quarter and say, "Don't come home until dark."
- It cost $0.14 for children under the age of 15 to get into the theater, leaving $0.11 for a snack.
- Raymond usually invested a nickel in a box of Jujyfruits, even though he didn't like the black or green ones.

Life at School and Work

- Raymond's aunt believed in education and would not discuss his dropping out of school; the children's father had forced the girls to leave school in the seventh grade, saying, "All they gonna do anyway is git married and have a bunch of babies."
- All three aunts wanted more for the children.
- Raymond's elementary school provided milk and graham crackers during the morning break, and he often was chosen to go to the pick-up area and get a half-pint carton of milk and graham crackers for each student in the class.
- For a class of 32 students, the school provided 16 half-pint cartons of regular milk and 16 of chocolate milk.
- Raymond would return and hand out the milk and crackers; the duty gave him real power, since he decided who got the chocolate milk.

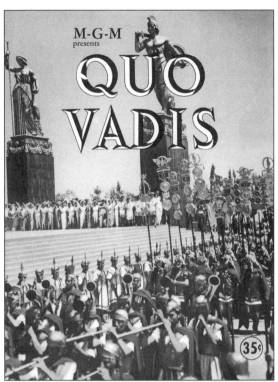

Raymond had a "Quo Vadis" hair cut, made popular by the MGM movie.

- Anyone who wanted chocolate milk worked hard to stay on Raymond's good side—an important shield provided by a teacher aware that children could be cruel to a classmate whose parents had died tragically.
- The school, like Raymond's home, constantly smelled of burning trash; the glow from the burning trucked-in garbage was a local landmark.
- In Junior High Raymond enjoyed a reputation as the class clown; he and his buddy were as much competitors as they were a team.
- Once Raymond's partner in comedy got in trouble for taping a mirror to his shoe so he could look up a classmate's dress.
- For many students, lunch at school was often last night's leftovers, ranging from fried fish heads to potted ham- or egg-salad sandwiches, which often smelled on a hot day.
- The school had books for the students to read while in class but not enough for each student to take one home for homework. Therefore the books were read aloud in class, with each student taking a turn.
- Raymond was aware of his poverty. He wore Converse sneakers to school every day, even during snowstorms.
- When a hole wore through the bottom of a sneaker, he stuffed it with cardboard to keep his feet dry.
- In the eighth grade, Raymond wore brogans with steel taps on the first day of school; this later became a school fad.
- In 1962 Raymond completed the ninth grade at an integrated school, having never attended school with whites before.
- At the beginning of the year, his aunt gave him $20 to buy clothes and supplies; he got two pairs of khaki pants and a couple of shirts from a surplus store, found shoes at a pawn shop, and still had enough money left to buy a loose-leaf notebook.
- But money issues remained.
- Following the Christmas break, the teacher asked each child to stand and talk about what they got for Christmas.
- He couldn't tell everyone that he got socks and underwear, so he created a fantasy Christmas for himself, complete with basketballs and his own record player.
- Once during the year, he stayed out of school for a week, embarrassed that he could not afford a haircut; when his teacher discovered the reason for his absence, she came to his house, gave him a dollar and took him to a barber.
- As they left the barbershop, she simply said, "I will see you at school tomorrow."
- Based on his test scores, but not his grades, Raymond was selected to attend Baltimore City College, the city's most prestigious public school for boys, the following fall.
- As the school year came to a close, though, he and his aunt fought over who had the right to the money sent by the Welfare Department, and Raymond finally moved out of the apartment.
- Then he had to carry his own weight.

- Raymond moved in with two friends in Cherry Hill and began work at the white country club across town.
- The first time he walked up the long road to the country club, the members of which were predominantly wealthy Jewish professionals, his stomach did flip-flops.
- Even though he was eager to be a caddie, Raymond had never been on a golf course before, let alone a course at a fancy country club.
- The club had opened in the summer of 1927 as a retreat for the wealthiest of the Eastern European Jews who had come to the United States around the turn of the century.
- Many of the newly arrived came to Baltimore, known as the American Jerusalem. Often, however, they did not see eye to eye with the German Jews who had emigrated a generation earlier. So the Eastern European Jews set up their own social clubs and eventually established their own country club, starting with 92 members and a nine-hole golf course.
- The club was an important center for the city's Jewish life; every Saturday night, parties for members were held at the club.
- On his first day, Raymond arrived a little after 7 a.m., with the morning dew soaking through his Converse sneakers and making his socks cling to his feet.
- The parking lot was filled with Cadillacs, Lincolns, and even a Jaguar and a Rolls-Royce.
- Three black men in their early twenties were taking turns chauffeuring cars to the parking lot.
- The senior caddie, who was past 60 years old, knew the rules of the club—including the unwritten rules, which were passed from caddie to caddie. These included keeping one's mouth shut, staying out of the golfer's way—and totally avoiding the pro shop.
- On Saturdays the urgency to "get a bag" was always apparent, even though it meant carrying a bag of clubs over nearly four miles of rolling terrain in the heat of summer.
- Most caddies carried two bags of clubs, one on each shoulder, and were paid $4 per bag for a full 18 holes of golf, which normally took four hours.
- A golf bag, with its many pockets, was filled not only with clubs but also with balls, tees, rain clothes, an umbrella, shoes, sweaters and hats—all combining to push the average weight of a bag to 50 pounds.
- If a caddie did not get any work during an entire day, he was given "caddie welfare"—$2 to cover lunch and the bus ride home.
- The club also provided a caddie class on Sunday mornings, from 6:30 a.m. until 8:30 a.m., so young men from "the Hill" could learn the rules of golf.
- At the class Raymond learned golf protocol, such as who goes first on the second shot, how to replace a divot, when to walk, when to talk and how to keep score.
- He was one of several kids from the Hill who had found their way to the country club that summer.
- Until then Raymond, like many from his community, had encountered white men mostly as policemen, mailmen and milkmen.
- Even though at the beginning he did not know his fellow black caddies very well, Raymond felt a brotherhood with them and with anyone else who came from the same public housing project.

Baltimore passed an equal employment ordinance, opening up more jobs to blacks.

Raymond had a reputation as the class clown, and was keenly aware that he stood apart from other children.

- In the caddie shack, where Raymond waited for work, the floor was rough and uneven, making the daily crap game a contest of nerves as well as of chance.
- Monday was Ladies' Day at the club; on other days there were restrictions on when women could play, but on Mondays the club belonged solely to them.
- When he caddied on Mondays, Raymond was even more careful about being polite.
- The murder of 14-year-old Emmett Till—in 1955, in Mississippi, after Till allegedly whistled at a white woman-and the pictures in *Jet* magazine of Till laid out in an open casket still haunted Raymond.
- Raymond learned that on most rounds, he had to be invisible; golfers—men and women—discussed extramarital affairs and generally behaved as if he were not there, without apology or acknowledgment.
- After work the caddies often went to a restaurant called Luigi's, where Raymond invariably ordered a plate of fried chicken, collard greens and potato salad.
- From there he regularly caught the number 37 bus back to Cherry Hill.
- Most evenings he hung out with two friends at the nearby shopping center, often in their favorite spot between the liquor store and the pool hall.
- Too young to go into either place of business, they occasionally convinced someone of legal age to buy them a bottle of Thunderbird, Purple Cow or Richards Wild Irish Rose. But Raymond only watched, because he did not like to drink.
- Not far away was the beauty parlor, where women went to get their hair "fried, dyed and laid on the side."
- Friday night was a busy night at the barbershop, where men and boys in need of a clipping sat waiting for their chance in the chair, well past the 9 p.m. closing.
- Raymond, like many boys his age, had a "Quo Vadis"—a hairstyle made popular after the 1951 MGM movie found its way into black theaters; after the hair was cut closely with clippers, a razor was used to produce a rounded look resembling the hairstyles in the movie.
- The barbershop became particularly crowded on the nights that heavyweight fights took place; everyone gathered to listen to the fights on the radio.
- When Sonny Liston became the world heavyweight boxing champion in September 1962, knocking out Floyd Patterson in the first round of their championship bout, men could be heard shouting up and down the street.

Life in the Community: Baltimore, Maryland

- The closeness of the apartments in the public housing project where Raymond lived promoted a strong sense of community.
- The mothers often talked to on another other over the backyard clotheslines or across the metal rails that divided the front porches.
- The men, few of whom owned a car, often walked together to and from the bus stop or sat side-by-side in the shade of the trees that dotted the small hill behind the row houses.
- A husband and wife, plus their children, occupied almost every apartment in his building; there were few single parents.

- Growing up, Raymond spent most afternoons on the tiny strip of land in back of the row houses, where he and the other boys shot marbles and played catch using a ball with no hide, held together only with tape.
- The girls spent their time jumping rope and playing jacks.
- Sometimes the street in front of the apartments would fill up with kids on skates-which would lead to forming a line, created when a kid skated down the middle of the street as fast as he could with a hand extended out behind him; quickly, other skaters grabbed hold and offered a hand to someone else.
- The last person was often a daredevil or naïve, because once the lead skater screeched to a stop, the line created a human slingshot that fired the last person down the street like a rocket.
- Raymond's first experience resulted in a bruised behind and a reputation for toughness that kept a lot of guys off his back.
- The neighborhood blended African American and Jewish culture; some people joked that Baltimore's Pennsylvania Avenue was the longest road in the world because it connected Africa to Israel.
- Raymond's mother had worked in a clothing store catering to working-class black women.
- The store was located near Pennsylvania Avenue and was owned by the son of a Jewish immigrant who had fled czarist Russia at the turn of the twentieth century.
- The owner let Raymond fold the boxes used to package the clothes, paying him a nickel, which Raymond immediately converted into a bag of candy corn or jellybeans.
- Baltimore's 1910 land-use ordinances mapped out black neighborhoods and white neighborhoods, designating undeveloped areas to be reserved for blacks or whites and in some cases converting black neighborhoods to white.
- These residential segregation ordinances, similar to laws passed in other Southern cities, prompted the founding of the National Association for the Advancement of Colored People (NAACP).
- By the 1930s segregation was well organized in the city, with blacks segregated by law into separate schools, hospitals, jobs, parks, restaurants and railroad cars.
- In 1952, after seven years of NAACP picketing, Ford's Theater agreed to admit African Americans.
- That same year downtown department stores agreed to sell to black customers, although they were not permitted to try on the clothing.
- The next year the municipal parks were desegregated and the first city department began hiring black employees.
- In 1956 the city passed an equal-employment ordinance, and the state ended the practice of listing separate job openings under "white" and "colored."
- By 1958 most movie theaters and first-class hotels accommodated African Americans.

"Colored admission" was still part of the landscape in the early 60s.

HISTORICAL SNAPSHOT
1962

- The late-night television show, *The Tonight Show*, with Johnny Carson, began

- Demonstrations against school segregation occurred throughout the South

- President John F. Kennedy contributed his salary to charity

- The Dow Jones Industrial Average reached a high of 767

- Movie premieres included *To Kill a Mockingbird*, *Long Day's Journey into Night*, *The Manchurian Candidate*, *The Longest Day* and *Lawrence of Arabia*

- The Students' Nonviolent Coordinating Committee (SNCC) organized the freedom ballot in the South, aggressively registering blacks to vote in Mississippi, Alabama and Georgia

- Astronaut John Glenn orbited the earth three times, saying, "It was quite a day. I don't know what you can say about a day when you see four beautiful sunsets."

- Popular songs included "Go Away, Little Girl," "What Kind of Fool Am I?", "I Left My Heart in San Francisco" and "The Sweetest Sounds"

- At nine New York daily newspapers, unions staged a strike that lasted five months

- Walter Cronkite replaced Douglas Edwards on the *CBS Evening News*

- Jackie Robinson was the first African-American inducted into the Baseball Hall of Fame

- *One Flew over the Cuckoo's Nest* by Ken Kesey, *Happiness Is a Warm Puppy* by Charles M. Schulz, *Sex and the Single Girl* by Helen Gurley Brown, and *Pigeon Feathers* by John Updike were all published

- *Mariner II* became the first successful interplanetary probe, confirming that the high temperatures of Venus were inhospitable to life

- Rachel Carson's book *Silent Spring* stated that more than 500 new chemicals were entering our bodies because of widespread insecticide use

- *Who's Afraid of Virginia Woolf?* opened on Broadway

- Inflation was at 0.4 percent, unemployment at 5.5 percent

- Eighty percent of households had a telephone

1962 ECONOMIC PROFILE

Selected Prices

Analgesic Powder, Stanback	$0.98
Automobile Seat Belts, Installed	$5.95
BB Gun, Daisy 1894	$12.98
Bed, Triple-Decker Bunk	$149.95
Can Opener, Electric	$8.44
Doll Clothes, Barbie Negligée	$3.00
Flower Delivery, FTD	$7.50
Ham, K-Mart, One Pound, Cooked	$0.46
Lawnmower	$98.99
Peanut Butter, Jif, 18 Ounces	$0.51
Pen, Scripto Tilt-Tip	$1.98
LP Record, Peter, Paul & Mary	$1.77
Shirt, Ban-Lon Knit	$2.97
Shoes, Classic Saddle	$3.97
Subway Token, New York City	$0.15

1966: African American Baseball Player

Luther Henderson was a natural athlete who turned down basketball and football college scholarships to play professional baseball—first base for the Washington Senators—because it would bring immediate cash to his family.

Life at Home

- Luther lived outside Washington, DC, in an apartment the Senators helped him locate; he wanted a house, but his teammates had told him to go slow with his spending because "rookie money" could disappear.
- During the season, he traveled with the team three to four days a week; he was excited about being in the majors but found Washington, DC, intimidating.
- Because he was afraid to drive in the city, he took cabs to work.
- He learned that city women were more aggressive than women he had known back home; when he was in the minor leagues, he had found it difficult to meet women, but as a Washington Senator, he was approached by women for dates.
- At age nine he had begun picking cotton 12 hours a day in Mississippi, alongside his mother; to forget the bleeding sores on his hands, he fantasized about becoming a major league baseball player.
- From an early age, it was his dream to help his mother escape poverty and picking cotton, which paid $2.50 for every hundred pounds.
- At age 14 he and his family left sharecropping and moved into the city of Greenville, on the Mississippi River.
- His mother did housework for others, making approximately $20 a week.
- To help support his mother, he dropped out of high school during his sophomore year, but the principal worked out a special arrangement that allowed Luther to work in a dry-cleaning plant and still attend classes on a rearranged schedule.
- Eventually he was able to play baseball, basketball and football in high school. Southern California offered him a football scholarship, while Oklahoma wanted him to play basketball; he selected professional baseball in part because he knew a contract would bring immediate cash to his family.
- Luther signed at the earliest possible moment: midnight of the day he graduated from high school.
- When he got the signing bonus of $10,000, he went home, asked his mother to sit at the kitchen table, and put a pile of money in front of her, telling her she would never have to work again.

Luther Henderson played first base for the Washington Senators.

219

At nine-years-old, Luther worked in the fields.

- Now that he was in the majors, he planned to build his mother a home.
- His only real interest was baseball, which he loved to talk about morning, noon and night—on trains and buses and in hotel lobbies.
- His tastes ran to brightly colored clothes; when he had money for the first time, he enjoyed spending it.
- While on a road trip, he bought himself a Sunbeam electric toothbrush for $14.99, and in the same store he found for his mother an electric knife with twin reciprocating blades for $16.99.

Life at Work
- A rookie baseball player with the Washington Senators, Luther was called up from the minor leagues after the season began.
- At 6'2" and 220 pounds, he was considered a big professional athlete, although he moved with the grace of a smaller man.
- Luther signed a professional contract at age 18, immediately following his high school graduation night in Greenville, Mississippi.
- Considering the potential he had shown, his signing bonus of $10,000 was low, probably owing to his lack of exposure in Mississippi.
- The scout who found Luther was the first African American scout ever employed by the team.
- Traditionally, when a scout found a promising prospect, he would write a letter to the director of the minor league system, but when the scout saw Luther play in high school, he raced to a telephone.
- Luther played in the minor-league system for four years, hoping for a shot at the major leagues.

- To gain additional experience, he played winter baseball in Nicaragua, increasing his confidence in his ability to play at the highest level of his sport.
- In high school and in the minor leagues he had played third base, but with the Senators he played first base.
- Over his first season in the majors, he improved his batting average by taking the advice of veteran players, who told him to use a heavier bat; he began to swing a 36-inch bat, which resulted in better control and fewer strikeouts.
- His teammates enjoyed telling stories about his power, including his game-winning home runs off the scoreboard in center field.
- His biggest weakness was chasing bad pitches just outside the strike zone, although he learned to be more patient at the plate.
- Competing managers predicted he would hit .340 to .350 once he learned the strike zone and understood how to read major-league pitchers.
- In his first season with the Senators, Luther batted sixth in the lineup and had a .289 average; but the Senators were given little chance of winning the pennant.
- The Senators never enjoyed the popularity in Washington of the National Football League's Washington Redskins, for whose games tickets were often as hard to get as a White House invitation.

Life in the Community: Washington, DC

- Washington was a city of amazing diversity and contrasts, ranging from the posh Georgetown section to the poverty of the inner city.
- Washington had two major products: government and tourism.
- Approximately 35,000 civil servants drove into the city every day from the Virginia and Maryland suburbs; the Washington metropolitan area comprised approximately 3 million people.
- Approximately 20 million people enjoyed the city's tourist attractions each year.
- Demonstrators, whose causes and concerns were numerous, were also attracted to the city in large numbers.
- In 1966 civil rights activists known as the Free DC Movement picketed and boycotted Washington retail businesses that were not supporting a move toward home rule for the city.
- Only 61 square miles in area, the federal city had a population of approximately 700,000, of whom 70 percent were black.
- The city's "bedroom" counties—Fairfax in Virginia and Montgomery in Maryland—had the highest median income level of any counties in the nation.

Luther was an excellent ball player.

- Lawyers made up the largest single group of professionals in the city; there were close to 20,000 attorneys in Washington, half of whom worked for the government.
- Until Brasília became the capital of Brazil in 1960, Washington was the only capital city in the world that was planned before it was built.
- In 1966 the area's 3,500 carpenters went on strike, affecting many heavy construction projects in the DC area.
- That year Congress approved $2.9 billion over three years to help build college classrooms.
- Howard University announced a plan to train 45 poor high-school dropouts as teacher's aides in Washington's elementary schools.
- Three African Americans ran for two council seats in the nearby town of Seat "Seat Pleasant" is the correct name.
- Pleasant, the first time a black had been on the ballot in the town of 6,800 across the District of Columbia line in Prince George's County; one black candidate won.

HISTORICAL SNAPSHOT
1966

- The term "Black Power" was introduced into the Civil Rights movement

- The exquisite playing of Jimi Hendrix helped popularize the electric guitar

- The President's Commission on Food Marketing reported that consumers pay 29 percent more for nationally advertised brands than for high-quality local brands

- The per capita consumption of processed potato chips rose from 6.3 pounds a year in 1958 to 14.2 pounds

- Blanket student military deferments were abolished; the draft demand for the Vietnam War was 50,000 young men a month

- Jackie Robinson, the man who broke the color barrier in major league baseball, became the general manager of the Brooklyn Dodgers of the Continental Football League

- The International Days of Protest against the war in Vietnam took place in seven American and seven foreign cities

- The Fillmore Theater in San Francisco popularized strobe lights, liquid color blobs, glow paint, and psychedelic posters

- Boxing Heavyweight Champion Cassius Clay became a Muslim and changed his name to Muhammad Ali

- Civil Rights activist James Meredith was shot during a march from Memphis, Tennessee, to Jackson, Mississippi

- The National Organization for Women (NOW) was formed

- 2,377 corporate mergers took place

- Tape cartridges, stereo cassette decks, lyrics on record albums, and the Rare and Endangered Species List all made their first appearance

- Haynes Johnson of the *Washington Star* won the Pulitzer for his coverage of the Selma, Alabama, Civil Rights conflict; the *Los Angeles Times* staff won the Pulitzer in the local reporting category for its coverage of the racially charged Watts riots

- Frank Robinson became the first baseball player to win a Most Valuable Player award in each league

- Los Angeles Dodger pitcher Sandy Koufax won his third Cy Young Award and retired

- The terms LSD, miniskirt, and Third World came into popular use

1966 ECONOMIC PROFILE

Income, Standard Jobs

Bituminous Coal Mining	$7,398.00
Building Trades	$7,363.00
Domestic Industries	$6,062.00
Domestics	$2,780.00
Farm Labor	$2,923.00
Federal Civilian	$8,170.00
Federal Employees, Executive Departments	$5,921.00
Federal Military	$4,650.00
Finance, Insurance, and Real Estate	$6,239.00
Gas, Electricity, and Sanitation Workers	$7,801.00
Manufacturing, Durable Goods	$7,228.00
Manufacturing, Nondurable Goods	$6,172.00
Medical/Health Services Workers	$4,565.00
Miscellaneous Manufacturing	$5,548.00
Motion Picture Services	$7,397.00
Nonprofit Organization Workers	$4,280.00
Passenger Transportation Workers, Local and Highway	$5,737.00
Personal Services	$4,551.00
Private Industries, Including Farm Labor	$6,098.00
Public School Teachers	$6,142.00
Radio Broadcasting and Television Workers	$8,833.00
Railroad Workers	$7,708.00
State and Local Government Workers	$5,834.00
Telephone and Telegraph Workers	$6,858.00
Wholesale and Retail Trade Workers	$7,345.00

Selected Prices

Antiques Magazine, Monthly
    for One Year $12.00
Black and Decker Drill, Electric $19.95
Bloomcraft Art Nouveau Cloth,
    per Yard....................... $3.50
Custom 7 Transistor Radio........... $12.95
Delta Airline Fare, Miami........... $74.70
Englander Mattress, Full Size $59.95
Florient Disinfectant Spray $0.59
Fred Astaire Dance Lessons,
    Eight Lessons.................. $13.95
Friden Model 132 Electronic
    Calculator $1,950.00
General Electric Alarm Clock $5.98
Goldblatts Air Conditioner.......... $498.00
Honeywell Slide Projector........... $149.50
Kutmaster, Two-Bladed Knife $1.00
Magnavox Television $650.00
Major League Warm-Up Jacket $12.95
Old Patina Polish, per Pint $2.25
Pittsburgh Plate Glass Mirror $7.00
Polaroid Color Pack Camera $50.00
Proctor Ice Cream Maker $16.95
Sheffield Candelabra, 22" High $425.00
Simonize Car Wax.................. $0.99
Stiffel Lamp, 22" Height............ $72.50
Tru-Dent Electric Toothbrush........ $12.50
Tyco Prairie Sante Fe Locomotive..... $16.77
Viking Chair $11.95
West Bend Coffee Maker $9.95

"College 'Sex Revolution' Overstressed," by Jean White, *The Washington Post*, May 1, 1966:

" 'Nice girls do, and that's that.' (Student at Reed College)

'I don't think there's been a sex revolution in what people are doing—just in the amount they talk about it.' (Radcliffe Co-ed)

'Promiscuity isn't a matter of the pill. . . . It may be easier to have an affair, but just because she's safe from pregnancy doesn't mean a girl is going to sleep with two dozen guys. Female psychology just doesn't work that way.' (University of Texas Co-ed)

'Who cares about a sex revolution? The thing is, how many dates do you have?' (Blonde at Ohio State University.)

Perhaps no revolution in history has been so minutely and flamboyantly reported as the so-called 'sexual revolution' of our time.

It has been debated in magazines and newspapers and on television panels. The scope of concern has ranged from the morality of it all to this fine point of etiquette raised in a question to an advice-to-the-lovelorn columnist: Should the man or woman pay for the pills for an affair?

The discussion has necessarily focused on the campus, where the first Post-Pill Generation has come of sexual age. Now even a best-selling book can be patched together from the quotes of 600 co-eds talking about their sex life on campus.

On the other hand, 'I'm not at all convinced that the activity matches the conversation,' says Clark E. Vincent, a family-life professor at the Bowman Gray School of Medicine at Winston-Salem.

Paul H. Gebhard, one of the authors of The Kinsey Report and Kinsey's successor as director of the Institute for Sex Research at Indiana University, agrees. He points to what he wryly calls the 'terrific amount of verbalization about sex' these days. . . .

With all the present ferment about campus sex, Gebhard feels that there is a need for 'hard data' beyond talk to document any revolution that has occurred. He has applied for a quarter-million-dollar federal grant to study sexual behavior on college campuses.

He shouldn't have any trouble collecting both views and experiences from the students, a survey of college correspondents of the *Washington Post* shows. They supplied most of the quotations and other material for this article, which was rounded out with observations from several specialists.

The survey report points to these conclusions:

The modern 'sexual revolution' has been inflated and overreported. One distortion has come from the overexposure of the sex life of the single student—and the brashest are always the most quotable.

'No one ever seems to write about the sex life of the 41-year-old truck driver or the 30-year-old matron these days,' complains Gebhard, 'and whoever interviews the girl who sits around the dorm and studies?'

Sociologist Vincent points out that an interviewer could talk to a half-dozen girls at each of 20 colleges and conclude that the sex has broken wide open; then go back and choose sets of six other girls and conclude that this is an age of prudery.

Or as a 22-year-old English major at Harvard put it: 'It's not really the "new moralists" who are talking, but the "new blabbermouths".'

The 'sexual revolution' is not all talk, however. Campus sex morals have been changing, and these changes must be taken seriously in contrast to the sensationalism of the free-love exhibitionists whose dirty words match their discarded dirty clothes at naked sex orgies.

In sex ethics, as in many other areas, young men and women are honestly questioning the relevance of old codes to contemporary society. The move is from stern 'thou-shalt-not' morality to more permissiveness and self-determination.

These changes are evident in two main areas: (1) freer discussion of sex, and (2) more

(continued)

"College 'Sex Revolution' . . ." *(continued)*

premarital sex between 'serious' couples and more open living together before marriage. . . .

In a recent report on 'Sex and the College Student,' a committee of the Group for the Advancement of Psychiatry (GAP) has this to say about campus sex:

'There is general agreement that premarital sexual relations among undergraduate college students are more frequent than they were a genera-tion ago. Certain students are more open in their activities and more vocal in their prerogatives.'

The report goes on to note a tolerance of behavior that would have been censured a few decades ago and even now is questioned in many quarters. Only 25 years ago, the GAP committee points out, the college boy went into 'town' for a sexual experience. Today, his partner is likely to be a college girl on campus."

1966: Army Private in the Vietnam War

Raised in Washington DC by his grandmother, Orlando Wright enlisted in the Vietnam War, and traded the inner-city streets for the brutality of the jungle, where he was forced to confront the death of a friend.

Life at Home

- When Orlando Wright arrived at Fort Jackson Army Base for basic training camp, he learned immediately that the drill instructor treated all the men, black or white, the same-badly.
- Also, marching through the sparsely wooded sandhills of Columbia, South Carolina, in the heat of August while carrying a full pack bore few similarities to the picture painted at his recruitment.
- Not only was he miserable, the always equally unkind drill instructor insisted that the jungles of Vietnam would only be worse.
- Imagine-worse than August at Fort Jackson!
- All the while, his grandmother continued to write regularly, reminding him often about everyone at his church praying for his safety and how proud she was that he was following in the footsteps of his grandfather, who had served in the 369th Infantry during World War I.
- Prior to joining the service and being shipped to South Carolina, Orlando had never traveled more than 30 miles from his home in Washington, DC.
- He grew up in the Anacostia neighborhood of the nation's capital.
- His father was never in the picture; Wright was the family name of Orlando's mother, who had persistent problems with drugs and alcohol.
- Orlando's maternal grandmother, "Mama Clem," took responsibility for his upbringing.
- Clementina Wright, who had cooked for a family in Georgetown for decades, was a prominent member of the African Methodist Episcopal (AME) Church, and a tough taskmaster.
- Even though her household consisted of an ever-changing number of children, grandchildren and great-grandchildren, she expected everyone to do chores and never, ever, use drugs, alcohol, tobacco or strong language in her home.
- In addition to God, she also worshipped education for her grandchildren and made

Orlando Wright traded his home in inner-city Washington DC for a tour in Vietnam.

Orlando finish high school, even after all his friends had dropped out.

- When he arrived at Fort Jackson, he knew nothing about the Viet Cong or communism, but being a soldier appealed to him; he had always been known for his toughness.
- At only 12 years old, he earned his nickname, "Hard Head," when a much larger boy had repeatedly smashed his head on the asphalt.
- As the older boy walked away, Orlando struggled to his feet demanding to finish the fight.
- His antagonist shouted back for all to hear, "Man, you got a hard head!"
- The biggest adjustment was dealing with white people.
- Everyone in his school, church and neighborhood had been black.
- Even though his drill instructor was not prejudiced, others saw black and white as an issue.
- At the end of training, Orlando was assigned to the 25th Infantry Battalion headed to Vietnam.
- His platoon, which included six African-Americans, was commanded by an Italian second lieutenant from Rhode Island, who had had no experience with blacks.
- However, the hostility he sensed from the commander didn't last long; they were all equally scared of what was ahead of them in the jungles of southeast Asia.

A lieutenant who had no experience with blacks commanded Orlando's platoon.

Life at Work

- During his first months in Vietnam, Private Orlando Wright's biggest shock was the brutality.
- During his first two weeks in the country, his unit entered a village looking for Viet Cong.
- It appeared to be clean, just old men, tired women and cautious children trying to eke out a living.
- But when the villagers would not answer questions, two women were beaten and a child shot when the soldier interrogating them was startled by something that turned out to be a stick.
- Then, when the men were leaving the village, a new guy tripped a booby trap wire and got a load of steel balls in his legs and gut.
- Immediately, the soldiers returned to the village for revenge, burning everything in sight and beating those who did not cooperate.
- Over time, Orlando has come to understand survival in Vietnam.
- He has seen several members of his unit-men he viewed as broth-ers-killed or maimed by ambush, infectious pongie stakes, or landmines.
- Though he tried to steel himself, he was revolted when, after a fire fight, two of the men in his squad-one white and one black-calmly cut the ears off the dead enemy and strung them from their dog tags like trophies.
- The lieutenant ordered the practice to stop when the ears began to stink; after that the men kept their collections hidden.

Orlando saw members of his unit killed or maimed.

- As days ever so slowly became weeks, Orlando was deeply depressed.
- The fever and loneliness were inescapable.
- He couldn't wait for each day to end, but especially feared the Viet Cong at night; for the first time in his life, he was unable to sleep more than an hour at a time.
- Only alcohol and marijuana-both in plentiful supply-made the time go more quickly.
- Another issue was the load he had to carry.
- It was not unusual to see a rifle company moving out of an operation with men carrying 50 to 60 pounds of equipment.

The soldiers walked cautiously to avoid land mines.

- Orlando himself carried his weapon, a double basic load of ammunition, two to four grenades, two canteens of water, and three to four C-rations.
- These were the essentials.
- When soldiers added to the pack a Claymore mine, smoke grenades and a few other "nice-to-have" items, mobility was reduced.
- Then there was the guilt.
- When the unit was pulled back to base camp for rest, Orlando found himself drawn to Cousin Eddie's, a club exclusively patronized by black soldiers, which featured attractive prostitutes, some of the best hash Orlando had ever smoked, and the chance to gamble with his paycheck.
- Mama Clem wrote him a letter three times a week, often including a prayer.
- Orlando found it hard to write back.
- With only eight weeks to go in his tour of duty, Orlando was confused, hurt and angry.
- He accomplished his first goal-staying alive-but everything else about his life and future was a jigsaw puzzle like the one his Mama Clem kept on a card table in her bedroom.
- Recently, as the unit moved through a narrow jungle trail, Orlando realized that he was still slightly stoned, but believed he had the experience to handle pot and the VC at the same time.
- In front of him was his friend Darryl Burrows, a guy from Harlem with a silly sense of humor and an innate goodness.

It was not unusual for men to carry 50-60 pounds of equipment.

- When Darryl suddenly froze, Orlando stopped immediately.
- With a slight grin and immense calm, Darryl explained that he had just stepped on the plunger of a land mine.
- If he allowed his foot to rise, he and anyone around him would be blown up.
- Cautiously, the soldiers gathered around.
- The platoon sergeant, a crusty Jewish New Yorker, cautiously dug around the mine with his bayonet and decided the mine could not be defused.
- All the while, Darryl was cracking jokes, acting cool-and sweating profusely.
- He was only 28 days from his tour's end.
- Quietly, the rest of the platoon eased back 30 yards, while the sergeant radioed for assistance.

"IT'S OK — ALL'S THEY GOT WUZ TH'
AMMO DUMP!! TH' BEER'S OKEY!!"

- The sun beating through the leaves made the jungle feel like a sauna.
- The soldiers stared at Darryl as if he were a bad accident.
- Forty-five minutes into the ordeal, and in the middle of a wise crack, Darryl's foot slipped.
- The silence of the jungle was shattered with the explosion.
- Darryl was lifted into the air; most of him was deposited in a lifeless heap at the feet of the platoon.
- Orlando was there and had done nothing; now that Darryl was gone, all he could do was scream.
- At camp, his first instinct was to get stoned.
- Before he had gotten a solid start, the chaplain arrived.
- First, Orlando screamed about a God who didn't care and loved cruelty.
- Then, he cried.
- Together, the two men began to sing hymns Orlando had learned growing up.
- When the chaplain departed, he left a copy of the Bible and a recommendation that Orlando tell God his thoughts and feelings.
- Orlando was not sure he knew how to talk with God, but he wanted to talk with his Mama Clem, so he wrote to her about all the good, the bad and the horrible of Vietnam.
- He confessed that he had indulged in drugs, alcohol and sex.
- Over and over in the letter, he said he wanted to come home.
- He also said he had decided to give up marijuana, and was ready to start a new life.
- Believing he had found his calling, he asked Mama Clem to show him how to become a minister.
- The loving letter he received in reply was stained with tears.

Life in the Community: Vietnam

- America's involvement in Vietnam began during WWII when American Office of Strategic Services (OSS) teams joined with Vietnamese guerrillas in fighting the Japanese invaders.
- Leading the guerrillas was a Vietnamese revolutionary named Nguyen Ai Quoc, widely known as Ho Chi Minh.
- After the Japanese were defeated, President Franklin Roosevelt declared that the country should not be handed back to the French, but to the Chinese, who declined the offer.
- After the death of Roosevelt, President Harry Truman was unwilling to risk a split with France and chose not to oppose the French occupation, despite Ho Chin Minh's desire for an independent Vietnam.
- In 1950, Truman officially recognized the French-supported Saigon government of Emperor Bao Dai and began sending aid to the country.
- The first Indochina war ended in May 1954 with the defeat of the French at Dien Bien Phu in northwest Vietnam.
- The Geneva Conference of 1954, which officially ended the war, divided Indochina into four parts; Vietnam was divided along the

Ho Chi Minh was a Vietnamese revolutionary.

17th parallel with Ho Chi Minh's government ruling the north; the Saigon government in the south; and Laos and Cambodia again made separate countries.

- By 1956, after France had withdrawn all of its troops from South Vietnam, the United States remained the only foreign power supporting the new regime of Ngo Dinh Diem.
- By 1959, the United States maintained in the country only 300 military advisors, whose main task was to prepare Diem's forces for the day the North Vietnamese invaded South Vietnam.
- During the next two years, the war heated up steadily.
- In 1961, President Diem requested newly elected President Kennedy to send more aid to fight the communist offensives of North Vietnam.
- Kennedy decided in December of that year to send 33 H-21C helicopters, bringing the total U.S. personnel to 1,500.
- Eleven days later, the first American soldier was killed by a Viet Cong bullet.

- On June 11, 1963, a 73-year-old Vietnamese monk immolated himself in front of a crowd of Buddhist monks to protest the Diem government.
- In response, Diem raided hundreds of temples and arrested thousands of Buddhist monks and nuns, thereby slowly losing the support of the United States.
- In November 1963, 14 dissident Vietnamese generals staged a coup, assured that the United States would support the new regime.
- Kennedy then ordered U.S. military forces from the 7th Fleet to protect the 16,500 American troops and 3,563 civilians in the country.

A 73-year old monk set himself on fire to protest the Diem government.

- Over the next 18 months, the Saigon government would change hands several times.
- By March 1964, approximately 20,000 troops were in the country, all of them restricted to advisory roles; soldiers arriving in Vietnam were told they were there only to help the South Vietnamese.
- By August 1964, nearly 300 Americans had died in Vietnam and 1,000 had been wounded.
- That same month, the U.S.S. Maddox reported a torpedo attack by North Vietnamese PT boats in the Gulf of Tonkin.
- In response, President Lyndon Johnson ordered air strikes against North Vietnam and called on Congress "to take all necessary measures to repel any armed attack against the forces of the United States and to prevent further aggression."
- In November, Viet Cong gunners hit Bien Hoa Air Base north of Saigon with mortars, killing five Americans and wounding 76.

- On Christmas Eve, terrorists bombed a Saigon hotel where American officers were staying, killing two and wounding 98.
- Responding to the coordinated attacks on bases in February 1965,
- U.S. fighter-bombers from the carriers Coral Sea, Hancock and Ranger attacked a guerrilla staging area in North Vietnam.
- The attack marked the official start of the American air war against North Vietnam and an expansion of U.S. involvement.
- Following a car-bomb attack on the American embassy in Saigon that killed or wounded more than 200, President Johnson tripled American troop strength in Vietnam to 75,000.
- In June 1965, the White House disclosed that General Westmoreland had the authority to send American troops into combat; the United States was no longer in an advisory role and could pursue the enemy.
- By the end of 1965, American troop strength topped 181,000.
- In the first three months of 1965, 71 Americans had been killed in Vietnam, and by the last quarter, the total was 920.
- In 1966, an average of 400 U.S. soldiers per month lost their lives.

US carriers launched fighter-bombers.

HISTORICAL SNAPSHOT
1966

- *Time* magazine named the "Twenty-five and Under Generation" its "Man of the Year"
- Blanket student military deferments were abolished; draft calls for the Vietnam War reached 50,000 a month
- A study showed that food prices were higher in poor neighborhoods than in affluent areas, where more variety was available
- The National Organization for Women was founded
- The per capita consumption of processed potato chips rose from 4.2 pounds a year in 1958 to 6.3 pounds
- Jimi Hendrix popularized the electric guitar
- The words "abort," "big-bang theory," "cable TV," "flashcube," "flower children," "miniskirt," "Third World" and "psychedelic" entered the language
- To combat smog, California imposed car-exhaust standards to take effect in 1969
- Bestsellers included *In Cold Blood* by Truman Capote, *A Thousand Days* by Arthur M. Schlesinger, Jr., *Valley of the Dolls* by Jacqueline Susann, *Capable of Honor* by Allen Drury and *All in the Family* by Edwin O'Connor
- Heavyweight boxing champion Cassius Clay became a Muslim and changed his name to Muhammed Ali
- Television premieres included *The Newlywed Game, Mission: Impossible, Star Trek, The Monkees, That Girl, The Dating Game* and *The Smothers Brothers Comedy Hour*
- Stokely Carmichael was elected head of the Student Nonviolent Coordinating Committee
- Sears introduced the Allstate Radial Tire with steel-cord tread plies for $30.80 to replace the unpopular two-ply tire.
- The approximately 80 million Americans born between 1946 and 1964 came to be called the Baby Boomer Generation
- Computer programming languages included FORTRAN for scientific and engineering applications, COBOL and ALGOL for business use, and BASIC for general use
- Procter & Gamble researchers Robert Duncan and Norma Baker came up with the wholly disposable diaper, test-launched as Pampers
- Total U.S. car registrations reached 78 million passenger cars and 16 million trucks and buses
- Black Power was introduced into the civil rights movement, differentiating SNCC and CORE from the pacifist followers of Martin Luther King, Jr.
- After years of debate, Congress passed the Traffic Safety Act to provide for auto safety standards and recalls
- The National Association of Broadcasters instructed all disc jockeys to screen records for hidden drug or sexual messages

Selected Prices

Automobile, Volkswagen Station Wagon..................... $2,602.00
Baseball Cards, Topps Complete Set................................. $11.95
Beer, Six-Pack.. $0.99
Carpet, per Yard.. $10.95
Catcher's Mask, Wilson.. $11.50
Coffee, Folger's, Two Pounds..$1.27
Electric Shaver...$13.97
Film Developing..$5.99
Gun Scope.. $34.50
Lawn Flamingo...$3.69
Table Tennis Set...$10.00
Table Tennis Table...$43.95
Tap Shoes, Child's...$5.77
Tool Set, Craftsman, 155 Pieces....................................$128.60
Tricycle... $7.95

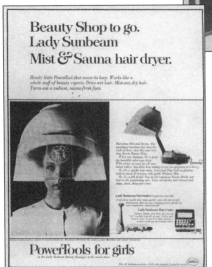

. . . and a Hard Rain Fell, A GI's true story of the War in Vietnam, John Ketwig:

Captain Benedict ordered a search-and-destroy patrol through the marshland outside what would be our new perimeter. I tried to talk my way out of it, to no avail. We lined up about six feet apart and headed into the tall grass in a pouring rain. Even at six feet, it was hard to keep track of the guy next to you. It was imperative that we maintain eye contact on both sides, because if you got ahead, you could be blown away by your own guys. I soon discovered that the elephant grass hid a tangle of twisted vines, thorns and razor-sharp leaves. You couldn't see your feet. You couldn't tell what you were stepping on, if it was solid or not. The wall of vegetation hid everything. We inched forward.

Whump! To my left, an explosion. I crouched, listening to sickening, heartrending screams. "Oh my God! Oh, God, it hurts! Momma! Oh, please! Momma, please! Oh, it hurts so bad! Pleeese help me!" I could feel my heart thumping against my ribs, the familiar shaking starting again. From the left came the cry, "Stay in place! Don't anybody move! We got a booby trap. Look for thin, clear wire, trip wire. Don't anybody move 'til we find out what they want us to do!" I could feel the cold rain dripping down the back of my neck, adding to the shivers already wracking my body. A thin, clear wire. I strained my eyes at the tall grass inches from my face. Crystal clear beads of water clung to the edges of the vertical blades, gathered, and trickled downward. The movement resembled a wire. A million straight edges of a zillion six-foot fronds, and I had to trust my water-spotted army-issue glasses to pick out a thread of clear wire or be blown away. If there was one booby trap, there were bound to be more. Jesus Christ.

"Move out! Stay awake!" Who could fall asleep? We edged forward, trying to inspect each waving blade of grass, but not wanting to take too much time and fall behind. You sure wouldn't want to be out here alone. We came to a stream. "Count off by twos. Ones cross, twos cover 'em. I slipped the safety off, and aimed blindly at the wall of shimmering green and brown while the two guys on my flanks plunged into the muck. I took off my ammo belt and held it and my rifle, safetied again, above my head. The stream was reddish-brown, swirling in and out among the base of the grasses. I waded forward, gritting my teeth, waiting for a pongie stick's point to drive itself into my leg or groin. Waiting for the big bang that would cut me in half. Praying for it to be over. My head went under. I clambered forward, more than a little panicky. There was a sharp bank of slimy mud on the other side, and I slipped twice before I hauled myself and my heavy, wet clothes up out of the goo. I wiped the grit off the lenses of my glasses, buckled the belt around my waist. I could only half-see. In the distance I heard the approach of an ambulance siren, coming to pick up the wounded. I thought they used helicopters. Next time I would tuck a clean rag inside my helmet so I could clean my glasses. We reached another stream. I was soaked. It was surprising how much heavier the wet gear had become, and how the belt seemed to have stretched 'til it was dragging my pants down off my waist. The pant legs were glued to my skin, a ponderous extra layer pulling my tired legs into the goo. My feet seemed to have shrunk, and the slipping from side to side was wearing blisters. Christ, how do some guys do this every day for a year?

"Reflections of a Battalion S3," *A Distant Challenge,* by Lieutenant Colonel Garold L. Tippin:

One of the enemy's favorite battlegrounds was the fortified village. This usually consisted of hamlets prepared with extensive fighting positions, trenchworks, connecting tunnels and spiderholes. The fighting bunkers often had five to seven feet of overhead cover and could take a direct hit from a 155-mm howitzer round. The bunkers were placed to cover avenues of approach and were interspersed throughout the village with tunnels connecting the bunkers and trenches, thereby allowing the enemy to disappear and reappear firing from another location. Trees, shrubs and even the earth itself were reshaped to conceal these positions.

At first glance, there seemed to be no logic or method to these defensive works. But upon closer investigation, one could find an intricate, well-planned defensive position that took advantage of existing cover and concealment, natural barriers and avenues of approach into and within the village.

The enemy elected to use a hamlet or a village as a battleground for one or more reasons:

- He expected to inflict enough casualties on U.S. troops during the attack to justify his making a stand.
- He knew that the U.S. soldier does not like to fire upon villages and populated areas.
- The village offered the enemy a labor source to prepare the fortifications.
- In the open valleys and coastal lowlands, the villages contained a great deal of natural cover and concealment.
- The hamlets in a village were usually spread out and their arrangement offered many avenues of escape.

The enemy's usual plan of battle followed the same pattern:

- He would allow U.S. troops to get as close as possible before opening fire, usually 15 to 25 meters. The purpose of these hugging tactics was to get the U.S. soldiers so closely engaged that they could not effectively use artillery and tactical air support.
- The enemy felt if he inflicted several casualties in his initial burst, the U.S. soldier would become involved in trying to get the wounded back to the rear for evacuation. He believed that when the U.S. troops started worrying more about getting their wounded buddies to safety than about the battle, they would become easy targets; in this respect, he was correct.
- Another facet of his battle plan was to fight viciously until dark; then, using the cover of darkness, he escaped by using one of his many preplanned escape routes, carrying off his dead, wounded, their weapons and even empty cartridges. . . . The enemy knew that we placed great emphasis on body count and weapons.

NAM, The Vietnam War in the Words of the Soldiers Who Fought There:

My platoon was pulled to do sentry duty at a place called Anu Tan, a rice mill surrounded by huts. Things weren't so safe at Anu Tan. People got killed. I was living in a bunker, but couldn't go in there at night because the rats were so bad you'd get bitten. If a rat bites you, you're sure not going to catch the rat and turn him over to find out if he has rabies. It was just assumed that all rats had rabies. You would undergo the shots. . . .

Once, early in the evening, before it was really dark yet, I was by myself on the top of the bunker when they started shooting at us. I didn't panic by this point in time. Calmly and methodically, but disconnected, like you're watching yourself do it—Clint Eastwood would have been proud of me—I moved my M-16 so that eventually the muzzle flashes from the graveyard lined up through my sights. The guy fired and I fired back on top of him, emptied eight or nine rounds right back at him.

I heard this scream, high in volume but like the stuff you use to scream with had been disconnected. I knew that I had really blasted somebody for the first time. The gurgling went on for 30 or 40 seconds, a retching scream for a long time. I felt strange. The consequences of pulling the trigger came home to me the next day when I found blood, hair and tissue all over this one tombstone. I probably killed the guy.

"AWOL," *The Noncom's Guide:*

When a man goes AWOL, he puts a black mark on your record as a leader. You may not be directly to blame, but you are responsible for "all our unit does or fails to do." A soldier absent without leave has committed a serious breach of discipline, and it is your duty to see that discipline is never broken.

During the war, a detailed study was made of the reasons why men go AWOL. Based on thousands of cases, this survey revealed that soldiers with little education and low mental ability are more likely to go "over the hill."

There is nothing the matter with this type of man except that he is not bright enough to make the grade in the army, even though he may not look "dumb" and may be strong, healthy and pleasant. The things that an average soldier learns easily, however, this man finds so difficult that he may become afraid and go AWOL. He does not seem to understand orders, he repeats mistakes over and over despite correction, and he is usually forgetful. Since he is unable to solve his personal problems, he takes what seems to be the easiest way out.

Accordingly, pay close attention to the least educated, least intelligent men in your outfit. They are the weakest and will need the most help and understanding.

Swanson N. Hudson, U.S. Army:

As a black kid straight from the farm in North Carolina, coming to Vietnam was a great adventure to me. I was looking forward to seeing the sights of southeast Asia. After all, what little I knew about Asia I had learned from movies such as *The World of Suzie Wong*. I knew there was some fighting going on, and I knew U.S. Marines had made a "peaceful landing" up in Da Nang, but to me, all this was exciting stuff. . . .

My platoon spent Christmas 1965 in guard duty up by the Man Yang Pass on Highway 19. We were guarding the few bridges that hadn't been blown up by roving bands of VC. In January, we started patrolling northeast of An Khe in places like Vinh Thanh Valley. I guess they were priming us new guys for the upcoming operation in Bong Son. At that time we "cherries" had never heard of the place. It wouldn't take long before we would never forget it.

After a few days of insignificant contacts, our company was flown back to base camp for rest. We were then choppered over to Qui Nhon on the coast for several more days. Then we went northwest to LZ [Landing Zone] Dog, about 2.5 miles north of Bong Son along Highway 1.

At LZ Dog, it really started looking like a war was going on. To this day, after three tours in Vietnam and more than 30 years later, the scene at Dog is still vivid in my mind. I remember setting up our pup tents in the cemetery. Heavy artillery was firing day and night, and an occasional incoming enemy mortar round was hitting in the distance. What really sticks in my mind, though, were the large piles of bloody G equipment, web belts, boots and helmets with bullet holes in them. Even now, that's what I remember about the Bong Son area. Seeing those piles gave me my first glimpses of death.

"Basic Pay," *The Noncom's Guide,* **Sixteenth Edition, The Military Service Division:**

Pay Grade	Monthly Basic Pay	
	Under two years	Over 10 years
Sergeant Major, E-9	$380	$380
Master Sergeant, E-8	310	320
Platoon Sergeant, E-7	206	285
Staff Sergeant, E-6	175	255
Sergeant, E-5	145	240
Corporal, E-4	122	190
Private, E-3	99	141
Private, E-2	86	108
Private, E-1	83	105

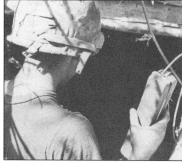

Norelco 'Flip-Top' Speedshaver® 20 for young shavers. With rotary blades that can't nick or pinch. A comfortable, close shave every time. Flip-top cleaning, too. And at a low price.

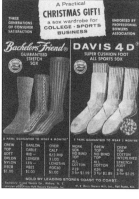

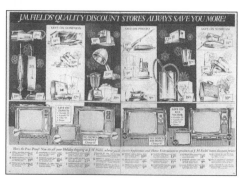

1968: Female Electronics Worker

Marian Whitley worked for a leading electronics manufacturer—one of the first corporations in Memphis to hire black workers—while her husband farmed the family land and hired himself out to neighboring farms.

Life at Home

- In addition to farming the family land, Richard hired himself out to neighbors, many of them white, in the spring and fall; he also sold fertilizer to earn extra income.
- In addition to growing vegetables for sale and use at home, he prided himself on his hunting skills; deer, squirrel and turtle were part of the family diet.
- Marian was one of the 40,000 people who drove into Memphis to work each morning.
- Developers were buying nearby farms for the expanding suburbs of rapidly growing Memphis; land speculation was rampant. The family had not decided whether or not to sell the family farm if asked.
- They were uncertain where they would move to if they agreed to sell the farm; most African Americans in Memphis—even those with money—lived in the often-substandard homes in the older section of town, because Memphis had few integrated neighborhoods.
- The approach of the suburbs also brought libraries; Memphis had nearly 20 library branches. Janet considered herself a good reader, and the library was important to her.
- Both parents believed that their third-grade daughter would have a better life with more opportunities than they had had, especially if she did well in school.

Marian Whitley worked at one of the first corporations in Memphis to hire black workers.

Life at Work

- Marian's employer, a nationally known electronics company, began manufacturing operations in Memphis in 1947, with 100 employees producing electronic components such as headphones and condensers.
- By 1968 the plant employed 1,200 workers, spread evenly over three shifts.
- Most of the workforce comprised middle-aged white women, who worked at machines producing small, delicate components.

- The first black employee had been hired in 1961, during a period of expansion.
- African American workers were added at the Memphis facility because of corporate pressure and a gradual change in the racial climate in Memphis as cafeterias, drinking fountains, public restrooms and similar facilities were desegregated.
- At the plant racial relationships were considered good by both black and white workers; in the cafeteria black workers normally sat together, apart from the white workers, out of tradition and choice.
- Black leaders thought that the changes in hiring practices took place not because of marches or demonstrations but because of the nondiscriminatory workplace requirements placed on government contracts.
- Most African Americans hired by the company had a high school diploma, and one-third had college experience; approximately one-fourth of the white workers did not have a high school diploma, and only seven percent had attended college.
- By 1968 half of all new hires were black women; only 16 black men were employed among the 1,200 workers.
- Typically the jobs required little training.
- The plant experienced little unionization.
- The electronics manufacturing industry, dominated by companies such as Westinghouse and General Electric, was growing rapidly.
- From 1923 to 1958, total employment in the electronics manufacturing industry grew threefold; electric-power consumption, measured in kilowatt hours, grew 16-fold.
- In 1968 sales of appliances and electronic products increased 9.0 percent, and profits, 18.2 percent, over the prior year.

Life in the Community: Memphis, Tennessee

- Memphis, at the extreme southwestern corner of Tennessee, sat high on a bluff overlooking the Mississippi River; it was the county seat of Shelby County.
- Memphis's economy had always been tied to the river; the city grew as a center where cotton bales were sold, loaded onto riverboats and shipped down the waterway.
- Firestone, RCA, International Harvester, General Electric and other well-known companies settled in the city, once known best for the blues, gambling and catfish.
- Over time, following a national pattern, neighborhoods near downtown Memphis became more African American, while new all-white suburbs sprang up around the city.
- With a population of nearly 550,000, Memphis was the largest city not only in Tennessee but in the region, including the bordering states of Mississippi and Arkansas.
- About 200,000 of Memphis's residents, or 40 percent of the city's population, were black.
- Many migrants from the cotton and soybean farms of the Mississippi delta settled in the city; just 56 percent of Memphis's population had been born in Tennessee, and

Memphis, Tennessee

more than 25 percent had lived in Memphis for fewer than five years.

- Approximately 57 percent of the African American families had incomes below the poverty level of $3,000 a year, while only 13.8 percent of white families lived below the poverty line.
- At the 1960 census, the median educational level of Memphis's African American residents over 25 years old was 6.7 years; the median educational level for whites over 25 was 11.1 years.
- Achievement tests showed black eighth-graders testing two grades behind white eighth-graders.
- The Shelby County school system was not desegregated until 1963; in 1968 the vast majority of the public schools were still de facto segregated.
- In 1968 only 3 of 13 city councilmen were black; just 5 percent of all school board members were African American.
- Early in 1968 civil rights activists encouraged black sanitation workers to strike, supported by the American Federation of State, County, and Municipal Employees' Union (AFSCME) and black ministers in the area; Reverend Martin Luther King Jr. took a leadership role.
- Pay for garbage workers was $70.00 a week; all of the supervisors were white, while workers typically were African Americans recruited from farms.
- The mayor considered the strike to be unwarranted, declaring "I don't make deals." King was branded an irresponsible rabble-rouser.
- From their pulpits Memphis's black ministers compared the strikers with Old Testament prophets who crusaded against injustice; they took up special collections for the workers and asked their congregations to join them in daily marches to downtown Memphis.
- In less than a week, $15,000 was raised to support the strikers; sales in downtown businesses dropped by 35 percent.
- On March 14, 1968, NAACP executive secretary Roy Wilkins spoke to a rally of 9,000; four days later, Reverend Martin Luther King Jr., spoke to an audience estimated at 25,000 and called for a one-day general strike of all workers.
- Riots broke out during a downtown march on March 28; a 16-year-old was killed, 60 people were injured and 300 demonstrators were arrested; the mayor called for martial law and brought in 4,000 National Guard troops.
- The president of the local Chamber of Commerce blamed the violence on activist preachers, saying, "If the Negro ministers would tend to their ministering instead of trying to stir things up, we wouldn't have had this trouble."
- King returned to Memphis from Atlanta on 3 April. Speaking to the sanitation workers and supporters, King told them, "I've seen the Promised Land. I may not get there with you. But I want you to know tonight that we, as a people, will get to the Promised Land."
- Reverend Martin Luther King Jr. was shot and killed on April 4, 1968, at the Lorraine Motel in Memphis. Memphis, along with cities across the nation, experienced rioting that night.
- The city eventually agreed to pay the garbage workers an extra $0.10 per hour and to permit union dues to be handled through a credit union and then paid to the AFSCME.

Civil Rights in Memphis

- On December 1, 1955, 42-year-old Rosa Parks helped launch a movement by refusing to surrender her bus seat to a White passenger; the federal courts ruled segregation of the Montgomery, Alabama, buses unconstitutional in 1956.
- In response Memphis post office employee O.Z. Evers filed a suit against the Memphis bus company in 1956 to desegregate that city's buses.
- Black banker and NAACP board member Jessie Turner filed a desegregation suit against the Memphis Public Library in 1958.
- John F. Kennedy promised during his 1960 presidential campaign to exercise "moral and persuasive leadership" to enforce the 1954 Supreme Court decision calling for desegregated schools.
- By 1960 a generation of high school Black students had grown up knowing that the Supreme Court had ruled the educational apartheid they were experiencing was against the law of the land.
- Resentment and frustration burst to the surface in the 1960s across the nation.
- Challenges to the official barriers to Blacks seeking public accommodations included sit-in demonstrations at drug stores, freedom rides on public buses across the South, and marches in hundreds of cities across the nation, although principally in the South.
- Student sit-ins began nationwide in 1960; 41 Memphis College students were arrested for entering two segregated libraries.
- The racially mixed Memphis Committee on Community Relations urged voluntary desegregation; the buses were desegregated in the fall of 1960, libraries in October, and the Overton Park Zoo in December of that year.
- To avoid a Black boycott, the Memphis downtown merchants agreed to volunteer desegregation in January 1962—provided that no changes were required during the 1961 Christmas season.
- Thirteen Black students integrated four Memphis schools in the fall of 1961 without incident; officials were so fearful of riots that even the teachers were not informed of the planned integration of their classrooms until the night before.
- In 1962 the movie theaters of the city were integrated secretly. With the cooperation of the theater managers, a Black couple was selected to integrate the Malco Theatre. When nothing happened to the couple, the following week two Black couples were sent to integrate another theater; by April, 1963, 14 theaters had been integrated in this way.
- When publicity about the progressive work of the Memphis Committee on Community Relations appeared in the Memphis newspaper, the White chairman, a respected former Memphis banker, received anonymous letters addressed to the "nigger lover" and stating, "race mixing is communism."
- As part of an agreement to voluntarily integrate the 20 largest restaurants in the city, and thus avoid picketing, the restaurant owners insisted that the *Memphis Appeal* not report that integration of the eating establishments was taking place.
- Until 1965 the Tennessee Department of Employment Security maintained segregated offices; employers who wanted White workers called one office, for Black workers, another separate facility.

Signs of segregation were throughout the city.

Historical Snapshot
1968–1969

- The U.S. gross national product reached $861 billion
- The Vietnam War and student protests intensified across the nation
- Richard Nixon was elected president
- 4,462 corporate mergers took place
- BankAmericard holders numbered 14 million, up 12 million in two years
- Civil Rights leader Rev. Martin Luther King, Jr., was assassinated at a Memphis, Tennessee, motel; riots occurred in over 199 cities nationwide
- Senator Robert F. Kennedy was assassinated in Los Angeles shortly after winning the California Democratic primary
- In response to the King and Kennedy assassinations, Sears & Roebuck removed toy guns from its Christmas catalog
- Automobile production reached 8.8 million
- Volkswagen captured 57 percent of the U.S. automobile import market
- Television advertising revenues hit $2 billion, twice that of radio
- First-class postage climbed to $0.06
- Inflation was now a worldwide issue
- Yale College admitted women
- The Uniform Monday Holiday Law was enacted by Congress, creating three-day holiday weekends
- Crimes of violence reportedly had increased 57 percent since 1960
- Nationwide 78 million television sets existed
- The average farm subsidy from the government was $1,000
- Neil Armstrong walked on the moon
- The average U.S. automobile wholesaled for $2,280
- Pantyhose production reached 624 million pairs in 1969, up from 200 million in 1968
- The average U.S. farm produced enough food for 47 people
- Blue Cross health insurance covered 68 million Americans
- *Penthouse* magazine began publication; *Saturday Evening Post* folded
- The National Association of Broadcasters began a cigarette advertising phase-out
- The U.S. began the first troop withdrawals from Vietnam; Vietnam casualties now exceeded the total for the Korean War
- Richard Nixon's 43.3 percent victory was the lowest presidential margin since 1912
- Pope Paul VI's ban on contraception was challenged by 800 U.S. theologians
- 20,000 people were added monthly to New York's welfare rolls; one-fourth of the city's budget went to welfare
- The Vietnam War became the longest war in U.S. history

1968 Economic Profile

Income, Standard Jobs

Bituminous Coal Mining $8,169.00
Building Trades $8,332.00
Domestic Industries $6,759.00
Domestics $3,254.00
Farm Labor $3,327.00
Federal Civilian $9,002.00
Federal Military $5,148.00
Finance, Insurance, Real Estate $6,994.00
Gas, Electricity, and Sanitation
       Workers $8,666.00
Manufacturing, Durable Goods $8,002.00
Manufacturing, Nondurable
       Goods $6,849.00
Medical/Health Services
       Workers $5,292.00
Miscellaneous Manufacturing $6,252.00
Motion Picture Services $7,946.00
Nonprofit Organization
       Workers $4,655.00
Passenger Transportation Workers,
       Local and Highway $6,279.00
Personal Services $4,960.00
Private Industries, Including
       Farm Labor $6,772.00
Public School Teachers. $7,129.00
Radio Broadcasting and
       Television Workers. $9,563.00
Railroads $8,663.00
State and Local Government
       Workers $7,255.00
Telephone and Telegraph
       Workers $7,506.00
Wholesale and Retail Trade
       Workers $8,142.00

Selected Prices

Argus 35-mm Cartridge Camera,
    with Flash $69.95
Black and Decker Drill, Electric $10.99
Child's Fruit of the Loom Briefs,
    Package of Three $2.65
Colgate Toothpaste, 6.75 Ounce Tube . . . $0.55
Custom 7 Transistor Radio $12.95
Cut-Glass Glasses, Includes Six
    Tumblers $2.49
Daisy Golden 750 Rifle $7.50
Davis Super Highway Tire,
    Six-Ply Rating $26.95
DeLong Red Worm Fishing Lure,
    Package of Three $0.49
Delta Airline Fare, Chicago
    to Miami $74.70
Dual-Exhaust Kit for Corvair $18.45
Goldblatt's Air Conditioner,
    Whole House $498.88
Hunts Catsup, 14-Ounce Bottle $0.22
Jarman Man's Dress Shoes $22.00
Lady Kenmore Electric Shaver $13.97
Mattel Teenage Barbie $2.29
Pepsi Cola, 10-Ounce Bottles, Six Pack . . $0.59
Seagram's VO Whiskey, 86.8
    Proof, Fifth $5.79
Solid-Oak Nightstand $25.95
Truetone Riviera Television,
    16" B&W $149.95
Western Auto Sunburst Wall Clock $16.25
Wizard Long Life Light Bulbs,
    Four Pack $1.29
Wizard Washer, 10-Pound Capacity $99.88

**"A New Cash Crop for Rural America," advertisement by
National Association of Real Estate Board, *Life Magazine*,
November 15, 1968:**

"The biggest migration of this century has been from America's small
towns to the big cities in search of jobs. The Make America Better program of the Realtors salutes Mountain Home, Arkansas, a small community that is successfully reversing this trend. Like most farming
communities, Mountain Home was steadily losing its people to the
cities. The economy slumped steadily until the town grabbed itself by
the bootstraps and began to pull. Though handicapped by limited assets, it succeeded in attracting two industries to locate in the county. As
a result, while most rural areas continue to lose population. Mountain
Home is gaining steadily. Now that good jobs are available at home, a
surprising number of former residents are coming back. And families
who otherwise would have emigrated to overpopulated cities are staying
at home...Help make America better. Join with the 85,000 Realtors in
their Make America Better Program."

1970: Earth Day Advocate

Miles Feimster didn't consider himself an environmentalist, but he did like the idea of honoring the natural world by setting aside one day in its honor, and joined Earth Day activities in his community.

Life at Home

- Miles Feimster was part of a furniture family from a furniture town in the heart of a furniture manufacturing region.
- He grew up in company-provided housing, substandard in many ways but extremely affordable: the rent was $8.00 a month.
- His father prided himself on being financially conservative; the family was permitted one window fan to battle the sometimes brutal summer heat of South-side Virginia.
- The monthly electric bill averaged $15.00 a month.
- Although the family was the proud owner of an electric range, the wood-burning "warm morning" cook stove was still used in the fall, winter and spring.
- Indoor plumbing had not yet arrived at the company housing in Martinsville, Virginia; therefore, the family outhouse was located on a hillside away from Indian Spring, the family's source of clean water for drinking, bathing and clothes washing.
- For washing clothes, the family relied upon a Maytag wringer washer.
- The water was heated in a galvanized steel tub placed over a fire pit; rinsing was done in the larger tub filled with cool, clean water.
- Both tubs were filled by carrying water from the spring in a 36-gallon aluminum bucket.
- The outhouse received a biannual Red Devil lye treatment to combat odor and disease.
- Every third year it was relocated, with precautions taken to integrate the abandoned latrine safely back into the landscape.
- Because the home was surrounded by streams on three sides, the family re-ditched every spring to insure proper drainage and reduce the mosquito breeding areas.
- To augment the family's food supply and hold down costs, Miles raised bantam chickens for meat and eggs.

Miles Feimster supported Earth Day.

Miles Feimster grew up in company-provided housing in the furniture manufacturing region of Martinsville, Virginia.

- Miles's young siblings, Allie, 14, and Hanson, 10, were entrusted with the job of selling surplus eggs to a neighbor.
- In addition, the family raised a Yorkshire hog each year that was located in a pen as far away from the house and water supply as possible.
- The family garden included tomatoes, corn, beans, potatoes, onions and greens.
- Miles's mother Addie's specialty was canning the crops at harvest; she also put up peaches, apples, jams and preserves for the coming winter.
- During the summer growing season, Addie Feimster enjoyed quilting, for which she had earned a highly esteemed reputation within the black and white communities of Martinsville.
- A Feimster quilt would fetch $30.00.
- Miles's favorite season was spring, which brought the opening of trout season on the Smith River.
- The rapidly moving river signaled new hope and opportunity.
- It was also the place where he began to understand the impact of man and his pollution on nature.
- At times, heavy industrial pollution gave the tender trout a metallic taste that diminished the joy of trout fishing and eating.
- But trout fishing was a cherished tradition in the Feimster household that improved the family table in all seasons.
- Miles Feimster's father, Nate, was a renowned local fisherman with many citation awards to prove his fish stories.
- He often credited his Cherokee heritage for his love of the wilds and his adeptness as a hunter.
- Every year he took down at least two deer, which were usually given to the local needy.
- Addie Feimster would not touch her husband's deer kills.

Miles's mother and sister.

Life at Work

- Eighteen-year-old Miles Feimster's participation in Earth Day, 1970, was ignited by a friend and classmate, Jan Lawless.
- Like Miles, she had grown up near the Smith River, playing along its banks and tributaries.
- It was she who had suggested that they participate in the Earth Day parade and teach-in at the local community college.
- Maybe this was a way to get people interested in the quality of the local air and water, Miles figured.
- He knew from experience that raw sewage was still pumped into the river in some places; on occasion the river changed color because of industrial discharges.
- And every teenager from the industrial areas of the town had seen the smokestack clouds rise and felt the resulting falling ash rainfall.
- Cleaning up the environment was not an abstract, theoretical concept for Miles.
- First, though, he would need approval to attend.
- Both his mother and grandmother wanted a promise that Earth Day was not going to be the type of protest in which a black teenager could be arrested, hosed or beaten.
- They had seen enough of that kind of protest.
- Miles's father and grandfather took for granted that something would go wrong.
- It was their nature to be cautious, especially with Miles pledging to ask hard questions about the very factories that supported the family.
- Pollution or not, the factories fed the community.
- Even though all wages were frozen by presidential mandate, to harness inflation, if a man could work 70 hours a week, that was prosperity.
- After Miles made the commitment to participate in the Earth Day environmental teach-in, he and his friend Jan were consumed by the possibilities.
- Most of their free time was spent in helping to prepare for the event scheduled for April 22, 1970.

Local schools held Earth Day programs.

Faculty from the community college coordinated local events.

- The date was part of a national campaign to raise awareness of environmental and conservationist issues.
- Significantly, the date was chosen by U.S. Senator Gaylord Nelson, a Democrat from Wisconsin, and Representative Paul R. McCloskey, a Republican from California.
- Environmental Teach-in Incorporated, a student-run organization, had been formed to coordinate the national campaign.
- Its goals and charter were clear and non-confrontational: organized by students with the approval of school authorities and political leaders, Earth Day sought to mobilize support for anti-pollution measures.
- Activities were created at more than 800 colleges and 2,000 high schools in every section of the nation.
- Even some of the nation's military bases, still on high alert because of the Vietnam War, elected to participate.
- In Martinsville, Virginia, biology instructor James M. McIntosh was named the local coordinator for Earth Day at Patrick Henry Community College.
- The announced topics for discussion included "What Is Pollution?," "What Is Being Done about It?," and "What Can the Individual Do to Help?"
- To kick off the teach-in, an Anti-Pollution Parade was scheduled for the afternoon of April 18, four days before Earth Day.
- Miles and Jan were eager to do their part.
- The parade was led by a hay wagon loaded with examples of pollutants, followed by students wearing gas masks and others carrying pollution protest signs.
- Jan and Miles both wore gas masks, which were hot.
- He was the only black teen in the parade and stayed toward the middle of the protest march in case the police decided to interrupt the proceedings.
- When the march ended, the 100 high school and college students who had participated were invigorated with the possibilities for change.

- To participate in the teach-in, which ran from 1:30 to 6:30 p.m. on Wednesday, April 22, Miles and Jan had to skip their afternoon high school classes—something they had never done before.
- The Earth Day protest had a high air of respectability—a far cry from the rag-tag anti-Vietnam War protests shown so prominently and so often on the nightly news.
- Virginia Assistant Attorney General, Gerald Bailes, was the keynote speaker, expounding on legal enforcement and pollution; local pediatrician Dr. John French spoke on the medical effects of pollution.
- Also included were speakers from the state Air Pollution Board and the Bureau of Solid Waste and Vector Control.
- For Miles, the impact of the day of protest began to sink in when he realized that he and Jan were part of a national movement, aimed directly at the burgeoning environmental crisis in the United States.

Miles' friend Jan encouraged him to participate in Earth Day.

- At Martinsville High School, two students condemned pollution by carrying signs and riding a tricycle before school to illustrate the effect of automobiles on the environment.
- As part of the Earth Day festivities at Patrick Henry Community College, an automobile engine was laid to rest before the start of the various antipollution seminars and speeches on the environment.
- Martinsville City Manager, Tom Noland, participated on a panel representing private citizens' groups, industry and government agencies, and others concerning the effect of pollution on the area.
- Miles and Jan stayed to the end, enthralled by the possibilities for change and the opportunities ahead.

Earth Day Around the United States

- To celebrate the kick-off of Earth Day, Virginia Governor Linwood Holton signed a statement designating a Virginia "Improved Environment Week."
- Senator William Spong, Jr., an early advocate of the anti-pollution cause, spoke at a program sponsored by the Department of Environmental Sciences at the University of Virginia in Charlottesville.
- At the College of William and Mary in Williamsburg, Virginia, Dr. William Sirl, a California research physicist and a member of the Sierra Club, spoke on the "value of the wilderness."
- Nationally, 10 million public school children participated in teach-in programs.
- In New York City, cars were banned on Fifth Avenue while a picnic was held.
- In Louisville, Kentucky, 1,500 students crowded into a concourse at Atherton High School to illustrate the problems of overpopulation.
- Nationwide, students rode horses, roller skates, and skateboards rather than cars or buses.
- While speaking at the University of California, Berkeley, Senator Gaylord Nelson, who had originated the Earth Day idea, proposed national policies on land use, herbicides and pesticides, national standards for air and water pollution, and a ban on oil drilling.

- New Jersey Governor William Cahill signed a bill creating a state Department of Environmental Protection.
- New York Governor Nelson Rockefeller signed a bill coordinating anti-pollution and conservation activities.
- Maryland Governor Marvin Mandel signed 21 bills and joint legislative resolutions dealing with the environment.
- During a speech in Philadelphia, Pennsylvania, Senator Edmond Muskie of Maine called for an environmental resolution against pollution.
- New York City Mayor John V. Lindsey rode an electric-powered car to his appointments that day, and told a Union Square rally, "There is a simple question: do we want to live or die?"
- In Washington, DC, Senator Bayh of Indiana called for a national environmental control agency to "conquer pollution as we have conquered space."
- Not all congressional speakers were received warmly: New York Senator Charles E. Goodell was greeted at a New York University by leaflets calling his speech "the biggest source of air pollution."
- Despite the participation of millions, arrests were few: in Boston a group protesting the air pollution of supersonic transport planes blocked the ticket counter at Logan International Airport, resulting in 13 arrests.
- While much of the nation observed Earth Day reverently, the Daughters of the American Revolution branded the environmental movement "distorted and exaggerated."

HISTORICAL SNAPSHOT
1970

- Woodstock, New York farmers sued Max Yasgur for $35,000 for damages caused by the Woodstock rock festival
- The Boeing 747 made its maiden voyage
- Diana Ross and the Supremes performed their last concert together, at the Frontier Hotel in Las Vegas
- President Nixon nominated G. Harrold Carswell to the Supreme Court, but the nomination was defeated because of controversy over Carswell's past racial views
- General Motors redesigned its automobiles to run on unleaded fuel
- The Chicago Seven defendants were found innocent of conspiring to incite riots at the 1968 Democratic National Convention
- A nuclear non-proliferation treaty went into effect, ratified by 43 nations
- The National Mobilization Committee to End the War in Vietnam organized a trip to Hanoi to meet with the prime minister of North Vietnam
- President Nixon signed a measure banning cigarette advertising on radio and television
- *Apollo 13* was crippled on the way to the moon, preventing a planned moon landing
- President Nixon announced to a national television audience that the United States was sending troops into Cambodia "to win the just peace that we desire," sparking widespread anti-war protests
- National Guardsmen fired at anti-war protestors at Kent State University, killing four and wounding 11 others, spawning campus protests nationwide
- The Beatles' film *Let It Be* premiered
- Two black students at Jackson State University in Mississippi were killed when police opened fire during student protests
- One hundred thousand people demonstrated in New York's Wall Street district in support of U.S. policy in Vietnam and Cambodia
- The federal government shut off power and fresh water supplies from the American Indians who had claimed Alcatraz Island
- Kenneth A. Gibson of Newark, New Jersey, became the first black person to win a mayoral election in a major Northeast city
- The Twenty-sixth Amendment, which lowered the voting age from 21 to 18, was signed into law
- The U.S. Senate voted overwhelmingly to repeal the Gulf of Tonkin resolution
- Heavyweight boxing champion Muhammed Ali's refusal of induction into the U.S. Army was heard by the Supreme Court
- Casey Kasem's *American Top 40* debuted on Los Angeles radio
- Gary Trudeau's comic strip *Doonesbury* first appeared
- The U.N. General Assembly accepted membership of the People's Republic of China
- The U.S. Senate voted to give 48,000 acres of New Mexico back to the Taos Indians
- The World Trade Center Towers in New York City were completed
- *Hello, Dolly!* closed at the St. James Theater on Broadway after a run of 2,844 performances

Selected Prices, 1970

Biofeedback Monitor Kit $125.50
Camera, Kodak Pocket $28.00
Hair Spray, Adorn $1.09
Hotel Room, Sheraton, New York City $22.00
Mattress, Queen Size, Two Pieces $399.95
Microwave Oven, Radarange $450.00
Pressure Cooker $18.99
Record Album, Simon & Garfunkel's *Bridge Over Troubled Water* $5.98
Telephone, Western Electric $6.95
Wheelbarrow $34.95

Environment Timeline

1898
Cornell became the first college to offer a program in forestry.

The U.S. Rivers and Harbors Act banned the pollution of navigable waters.

1902
The U.S. Bureau of Reclamation was established.

1903
The nation's first wildlife refuge was formed when President Theodore Roosevelt protected Pelican Island, Florida, from hunters decimating the island's bird population.

1905
The United States Forest Service was established within the Department of Agriculture to manage forest reserves.

1908
The Grand Canyon in Arizona was set aside as a national monument.

President Theodore Roosevelt hosted the first Governors' Conference on Conservation to inventory America's natural resources.

Chlorination was first used extensively at U.S. water treatment plants.

1911
Canada, Japan, Russia, and the United States signed a treaty to limit the annual harvest of northern fur seals.

The Weeks Act appropriated $9 million to purchase six million acres of land in the eastern United States for the purpose of establishing national forests.

1913
President Woodrow Wilson approved a plan to dam the Hetch Hetchy Valley to serve as a reservoir for the city of San Francisco.

1914
Martha, the last passenger pigeon, died in the Cincinnati Zoo and became a symbol of species extinction.

1915
Dinosaur National Monument was established in Colorado.

1916
The National Park Service and the National Park System were established to conserve scenery, wildlife and "historic objects" for future generations.

1917
President Woodrow Wilson created Alaska's Mount McKinley National Park.

1918
The Save-the-Redwoods League was created.

The hunting of migratory bird species was restricted by a treaty between the U.S. and Canada.

continued

Timeline . . . *(continued)*

1919
Congress established the Grand Canyon National Park in Arizona.

1920
The U.S. Mineral Leasing Act regulated mining on federal lands.

1922
The Izaak Walton League was established as a nonprofit research and advocacy organization.

1924
Naturalist Aldo Leopold secured the designation of Gila National Forest in New Mexico as America's first extensive wilderness area.

1928
The Boulder Canyon Project (Hoover Dam) was authorized to bring irrigation, electric power and flood control systems to the Western United States.

1930
Chlorofluorocarbons (CFCs) were hailed as safe refrigerants because of their nontoxic and non-combustible properties.

1933
The Tennessee Valley Authority was created lo develop the Tennessee River for flood control, navigation, electric power, agriculture and forestry.

1935
Aldo Leopold, Robert Marshall, Benton MacKaye, Robert Sterling Yard and others joined to form the Wilderness Society.

1947
Everglades National Park was established in Florida.

Effigy Mounds National Monument was established in Iowa.

1956
Congress passed the Colorado River Storage Project Bill halting dam construction within any national park or monument.

1961
Investigators in the U.S. Adirondacks confirmed that acid rain was killing some animal species living in and around the lakes.

1962
Silent Spring by Rachel Carson exposed the dangers of pesticides.

The Padre Island National Seashore was established in Texas.

continued

Timeline . . . *(continued)*

1963
Congress passed the first Clean Air Act.

1964
Congress passed the Wilderness Act, setting up the National Wilderness Preservation System.

1965
Congress passed the Solid Waste Disposal Act, the first major solid waste legislation.

1966
Congress passed the Rare and Endangered Species Act.

1967
Scientists predicted that increased amounts of carbon dioxide in the atmosphere would lead to global warming.

The bald eagle, California condor, whooping crane, gray wolf, and grizzly bear were placed on the Endangered Species List.

Congress passed the Air Quality Act.

1968
Congress passed the Wild and Scenic Rivers Act, identifying areas of scenic beauty for preservation and recreation.

President Lyndon Johnson signed the Central Arizona Project into law, protecting the Colorado River from damming.

North Cascades National Park was established in Washington State.

Redwoods National Park was established in California.

1970
An estimated 20 million people participated in the first Earth Day demonstrations and activities across the country.

The National Environmental Policy Act was signed into law, which required an analysis of the environmental impacts of federal actions.

The U.S. Environmental Protection Agency began operations.

American and peregrine falcons were placed on the Endangered Species List.

"Sky Spies to Watch Pollution," *Martinsville Bulletin* **(Virginia), March 3, 1970:**

Air and water pollution can be monitored effectively and traced to the source by survey satellites being developed by the United States, researchers reported today.

Two teams of researchers who are testing camera and sensor systems for the satellites, the first of which will be launched in March 1972, made their report to an Earth Conference. . . .

The application with the broadest current user interest is detecting elements of water pollution, tracing them to their source, and measuring the dispersion and concentration of the pollutants.

To illustrate, the MIT-NASA team showed a picture of Massachusetts Bay, near Salem, and identified a plume-like image as the flow from a combined sanitary and storm sewer and a smaller plume as a surface slick created by a power plant coolant.

"Pollution Clean-up of Nation Will Take Time, Experts Warn," by Alton Blakeslee,
Martinsville Bulletin, **March 19, 1970:**

The galloping popular campaign to clean up the nation's polluted environment won't witness some magical quick fix.

And that is worrying some experts in pollution control.

They are concerned that enthusiasm will fade when the drive to clean up air, water and land runs into inevitable practical realities, even if given all the goodwill in the world to do the job.

Disappointment and fading interest could deflate the pressures to do what is really required—a continuing commitment and motivation to raise the money, to pass and enforce the laws, to develop technology and to do all the work first to halt and then correct manmade insults to the environment. And then to keep improving antipollution controls as population expands.

As one reality, take a river basin which is being polluted by raw sewage from a number of towns.

By popular demand, even law, all towns are asked to halt their pollution, right now. People along other rivers make similar demands.

But would there be enough engineers to make the essential surveys, then to plan and design the sewage treatment plants, or would there be enough skilled construction firms—given contracts for the lowest bid—to build all the plants for all the towns and cities at the same time?

The point is raised by Reinholt W. Thieme, a deputy assistant secretary of the Interior, not in terms of suggesting any slowdown, but merely to point out that some cities might have to wait their turn to complete the clean-up of the entire river.

Seventy percent of the solid particles contaminating urban air have not been identified, and even if we had limitless resources we could not formulate really effective control programs because we know so little about the origin, nature and effects of most air pollutants.

—Dr. Rene Dubos of Rockefeller University

"Conservationists Disappointed," *Martinsville Bulletin*, April 2, 1970:

Conservationists have expressed disappointment at President Nixon's failure to appoint a clearly qualified environmentalist as undersecretary of the Interior.

But they withheld judgment on Nixon's choice of multimillionaire Fred J. Russell, an unknown in the field of environment and resources, to succeed the highly respected Russell E. Train, the No. 2 job at Interior.

In a sense, some prominent conservation spokesmen said, the calm greeting of Russell amounts to a vote of confidence in Interior Secretary Hickel.

"Leaded Gasoline Fights Critics as Anti-Pollution Drive Grows," *Martinsville Bulletin*, March 17, 1970:

The automobile industry is urging the petroleum industry to get the lead out—literally—to help clean up the nation's air. The lead is tetraethyl lead, which has been used in gasoline since its anti-knock qualities were discovered by Thomas Midgley, Jr. in 1921.

The petroleum people say they will be happy to supply unleaded gasoline any time Detroit mass-produces engines that can use it. The automakers say they will start building the engines as soon as the oil men give them the specifications of the fuel.

Now a third interested party has gotten into the act.

J. L. Kimberley, executive vice president of the Lead Industries Association, claims that no studies have shown any health hazard to the public from the lead in gasoline. Not only that, we don't know what health hazards might result from widespread use of unleaded gasoline, he says.

1975: Jamaican Immigrant and Caregiver

Andrea Spencer emigrated from Jamaica to New York where, after seven years and several jobs, she found an ideal position caring for two elderly sisters.

Life at Home

- Jamaica, the land of sunshine and laughter, had been hard on Andrea Spencer, even as a child.
- "All my years I been working, since I was 13."
- Seven years earlier, at age 38, she was ready for a change in a place called New York City.
- Her goal was not to leave Jamaica for America; rather, it was to exchange Jamaica for New York City where most Jamaican immigrants had settled.
- Friends who had worked there came back and said the same thing: "Twasn't bad; but 'twasn't good'; I knew it had to be better than Jamaica."
- While Andrea was still a small child, her mother died; her father left her in the care of her grandmother and disappeared.
- At 13 she left school to work as a domestic servant in a boarding school for boys.
- Her job was to clean up and feed the younger boys, some of whom were very young.
- She made $0.30 a week plus free room and board.
- Once a year she rode a bus for four hours each way to visit her grandmother in the country—"Once a year was all I could go."
- Her next job was decidedly a step up, working for "a nice, white woman" in Kingston, Jamaica.
- Next, she took a job at a wholesale dealer, where she cleaned the lobby and the shelves.
- "All my life I work for white folks and never had any trouble."
- By the time Andrea made the decision to leave, she had three children, two of whom were on their own; the youngest was left with an aunt.
- Andrea was determined to come alone: "No man come with me. I like being alone, choosing my own friends. Doing what I want. I'll never marry nobody again."
- Her ticket out was a scheme that involved New York housewives, Jamaican lawyers and women like herself.

Andrea Spencer left Jamaica for New York City when she was 38-years-old.

- The 1965 U.S. Immigration law included a work certificate provision that permitted individuals to enter the United States to take jobs that could not be filled from the resident workforce.
- The employer in each case had to provide evidence that he had unsuccessfully tried to find suitable workers from inside the country.
- Often employers did not try very hard, but most ran an advertisement in the local newspaper.
- Andrea paid 100 Jamaican dollars to a lawyer in Kingston; in exchange she received the work certification permit, a plane ticket, and placement as a live-in servant with a family in New York.
- She agreed to work one year at $55 per week plus room and board; the remainder of what she

would have earned went to the officials who financed her trip and processed her papers.
- The agreement ended after 12 months, after which time she could negotiate her own working and living arrangements.
- The employment plan was similar to the managed service system used in the colonial era to bring employees to the Americas.
- The twentieth-century version was modified to bring a large number of domestic servants to wealthy U.S. homes in search of a maid or a cook.
- Jamaicans were particularly suited to this form of immigration; as native English speakers, they were attractive for families seeking domestic help.
- In 1968, the year Andrea emigrated, 17,000 Jamaicans entered the United States, 13,000 of whom were female; one in three of the women was a "private household worker." life at Work
- After seven years in New York, Andrea Spencer finally found the ideal job caring for two elderly sisters.
- The two women, both in their seventies, lived in a nice, overly decorated home, paid her well and, most important of all, treated her with respect.
- Her life in America had not begun that way.
- Andrea's first assignment upon arrival in America was caring for an upwardly mobile couple and their four children, who were accustomed to having their own way.

- The couple, who loved parties, dressing up and being seen, went out four to five times a week, leaving the children with babysitters or nannies.
- On the day Andrea arrived, the children were bold enough to lay bets in her presence on how long she would survive before quitting.
- Previously, the longest tenure of a nanny was 16 months; the shortest was 10 days.
- The two younger girls bet that Andrea would make it three to four months; the boys were determined to break their own record and see her gone in under 10 days.

Top and above: Andrea's birthplace, Jamaica.

- Quickly, it became clear they had overestimated the sweetness of her Jamaican accent and underestimated the strength of her Jamaican upbringing.
- When she hit the one-year mark and was free to seek other employment, the couple offered to double her pay and guaranteed one weekend a month off.
- Flattered, she accepted the raise and immediately regretted her decision; she lasted another seven months before moving on.
- Her next job was as a live-in maid to two wonderful children and their four horrid dogs.
- Every morning she awoke with eager anticipation of the children's new day and dreading the task of taking the four dogs for their walks.
- Invariably one of the little beasts would pee in the elevator on the way down from their ninth-floor apartment.
- Then at least two of the dogs would begin yapping as they walked through the marble lobby, attracting attention and humiliation.

Andrea's determination and hard work afforded her a comfortable life in New York City.

- She tried taking the dogs out one at a time instead of as a group, but that took too much time away from the children, who were her primary responsibility.
- So she moved on and discovered that working with two elderly sisters reminded her of Jamaica, where she had spent so much time around her grandmother.
- Also, it was less painful; working with children sometimes reminded her of her own kids, whom she had not seen in years.
- The women's Manhattan apartment was very Victorian in fashion, simply jammed tight with their travel memories; at every turn were souvenirs from their many trips abroad with their husbands when they were still alive.
- Every day was an education for an impoverished girl from Jamaica.
- In addition, the two women planned their day around the civilized habit of holding high tea most afternoons at 4 o'clock.
- This quaint habit also reminded her of Jamaica and the classic culture of the former British possession, where residents liked to believe that Bach lived in every Episcopal hymn and Shakespeare was still a living force.
- Another plus was the sisters' preference that she not live in-marking the first time since she'd come to America that she had her own place.
- Andrea proudly picked Bedford-Stuyvesant, which seemed to have attracted enough West Indians to be an inland Caribbean island all by itself.

Bedford-Stuyvesant was home to a vast influx of West Indian immigrants, including Jamaicans.

Women's roles evolved into less traditional paths.

- She arrived at 7 each morning, woke the sisters, prepared a light breakfast, and settled in for the first political argument of the day.
- The older sister, Marlene, had once danced with Vice President Richard Nixon at the inaugural ball in 1957, believed that Watergate was "a big nothing," and that he was being hounded for political purposes.
- The younger sister, by two years and 11 months, was once married to a Cabinet undersecretary in the Kennedy Administration and vehemently believed that Nixon was only getting his "just desserts."
- From there the arguments would move to the cause of inflation, the impact of the Vietnam War and the role of women in tomorrow's America.
- Marlene was particularly proud of her granddaughters, who were focused on careers in law and medicine "if the men don't block their way."
- The younger one, Jill, would then talk about her grandchildren and how arts and motherhood were still a good combination in the twenty-first century.
- "In my day, home cooking is what kept the boys coming back," she would say and then laugh.
- Once a month the sisters hosted the Thursday Bridge Club, an event that included drinks, dinner, cigarette smoking, exuberant conversation, and cards.
- Andrea relished the exacting preparation, the elaborate meals and the carefree conversation.
- "Truly Americans have created Heaven on Earth and given it to themselves," she often thought.
- Life in Manhattan was quite a contrast to Bedford-Stuyvesant, where the music pulsed from every building, the food smells leapt from every kitchen and she thought of herself as a Jamaican.
- On any given Sunday afternoon, Jamaican teenage boys would be competing with the kids from Barbados on who could produce the best music.
- All the time the goal was to impress the girls.
- "In my day," Andrea thought to herself, "the goal was the same—to impress the girls—only I was too young to know and now I'm too old to care."

Life in the Community: New York City

- Andrea Spencer loved her apartment in the nation's second most populous black community, the Bedford-Stuyvesant section of New York City.
- Bedford-Stuyvesant was also home to the nation's largest concentration of voluntary black West Indian immigrants, a designation that included Jamaicans.

- For more than 35 years, Caribbean immigrants from Trinidad, Jamaica, Barbados, Granada, St. Vincent, and Montserrat had been congregating in Bedford-Stuyvesant's 653 square blocks.
- And for most of this time the cultural differences between West Indians and African Americans had been lost on outside observers.
- Inside Bedford-Stuyvesant, geographic distinctions and cultural habits were clearly defined and strictly noted, cultivated and respected.
- Four of the six elected officials from Bedford-Stuyvesant were West Indian, including Representative Shirley Chisholm.
- In the arts, every West Indian was openly proud of the national success of West Indian stars Harry Belafonte and Sidney Poitier.
- A quarter million Jamaicans inhabited New York City.
- Bedford-Stuyvesant was also the place to see the split between American blacks and West Indians.

A quarter million Jamaicans lived in New York City.

- West Indians were said to work harder and succeed more than American blacks, who resented the comparisons.
- Mostly, the two groups stayed away from each other; mixing only brought trouble.

Historical Snapshot
1975

- A national opinion survey in the aftermath of Watergate indicated that 69 percent of the population believed that "over the last 10 years this country's leaders have consistently lied to the people"

- Former CIA Director Richard Helms divulged that the CIA had sponsored foreign assassinations, including a plan to kill Premier Fidel Castro of Cuba

- The Atomic Energy Commission was dissolved

- A whooping crane born in captivity, a hotel for dogs, the individual's right to buy gold again, an electronic watch and the awarding of the Pulitzer Prize for cartoon *Doonesbury* all made their first appearance

- To counter record low automobile sales, Chrysler introduced the concept of rebates

- Movie premieres included *One Flew Over the Cuckoo's Nest, Dog Day Afternoon, Jaws, Nashville, Monty Python* and the *Holy Grail*, and *Three Days of the Condor*

- The Brewers Society reported that Americans consumed an average of 151 pints of beer per year

- The Rolling Stones concert tour grossed $13 million

- In an effort to popularize soccer in America, the New York Cosmos soccer team signed Brazilian star Pelé to a $1 million contract

- The Khmer Rouge in Cambodia began evacuating people from its cities, which led to the intentional killing of millions

- Author Maribel Morgan declared, "A total woman caters to her man's special quirks, whether it be in salads, sex, or sports."

According to reports, Americans consumed an annual average of 151 pints of beer.

- Television premieres included *Baretta, The Jeffersons, Barney Miller, Starsky and Hutch, One Day at a Time* and *Welcome Back, Kotter*

- The Heimlich maneuver, designed to assist people who choke on food, gained government approval

- Atari of Japan introduced the first low-priced integrated circuit for TV games

- *Humboldt's Gift* by Saul Bellow won the Pulitzer Prize for fiction, while *Why Survive? Being Old in America* by Robert N. Butler won for nonfiction

- Artist Willem de Kooning completed *Whose Name Was Writ in Water*

- The so-called typical nuclear family with a working father, housewife and two children represented only 7 percent of the total American population

- Rape laws were changed in nine states, narrowing the level of collaborative evidence necessary for conviction and restricting trial questions regarding the victim's past sex life

- Bantam books paid a record $1.8 million for the paperback rights to E. L. Doctorow's *Ragtime*

- Professional golfer Jack Nicklaus won the Masters and PGA to capture his fifteenth and sixteenth major tournaments

Selected Prices

Bathroom Scale $17.99
Food Processor $39.99
Hair Dryer $3.88
Home, Six Rooms, Flushing, NY $48,500
Ice Bucket $80.00
Maternity Top $8.00
Radio, AM $6.99
Stereo Cassette System $400.00
Watch, Woman's Movado $925.00
Woman's Jumpsuit $32.00

Jamaican Immigration Timeline

1619
Twenty indentured workers from the Caribbean islands arrived in Jamestown, Virginia, where they worked as free persons.

1850s
Large numbers of Jamaicans were recruited by American and European companies to harvest sugar in Panama and Costa Rica.

1869
Jamaican workers were imported as "swallow migrants" to harvest crops in the American South after the end of slavery; most returned home when the harvest was complete.

1881-1914
A total of 90,000 Jamaicans were recruited by the United States to work on the Panama Canal.

1930
The Census Bureau reported that 100,000 documented first-generation Caribbean immigrants and their children lived in the United States.

1965
Britain restricted the number of immigrants accepted from the newly independent black majority colonies, including Jamaica.

The Immigration Reform Act opened the way for a new surge of immigrants from the Caribbean.

1966-1970
The United States legally admitted 62,700 Jamaicans.

1971-1975
The United States legally admitted 80,600 Jamaicans.

When the West Indians came here they were aware of discrimination, but they were not conditioned to accept it without making a try.

—Dr. Elliot Skinner, Trinidad-born anthropologist,
Columbia University, 1970

What this shows is that the American Southern black did not receive the incentive and certainly not the education, in most cases, to motivate him to compete. It's not that anyone is superior; we're all black, we're all the descendents of slaves. The point is that because I was born in Halfway Tree Parish in Kingston, Jamaica, I was far better equipped to cope with the American system than, say, the woman across the hall who was born in Due West, South Carolina.

—Madge Josephs, Jamaican-born city social worker, 1970

"Dialing Butterfield Hate," *Time*, February 10, 1975:

When he revealed the existence of Richard Nixon's tapes, Alexander Butterfield doomed the president. A former White House aide, Butterfield was only truthfully replying to the questions of the Senate investigators, but he incurred the enduring hatred of Nixon loyalists, who thought that he should have covered up for his old boss.

Nearly two years later, Butterfield is still being hunted down by hard-core Nixonians. Now head of the Federal Aviation Administration, which is under attack for neglecting safety standards, he has been hampered by the undercutting and sandbagging Nixon allies at the Department of Transportation, the parent body of the FAA. What is more, Butterfield has been getting midnight phone calls from old associates who berated him for coming clean about the White House tapes. One call came from Rose Mary Woods, the former president's longtime secretary, who angrily assailed Butterfield as a "son of a bitch" and charged: "You've destroyed the greatest leader this country has ever had."

But outside Washington, Butterfield has found his forthright revelation of the tapes has created quite a different reaction. On trips, Butterfield is constantly sought out by people who want to congratulate him for his honesty and candor. In Los Angeles, one woman asked him if he would shake her son's hand. "His father was killed in Vietnam," she said. "You're the kind of man he would want his son to grow up to be."

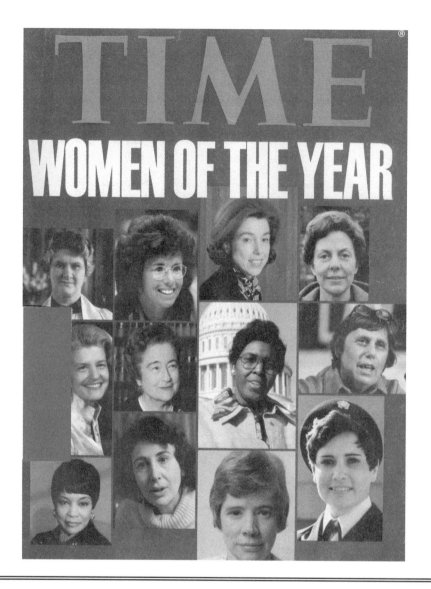

"Women of the Year, Great Changes, New Chances, Tough Choices,"
***Time*, January 5, 1976:**

They have arrived like a new immigrant wave in male America. They may be cops, judges, military officers, telephone linemen, cab drivers, pipe fitters, editors, business executives or mothers and housewives, but not quite the same subordinate creatures they were before. Across the broad range of American life, from suburban tract houses to state legislatures, from church pulpits to army barracks, women's lives are profoundly changing, and with them, the traditional relationships between the sexes. Few women are unaffected, few are thinking as they did 10 years—or even a couple of years—ago. America has not entirely repealed the Code of Hammurabi (women as male property), but enough U.S. women have so deliberately taken possession of their lives that the event is the spiritual equivalent to the discovery of a new continent. Says critic Elizabeth Janeway: "The sky above us lifts, the light pours in. No maps exist for this enlarged world. We must make them as we explore."

continued

"Women of the Year, Great Changes, New Chances, Tough Choices," . . . *(continued)*

It is difficult to locate the exact moment when the psychological change occurred. A cumulative process, it owes much to the formal feminist movement of the Friedans and Steinems and Abzugs. Yet feminism has transcended the feminist movement. In 1975 the women's drive penetrated every layer of society, matured beyond ideology to a new status of general and sometimes unconscious acceptance.

Women's changing career options.

"West Indies," *Compton Yearbook*, 1976:

The Bahamas, Barbados, Grenada, Jamaica, Trinidad, and 40 other countries signed a five-year agreement with the European Economic Community in 1975. The pact called for economic aid for the less developed countries and for preferential treatment for their exports. The government of Guyana nationalized the U.S.-based Reynolds Metals Co. during the year, paying the firm $14.5 million as compensation. Guyana was a sponsor of a United Nations resolution to bar arms to South Africa, vetoed by the U.S., Great Britain, and France. Gulf Oil Corp. signed a consent decree charging the company with using the now defunct Bahamas Exploration Company to channel secret contributions to U.S. politicians.

Puerto Rico suffered from the U.S. recession in 1975 and made large cuts in its budget. It was revealed that the Federal Bureau of Investigation had in the past harassed Puerto Rican independence groups.

"Families," *Compton Yearbook*, 1976:

In 1975 the U.S. Census Bureau reported that U.S. family size has decreased to a record low in 1974 of 2.97 persons. The decrease was not an isolated event but was part of a long-term trend.

The declining birthrate was only one factor in the decrease in family size. Patterns of family living were changed; for example, fewer young people stayed home with their parents after leaving school, although many later returned for economic reasons. Also, older people tended to live alone rather than join in their children's families.

The U.S. divorce rate continued to rise, while the marriage rate, which was then rising, decreased for the first time in 16 years. About 2.2 million marriage ceremonies were performed in 1974, a decrease of 2.4 percent from 1973.

Some observers noted a trend still small but steadily increasing toward households headed by fathers only. This resulted partly from the fact that child custody was being awarded to fathers in an increasing number of divorce cases, and also from an increase in single-parent adoptions by males.

"Havana Jamboree," *Time,* January 5, 1976:

Not since the revolution of 1958 has Havana sparkled so elegantly. For two months, volunteer workers have hauled away debris, cleaned vacant lots to build parks and playgrounds, and given 38,100 houses the first coat of paint since Fidel Castro came to power. Cuban flags and bunting decorated the streets of the capital; there were even ranks of shiny new Ford Falcons, imported from Argentina, waiting at the José Marti Airport to chauffeur delegates from 87 countries to their hotels. The foreign visitors included Soviet Party ideologue Mikhail Suslov, North Viet Nam's General Vo Nguyen Giap and others who were joining 3,136 Cuban delegates for a spectacular six-day jamboree in suburban Havana's Karl Marx theater. The occasion: the first Congress of Cuba's Communist Party.

The purpose of the Congress, which ended early last week, was to "institutionalize a revolutionary process," as Castro put it in his closing address. The intention was to put the party's legal approval on the present political structure and thus ensure that whatever happens to Castro or his top lieutenants, Cuba's peculiar style of communism will survive unchanged. "Men are very fragile," said Castro, who abandoned his customary battle fatigues and appeared in a newly tailored uniform. "We disappear and go up in smoke for almost any reason."

Cuba's Fidel Castro.

1983: Music Promoter and Innovator

The decades-long musical career of George Clinton, known as the Prince of Funk, started by playing doo-wop and ended by transforming popular black dance music with locomotive poly-rhythms and screaming guitars.

Life at Home

- Although George Clinton started his musical career playing doo-wop, his legacy was the transformation of black popular dance music using locomotive poly-rhythms, screaming guitars, R&B vocal harmonies and the down-home soul sounds of James Brown.
- Born July 22, 1941, in Kannapolis, North Carolina, George grew up in Plainfield, New Jersey, where his band the Parliaments first appeared on the music scene with its recording of "Sunday Kind of Love" in 1956.
- When the song was released, George was still attending junior high school and running a neighborhood barbershop where he cut and straightened hair.
- Two years later the band recorded and released "Poor Willie" and continued to play in the area, with its most regular gig coming from The Silk Palace, a barbershop, where they shared the spotlight with the Monotones and the Fiestas.
- Known in later years for his outlandish costumes and multicolored dreadlocks, George believed it was crooner Frankie Lymon and the Teenagers who originally inspired him to become a singer when, "Frankie Lymon's was the devil's music," he said.

George Clinton transformed black dance music with poly-rhythms and screaming guitars.

- "Even 'bop-bap-ba-do-la-ba-bop-bam-boom' was considered to be bad. Then when the '60s came around, with Jimi Hendrix playing a loud guitar with all this feedback, then that was the devil's music. Now we got rappers, and they're the devil's music. So I never played what you could call safe music."
- "If you listen close you can hear Motown in what I do, and doo-wop evolved into Motown. Then funk became the DNA for hip-hop. Rock and roll, R&B, blues, gospel, you see them as different, but funk is the thread that goes through all of them."
- His first band may have started out as a doo-wop group, like the Temptations, who performed romantic ballads and four-part harmonies like "Goodnight, Sweetheart, It's Time to Go," but his

musical statements had moved a long way by the time he recorded the raucous "Flashlight" and "The Atomic Dog" in the 1980s.

- Or, as George said, "In the beginning there was funk."
- Lured by the success of Motown in the 1960s, George sold the barbershop and drove to Detroit so the Parliaments could camp out on the steps of the Berry Gordy's hit machine.
- Once there, George became a staff songwriter for Motown and learned the entertainment craft, including the role of clichés, puns and hooks to boost a song's appeal.

Rappers were considered the devil's musicians.

- "I just went stupid with it. Instead of one or two hooks, we'd have 10 hooks in the same song. And puns that were so stupid that you could take it three or four different ways."
- He also recorded his first major hit single, "I Wanna Testify," in 1967, that scored on both the pop and soul charts for the Parliaments.
- While in Detroit, George also worked with Golden World where he co-produced Barbara Lewis's hit, "Hello Stranger," and Darrell Banks's "Open the Door to Your Heart."
- But when American cities began to go up in flames in the summer of 1968, George was inspired to produce music as fiery as the racial riots outside his door.
- Out went the perfectly matched tuxedos; in came psychedelic-influenced pink jackets, diapers made from hotel towels, outfits created from their suit bags—anything outrageous and over the top would do. Anything: rude carvings in his hair, language designed to shock, drugs. Their music also took on a new sound.
- One night after their equipment was late in arriving, they borrowed a double stack of Marshall amps, a triple stack of SVTs—high performance bass amps—and an oversized set of fiberglass drums from the front band Vanilla Fudge.

Outrageous outfits replaced tuxedos.

- After that, super loud and utterly outrageous were also part of their zany repertoire.
- At about the same time, due to trademark issues with Revilot Records, George changed the name of the Parliaments to Funkadelic and scored a hit with the song ""A New Day Begins."
- Same band—different name.
- Then in 1970, after George reclaimed the rights to the original name, he changed the group's name once again to simply Parliament and enjoyed a minor hit with "The Breakdown" and expanded his largely black, very loyal following.
- Over time, with the constant name and lineup changes, the group became known as simply P-Funk—short for Parliament-Funkadelic— and were discussed in the same breath as Jimi Hendrix, Sly and the Family Stone, Cream, and James Brown while exploring different sounds, technology, and lyrics.

- He mixed and matched musicians and singers into several groups, including the Parlettes, Parliament, Funkadelic, and P-Funk.
- Although essentially made up of the same personnel, the groups recorded in different styles, often on different labels.
- At one point, the same group formed Parliament on Casablanca Records, with a hot horn section and complicated vocal lines, while also being Funkadelic at Warner Brothers, a straight rock band with a blazing rhythm section.
- Detroit drummer Sam Dinkins explained, "By giving them different names, even though it was the same group, he was able to take one product and make it into several, if you would, but it was the same lineup."
- During their heyday in the mid-to late 1970s, following the success of their platinum-selling album, 1975's *Mothership Connection*, George and his band Parliament-Funkadelic engaged in a series of high-profile, noexpenses-spared stadium tours around the United States, culminating in the P-Funk Earth Tour.
- At these gigs, the much-referenced Mothership was seen to land on stage amongst the band before a baying and expectant crowd.
- At this point in the show, George would emerge from the Mothership in the form of Dr. Funkenstein, the "cool ghoul with the funk transplant," in order to better administer funk to the audience.
- During the 1970s, George and Parliament-Funkadelic produced over 40 R&B hit singles—including three number ones—and three platinum albums.

Life at Work

- The early 1980s were not kind to George Clinton. George went from the musical magician to industry pariah for three years, thanks to the same legal system that had tied his hands earlier in his career.
- As the decade opened, the 39-year-old showman/producer was the writer, producer and brains behind half a dozen different bands—each with their own sound.
- Some were described as Sly Stone Meets the Temptations, while others sounded like Stevie Wonder an acid, critics drooled.
- A night's entertainment with the Prince of Funk was designed to be an adventure; on stage "we were James Brown, the Temptations and the Three Stooges on acid," George himself claimed.

Bootsy, of Funkadelic's Bootsy Rubber Band

- On stage, George performed and preached his personal gospel of psychedelic funk, sexual liberation, ghetto realism, mind-expanding drugs, along with a God-given right to have a good time. Having sold 10 million albums within five years, George was the king of funk. That's when he challenged the musical establishment and filed three separate lawsuits for breach of contract, claiming a total of $100 million in damages against Warner Brothers, the label which had signed Funkadelic's Bootsy Rubber Band and Zapp. Warner Bros. then decided not to distribute George's Park Place label. Several other record producers followed suit, and George's wild, funkadelic world became tied up in the courts. So many deals fell through in such a short time that George was quickly broke. It was costing him more than $150,000 a week to keep his 88-man entourage of musicians, singers and crew on the road.

George Clinton, center right.

- Without new hits to keep the fans coming and his royalties tied up in courts, there was no money to pay his personnel, and his debts accumulated. George added free-base cocaine to his drug diet, which already included Quaaludes, acid, marijuana and cocaine. For several years he was locked out of recording studios because of unpaid bills. No major label would deal with him. Then Capitol Records signed on to a deal and advanced George $300,000 to relaunch. Despite his legal entanglements with Warner Bros., George was given an opportunity to make music again. Jettisoning both the Parliament and Funkadelic names (but not the musicians), George signed to Capitol both as a solo act and as the P-Funk All-Stars. His first solo album, 1982's Computer Games, contained the Top 20 R&B hit "Loopzilla." Several months later, the title track from George's *Atomic Dog* hit number one on the R&B charts and stayed at the top spot for four weeks.

- The funkmeister was back in all his outrageous glory.

- And once again, when the fans demanded an encore at the end of a concert, everyone knew that Dr. Funkenstein had one requirement—a rain shower of joints as a show of appreciation.

Life in the Community: Detroit, Michigan

- Although the powerful music of Motown was indelibly linked to Detroit, the Motor City spent decades developing a distinct musical heritage.

- Even before Motown opened its doors, Detroit was already well on its way to being an R&B and soul hotbed.

- In 1955, the influential soul singer Little Willie John made his debut; then in 1956, the Detroit-based R&B label Fortune Records enjoyed success with Nolan Strong & The Diablos.

- In 1959, The Falcons, featuring Wilson Pickett and Eddie Floyd, released "You're So Fine," considered to be the first true soul record.

- Also that year, Jackie Wilson had his first hit with "Reet Petite," which was co-written by a young Berry Gordy Jr.

- The Volumes had a hit single in 1962 for Chex Records with the single "I Love You," and singer/songwriter Barbara Lewis found success with the single "Hello Stranger."

Detroit's musical heritage was R&B and soul.

- Digging back further, following the Roaring Twenties, Detroit's former "Black Bottom" area on the city's east side became nationally famous for its music; major blues singers, big bands, and jazz artists—such as Duke Ellington, Billy Eckstine, Pearl Bailey, Ella Fitzgerald, and Count Basie—regularly performed in the nightclubs of the Paradise Valley entertainment district.
- The Detroit blues scene in the 1940s and 1950s was centered around bars on Hastings Street and featured artists on the local JVB and Sensation labels such as Eddie "Guitar" Burns, John Lee Hooker, Bobo Jenkins, Boogie Woogie Red, Doctor Ross, Baby Boy Warren and Washboard Willie.
- Detroit also produced some excellent gospel singers.
- In the 1940s, Oliver Green had formed the popular gospel group The Detroiters, followed in the 1950s by Della Reese just launching her long career, while Mattie Moss Clark was pioneering three-part harmony into gospel choral music.
- In the 1960s, the Reverend C.L. Franklin found

Madonna, born and raised in Detroit, hit the music scene in the early 80s.

success with his recorded sermons on Chess Records' gospel label, and with an album of spirituals recorded at his New Bethel Baptist Church that included the debut of his young daughter, Aretha Franklin.
- In the 1980s, the Winans dynasty produced Grammy winners CeCe and BeBe Winans, as well as Bill Moss & The Celestials, and Fred Hammond.
- During the development of jazz, Detroit emerged as an important musical center, alongside New Orleans, Chicago, and St. Louis.
- Among the musicians who relocated to Detroit were drummer William McKinney, who formed the seminal big band McKinney's Cotton Pickers, with jazz great Don Redman.
- In the 1980s, pop icon Madonna—who was born and raised outside of Detroit— emerged.
- The star in Detroit's musical history was the success of Motown Records during the 1960s and early 1970s.
- Originally known as Tamla Records, Motown was founded by auto plant worker Berry Gordy and became home to some of the most popular recording acts in the world, including Marvin Gaye, the Temptations, Stevie Wonder, Diana Ross and the Supremes, Smokey Robinson and the Miracles, the Four Tops, Martha and the Vandellas, Edwin Starr, Little Willie John, the Contours, and the Spinners.
- In 1967, longtime backroom barbershop doo-wop group the Parliaments, featuring George Clinton, scored a hit with "I Wanna Testify" for Revilot Records, and marked the beginning of funk in mainstream R&B.
- In 1978, George Clinton's bass player Bootsy Collins had a top charting hit with Bootzilla.
- Then, in the late 1960s, Metro Detroit became the epicenter for high-energy rock music with the MC5 and Iggy and the Stooges, whose sound was equal parts anger, determination and attitude.
- This was followed by hardcore punk, which was louder, harder and more aggressive.

HISTORICAL SNAPSHOT
1983

- Björn Borg retired from tennis after winning five consecutive Wimbledon championships
- Lotus 1-2-3 was released for IBM-PC-compatible computers
- The U.S. Environmental Protection Agency announced its intention to buy out and evacuate the dioxin-contaminated community of Times Beach, Missouri
- The final episode of M*A*S*H set records for the most watched episode in television history
- "Menudomania" arrived in New York as 3,500 screaming girls crowded Kennedy Airport to catch a glimpse of Puerto Rican boy band Menudo, who were playing six sold-out shows at the Felt Forum
- The Rolling Stones concert film *Let's Spend the Night Together* opened in New York
- Michael Jackson's *Thriller* album tracked 37 weeks as #1 on the U.S. charts
- Compact discs, which had first been released in Japan the previous October, went on sale in the U.S.
- Ellen Taaffe Zwilich became the first woman to win the Pulitzer Prize for Music
- Michael Jackson unveiled his version of the moonwalk during a performance of "Billie Jean" on the *Motown 25 Special* aired on NBC

A tale of two Michaels: A complex genius reigned as our King of Pop

- Johnny Ramone suffered a near-fatal head injury during a fight over a woman
- The members of Kiss showed their faces without their makeup for the first time on MTV
- Quiet Riot's *Metal Health* album became the first heavy metal album to hit #1 in America
- The Space Shuttle *Challenger* carried Guion S. Bluford, the first African-American astronaut, into space
- The Global Positioning System (GPS) became available for civilian use
- The Red Hot Chili Peppers launched their first, self-titled album
- Simultaneous suicide truck-bombings destroyed both the French and the U.S. Marine Corps barracks in Beirut, killing 241 U.S. servicemen, 58 French paratroopers and six Lebanese civilians
- Immunosuppressant cyclosporine was approved by the FDA, leading to a revolution in the field of transplantation
- *Flashdance* and *Star Wars Episode VI: Return of the Jedi* were box-office hits
- McDonalds introduced the McNugget

Selected Prices

Apple Macintosh Computer	$2,500.00
Butter, per Pound	$1.99
China, 10-Piece Tea Set	$69.00
Coffee, per Pound	$2.19
Gas Grill	$179.99
House, Four-Bedroom, New York	$156,000
Lawn Mower, Craftsman	$299.99
Screwdrivers, Stanley Set of Four	$26.95
Shotgun, Winchester 12-Gauge	$1,200.00
Woman's Leather Bag	$49.00

an Apple after school

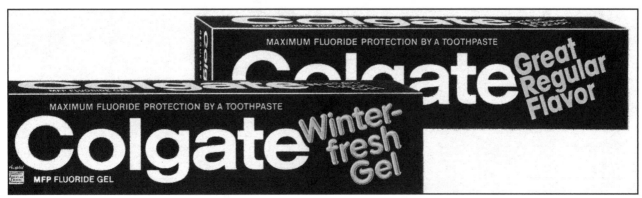

Trying to put the thang called Funk into words is like trying to write down your orgasm. Both thrive in that gap in time when words fall away, leaving nothing but sensation.

—Barry Walters, *The Village Voice*

"George Clinton Returns to the Limelight," *Lubbock Evening Journal,* (Texas), June 24, 1983:

Heads turn when George Clinton enters a room. Any room.

At the moment, the people in the lobby of the Beverly Hills Hotel are staring at him. It is a lobby designed for legendary movie stars; there is nothing funky about it. Except for George Clinton.

The 41-year-old mastermind behind Funkadelic, Parliament, Bootsy's Rubber Band, Zapp, the P-Funk All-Stars and so many other acts is wearing blue jeans, Nike running shoes, a black leather jacket and a gray sweatshirt. He is taking gulps from a bottle of Beck's and giggling. It is the giggle of a man who is stoned: stoned on life, stoned on drugs. A religious man, if you will. And right there, on the front of the sweatshirt printed in black, six-inch letters is the gospel of George Clinton: FUNK!

Here in the lobby, most people have not noticed the bottle of beer. They are too busy eyeing the hair. The two-inch wide Mohawk. The luminous purple Mohawk. And the rows of luminous purple cornrow braids. But George Clinton doesn't worry about what these people think of him. "Too many beautiful people in Los Angeles," he says. "That's why I can't stay in LA." He laughs again. "'Cause everyone comes here to be a star, and so everybody looks especially good. Too much of a good thing in LA. So I had to move."

That may be why, when he is not on the road or in the recording studio or taking care of business, Clinton leads a reclusive life with his wife Stephanie on a farm outside Detroit that has no phone. There he hunts and fishes and plays video games and reads science fiction novels and meditates and practices yoga and dreams up the strange concepts for his albums.

Clinton leaves the lobby and walks to his limo. A movie producer is getting out of a car parked directly in front of Clinton. He stares at Clinton, shakes his head, smiles.

"You laugh," someone says to the movie producer. "But at the moment, he's got a number one record."

Inside the limo, Clinton is laughing, too. He takes a sip of the Beck's and stretches out his legs. How does it feel to be back? he is asked. "I don't even know yet," he says with a grin.

Ah, but he knows. And it feels good, mighty good, to be back, to be out on the road again, playing to crowds of up to 20,000 fans, six nights a week. It feels fine to be back on the charts with a hit single, "Atomic Dog," and a hit album *Computer Games.*

1985: Haitian Immigrant and Artist

After a lifetime of dreaming and years of planning, artist Edwidge Dominique emigrated from Haiti to Florida, determined to become a successful and recognized artist.

Life at Home

- Twenty-three year-old Edwidge Dominique's anger was on the edge of bitterness.
- Since he was a small boy, Edwidge had been fascinated by the vibrant colors of Haiti's landscape and had grown adept at using paint to differentiate shadow from dimness, light from brightness.
- Color subtlety was so fascinating to Edwidge, he spent nearly a month doing six paintings of an acacia tree illuminated by different light cast at various times during the day.
- His older brothers and sisters thought the tree series was an enormous waste of time; "Pretty pictures will not feed you or get you a wife," his older sister Kaiama hissed.
- But his grandmother, the only parent he had ever known, loved his artwork and said over and over, "One day you will be famous."
- That was Edwidge's dream.
- How this fire could be quenched became clear when he met an American couple who were in Les Cayes to visit the Sisters of Charity Orphanage in the middle of the city.
- As was his habit, Edwidge was selling his latest paintings that day in the market alongside fruit vendors, woodworkers and dressmakers when the Americans stopped, admired, and then bought everything he had on display without haggling over the price.
- He trembled at the sight of US$85.00 in his hand.
- Unable as he was to understand English, only later did Edwidge learn from an old fruit dealer that the woman had said, "These will sell for five times more in America. He is very talented and should display his work in New York and Miami."
- Edwidge had never experienced such happiness; her words were burned in his soul.
- In America, he told himself, "I can be an artist who is famous and rich."
- So for the next two and a half years, Edwidge was consumed by the idea of America, particularly Miami, where his second cousin was living and doing well enough so that every month he sent money home.

Edwidge Dominique was a Haitian artist who moved to Florida.

- Everyone was in agreement that he should go, especially if he planned to send money back; even his doctor, who was trained in Cuba, said, "I think you should go."
- Since the late 1970s thousands had fled Haiti with no money, using makeshift boats and totally lacking any documentation, taking only their fervent prayer "God is good" as a sign that somehow they would be admitted to the United States.
- Most were not.
- Thousands drowned during the journey; more were caught by the Coast Guard or Immigration officials and unceremoniously sent back to Haiti.
- Some made it to America and asked for asylum or at least the same privileges offered Cubans fleeing that neighboring Caribbean island.
- Terrified that an all-volunteer army of unemployed, illiterate Haitians was about to descend on America's privileged Gold Coast, Florida's residents fought back.

Painting by Dominique.

- Cubans should have special privileges because they were fleeing Castro's communism, they said; Haitians, they remarked, were running from poverty and would only bring more crime, AIDS, drugs and additional burdens for the area schools.
- But after a series of battles in American courts, some Haitians were given the status of "Cuban/Haitian entrant," which provided an ambiguous legal position in the United States, but did allow them to stay.
- More Haitians, most of whom could not swim, transformed themselves into "boat people" in hopes of gaining entry into the U.S.; the U.S. Coast Guard was instructed to seek them out and make sure they didn't arrive.
- Those who were captured at sea were rapidly repatriated to Haiti with the cooperation of the Haitian government and the Reagan Administration.
- By 1983, Edwidge knew that unrest was rumbling throughout Haiti and that the Duvalier family might one day be dethroned.
- Now was the time to chase his dream, he decided.
- In all, he had gathered together $480, which he gave to a well-dressed man from Portau-Prince who promised that Edwidge would land safely in Miami "without even getting your feet wet."
- It was not the first lie Edwidge would be told.

Life at Work

- Edwidge Dominique's boat trip to America began in a rubberized raft loaded to overflowing with desperate people; 14 nervous men were jammed into a raft designed to hold eight.
- Upon hitting the first wave, the raft sagged into the sea and everyone was soaked within minutes.
- Edwidge was able to keep his spare clothing dry but the art supplies he had packed so carefully were ruined.

- The raft was then paddled very slowly into the inky night to a waiting trawler that had seen better days and soon was overwhelmed by the number of rafts that congregated at its side.
- The trawler, operating mostly at night, drifted toward Miami for more than two weeks; Edwidge's many questions went unanswered even when a group of men threatened the captain's life if land was not found soon.
- The final stage of the trip was by a small speedboat, with a faulty motor, that was intended to take the illegal immigrants to an isolated dock south of Miami near Homestead.
- Underpowered and overloaded, the boat accidentally dumped Edwidge into the water when they were just within sight of land.
- Edwidge swam for his life, guided only by lights at the dock.
- Exhausted by the long trip and the arduous swim, he offered no resistance to the police awaiting his arrival.
- Altogether the voyage had taken 18 days; the boat carried supplies for about 10 days and the trip ended in a detention facility, courtesy of the United States Government.
- For 11 months, Edwidge was held at the Krome Center in Miami while politicians and federal agencies considered whether he and nearly 15,000 other Haitian refugees should be allowed to stay in the country.
- His family did not know whether he had arrived or was lost at sea.
- No paints, no privacy and few lawyers who spoke Creole were available.
- Then, he was freed from detention without any explanation he could understand.
- He was given special permission to stay temporarily in America but denied all immigration papers that would allow him to work.
- Housing was provided until his case was settled.
- Edwidge felt listless and unable to paint; without the special light of Haiti his paintings grew dark, less vibrant and apparently unsellable.
- Every day he waited for the knock on the door that said he would be sent back; maybe it was a knock he would embrace, he repeatedly told himself.

Life in the Community: Haiti and Miami, Florida

- Even though Haiti was one of the poorest countries in the Western Hemisphere, Haitians had a rich culture and historical heritage.
- Haiti was the second-oldest republic in the Americas, established by slaves in a revolt against the French, grounded on the "rights of man" in 1804.
- Historians believe that the defeat of Napoleon's forces by the Haitian slave rebellion paved the way for the Louisiana Purchase, which doubled the size of America and dramatically reduced the holdings of the French on the continent.
- The French took possession of Santo Domingo, as colonial Haiti was known, at the end of the seventeenth century.
- By the middle of the eighteenth century, when 400,000 imported African slaves worked at the sugar cane, coffee, cotton and indigo plantations, Haiti was the most profitable colony in the world, far more valuable to the French than 13 North American colonies were to the British.
- But little of that wealth remained after the land was divided into subsistence farms and Western powers, including the United States, established punitive policies against the only country in the Americas to be established through a slave revolt.
- Situated between Spanish-speaking Cuba and the Dominican Republic, mountainous Haiti retained its distinct linguistic and cultural identity; French Creole and French remained the major languages.
- Haiti was at once the most densely populated and the most rural nation in the Caribbean region; peasant agriculture dominated the economy.

- Even in the southern seaport city of Les Cayes, with a population of 36,000, the electricity was unreliable, sometimes only working four hours a day.
- At night the entire city was dark except for a few dozen homes and businesses outfitted with solar power collectors.
- Locally made charcoal was used for heating, and clean water was a luxury; hundreds of children died yearly from waterborne diseases.
- To escape the poverty of Haiti, a growing body of Haitians, including the country's educated elite, gravitated to Miami and created the nucleus of a community that needed Creole-speaking teachers, professionals and entrepreneurs.
- Officially, 50,000 Haitians were said to live in the Miami area; Haitian community leaders put the figure closer to 75,000.
- Educated Haitians found in Miami an agreeable climate and a sense of community that had been denied them in exile elsewhere.
- Haitians who grew up in other parts of the U.S. were often ashamed of their nationality; Miami changed that, especially for professionals.
- However, the people who came by boat encountered a stream of legal and social problems in the United States, principally, the inability to gain asylum as political refugees.
- Twenty-five thousand Haitians in south Florida faced proceedings that could lead to their departure from the United States.
- The Haitian boat people were catapulted into the national spotlight in 1980 when some 15,000 began arriving in south Florida on the heels of the larger Cuban refugee boatlift.
- The United States 1980 Census found 90,000 people who said one or both parents were of Haitian ancestry, and the Immigration and Naturalization Service estimated that there were probably an equal number of Haitians in America illegally.
- A survey published by the Behavioral Science Research Institute of Coral Gables estimated that 22,800 Haitians resided in the Edison-Little River community, which included Little Haiti.
- The survey concluded that half were unemployed, half could not converse in English and two-thirds had a household income of less than $150 a week.
- Despite the high unemployment rate among Haitians, four times that of the U.S., the study noted that there was no greater dependency upon public agencies for assistance among Haitians than other groups.
- The report said this reflected the strong desire among many Haitians to be self-sufficient rather than depend on agencies for help.
- But the Haitian community had found few ways to confront the public reaction to the discovery that some victims of AIDS were Haitian.
- Of the 1,641 AIDS cases reported in the United States, 5 percent were Haitian, yet AIDS was being identified as a disease associated with homosexuals, drug users and Haitians.

HISTORICAL SNAPSHOT
1985

- A highly addictive, inexpensive cocaine derivative known as crack began appearing in America
- The Live Aid concert in Philadelphia and London was viewed by 1.6 billion people worldwide on television and grossed $70 million for famine-starved Africa
- A Nielsen study on television watching reported that young children spent more than 27 hours a week in front of the TV
- After Coca-Cola introduced a new formula known as New Coke, public reaction forced it to reintroduce the Coca-Cola Classic
- In professional baseball, Pete Rose broke Ty Cobb's record with his 4,192nd hit
- Milk cartons with photos of missing children, the Ford Taurus, a female Harlem Globetrotter, Wrestlemania and the Rock and Roll Hall of Fame all made their first appearance
- The Nobel Peace Prize went to the International Physicians for the Prevention of Nuclear War founded by two cardiologists
- The discovery of a 4.4 million-year-old anthropoid jawbone in Burma created speculation that our human ancestors may have originated in Asia and migrated to Africa
- Television premieres included *The Golden Girls, Spencer for Hire,* and *The Oprah Winfrey Show*
- Studies indicated an estimated 27 million American adults were functionally illiterate
- ABC was acquired by Capital Cities Communications for $3.43 billion
- American spy John Walker was turned in by his wife and daughter
- General Westmoreland dropped his $120 million libel suit against CBS for its documentary alleging that he deceived the public during the Vietnam War
- Movie premieres included *Out of Africa, The Color Purple, Kiss of the Spider Woman, Back to the Future, Rambo,* and *The Breakfast Club*
- Worldwide, more than 2,000 people died in plane crashes, marking it the worst year in civil air travel
- *ARTnews* magazine pressured the Austrian government to return 3,900 works seized by the Nazis during World War II
- Top albums of the year included *Born in the U.S.A.* by Bruce Springsteen, *Like a Virgin* by Madonna, *Private Dancer* by Tina Turner and *No Jacket Required* by Phil Collins
- *Lonesome Dove* by Larry McMurtry won the Pulitzer Prize for fiction; *The Flying Change* by Henry Taylor captured the prize for poetry

Selected Prices

Bicycle, Aero Urban Cowboy	$600.00
Briefcase, Leather	$565.00
Camcorder	$994.00
Coca-Cola, Two-Liter	$1.00
Doll, Playskool	$24.97
Ice Cream, Dove Bar	$1.45
Martini for Two	$1.08
Modem	$119.95
Synthesizer, Yamaha	$188.88
Walkman, Sony	$19.95

"Employing Micro-credit in the Community of Les Cayes, Haiti," by the Rev. Kenol Rock, Episcopal priest:

The first time that I had the intention to start the micro-credit was when I went to worship in one of the congregations located in the countryside named Savanette.

I met some women who told me: "Fr. Rock, how can you find some money to borrow so we may open even a small business to survive? We are helpless." I said, "Well, I can find some money to loan you and we can create an activity named micro-credit; however, the first thing that we are going to do is to gather together and learn the rules that you need to follow."

I taught them the rules which were based on honesty and trusting. Also in this gathering I motivated them that the more they managed well the loan received, the more they will have opportunity to change their life of dependency into a life of interdependency in the family. It was our first start; since then, the life of the women has been rewarded. The following ideas will give not only the impacts but also the manner to use the micro-credit for the benefit of the poorest.

After training based on honesty and trusting, I found some money from the generous partners in the USA, particularly in Kansas City. I did the distribution of the credit according to what each person listed. I realized that the best way to decrease the

Rev. Kenol Rock.

level of poverty was by extending this activity of economic development from below. Since the micro-credit has been started in the community of Les Cayes, remarkable progress has been made. With a small step, we can make a big step; also with the micro-credit we can make a positive difference by ameliorating gradually the poverty in the world.

The micro-credit can bring a new paradigm in the family where the wife becomes a real partner for the husband, rather than an object. For instance, since the program began, the women retrieve a certain dignity by having the opportunity to not depend totally on the husband in the house. They can even make decisions as needed, as well the men. There is, now between woman and man, a real partnership based upon mutual respect, which is a good model for the children in the house. Therefore, micro-credit is a key tool of transformation of the community of the poor into a community of justice and equity.

The women are more successful in the micro-loan activities than men, according to the experiences that I had during my period in the south part of Haiti. In the five congregations of the missions of Les Cayes, which had the opportunity to participate in such activity, there were 60 women and 40 men who were enrolled; 80 percent of the women have made success and only 15 percent of men have made success.

As a result, in the poor community the women manage money much better than men. With simple sewing they can make clothing, or they can buy a bag of rice to resell it and make a quick profit. So, there are tremendous activities that the women can make even a tiny profit in the community. We reward the women who are the best workers of the year in the micro-credit, and also we augment the rate of the loan. This is a strategy that we use to encourage them to move forward, and this is the best reason we have been successful.

1993: University Student and Music Promoter

Anwar X. Holliday promoted popular New York City rap and hip-hop music to his fellow students at Howard University by organizing concerts on campus and encouraging students, especially New Yorkers, to attend.

Life at Home

- Anwar X. Holliday was born on a Monday in Queens, New York, October 16, 1971.
- His father John 23X Holliday immediately associated his son's Monday birth with the lead character in the 1970s blaxploitation film *Black Caesar*.
- *Black Caesar* starred ex-NFL player Fred "The Hammer" Williamson, who portrayed "Bumpy" Johnson's rise to the top of the Harlem numbers rackets.
- The theme song by soul singer James Brown began with the famous line "I was born in New York City on a Monday," hence, the connection between Anwar and his father's favorite song and favorite movie.
- She and several cousins had made the natural transition from church choir to performing covers of songs by popular girl groups of the 1960s, like the Supremes and Martha and the Vandellas at block parties and recreational halls around Queens.
- In 1969, Juanita and John Holliday met, and later that year the couple settled into a walk-up duplex in the Hollis section of Queens.
- When Anwar's grandparents migrated from the South in the 1950s, Queens was a magnet for blacks seeking upward mobility.
- Harlem had been the original black Mecca during the great South and North migration in the early part of the twentieth century.
- Due to deterioration and overcrowded conditions in Harlem, the focus shifted to Brooklyn during the 1930s and 1940s.
- By the 1950s, Queens had become home to jazz legends like Count Basie, Louis Armstrong, Ella Fitzgerald, and Dizzy Gillespie.
- By the 1960s, the tremendous influx of blacks and Latinos from the other boroughs triggered "white flight" from Queens to the more suburban Nassau and Suffolk County on Long Island.
- During the fall of 1978, eight-year-old Anwar started third grade at St. Pascal-Baylon Elementary School, a Catholic school that required its students to wear a blue and yellow uniform every day.

Anwar Holliday began promoting rap and hip-hop while still a student at Howard University.

- While raising Anwar within the Five Percent Nation at home, his parents felt that a Catholic school would provide their son with a better education than the public school system.
- Anwar quickly learned to avoid the older bullies who waited outside the school each day to rob the younger kids of their possessions.
- At the same time, the hip hop culture was forming in New York City as block parties became increasingly numerous, especially when they incorporated DJs who played popular genres of music, especially funk and soul music.
- Soon DJs began isolating the percussion breaks of popular songs, a technique then common in Jamaican dub music, and developed turntable techniques, such as scratching, beat mixing/matching, and beat juggling that created a base that could be rapped over.

- Rapping was a vocal style in which the artist speaks lyrically, in rhyme and verse, generally to an instrumental or synthesized beat, which is almost always in 4/4 time.
- Anwar's father believed hip hop had emerged as a direct response to the watered-down, Europeanized disco music that permeated the airwaves.
- The first hip hop recording Anwar heard was The Sugarhill Gang's "Rapper's Delight," initially at home and then throughout the neighborhood.
- Hollis was a working middle-class neighborhood south of the Grand Central Parkway and east of 184th Street.
- Anwar grew into his teens in a neighborhood filled with private homes and busy main streets with stores and movie theaters.
- By the mid-1980s, a trend developed among black youngsters nationwide in which academic achievement lost its importance and was replaced by "street credibility," represented by various forms of thuggery in the pursuit of a cool image.
- Despite being from solid homes where good grades were expected, Anwar and his crew of friends shared many of the same ideas as their peers and allowed their grades to slip in solidarity.
- When the crew played basketball at 205th Street Park, they couldn't help noticing the drug dealers and other hustlers with their Mercedes and BMW cars, gold watch chains, and Movado watches.
- They also surrounded themselves with rap music.
- Anwar's infatuation with street life came to an abrupt end when his best friend's grandfather was abducted and shot in an attempted robbery and drug extortion scheme.
- In 1989, Anwar graduated from Harlem Brothers Rice Catholic High School with plans to attend Howard University in Washington, DC.

Life at Work
- The fall of 1989 found Anwar X. Holliday as a member of the freshman class at Howard University in Washington, DC.
- Howard was founded in 1867 to educate freed slaves and their descendents. Anwar was joined at Howard by his cousin Malik, who, like Anwar, had chosen radio and television media studies as a major.
- Like most college students, Anwar and his cousin were plagued by cash flow shortages and were constantly brainstorming for a solution to this problem.
- They decided to be entrepreneurs, moving from project to project.

- Along with his brother Raymond, Malik's father had ridden the popularity wave of vinyl siding and window installation to achieve middle-class stability.
- So the two enterprising young men secured a $500 loan from their fathers to purchase the Supreme Bean Pies and Cookies concern from the Nation of Islam Bakery in Newark.
- They also arranged to distribute *The Final Call* newspaper, published by the Nation of Islam on campus.
- After that, the two young men roamed the campus selling pies, cookies and newspapers—it was a great education in business, human psychology and accounting.
- Not only did the venture provide snacks and much-needed income, but it gave the pair a high level of exposure and visibility.
- Then, when Anwar repaid the loan on time-with interest- he elicited a look of respect from his father that he had been seeking his entire life.
- Being a New Yorker, Anwar noted that the Howard student body included a substantial percentage of New Yorkers who missed the rap and hip hop performances so common in the city's parks and squares.
- So Anwar decided on his summer break that he would get into the promotion of music on campus.
- In the fall, when the pair returned to Howard with the summer money they had earned working with their fathers, they began to stage special events on campus, especially parties at the fraternity houses.
- With his Five Percent connections, Anwar was able to bring the highly popular Big Daddy Kane to Howard for his football homecoming party.
- From that point on, their parties and events became the most popular on campus; Anwar quickly learned to balance the risks associated with an event, such as a concert, with the financial rewards it might bring.
- After two years of working in special events, Anwar knew he wanted a career in music.
- In 1991, he got his start as an assistant to Dante Ross, who was an artists and repertoire (A&R) man for a group called Brand Nubian, a Five Percent group that came to prominence in the 1980s.
- The Five Percent belief that white men were devils while black men were gods echoed loudly in hip hop lyrics.
- A white man, Dante Ross, seemed highly unlikely to sponsor and support groups that espoused such beliefs.
- However, Ross was a professional, and Anwar took note of his dedication to the groups under his care.
- More than just talent scouts, A&Rs were responsible for shaping the artists' sound, finding material to record, and generally nurturing an artist's career.

- They also attempted to predict musical trends, discover new artists, and then mold them into the image that maximized their talent.
- At smaller labels, the job might consist of seeking out new talent the hard way: going to shows, scouring the Internet, sifting through endless demos, and then bringing the artists to the label, signing them, and bringing an album to fruition.
- Often, A&R professionals were a sort of liaison between the label and the artists.
- They oversaw most of the interaction between an artist's management and the label, lawyers, and publishing/ distribution companies.
- It was the "Golden Age" in mainstream hip hop, characterized by its diversity, quality, innovation and influence.
- Its strong themes of Afrocentricity and political militancy blended well with music that was highly experimental and whose sampling was eclectic.
- "It seemed that every new single reinvented the genre," according to *Rolling Stone*.
- The artists most often associated with the period were Public Enemy, Boogie Down Productions, Eric B. & Rakim, De La Soul, A Tribe Called Quest, Gang Starr, Big Daddy Kane, and the Jungle Brothers.

The music of rapper Ice-T depicted the violent lifestyles of inner city youth.

- The freedom and creativity also spawned gangsta rap, a subgenre of hip hop that reflects the violent lifestyles of inner-city American black youths, best epitomized by rappers such as Schoolly D and Ice T.
- By the early 1990s, gangsta rap became the most commercially lucrative subgenre of hip hop.
- In 1992, Dr. Dre released *The Chronic,* an album that founded a style called G Funk, which was further developed and popularized by Snoop Dogg's 1993 album *Doggystyle.*
- The Wu-Tang Clan shot to fame around the same time and brought the East Coast back into the mainstream of rap, when the West Coast dominated.
- Another act Ross had worked with at Def Jam was 3rd Bass, one of the first successful interracial hip hop groups, featuring Michael Berrin, also known as MC Serch.
- Michael Berrin, who was raised in mostly black Far Rockaway, Queens, spent his teenage weekends facing initially hostile crowds at the Latin Quarter.
- Berrin continued getting to the mike and finally earned respect for his rhyme skills and give-no-quarter attitude.
- Through Dante Ross, Anwar met Michael Berrin.
- Ross, after his successful experience with 3rd Bass, had moved into management and production, while Anwar, following his internship under Ross of Def Jam, had moved into A&R with Sony.
- In his management and production capacity, Berrin came into contact with Nas, a young rapper with a reputation as one of the best lyricists ever.
- As Nas's manager, Berrin brought demos to Anwar's office.
- It was Anwar's first major signing.

Life in the Community: Queens, New York

- Hollis was a neighborhood within the southeastern section of the New York City borough of Queens.
- The boundaries of the predominantly African-American community were considered to be the Far Rockaway Branch of the Long Island Rail Road to the west, Hillside Avenue to the north, and Francis Lewis Boulevard to the east.
- The first European settlers were Dutch homesteaders in the seventeenth century.
- A century later, early in the American Revolutionary War, it was the site of part of the Battle of Long Island, a conflict in which the rebel Brigadier General Nathaniel Woodhull was captured at a tavern.
- The area remained rural until 1885, when developers built houses on 136 acres, and three years later it became a part of New York City with the rest of the borough of Queens.
- Since the end of the Korean War, the neighborhood had been settled primarily by African-American middle class families.
- Since the rise of hip hop, the neighborhood has been a hotbed of rap talent, sparked primarily by the fact that hip hop producer and icon Russell Simmons was from this community, as was his brother Joseph, who along with two other neighborhood residents, formed the rap group Run-D.M.C.
- Young MC—winner of the second and final Grammy Award for Best Rap Performance—Ja Rule, and DJ Hurricane were also from Hollis.
- LL Cool J was from nearby St. Albans.
- Anwar X. Holliday grew up in the Hollis community during a radical shift in the outlook of black youth.
- Although Hollis was a working middle-class neighborhood, its young people took on the attitudes of the more impoverished and crime-ridden areas like the Bronx.
- Hip hop's beginning flowed from the Bronx through people like Afrika Bambaataa a DJ known as the Amen Ra of Universal Hip Hop Culture as well as the Father of The Electro Funk Sound.
- Through his co-opting of the street gang the Black Spades into the music and culture-oriented Universal Zulu Nation, he was responsible for spreading hip hop culture.
- Zulu nation was a collective of DJs, break dancers and graffiti artists who filled the void once occupied by gang culture by de-emphasizing violence and crime in the mid-seventies.
- In the mid-1980s, when Anwar was in his teens, the crack cocaine epidemic emerged and changed the nation.
- Young men and women like Anwar were affected by the glamorization of the violent, cash-fueled cocaine culture glorified through hip hop music and images he saw on the streets of Hollis.
- The price of a kilo of cocaine dropped from $35,000 in 1982 to $12,000 in 1984, when it was estimated that 650,000 people were employed in New York City drug trade.
- In the fashion world, Run-D.M.C.'s My Adidas set the tone for a very high premium to be placed on the hippest sneakers and athletic wear.
- Michael Jordan was already on his way to revolutionizing sports apparel with his landmark Nike deal. By 1987, Run-D.M.C.

Fab 5 Freddy hosted the highly rated MTV show, Yo!MTV Raps.

had negotiated a $1.7 million sneaker deal with Adidas—the same shoes kids were fighting life-and-death battles over in the streets of Hollis.

- Many diverse influences affected the evolution of hip hop: cash, corporations, sampling, crime, violence, but none more important than the music video.

- As rap videos emerged as a viable business, two black-owned companies rose to prominence in New York: Atlantis and Classic Concept.

- *Yo! MTV Raps* debuted in September 1988 and scored the highest ratings of any show in MTV history.

- *Yo! MTV Raps* forced the more conservative Black Entertainment Television network to introduce *Rap City* a year later.

- Exposure and sales were increased dramatically by bringing the images of the clothes, cars, jewelry and attitudes into the average American home.

HISTORICAL SNAPSHOT
1993

- Cream reunited for a performance at their Rock and Roll Hall of Fame induction ceremony in Los Angeles; other inductees included Creedence Clearwater Revival, Ruth Brown, the Doors, Van Morrison, and Sly & the Family Stone

- In Super Bowl XXVII the Buffalo Bills became the first team to lose three consecutive Super Bowls when they were defeated by the Dallas Cowboys, 52–17

- Bobby Brown was arrested in Augusta, Georgia, for simulating a sex act onstage

- Oprah Winfrey interviewed Michael Jackson during a television prime time special; it was Jackson's first television appearance in 14 years

- A van bomb parked below the North Tower of the World Trade Center in New York City exploded, killing six and injuring over 1,000

- Whitney Houston's single "I Will Always Love You" became the longest-running number one single of all time

- Willie Nelson, John Cougar Mellencamp, Neil Young and more than 30 other artists performed at Farm Aid 6 in Ames, Iowa

- Janet Jackson's *Janet* debuted at #1—the first to do so by a female artist in the era of Nielsen SoundScan, an information and sales tracking system; the album included the single "That's the Way Love Goes"

- The Intel Corporation shipped the first P5 Pentium chips

- On his thirty-fifth birthday, Prince announced that he was changing his name to an unpronounceable symbol, which led to him being called The Artist Formerly Known as Prince

- Billy Joel released his final studio album before quitting music after 20 years

- Pearl Jam's second album *Vs.* sold 950 000 copies in one week to set a new record

- Wu-Tang Clan released *Enter the Wu-Tang (36 Chambers)*

- Bureau of Alcohol, Tobacco and Firearms agents raided the Branch Davidian compound in Waco, Texas, with a warrant to arrest leader David Koresh on federal firearms violations; four agents and 81 Davidians died

- *Unforgiven* won the Academy Award for Best Picture

- Andrew Wiles won worldwide fame after presenting his proof of Fermat's Last Theorem a problem that had been unsolved for more than three centuries

Selected Prices

Alarm Clock $9.99
Car Seat.. $65.00
Christmas Tree, Artificial...................................... $124.99
Comforter.. $26.88
Lawn Mower.. $289.00
Leggings $15.00
Light Bulb, Halogen $8.96
Microwave Oven... $99.00
Shower Curtain $19.77
Videotape, Three Blank $8.49

2008: Surfer and Surfboard Entrepreneur

Surfer and materials scientist Rey Banatao and his brother, encouraged by their venture capitalist father, built surfboards using sugar beet oil instead of the industry's traditional, potentially carcinogenic materials.

Life at Home

- Thirty-four-year-old Rey Banatao and his brother Desi wanted to fundamentally change the way surfboards were built.
- The secret, they believed, was sugar beet oil.
- For decades the surfboard industry had been ripping through polyurethane foam cores, known as blanks, coated in petrochemical solvents and polyester resin—all wrapped in fiberglass.
- In most cases, modern surfboard blanks were so heavily packed with chemicals, including volatile organic compounds, they could be deemed carcinogenic by the EPA.
- This gave the impression that surfers, shapers, and glassers were willing participants in the destruction and soiling of the environment their lifestyle depends upon.
- Surfboard manufacturering, which had long been a garage-scale business, was dominated by shapers, who turned out a few hundred surfboards a year, priced at around $700 each, and netted maybe $40,000 a year.
- Rey and his brother, both surfers and materials scientists, were convinced that their semi-natural boards performed as well as those made from fiberglass.
- Now they had to prove it to the surfing community.
- When the two brothers began the project, they were definitely outsiders.
- Rey was finishing up postdoctoral research on nanomaterials at the University of California, Los Angeles.
- Desi had a master's degree in materials science from Berkeley, and had just lost his job at a Portland Oregon engineering company when his projection TV technology became obsolete.
- Their father, a venture capitalist and semiconductor engineer, proposed that they start a company to make use of their tech degrees.
- Growing up, the brothers fell in love with board sports: snowboarding, skateboarding and surfing.

Rey Benatao and his brother, Desi, resolved to make a better, greener surfboard.

- They started Entropy to make equipment for all these sports.
- They also wanted to understand and respect the traditions that had brought board sports like surfing to prominence.
- The ancient Hawaiian people did not consider surfing a mere recreational activity, but something to be integrated into their culture.
- Prior to the surfer entering the ocean, the priest would bless the undertaking with a spiritual ceremony devoted to the construction of the surfboard.

Entropy was the surfboard company started by the Benatao brothers.

- Hawaiians would carefully select one of three types of trees, including the koa, then dig the tree out and place a fish in the hole as an offering to the gods.
- Selected craftsmen of the community were then hired to shape, stain, and prepare the boards, employing three primary shapes: the *'olo, kiko'o,* and *alaia.*
- The *'olo* was thick in the middle and gradually got thinner towards the ends.
- The *kiko'o* ranged in length from 12-18 feet, while the *alaia* board was around nine feet long and required great skill to ride and master.
- Aside from the preparatory stages prior to entering the water, the most skilled surfers were often of the upper class, including chiefs and warriors who surfed the best waves on the island.
- These upper-class Hawaiians gained respect through their enduring ability to master the waves and this art the Hawaiians referred to as surfing.
- In 1907, George Freeth was brought to California from Hawaii to demonstrate surfboard riding as a publicity stunt to promote the opening of the Los Angeles-Redondo-Huntington Railroad owned by Henry Huntington.
- Surfing on the East Coast of the United States began in Virginia Beach, Virginia, in 1912, when James Matthias Jordan, Jr. captivated the locals astride a 110-pound (50 kg), nine-foot Hawaiian redwood.
- Around the same time, Hawaiians living close to Waikiki began to revive surfing, and soon reestablished surfing as a sport.
- Duke Kahanamoku, "Ambassador of Aloha," Olympic medalist, and avid waterman, helped expose surfing to the world.
- Author Jack London, already famous for his adventure books, wrote about the sport after having attempted it on his visit to the islands.
- As surfing progressed, innovations in board design exploded.
- In the 1960s, the release of the film *Gidget* boosted the sport's popularity immensely, moving surfing from an underground culture into a national fad and packing many surf breaks with previously unheard-of crowds.

Author Jack London tried surfing while in Hawaii.

Popular movies and music helped to increase interest in surfing.

- B-movies and surf music authored by the Beach Boys and Surfaris formed the world's first ideas of surfing and surfers, while the 1980s included portrayals of surfers represented by characters like Jeff Spicoli from *Fast Times at Ridgemont High*.
- The evolution of the short board in the late 1960s to the performance hotdogging of the 1980s and the epic professional surfing of the 1990s brought more and more exposure.

Life at Work

- The Banatao brothers began working on bio-boards in 2006, opening a makeshift office in the basement of an office building owned by their father.
- They first focused on snowboards by combining epoxy resins with carbon nanotubes to create materials that would resist cracking.
- The nanotubes acted as barriers to a crack, preventing it from lengthening, but too many nanotubes make some materials unworkable.
- With the help of a Ph.D. student from Berkeley, they found the optimal concentration of tubes and proudly crafted a prototype for a custom snow ski company in Idaho.
- The technology was a success, but the company didn't like the design, so the brothers turned to surfboards created with nanotube technology and then shaped with simple hand tools.

- Again the bio-board was a success, but the grayish boards were a sleeper.
- That's when Rey went green.
- In December 2005, the surfboard blank manufacturing company Clark Foam shut its doors without warning, reportedly due to a mass of workers' compensation lawsuits and strict Environmental Protection Agency regulations.
- The vacuum left by Clark Foam's demise opened a giant door for new innovations in surfboard construction, including the manufacturing of "greener" surfboard materials.

- "It forced the industry to be open-minded," Rey said.
- Innovations included ways to effectively use bamboo in surfboard construction, as well as bio-plastic leash plugs and removable fin systems.
- For the committed, surfing was a spiritual enterprise—a connection with a divine energy unleashed by the interaction of wind, water and ocean-floor geography.
- The fact that the board used to tap into this energy was made from petroleum-based foam, polyester resins and chemically treated fiberglass had long been surfing's quiet contradiction.

Entropy's surfboards performed well and looked good.

- A broken board tossed in a landfill will take generations to biodegrade; the plastic fins probably never will.
- Even the thin strip of wood that runs down the middle to provide strength came at an environmental cost—a minuscule yield from the raw material from which it is milled.
- A wave of experimentation sought to detoxify surfboards by using materials that suggested the Whole Earth catalog rather than the periodic table of elements: hemp, bamboo, kelp and silk instead of fiberglass; foam made from soy and sugar rather than polyurethane, which is composed of toluene diisocyanate, or TDI, a possible carcinogen that can be inhaled and absorbed through the skin; and adhesive resins made from linseed, pine and vegetable oils.
- But changing the way surfboards were made had proved difficult.
- The few who have sought to go greener have struggled not only with finding just the right materials, but also with overcoming resistance from shapers and professional surfers reluctant to fix what they don't consider broken.
- Making a performance surfboard—one that flexes and maneuvers correctly—was a black art.
- Shapers work quickly; their tools and techniques have been refined by years of working with Clark Foam.
- Rey had chosen to have their foam blanks made from sugar beet oil instead of polyurethane because chemically, the beet polymer was almost identical to polyurethane, but could be processed using much less toxic chemicals.

A few broken boards were to be expected.

- Rey then wrapped the blanks in the layer of hemp cloth to fine-tune their flex and feel; the hemp rendered each board a yellowish color.
- Ray learned the craft from a do-it-yourself website and asked his friends to test his early efforts.
- "There have been a couple of boards breaking in bad situations, but everyone is still alive" said Desi.
- They finished developing the bio-board two years later, completing several dozen samples in their Santa Monica garage that doubled as the company headquarters.

- The challenge was then winning the respect of California surfers, who often maintained long-standing relationships with local shapers.
- The brothers had spent $150,000 on the bio-board, mostly borrowed from their wives; thus far, only two dozen boards had been sold.
- The company needed to move 300 boards to gross $200,000 and break even.
- Rey was hoping that several of the local superstars of the sport would embrace his enviro ethic and help launch the green board revolution.
- After all, Rey knew his philosophy was sound and the quality of his boards excellent; the only thing he didn't know was whether enough surfers would be willing to pay for them.
- Timing, Rey understood, was everything in surfing and in business.

Life in the Community: Santa Monica, California

- Santa Monica, California, situated on Santa Monica Bay and surrounded on three sides by Los Angeles, had always been known as a resort town.
- Named for Saint Monica of Hippo, the area was first visited by Spaniards on her feast day.
- First incorporated in 1886, Santa Monica waged a battle with Los Angeles in the 1890s to be designated as the Southern Pacific Railroad's seaport and lost, thereby preserving the charm of the town.
- In 1895, Ocean Park was developed as an amusement park and residential projects, followed by a race track and a golf course.
- By 1900, amusement piers were becoming enormously popular, stimulated by the Pacific Electric Railroad's ability to transport people from across the Greater Los Angeles area to the beaches of Santa Monica.
- At the same time, Santa Monica experienced a growing population of Asian-Americans, primarily Japanese fishermen and Chinese laborers; white Americans were often well disposed towards the Japanese but condescending to the Chinese.

Amusement piers have been popular in California since the early 1900s.

Arcadia in Los Angeles County was home to the rich and famous.

- After the Ocean Park Pier burned down in 1912, Fraser's Million Dollar amusement pier was built, which claimed to be the largest in the world at 1,250 feet long and 300 feet wide.
- The pier housed a spacious dance hall, two carousels, the Crooked House fun-house, the Grand Electric Railroad, the Starland Vaudeville Theater, Breaker's Restaurant and a Panama Canal model exhibit.
- Next came auto racing, culminating in events that by 1919 were attracting 100,000 people, at which point the city halted them.
- In the 1920s, Donald Wills Douglas, Sr. founded the Douglas Aircraft Company and built a factory.
- In 1924, two Douglas-built planes circumnavigated the globe, covering 27,553 miles in 175 days, and were greeted on their return on September 23, 1924, by a crowd of 200,000.
- The prosperity of the 1920s also fueled a population boost from 15,000 to 32,000 and a downtown construction boom.
- Beach volleyball is believed to have been developed in Santa Monica during this time.
- Surfing guru Duke Kahanamoku brought a form of the game with him from Hawaii when he took a job as athletic director at the Beach Club.
- Competitions began in 1924 with six-person teams, and by 1930 the first game with two-person teams took place.
- The La Monica Ballroom, which opened in 1924 on the Santa Monica Pier, was capable of accommodating 10,000 dancers in its over 15,000-square-foot area and hosted many national radio and television broadcasts in the early days of these networks.
- From 1958 to1962, the ballroom became one of the largest roller-skating rinks in the western U.S.
- Comedian Will Rogers bought a substantial ranch in Santa Monica Canyon in 1922, where he played polo with friends Spencer Tracy, Walt Disney and Robert Montgomery.

- Upon his untimely death, it was discovered that he had generously deeded to the public the ranch now known as Will Rogers State Historic Park, Will Rogers State Park, and Will Rogers State Beach.
- The Great Depression hit Santa Monica hard; numerous resort hotels went bankrupt.
- Muscle Beach, located just south of the Santa Monica Pier, started to attract gymnasts and body builders who put on free shows for the public, and continues to do so today.
- At the outbreak of World War II, the Douglas plant's business grew astronomically, employing as many as 44,000 people in 1943.
- To defend against air attacks, set designers from the Warner Brothers Studios prepared elaborate camouflage that disguised the factory and airfield.
- Never fully shedding its resort personality, Santa Monica was also home to the rock and roll club, The Cheetah, which featured performers such as the Doors, Alice Cooper, Pink Floyd, Love, the Mothers of Invention, the Seeds, Buffalo Springfield and others.
- The completion of the Santa Monica Freeway in 1966 brought the promise of new prosperity, though at the cost of decimating the Pico neighborhood that had been a leading African-American enclave on the Westside.
- The Douglas plant closed in 1968, depriving Santa Monica of its largest employer.
- During the 1970s, a remarkable number of notable fitness- and health-related businesses started in the city, creating the Supergo bicycle shop chain, the Santa Monica Track Club, which trained Olympians such as Carl Lewis, and Gold's Gym.
- The city's economy began to recover in the 1980s and with it, the resort feel of Santa Monica.
- After a hurricane badly damaged the pier, rundown stores and bars, the pier and shopping areas were extensively renovated.
- The failed Santa Monica Mall was transformed into the Santa Monica Promenade, and between 1988 and 1998, taxable sales in the city grew 440 percent, quadrupling city revenues.
- The increasingly upscale nature of the city was the cause of some tensions between newcomers and longtime residents nostalgic for the more bohemian, countercultural past.
- Nevertheless, with the recent corporate additions of Yahoo! and Google, gentrification continued.

HISTORICAL SNAPSHOT
2008

- During a nearly 40-minute speech, presidential candidate Barack Obama explained the complexities of race in America
- Three men wearing ski masks stole artwork from the Zurich Museum, including a Cezanne, a Degas, a van Gogh, and a Monet, with a combined worth of $163 million

- At a news conference in Baghdad, a reporter for a Cairo-based satellite television network hurled his shoes at President George W. Bush and called him a "dog"
- New York Governor Eliot Spitzer, known as a crusader against white-collar crime, was pressured to resign after he confessed to hiring prostitutes
- Danica Patrick won the Indy Japan 300, becoming the first woman to win an IndyCar race
- The U.S. Supreme Court ruled five to four that prisoners at Guantánamo Bay, Cuba, had a right to challenge their detention in federal court
- American swimmer Michael Phelps won eight gold medals at the Summer Olympics in China to beat a 36-year-old record set by countryman Mark Spitz
- A five-year inquiry by the Intelligence Committee found that President George W. Bush and his staff repeatedly overstated evidence that Saddam Hussein possessed nuclear, chemical, and biological weapons and misled the public about ties between Iraq and al-Qaeda
- Bill Gates ended his day-to-day management of Microsoft, the computer giant he founded
- The Supreme Court ruled five to four that the Constitution protected an individual's right to possess a gun, but insisted that the ruling "is not a right to keep and carry any weapon whatsoever in any manner whatsoever and for whatever purpose."
- Barack Obama won the presidential election against Senator John McCain, taking 365 electoral votes to McCain's 162
- Notable books for the year included *The Appeal* by John Grisham; *The Audacity of Hope* by Barack Obama; *Diary of a Wimpy Kid: Rodrick Rules* by Jeff Kinney; *Eat, Pray, Love* by Elizabeth Gilbert; *The Last Lecture* by Randy Pausch and Jeffrey Zaslow; and *Three Cups of Tea* by Greg Mortenson
- Researchers decoded the genome of a cancer patient and found mutations in the cancer cells that may have either caused the cancer or helped it to progress
- Mortgage giants Freddie Mac and Fannie Mae collapsed just days before investment bank Lehman Brothers declared bankruptcy
- The Iraqi government took command of 54,000 Sunni fighters who turned against al-Qaeda in Mesopotamia in 2007 and began siding with the United States

Selected Prices

Backup Hard Drive $44.71
Book, Paperback $10.20
Business Cards, 250 Count $19.99
Coffeemaker, Krups $90.00
Combination Router/Modem $160.00
Phone Service, Land Line, Monthly $70.00
Printer Ink, Three-Pack $71.00
Surfboard $735.00
Toaster, Krups $90.96
Trimline Corded Telephone $14.72

"How to Shape a Surfboard," Jay DiMartino,
About.com Guide, 2008:

Watching your surfboard as it's shaped is a bit like watching your baby being born...just a little. If you haven't stood in the shaping room during this wondrous birth and felt foam dust waft up your nostrils as it blank to fully designed, you are missing out on a special moment. It takes the relationship between you and your surfboard to a deeper level, and may just lift your surfing to another level.

For those not familiar with the latest craze to invade the sun-drenched Pacific coast of Southern California, here is a definition of "surfing"—a water sport in which the participant stands on a floating slab of wood, resembling an ironing board in both size and shape, and attempts to remain perpendicular while being hurtled toward the shore at a rather frightening rate of speed on the crest of a huge wave (especially recommended for teen-agers and all others without the slightest regard for either life or limb).

—Sleeve notes on The Beach Boys' 1962 album *Surfin' Safari*

Our goal is to create high-performance resin systems that optimize the sustainability of endproducts by replacing petroleum-based chemicals with bio-based renewable resources. By employing bio-derived materials such as pine oil components sourced as a co-product from wood pulp processing and vegetable oil components sourced from the waste stream of bio-fuel processing, we are able to lower our resins' environmental impact from processing and improve the overall health and safety of our products.

—Entropy website (www.Entropyresins.com)

Walking on Water

2015: Field Service Scheduling Supervisor

After a self-indulgent youth, David Mitchell joined the Marine Corps where he learned the value of discipline and hard work, the foundation of his successful career as a service scheduling supervisor.

Life at Home

- David Mitchell was born in 1958 in the South End of Boston, Massachusetts, where his parents lived for most of their lives.
- In spring of 1959, when David was six months old, the family moved to Dorchester, an inner city section of Boston.
- David was one of two sons born to his parents, who adopted six other children.
- The eight children were brought up in a very strict household.
- David has a tattoo that reads "A.E.M," which are the initials of his father, brother, sister, and nephew.
- Through the eighth grade, David was taught at St. Mary's of the Assumption by Catholic nuns, who were extremely strict and applied severe corporal punishment to the children.
- In 1972, he attended Don Bosco, an all-boys Catholic high school, but having had enough of Catholic education, he transferred to Boston's Roxbury Medical Technical Institute, run by the Nation of Islam in America.
- Today, this type of school is called a pilot school.
- David felt the teachers made young African-American men feel as if Black was the thing to be.
- Being a typical teenager in the early 1970s, he wore wide-bottom pants and high platform shoes: one of the heels broke while David was going down a flight of stairs and he nearly broke his neck.
- After graduating in 1975 with his neck intact, he attended Howard University in Washington, DC.

David Mitchell's crooked education and career path led to his wife and a successful career.

- Living in extreme poverty and having way too much fun made for a very short stay in DC, so David headed back home to Boston.
- He indulged in drinking, smoking pot, driving around in stolen cars, and singing and partying in abandoned houses.
- In 1977 he decided to join the U.S. Marine Corps.
- His first stop was Parris Island, South Carolina, the U.S. Marine Corps Bootcamp, where he learned to keep his eyes and ears open, and his mouth shut.
- Recruits are stationed there for three months while enduring extreme psychological and physical training.
- The USMC Bootcamp produces the most elite and combat-ready regiments in the world.

"Pop Pop" with one of his eight grandchildren.

- David spent three months training to be a Marine and two years serving.
- He received an Honorable Discharge in 1979 due to a genetic disorder that led to degenerative arthritis in his hip joints.

Life at Work

- In 1979, David enrolled in the O.I.C. Electronic School, an inner-city electrical trade program.
- Upon completing the program in 1980, he obtained his first professional job at Honeywell, Inc.
- As a field service technician for the company, he fixed computers.
- During the 10 years he worked for the company, his daughters Ashlei Elizabeth and Brenda Stacey-Janice were born.

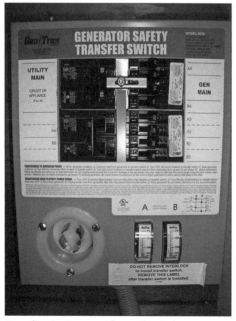

Russelectric, Inc. manufactured switch gear.

- In 1990, David left Honeywell and began working for Sullivan & Cogliano IT Contract Staffing doing odd jobs to make ends meet.
- In 1993, he became a temporary employee at Russelectric, Inc., Weymouth, Massachusetts, manufacturer of state-of-the-art switchgear and automatic transfer switches for hospitals, schools, data centers, water treatment plants, phone companies, etc.
- After a three-month trial, he was hired full time as the field service scheduling supervisor for projects west of the Mississippi River.
- David scheduled field service engineers for start-up, emergency response, modifications, etc., for all Russelectric-manufactured equipment.
- This job gave him much more than simply employment.
- One week after David's 36th birthday in 1994, he met his fiancée, Dotti, who worked in the purchasing department at Russelectric.

- "Lucky for me our paths crossed at the right place at the right time. She has always been my ray of sunshine and hope, right up to now and far into the future," said David.
- Between them, they had three daughters, two sons, and eight grandchildren.
- David is known by the affectionate name of "Pop-Pop" to all their kids and grandkids.

Life in the Community: Weymouth, Massachusetts

- Although Weymouth, Massachusetts, has a city government, it opted to keep the "Town of Weymouth" as its official name.
- It is the second-oldest township in Massachusetts, dating back to 1622.
- The remnants of early roads can be traced in some of the town's existing streets; Commercial Street has been identified as an original Native American trail.
- In 1837, when enough natural bog iron was discovered to support a local factory, the Weymouth Iron Works was built.
- During this time, the city's maritime and agricultural society transformed into a culture of manufacturing and trade.
- By the mid-1800s, Weymouth was experiencing a period of economic stability, thanks to the expansion of the railroad and local financial institutions.

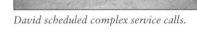

David scheduled complex service calls.

- After World War II, rising incomes led to a boom in automobile ownership, and the federal and state governments responded with aggressive highway improvement programs.
- Bisecting Weymouth in 1956, Route 3 had a major impact on the city, since the new highway allowed more people to commute to work in Boston.
- As a result, the local economy shifted dramatically to small service retail businesses and some wholesale operations.
- By the late 20th century, Weymouth was transformed into a mature suburb of Boston.

The Russelectric campus.

HISTORICAL SNAPSHOT
2015

- Paris, Damascus, and Beirut terrorist attacks left hundreds dead

- Flowing liquid water was found on Mars

- Iran and a coalition that included the United States came to an agreement that lifted the United Nations Security Council's sanctions against Iran in exchange for the reduction of Iran's stockpile of enriched uranium by about 98 percent for the next 15 years

- President Obama signed into law the USA Freedom Act, ending the U.S. government's gathering of telephone records

- Amid controversies and accusations of cheating, the New England Patriots beat the Seattle Seahawks 28-24 in Super Bowl XLIX

- *Birdman* won four Academy Awards, including Best Picture

- Governor Jerry Brown of California signed an executive order mandating that the state reduce its water use by 25 percent in an effort to confront severe drought conditions

- Dzhokhar Tsarnaev—the Boston Marathon Bomber—was sentenced to death for planning the 2013 attack

- William C. Campbell, Satoshi Omura, and Youyou Tu, who developed therapies against parasitic infections, won the Nobel Prize in Physiology or Medicine

- Police killings of unarmed African-American women and men totaled 986

- In a 5-4 decision, the Supreme Court ruled that the Constitution guarantees a right to same-sex marriage in the United States

- President Barack Obama announced the full re-establishment of diplomatic ties with Cuba, including reopening both embassies

- The South Carolina State House formally removed the Confederate battle flag from its grounds

The White House lit up in rainbow colors.

- President Obama announced the Clean Power Plan, which included the first-ever Environmental Protection Agency standards on carbon pollution from U.S. power plants

- A gunman opened fire at a Planned Parenthood clinic in Colorado Springs, Colorado, killing three, including a police officer, and injuring nine

- Defense Secretary Ashton Carter announced that all combat roles in the United States military must be opened to women by April 1

Selected Prices

2015 Ford Focus $25,900

Bed Sheet Set. $27.79

Insect Repellent. $10.99

Lee Women's Skinny Jeans $32.90

London Fog Trench Coat with Hood . . . $133.44

Nikon D3300 2 Digital SLR Camera . . . $446.95

Q-tips Cotton Swabs, 500 Count $12.58

Stainless Steel Sauce Pan with Glass Lid . $22.13

Stainless Steel Whistling Tea Kettle $31.95

Trader Joe's Toothpaste, 12 Ounces. $12.29

U.S. Marine Corps Bootcamp

Phase One

Receiving Week: Recruits arrive on Parris Island late at night and are immediately thrust into the stressful whirlwind of in-processing, haircuts, uniform and gear issue and medical evaluations. Recruits undergo an initial strength test to ensure they are prepared for training. At the end of the week, they meet the team of drill instructors who will be responsible for them for the rest of training.

Weeks 1-3: Recruits receive instruction on military history, customs and courtesies, basic first aid, uniforms, leadership and core values. They begin to learn discipline through close-order drill and hand-to-hand combat skills through the Marine Corps Martial Arts Program, which is made up of various martial arts styles.

Week 4: Swim Week. True to their name, Marines need to know how to survive in the water. Recruits learn to leap into deep water, tread water, use issued equipment to stay afloat and to shed heavy gear that could pull them under water.

Phase Two

Week 5: Recruits take their initial written test and compete in an initial drill competion against the other platoons of their company. They also learn to rappel and properly use a gas mask.

Week 6: Grass Week. Recruits hike to the rifle range and begin to learn the fundamentals of Marine Corps marksmanship. Recruits learn the proper firing positions and spend hours sitting in grass fields sighting in on practice targets.

Week 7: Firing Week. Recruits finally fire live rounds with their M16-A4 rifles. Recruits practice firing from different distances in the sitting, standing, kneeling and prone positions.

Week 8: Team Week. The recruits take a short break from nonstop training to help out around the island. Recruits do laundry, help in supply warehouses and clean buildings around the depot before beginning the final phase of training.

Phase Three

Week 9: Basic Warrior Training. They are taught basic skills of survival in combat, such as combat marksmanship skills, land navigation and how to manuever under enemy fire.

Week 10: The recruits undergo practical application evaluations. They complete a combat fitness test and face the challenges of the Confidence Course for the last time.

Week 11: Recruits face the final challenges they must overcome to earn the title of Marine. The week begins with a physical fitness test and a written exam before the final drill evaluation. The recruits then face the Crucible, a final 54-hour field event that tests the recruits on the knowledge, skills and values they have been taught throughout training. Those who complete the final challenge are awarded their Eagle, Globe and Anchors, symbolizing their transformation from recruits to Marines.

Week 12: The new Marines are inspected by their commanding officers. They complete final administrative tasks on the island before their graduation ceremony. The new Marines get 10 days of leave before reporting to the Camp Lejeune, N.C., for additional combat training, and then to various military occupational specialty schools across the country.

Automatic Transfer Switch

An Automatic Transfer Switch (ATS) is often installed where a backup generator is located, so that the generator may provide temporary electrical power if the utility source fails.

As well as transferring the load to the backup generator, an ATS may also command the backup generator to start, based on the voltage monitored on the primary supply. The transfer switch isolates the backup generator from the electric utility when the generator is on and providing temporary power. The control capability of a transfer switch may be manual only, or a combination of automatic and manual. The switch transition mode (see below) of a transfer switch may be Open Transition (OT) (the usual type), or Closed Transition (CT)) .

For example, in a home equipped with a backup generator and an ATS, when an electric utility outage occurs, the ATS will tell the backup generator to start. Once the ATS sees that the generator is ready to provide electric power, the ATS breaks the home's connection to the electric utility and connects the generator to the home's main electrical panel. The generator supplies power to the home's electric load, but is not connected to the electric utility lines. It is necessary to isolate the generator from the distribution system to protect the generator from overload in powering loads in the house and for safety, as utility workers expect the lines to be dead.

When utility power returns for a minimum time, the transfer switch will transfer the house back to utility power and command the generator to turn off, after another specified amount of "cool down" time with no load on the generator.

A transfer switch can be set up to provide power only to critical circuits or to entire electrical (sub)panels. Some transfer switches allow for load shedding or prioritization of optional circuits, such as heating and cooling equipment. More complex

Intelligent transfer switch

emergency switchgear used in large backup generator installations permits soft loading, allowing load to be smoothly transferred from the utility to the synchronized generators, and back; such installations are useful for reducing peak load demand from a utility.

Homes with standby generators may use a transfer switch for a few circuits or the whole home. Different models are available, with both manual and automatic transfer. Often small transfer switch systems use circuit breakers with an external operating linkage as the switching mechanism. The linkage operates two circuit breakers in tandem, closing one while opening the other.

Med School Dean Lauds Performance of Roxbury
Educational Organization, *The Harvard Crimson*, March 23, 1973*

Robert H. Ebert, dean of Harvard Medical School, said yesterday that recruitment of minorities into educational programs is an important responsibility of medical schools.

Ebert spoke at a luncheon sponsored by the Med School to attract financial support for the Roxbury Medical Technical Institute (RMTI), an educational and social service organization.

"The RMTI is a valuable institution with great viability because it arises from a grass-roots effort," Ebert told the 40 guests.

RMTI provides educational opportunities and facilities for disadvantaged students from the Roxbury-Dorchester area. The institute is also attempting to increase the quality and amount of health care in the Roxbury-Dorchester area.

Back Into the Community
Octavius Rowe, executive director of RMTI, said that the function of the institute is to encourage community participation in social services. "RMTI is self-help personified, because it attracts black people back into the community," he said.

At present, only four black doctors are practicing in Roxbury and Dorchester, Rowe said.

The institute's program enables 8 to 18-year-old students to work with educators, students and pre-medical students at Boston hospitals and educational institutions, in order to motivate them to enter the medical profession.

"Many of our students do not see the possibilities because they do not have the proper role models," he said.

Profile subject David Mitchell graduated from RMTI.

2016: Family Therapist

Cindy Constant, the ninth of ten children, was born in Dallas to Haitian parents. The family moved around a lot, struggling to find a place to settle down in, which developed Cindy's wandering spirit.

Life at Home

- Cindy Constant was born to working middle class parents.
- Her mother was the main provider for the family and worked multiple positions, while Cindy's father garnered frequent but unstable employment.
- Cindy's was the ninth of 10 children: seven boys and three girls.
- Since there were huge age gaps from the oldest to the youngest, Cindy was actually raised with only her younger brother.
- Only three of her siblings lived in America with Cindy, but two of them were already married with their own families while Cindy was still a young girl.
- For her younger brother, she carried out an elder sibling's responsibilities.
- Education was always a primary focus within the family.
- Cindy was involved in many extracurricular activities but excelled in dance and playing the violin.
- A favorite with most of her teachers, she always received A's in school, and was placed in accelerated learning programs.
- Her home life, however, was unhealthy, with abusive parents.
- Cindy sought escape with friends, dance, and school.
- By age 13, she was running away from home often.
- By 16, she was pregnant and living in a teen housing program.
- Cindy left high school but obtained her GED.
- Wasting no time, she began college right away but changed majors often.
- After finally deciding on a major, Cindy finished college with a bachelor of science degree in business.

Cindy Constant's own teen-age struggles and the needs of her children led to a career in human services.

- She accomplished this while raising a family and experiencing several personal tragedies.
- By 2005, she had four children—two boys and two girls.
- Although her degree was in business, Cindy had always felt the need to help others.
- This is what led to her career in the human services field.

Life at Work

- After working at numerous jobs, Cindy began her business career in recruiting, but was eventually laid off.
- She then focused on her son who had mental health issues.
- Enrolling him in an appropriate school for his needs was a year-long process.
- Cindy then created and ran a support group for parents of children with mental health problems in Fitchburg, about 40 miles west of Boston.
- As a result, she changed her career to human services and continued her education, acquiring a master's degree in counseling.
- She worked at an agency that served predominantly minorities in Worcester, Massachusetts, 25 miles south of Fitchburg.
- Under the Child Health Behavioral Initiative, family therapy took place in the home for children who were diagnosed with severe emotional disturbances.
- Through her work at Bay Cove Human Services, Cindy recognized the systemic failures that led to problematic children, dysfunctional families, and chaotic lives for many minorities.
- She realized that help could not happen within a failed system.
- She was frustrated by the system's inability to help unite families so that children could be kept at home rather than being sent to the Department of Youth Services, the Department of Children and Families, or to a hospital.
- Cindy watched helplessly as families lost control and children suffered.
- Despite her struggle in this role, Cindy continued to work to improve the system.
- Cindy has seen some improvement for many families, with children gaining self-esteem and goals for success while struggling with

Cindy's four children.

discrimination, high-crime neighborhoods, and poor schools.

Life in the Community: Worcester, Massachusetts

- The city of Worcester is located about 45 miles west of Boston, Massachusetts.
- The area was first inhabited by the Nipmuc tribe.
- Incorporated as a city in 1722, Worcester was chosen as the county seat of the newly founded Worcester County government in 1731.
- Between 1755 and 1758, future President John Adams worked as a schoolteacher and studied law in Worcester.
- The Worcester State Insane Asylum Hospital (1833) was the first hospital in the United States established to treat mental illnesses.
- The Jesuit College of the Holy Cross was founded in 1843 and is the oldest Roman Catholic college in New England, and one of the oldest in the United States.
- At the turn of the 19th century, Worcester's economy became based on the manufacturing of textiles, shoes, and clothing.

As a therapist at Bay Cove Human Services, Cindy helped families benefit from the system.

- After World War II, the city began to fall into decline as it lost its manufacturing base to cheaper options across the U.S. and overseas.
- In the mid-20th century, large urban renewal projects were undertaken to try to reverse the city's decline.
- A huge area of downtown Worcester was demolished for new office towers and the one million-square-foot Worcester Center Galleria shopping mall.
- However, after only 30 years the Galleria would lose most of its major tenants to more suburban shopping malls around Worcester County.
- In the 1960s, Interstate 290 was built right through the center of Worcester, thus permanently dividing the city.
- In the late 20th century, Worcester's economy began to recover as the city expanded into the biotechnology and healthcare fields.
- The University of Massachusetts Medical School became a leader in biomedical research, while the Massachusetts Biotechnology Research Park has become a center of medical research and development.
- On December 3, 1999, a homeless man and his girlfriend accidentally started a five-alarm fire at the Worcester Cold Storage & Warehouse Company; the fire killed six firefighters and drew national attention as one of the worst firefighting tragedies in the late 20th century.
- A Convention Center was built in downtown Worcester in 1997.
- In 2000, Worcester's Union Station reopened after 25 years of neglect and a $32 million renovation; in the same year, the Massachusetts College of Pharmacy and Health Sciences built a new campus in downtown Worcester.
- A multimillion-dollar renovation converted the old Franklin Square Theater into the Hanover Theatre for the Performing Arts.
- Despite all these improvements, however, the city's problems have persisted.

- Worcester's drug fatalities have surged in the past year as the city's heroin use rose to twice the U.S. average.
- Waiting lists at homeless shelters have risen to more than 60 people in some cases.
- One of the goals of these shelters is to help with job hunting, but there are not enough facilities to cater to the city's needs.
- In Worcester's public high schools, the average number of students who are chronically absent is nearly 20 percent.
- Throughout the entire city school system, the percentage of chronically absent students is 14.4.

HISTORICAL SNAPSHOT
2016

- Winter storm Jonas brought record-breaking amounts of snow and wind throughout the northeastern and mid-Atlantic United States in late January

- Scientists discovered that the fault beneath the Himalayas is kinked, making the mountains taller between major earthquakes

- The solar power industry grew 12 times faster than overall U.S. employment

- The federal deficit was at $486 billion this year-about a third of what it was in 2009

- Films premiering this year included *Batman v Superman: Dawn of Justice, Risen,* and *The Choice*

- Roger Goodell, the commissioner of the National Football League, announced that at least one woman be interviewed for all executive positions in an effort to diversify leadership

- Bestselling books included *When Breath Becomes Air* by Paul Kalanithi, *Between the World and Me* by Ta-Nehisi Coates, and *The Nightingale* by Kristin Hannah

- A fast-loading format developed by Google sped up mobile web pages on smartphones

- South Korea and the People's Republic of China held talks to develop a joint response to North Korea's nuclear test

- After diverting Flint's water source from Lake Huron to the Flint River, Michigan Gov. Rick Snyder faced a class-action lawsuit allowing lead-tainted water into the city's homes

- The Black Lives Matter movement forced U.S. presidential candidates to deal with the issue of racial inequality

- Hurricane Alex became the first January hurricane to form in the Atlantic Ocean since 1938

- The Zika virus—a flulike illness that normally causes mild symptoms but can be severe—quickly spread throughout Latin America; Brazil estimated close to one million cases by mid-February

- The unemployment rate fell to an eight-year low of 4.9 percent

- Through the Affordable Care Act, 15 million more Americans are covered than in 2014

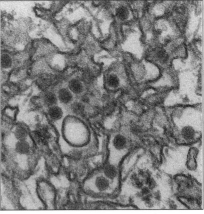

A transmission electron micrograph (TEM) of Zika virus, which is a member of the family Flaviviridae.

Selected Prices

2016 Toyota Prius $24,200

60-Watt Bulbs, Soft White, 4-Pack $5.71

6-Piece Towel Set. $79.99

Brandy Glasses, Set of 4 . . . . $23.99

Cat Litter, Clumping, 27-Pounds $9.99

Drywall Anchors, Pack of 20 . . . . $7.75

Magnetic Stud Finder $9.99

Three-piece patio set. $284.56

Swivel Top Entertainment Console $109.39

Witch Hazel 16 ounces $8.58

Early Intervention Services

The Bay Cove Early Intervention (EI) program serves more than 400 children under three years of age, who are developmentally delayed, or have a known disabling condition, or are at risk of developmental delays due to biological or environmental factors. The program's goal is to promote the physical, mental and emotional development of eligible children. Services are provided in the children's homes, in the community and at the program site on Victory Road. Bay Cove's EI program has been providing such services to children and their families since 1976.

Staff and Services Provided

Once eligibility has been determined by a multidisciplinary developmental assessment team, an Early Intervention Specialist is assigned to develop an Individualized Family Service Plan with the child's parents. This plan outlines the steps that will be taken to address the child's specific needs. The program's staff is made up of a team of over 40 full- and part-time professionals including Early Childhood Educators, Social Workers, Psychologists, Nurses, Speech/Language Pathologists, Occupational and Physical Therapists. The Bay Cove approach to working with children is very "family-centered," meaning that parents are actively involved in all phases of both service planning and service delivery for their child. The type and frequency of services provided are determined by the needs of each particular child and family, but usually include some combination of the following:

- Multidisciplinary developmental assessments
- In-home developmental play stimulation
- Toddler developmental play groups, including transportation, if needed
- Parent education and support groups
- Individual or family therapy
- Speech therapy, occupational therapy and physical therapy
- Service coordination and advocacy

Community Involvement

The Early Intervention staff members work closely with other service providers such as day care centers, pediatricians and other healthcare providers, food pantries and homeless/domestic violence shelters.

"Drug Overdoses Rampant in Worcester, City Issues Health Advisory," by Nicholas Handy, *GoLocalWorcester*, August 7, 2014

After reporting nine deaths from August 1st to August 6th with a possibility of a tenth, the city of Worcester has a growing concern that the local heroin problem is increasing to an epidemic like status.

After issuing a public health advisory on Wednesday August 6th warning citizens that contaminated heroin may be available on the streets, city officials announced that they are devoting a wealth of resources to respond to the growing issue.

"The city of Worcester is taking this spike in opiate related deaths very seriously," said City Manager Ed Augustus. "It certainly is a drastic and alarming spike in deaths. We are working on two fronts, one being the public safety and investigative element. We are also looking at it as a public health issue. The Public Health Department has issued a public health advisory, which we are sharing with our community partners. We want to try to get to the bottom of where this is coming from and how we can stop it."

Worcester Police confirm that eight of the nine or ten overdose deaths are suspected to involve heroin. These are in stark contrast to 2011, where the city of Worcester only saw 22 drug-related deaths throughout the whole year. The Worcester Police have responded to roughly 300 overdose calls since the beginning of the year and have responded to 33 overdose calls since August 1st.

Stay Away from It

According to Worcester Police Chief Gary Gemme, the Worcester Police Department is working to investigate the recent string of deaths, which highlights a growing problem in the city.

Gemme says that the problem appears to be local and that investigators are currently working to determine the purity of the narcotic and whether or not it is cut with another substance. Additionally, the Police Department is working to equip their police cruisers with Narcan; Gemme says that $13,000 will be spent on Narcan and all cruisers should be equipped in the next two weeks.

City Director Brindisi, Police Chief Gemme, City Manager Augustus, and Mayor Petty at a briefing about the heroin epidemic

City Director Brindisi, Police Chief Gemme, City Manager Augustus, and Mayor Petty at a briefing about the heroin epidemic

"There's something going on with the heroin. Stay away from the heroin; it's as simple as that," said Gemme at a media briefing. "When you buy heroin off the street, you don't know who mixed it, you don't know who cut it, and you don't know the quality of it. We're not going to solve this overnight, but we are going expend the resources to get to the bottom of this and hopefully identify the individuals and bring this to some conclusion."

"Drug Overdoses..." *(continued)*

A Public Health Emergency
Worcester Police and Public Health officials are also working to warn known drug users in the hopes that the message can be spread throughout the community, alerting everyone about the current dangers of using the drug, which sells for about $8 in the city right now, according to Police Chief Gemme.

The city has also reached out to community partners like AIDS Project Worcester, AdCare Hospital and Spectrum Health Systems, who have all agreed to help the city battle against drug addictions and overdoses.

There are currently beneficial programs in place in Worcester like AIDS Project Worcester's Overdose Prevention and Narcan Distribution Program, which helps to train opiod users and families how to use Narcan, which can help to reverse an overdose. The program – which has been running for a few years—has seen over 100 reversals according to Derek S. Brindisi, the City Director of Public Health.

"We are in the midst of a public health emergency," said Brindisi. "We've been monitoring the overdoses and their totality and certainly the most recent deaths, which have raised many concerns. We have asked for the help of our community partners and they have agreed to be part of the solution. We are going to use our community partners to help work with and provide outreach for this issue."

"Grant Will Fund Planning to Improve Refugee Resettlement in Worcester,"
by Bob Kievra, *Telegram & Gazette*, March 5, 2015

WORCESTER—Refugees by the thousands have found a welcoming environment in Worcester, as low-cost housing, public transportation and available jobs provide the required building blocks sought by the U.S. State Department.

But integrating refugees into the community remains a struggle, with gaps in various services, fragmented integration of others and outdated procedures that don't reflect the current influx, officials said this week.

Armed with a $170,722 grant from the Health Foundation of Central Massachusetts, Ascentria Care Alliance hopes to reshape the integration template.

The planning grant, announced this week, will fund a yearlong effort to create a collaborative integration model—one that focuses on resettled refugees' overall well-being and not just employment and self-sufficiency.

"How do we unify services around these people?" said Angela B. Bovill, president and chief executive officer of Ascentria, formerly Lutheran Social Services of New England, a $59 million human service agency. "There are gaps and fragments and pressures that are not being met."

Worcester is the largest site for refugee resettlement in Massachusetts, with more than 1,600 refugees resettled in the city in the past five years, including Bhutanese, Burundians, Congolese, Liberians, Iraqis, Russians, Somalis and Vietnamese. Over the past three years, the majority (51 percent) have come from Iraq, with Bhutan second at 28 percent.

The State Department normally provides about eight months of assistance to refugees, with the major emphasis on securing a job and finding a place to live.

But many refugees arrive with many health and social needs because of years spent in crowded refugee camps, separation from families and unfamiliarity with the English language.

Building a framework that assesses and connects the refugee population to those services will be a focus of the planning grant, which usually turns into multiyear support totaling about $2 million.

"This issue has bubbled up a couple of times," said Janice B. Yost, president of the Health Foundation. "Worcester has the opportunity to be an excellent pilot for the rest of the U.S. to follow."

The planning grant will build relationships with the city of Worcester, the state Office of Refugees and Immigrants, Community Legal Aid, Family Continuity, the Edward M. Kennedy Community Health Center, Quinsigamond Community College and Worcester Public Schools.

The current system has gaps in mental health services and emphasizes employment over language education, which may inhibit a refugee's long-term economic prospects, Ms. Bovill said. Highly educated refugees often have to quickly find work that doesn't necessarily match their skill set, she said.

"There is very little flex in the system," she said. "Right now everyone is pretty much treated the same. Unlike years past, we now have refugees from many different countries with nothing in common."

Ms. Bovill said the planning grant bodes well for the city.

"From our vantage point Worcester is on the cusp of being that mecca of taking cultural diversity and turning it to our competitive advantage as a society."

"Officials, Residents Ponder Worcester's Problems, Potential," by Brad Petrishen, *Telegram & Gazette*, September 21, 2014

WORCESTER—As Edward M. Augustus Jr. looks to become the city's sixth permanent manager since 1950, the problems to solve and the potential to nurture growth seem as diverse as the city itself, civic leaders and residents said last week.

"Homelessness," a couple living on the street for the past two months pegged as the city's biggest problem.

"Infrastructure," opined a retired mail carrier, echoing the sentiments of many residents who say potholes and traffic are out of control.

The skyline of Worcester is seen from the upper half of Orient Street near Grafton Hill. (T&G Staff/Christine Peterson)

"We need a strong mayor," one man said at the Webster Square Towers, charging the city with wasting money on repetitive cosmetic makeovers.

From the towers to Elm Park, those asked to ponder the city's problems and possibilities talked mostly about street-level, customer-service issues. Those in the business and research spheres focused on economics and education, highlighting a divide in thinking some say city leaders need to address.

"We need to have more engagement," said Timothy J. McGourthy, executive director of the Worcester Regional Research Bureau.

The city has real financial challenges, yet many residents don't know about them, Mr. McGourthy said.

The city's Other Post-Employment Benefits Liability, which anticipates life insurance and health care costs that will need to be paid to future retirees, rests at $656 million, more than twice its pension liability.

"It's the Sword of Damocles hanging over our head," Mr. McGourthy said, yet one of a host of issues most people know little to nothing about.

In addition to looking at fiscal problems—one estimate puts one-third of the city's revenue going toward retiree benefits by 2020—the Research Bureau is studying ways of getting Worcester voters more engaged, Mr. McGourthy said.

"We can't accept a turnout of 15 or 20 percent," he said, acknowledging city government has been slow to adapt to changes in demographics.

According to census figures, whites made up 69.4 percent of the city's 181,045 residents in 2010, down from 77.1 percent of the city's 172,648 residents in 2000.

Over those same years, the African-American population grew from 6.9 percent to 11.6 percent, the Asian population from 4.9 percent to 6.1 percent and the Hispanic/Latino population from 15.1 percent to 20.9 percent.

"Officials, Residents Ponder... *(continued)*

"The key to our city is its diversity," said Juan A. Gomez, president and CEO of Centro Las Americas, a Latino social services provider.

Mr. Gomez, a former city councilor, threw his support behind Mr. Augustus because he said he believes he's committed to making city government more reflective of its demographics.

Mr. Gomez said the city needs more minorities on its fire and police forces and among the rest of its 6,867 full- and part-time employees.

Inclusivity was one of a wide range of topics Mr. Augustus mentioned Thursday upon accepting the City Council's request to extend his employment.

"We are one city. That's a theme I've tried to (stress)," he said.

In addition to securing the city's financial footing, Mr. Augustus spoke of strengthening the schools, redeveloping neighborhoods, prioritizing young people and revitalizing downtown.

"I see a city where we see a vital, vibrant downtown—an 18-hour day where people are living and working and having experiences that people expect of a city the size and caliber of Worcester," he said.

Francesco C. Cesareo, president of Assumption College and a supporter of Mr. Augustus, said he believes the city needs to follow through on such a vision.

"If you're going to have a vibrant city, you've got to have a vibrant downtown," Mr. Cesareo said. He noted that, despite the presence of 35,000 college students, the city "does not feel like a college town."

"Students need to begin to see the city as alive, as a place they want to be," Mr. Cesareo said — tough to do with the state of its downtown.

Upperclassmen at Worcester Polytechnic Institute Friday agreed.

Junior Stephanie Esmond said it would behoove the city to better advertise its destinations to students on college campuses.

"Every once in a while we'll stumble on something (cool)," she said, but other than that a lot of students simply don't know what's out there.

Longtime city residents Jack King and Evelyn Gorham don't have trouble figuring out where they want to go in the city. They do have trouble getting there.

"They need to fix the roads," Mr. King said as he and his friend sat outside their home, the Webster Square Towers, Friday morning.

Mr. King said he can't stand inconsistencies in the way the city approaches public works projects, such as "cheap-looking" blacktop sidewalks on Park Avenue instead of cement.

"It looks disgusting," he said. "We have a lot of nice things (in Worcester), but also a lot of crap."

Mr. King said he's seen Elm Park get done over several times while Institute Park, near his boyhood home, has "gone to the dogs."

"Officials, Residents Ponder... *(continued)*

"It's like no research goes into the projects they do," Ms. Gorham said. "How many times have they redone the Common?"

The pair said they think the city should change its form of government to a strong-mayor system to ensure the person at the top is accountable to voters.

Ronnie Clarkson, who also lives at the tower and uses a wheelchair, said he wishes the city would enforce ordinances requiring property owners to shovel sidewalks.

"I'm out there in the street like this when I need to get to Price Chopper," he said, raising his hands in response to implied beeping drivers.

Ms. Gorham said she believes the city also needs to do a better job of attracting tax-paying businesses. According to the Research Bureau, more than 35 percent of Worcester's land area is tax exempt.

"They're raking it in," Ms. Gorham said of religious schools exempt from paying taxes.

While Mr. King and Ms. Gorham follow city politics, most people at Elm Park Thursday said they generally don't pay too much attention to the doings at City Hall.

Saeed Siamak, 26, said many of the things he finds fault with in Worcester may not be fixable by politicians or administrators.

"Crazy drivers," Mr. Siamak identified as his biggest pet peeve as he pushed his young niece on a swing.

At a nearby bench, Ray Allard, a recently retired mail carrier and Lanesboro Road resident, said the city's biggest problem is infrastructure.

"It seems like instead of fixing the problem before it gets worse, they let the problem get worse before they fix it," he said, leading to a lot of people damaging their cars in gaping potholes.

Elaine Blair and John Cook were at Elm Park Thursday because it's where they spend most of their day. The couple said they lost their Virginia home to foreclosure and, after getting evicted from a "rathole" of an apartment in Worcester after complaining, have found themselves on the streets.

"It's absolutely out of control," Mr. Cook said of homelessness in the city. He said in the past two months he's seen people of all ages and with all kinds of problems struggling to survive.

Ms. Blair said there isn't enough subsidized housing or other social programs available for couples in the city. She said she and Mr. Cook may have to live in a tent community this winter to avoid the cold.

"We're not looking for a handout," Ms. Blair said. "We need a hand up."

According to figures from the U.S. Census Bureau, the percentage of Worcester families below the poverty line has risen from 14.1 percent to 16 percent from 2000 to 2012, while the percentage of individuals below the poverty level has risen from 17.9 percent to 20.1 percent.

Some of those on the street are those who have become addicted to drugs like heroin, a bad batch of which was blamed for causing a spate of deadly overdoses last month.

"Officials, Residents Ponder... *(continued)*

Jesse Pack, director of prevention and screening at AIDS Project Worcester, said the city needs to make overdose-reversing drug Narcan available to as many people and agencies as possible.

"I think focusing on preventing overdoses, and preventing fatal overdoses in particular, should be a priority," he said.

Michael P. Angelini, chairman of the law firm Bowditch & Dewey, said the most important thing Mr. Augustus needs to do is set an overall tone of excellence for the city.

"To me, what's most important is to say, 'We need to be a place of unmitigated excellence,' " said Mr. Angelini, whether that comes to roads, sidewalks or schools.

Mr. Angelini, who supports Mr. Augustus, said he appreciates the city manager's commitment to better serving the city's youth.

The 71-year-old lawyer said the city needs to improve its schools and should look to spend less on its older population if need be, noting students are the city's future.

Mr. Angelini also stressed the importance of investing in public safety and doing whatever it takes to bring in big employers, including offering tax breaks.

"We are not as competitive as we need to be," he said. "I think we need to take some risks."

Craig L. Blais, president & CEO of the Worcester Business Development Corp., said one of the first things the city needs to do is find a permanent chief development officer.

The city has an interim chief development officer after Mr. McGourthy left that post in February.

Another important discussion is reducing taxes on businesses at the expense of residents, Mr. Blais said — a difficult political move, but one that may be needed to continue economic growth.

Mr. Blais said he also looks forward to implementation of the urban revitalization plan for the city's theater district.

"That area is a key connection between CitySquare and Main Street," Mr. Blais said. "It's going to be high on the agenda for the next couple years."

Though most residents said the city's challenges are going to be difficult to meet, none of them said it was worse off than any other big city.

"I'm proud to live in this city," Mr. Allard said. "I started in this city, and I'm probably going to end in this city."

Frederick H. Eppinger, president and CEO of The Hanover Insurance Group and a city benefactor, said he sees "great things ahead" for the city under Mr. Augustus.

"He has a vision of Worcester as an even stronger, healthier and more vibrant community, and he has the management and leadership skills needed to take the city forward," he said.

The Black Population: 2010

2010 Census Briefs

Issued September 2011

C2010BR-06

By
Sonya Rastogi,
Tallese D. Johnson,
Elizabeth M. Hoeffel,
and
Malcolm P. Drewery, Jr.

INTRODUCTION

This report provides a portrait of the Black population in the United States and discusses its distribution at the national level and at lower levels of geography.[1,2] It is part of a series that analyzes population and housing data collected from the 2010 Census. The data for this report are based on the *2010 Census Redistricting Data (Public Law 94-171) Summary File*, which was the first 2010 Census data product released with data on race and Hispanic origin and was provided to each state for use in drawing boundaries for legislative districts.[3]

UNDERSTANDING RACE DATA FROM THE 2010 CENSUS

The 2010 Census used established federal standards to collect and present data on race.

For the 2010 Census, the question on race was asked of individuals living in the United States (see Figure 1). An individual's response to the race question was based upon self-identification. The U.S. Census Bureau collects information on race following the guidance of the U.S. Office of Management and Budget's

Figure 1.
Reproduction of the Question on Race From the 2010 Census

6. **What is this person's race?** *Mark* $\boxed{X}$ *one or more boxes.*

☐ White
☐ Black, African Am., or Negro
☐ American Indian or Alaska Native — *Print name of enrolled or principal tribe.* ⬎

[   ]

☐ Asian Indian   ☐ Japanese   ☐ Native Hawaiian
☐ Chinese   ☐ Korean   ☐ Guamanian or Chamorro
☐ Filipino   ☐ Vietnamese   ☐ Samoan
☐ Other Asian — *Print race, for example, Hmong, Laotian, Thai, Pakistani, Cambodian, and so on.* ⬎   ☐ Other Pacific Islander — *Print race, for example, Fijian, Tongan, and so on.* ⬎

[   ]

☐ Some other race — *Print race.* ⬎

[   ]

Source: U.S. Census Bureau, 2010 Census questionnaire.

(OMB) 1997 *Revisions to the Standards for the Classification of Federal Data on Race and Ethnicity.*[4] These federal standards mandate that race and Hispanic origin (ethnicity) are separate and distinct concepts and that when collecting these data via self-identification, two different questions must be used.[5]

---

[1] The terms "Black" and "Black or African American" are used interchangeably in this report.
[2] This report discusses data for the 50 states and the District of Columbia, but not Puerto Rico.
[3] Information on the *2010 Census Redistricting Data (Public Law 94-171) Summary File* is available online at <http://2010.census.gov/2010census/data/redistricting-data.php>.

---

[4] The 1997 *Revisions to the Standards for the Classification of Federal Data on Race and Ethnicity,* issued by OMB, is available at <www.whitehouse.gov/omb/fedreg/1997standards.html>.
[5] The OMB requires federal agencies to use a minimum of two ethnicities: Hispanic or Latino and Not Hispanic or Latino. Hispanic origin can be viewed as the heritage, nationality group, lineage, or country of birth of the person or the person's parents or ancestors before their arrival in the United States. People who identify their origin as Hispanic, Latino, or Spanish may be of any race. "Hispanic or Latino" refers to a person of Cuban, Mexican, Puerto Rican, South or Central American, or other Spanish culture or origin regardless of race.

U.S. Department of Commerce
Economics and Statistics Administration
U.S. CENSUS BUREAU

Starting in 1997, OMB required federal agencies to use a minimum of five race categories: White, Black or African American, American Indian or Alaska Native, Asian, and Native Hawaiian or Other Pacific Islander. For respondents unable to identify with any of these five race categories, OMB approved the Census Bureau's inclusion of a sixth category—Some Other Race—on the Census 2000 and 2010 Census questionnaires. The 1997 OMB standards also allowed for respondents to identify with more than one race. The definition of the Black or African American racial category used in the 2010 Census is presented in the text box on this page.

Data on race have been collected since the first U.S. decennial census in 1790.[6] For the first time in Census 2000, individuals were presented with the option to self-identify with more than one race and this continued with the 2010 Census, as prescribed by OMB. There are 57 possible multiple race combinations involving the five OMB race categories and Some Other Race.[7]

The 2010 Census question on race included 15 separate response categories and three areas where respondents could write in detailed information about their race (see

---

DEFINITION OF BLACK OR AFRICAN AMERICAN USED IN THE 2010 CENSUS

According to OMB, "Black or African American" refers to a person having origins in any of the Black racial groups of Africa.

The Black racial category includes people who marked the "Black, African Am., or Negro" checkbox. It also includes respondents who reported entries such as African American; Sub-Saharan African entries, such as Kenyan and Nigerian; and Afro-Caribbean entries, such as Haitian and Jamaican.*

*Sub-Saharan African entries are classified as Black or African American with the exception of Sudanese and Cape Verdean because of their complex, historical heritage. North African entries are classified as White, as OMB defines White as a person having origins in any of the original peoples of Europe, the Middle East, or North Africa.

Figure 1).[8] The response categories and write-in answers can be combined to create the five minimum OMB race categories plus Some Other Race. In addition to White, Black or African American, American Indian and Alaska Native, and Some Other Race, 7 of the 15 response categories are Asian groups and 4 are Native Hawaiian and Other Pacific Islander groups.[9]

For a complete explanation of the race categories used in the 2010 Census, see the 2010 Census Brief, *Overview of Race and Hispanic Origin: 2010.*[10]

---

[8] There were two changes to the question on race for the 2010 Census. First, the wording of the race question was changed from "What is this person's race? Mark ⊠ one or more races to indicate what this person considers himself/herself to be" in 2000 to "What is this person's race? Mark ⊠ one or more boxes" for 2010. Second, in 2010, examples were added to the "Other Asian" response category (Hmong, Laotian, Thai, Pakistani, Cambodian, and so on) and the "Other Pacific Islander" response category (Fijian, Tongan, and so on). In 2000, no examples were given in the race question.

[9] The race categories included in the census questionnaire generally reflect a social definition of race recognized in this country and are not an attempt to define race biologically, anthropologically, or genetically. In addition, it is recognized that the categories of the race question include race and national origin or sociocultural groups.

[10] Humes, K., N. Jones, and R. Ramirez. 2011. *Overview of Race and Hispanic Origin: 2010*, U.S. Census Bureau, 2010 Census Briefs, C2010BR-02, available at <www.census.gov/prod/cen2010/briefs/c2010br-02.pdf>.

RACE ALONE, RACE IN COMBINATION, AND RACE ALONE-OR-IN-COMBINATION CONCEPTS

This report presents data for the Black population and focuses on results for three major conceptual groups.

People who responded to the question on race by indicating only one race are referred to as the *race alone* population, or the group who reported *only one* race. For example, respondents who marked only the "Black, African Am., or Negro" category on the census questionnaire would be included in the *Black alone* population. This population can be viewed as the minimum number of people reporting Black.

Individuals who chose more than one of the six race categories are referred to as the *race in combination* population, or as the group who reported *more than one race.* For example, respondents who reported they were Black or African American *and* White or Black or African American *and* Asian *and* American Indian and Alaska Native would be included in the *Black in combination* population. This population is also referred to as the *multiple-race Black* population.

---

[6] For information about comparability of 2010 Census data on race and Hispanic origin to data collected in previous censuses, see the *2010 Census Redistricting Data (Public Law 94-171) Summary File—Technical Documentation* at <www.census.gov/prod/cen2010/doc/pl94-171.pdf>.

[7] The 2010 Census provides data on the total population reporting more than one race, as well as detailed race combinations (e.g., Black or African American *and* White; Black or African American *and* Asian *and* American Indian and Alaska Native). In this report, the multiple-race categories are denoted with the conjunction *and* in bold and italicized print to indicate the separate race groups that comprise the particular combination.

Table 1.

Black or African American Population: 2000 and 2010

(For information on confidentiality protection, nonsampling error, and definitions, see *www.census.gov/prod/cen2010/doc/pl94-171.pdf*)

Race	2000		2010		Change, 2000 to 2010	
	Number	Percent of total population	Number	Percent of total population	Number	Percent
Total population	281,421,906	100.0	308,745,538	100.0	27,323,632	9.7
Black or African American alone or in combination	36,419,434	12.9	42,020,743	13.6	5,601,309	15.4
Black or African American alone	34,658,190	12.3	38,929,319	12.6	4,271,129	12.3
Black or African American in combination	1,761,244	0.6	3,091,424	1.0	1,330,180	75.5
Black or African American; White.........................	784,764	0.3	1,834,212	0.6	1,049,448	133.7
Black or African American; Some Other Race................	417,249	0.1	314,571	0.1	−102,678	−24.6
Black or African American; American Indian and Alaska Native ..	182,494	0.1	269,421	0.1	86,927	47.6
Black or African American; White; American Indian and Alaska Native.........................	112,207	–	230,848	0.1	118,641	105.7
Black or African American; Asian.........................	106,782	–	185,595	0.1	78,813	73.8
All other combinations including Black or African American	157,748	0.1	256,777	0.1	99,029	62.8
Not Black or African American alone or in combination	245,002,472	87.1	266,724,795	86.4	21,722,323	8.9

– Percentage rounds to 0.0.

Note: In Census 2000, an error in data processing resulted in an overstatement of the Two or More Races population by about 1 million people (about 15 percent) nationally, which almost entirely affected race combinations involving Some Other Race. Therefore, data users should assess observed changes in the Two or More Races population and race combinations involving Some Other Race between Census 2000 and the 2010 Census with caution. Changes in specific race combinations not involving Some Other Race, such as Black or African American *and* White or Black or African American *and* Asian, generally should be more comparable.

Sources: U.S. Census Bureau, *Census 2000 Redistricting Data (Public Law 94-171) Summary File*, Table PL1; and *2010 Census Redistricting Data (Public Law 94-171) Summary File*, Table P1.

The maximum number of people reporting Black is reflected in the *Black alone-or-in-combination* population. One way to define the Black population is to combine those respondents who reported Black alone with those who reported Black in combination with one or more other races. This creates the *Black alone-or-in-combination* population. Another way to think of the *Black alone-or-in-combination* population is the total number of people who reported Black, whether or not they reported any other races.

Throughout the report, the discussion of the Black population compares results for each of these groups and highlights the diversity within the entire Black population.[11]

[11] As a matter of policy, the Census Bureau does not advocate the use of the *alone* population over the *alone-or-in-combination* population or vice versa. The use of the *alone* population in sections of this report does not imply that it is a preferred method of presenting or analyzing data. The same is true for sections of this report that focus on the *alone-or-in-combination* population. Data on race from the 2010 Census can be presented and discussed in a variety of ways.

THE BLACK POPULATION: A SNAPSHOT

The 2010 Census showed that the United States population on April 1, 2010, was 308.7 million. Out of the total population, 38.9 million people, or 13 percent, identified as Black alone (see Table 1).[12, 13] In addition, 3.1 million people, or 1 percent, reported Black in combination with one or more other races.

Together, these two groups totaled 42.0 million people. Thus, 14 percent of all people in the United States identified as Black, either

[12] Percentages shown in text generally are rounded to the nearest integer, while those shown in tables and figures are shown with decimals. All rounding is based on unrounded calculations. Thus, due to rounding, some percentages shown in tables and figures ending in "5" may round either up or down. For example, unrounded numbers of 14.49 and 14.51 would both be shown as 14.5 in a table, but would be cited in the text as 14 and 15, respectively.

[13] For the purposes of this report, the terms "reported," "identified," and "classified" are used interchangeably to refer to the response provided by respondents as well as responses assigned during the editing and imputation process.

alone, or in combination with one or more other races.

The Black population increased at a faster rate than the total population.

The total U.S. population grew by 9.7 percent, from 281.4 million in 2000 to 308.7 million in 2010 (see Table 1). In comparison, the Black alone population grew by 12 percent from 34.7 million to 38.9 million.[14]

The Black alone-or-in-combination population experienced more growth than the total population and the Black alone population, growing by 15 percent. However, both groups grew at a slower rate

[14] The observed changes in the race counts between Census 2000 and the 2010 Census could be attributed to a number of factors. Demographic change since 2000, which includes births and deaths in a geographic area and migration in and out of a geographic area, will have an impact on the resulting 2010 Census counts. Additionally, some changes in the race question's wording and format since Census 2000 could have influenced reporting patterns in the 2010 Census.

Table 2.

Most Frequent Combinations of Black or African American Population With One or More Other Races by Hispanic or Latino Origin: 2000 and 2010

(For information on confidentiality protection, nonsampling error, and definitions, see *www.census.gov/prod/cen2010/doc/pl94-171.pdf*)

Black or African American in combination	2000		2010		Change, 2000 to 2010	
	Number	Percent	Number	Percent	Number	Percent
Total number reporting Black or African American and one or more other races	1,761,244	100.0	3,091,424	100.0	1,330,180	75.5
Black or African American; White	784,764	44.6	1,834,212	59.3	1,049,448	133.7
Black or African American; Some Other Race.	417,249	23.7	314,571	10.2	−102,678	−24.6
Black or African American; American Indian and Alaska Native	182,494	10.4	269,421	8.7	86,927	47.6
Black or African American; White; American Indian and Alaska Native	112,207	6.4	230,848	7.5	118,641	105.7
Black or African American; Asian	106,782	6.1	185,595	6.0	78,813	73.8
Black or African American; White; Some Other Race	43,172	2.5	46,641	1.5	3,469	8.0
All other combinations including Black or African American . . .	114,576	6.5	210,136	6.8	95,560	83.4
Hispanic or Latino						
Black or African American in combination	325,330	100.0	653,747	100.0	328,417	100.9
Black or African American; White.	87,687	27.0	245,850	37.6	158,163	180.4
Black or African American; Some Other Race.	161,283	49.6	227,648	34.8	66,365	41.1
Black or African American; American Indian and Alaska Native.	14,472	4.4	31,571	4.8	17,099	118.2
Black or African American; White; American Indian and Alaska Native.	18,046	5.5	50,000	7.6	31,954	177.1
Black or African American; Asian.	7,269	2.2	15,451	2.4	8,182	112.6
Black or African American; White; Some Other Race	15,481	4.8	33,554	5.1	18,073	116.7
All other combinations including Black or African American.	21,092	6.5	49,673	7.6	28,581	135.5
Not Hispanic or Latino						
Black or African American in combination	1,435,914	100.0	2,437,677	100.0	1,001,763	69.8
Black or African American; White.	697,077	48.5	1,588,362	65.2	891,285	127.9
Black or African American; Some Other Race.	255,966	17.8	86,923	3.6	−169,043	−66.0
Black or African American; American Indian and Alaska Native.	168,022	11.7	237,850	9.8	69,828	41.6
Black or African American; White; American Indian and Alaska Native.	94,161	6.6	180,848	7.4	86,687	92.1
Black or African American; Asian.	99,513	6.9	170,144	7.0	70,631	71.0
Black or African American; White; Some Other Race	27,691	1.9	13,087	0.5	−14,604	−52.7
All other combinations including Black or African American.	93,484	6.5	160,463	6.6	66,979	71.6

Note: In Census 2000, an error in data processing resulted in an overstatement of the Two or More Races population by about 1 million people (about 15 percent) nationally, which almost entirely affected race combinations involving Some Other Race. Therefore, data users should assess observed changes in the Two or More Races population and race combinations involving Some Other Race between Census 2000 and the 2010 Census with caution. Changes in specific race combinations not involving Some Other Race, such as Black or African American *and* White or Black or African American *and* Asian, generally should be more comparable.

Sources: U.S. Census Bureau, *Census 2000 Redistricting Data (Public Law 94-171) Summary File,* Tables PL1 and PL2; and *2010 Census Redistricting Data (Public Law 94-171) Summary File,* Tables P1 and P2.

than most other major race and ethnic groups in the country.[15]

---

[15] Humes, K., N. Jones, and R. Ramirez. 2011. *Overview of Race and Hispanic Origin: 2010,* U.S. Census Bureau, 2010 Census Briefs, C2010BR-02, available at <www.census.gov/prod/cen2010/briefs /c2010br-02.pdf>.

MULTIPLE-RACE REPORTING AMONG THE BLACK POPULATION

Blacks who reported more than one race grew at a much faster rate than the Black alone population.

In the 2010 Census, 3.1 million people reported Black in combination with one or more additional races (see Table 2). The multiple-race Black population grew at a considerably faster rate than the Black alone population, growing by more than three-fourths in size since 2000.

The largest multiple-race combination was Black *and* White.

Among people who reported they were Black and one or more additional races, the majority identified as Black *and* White (59 percent) (see Table 2). This was followed by Black and Some Other Race (10 percent), Black *and* American Indian and Alaska Native (9 percent), and Black *and* White *and* American Indian and Alaska Native (7 percent). Together, these four combinations comprised over 85 percent of all Blacks who reported multiple races.

The Black *and* White population contributed to most of the growth among Blacks who reported multiple races.

Among people who reported their race as Black and one or more additional races, those who reported Black *and* White more than doubled in size from about 785,000 in 2000 to 1.8 million in 2010. This combination constituted the greatest increase in the multiple-race Black population. The Black *and* White population's share of all multiple-race Blacks also increased substantially, from 45 percent in 2000 to 59 percent in 2010, about a 15 percentage-point difference.

The Black *and* Some Other Race population decreased between 2000 to 2010. This decrease was likely due to a data processing error in the Two or More Races population, which largely affected the combinations that included Some Other Race, overstating the

Black *and* Some Other Race population in 2000.[16]

The Black *and* American Indian and Alaska Native population grew by nearly one-half its size, increasing from 182,000 in 2000 to 269,000 in 2010. However, the Black *and* American Indian and Alaska Native population decreased as a proportion of the Black in combination population, from 10 percent to 9 percent.

The Black *and* White *and* American Indian and Alaska Native population increased both numerically and as a proportion of the Black in combination population. This population more than doubled in size from 112,000 in 2000 to 231,000 in 2010.

The Black *and* Asian population increased numerically from 107,000 in 2000 to 186,000 in 2010, an increase of 74 percent or nearly three-fourths in size. However, the Black *and* Asian population as a proportion of Blacks who reported multiple races remained at about 6 percent.

PATTERNS AMONG THE NON-HISPANIC BLACK POPULATION AND THE HISPANIC BLACK POPULATION

According to the 1997 OMB standards, Hispanics may be of any race. The 2010 Census results reflect this, demonstrating that

Hispanics report a diversity of races (White, Black, American Indian or Alaska Native, etc.), or may also report that they are "Some Other Race" (self-identifying their race as "Latino," "Mexican," "Puerto Rican," "Salvadoran," or other national origins or ethnicities), or identify with various combinations of races. For more details on the race reporting patterns of Hispanics, see the 2010 Census Brief, *The Hispanic Population: 2010*.[17]

This section presents data for the Black population, highlighting patterns for Blacks who reported a Hispanic origin and Blacks who did not report a Hispanic origin.

About 97 percent of the Black alone population reported that they were non-Hispanic.

In 2010, the overwhelming majority of the Black alone population was non-Hispanic—about 97 percent of the Black alone population reported as non-Hispanic and 3 percent as Hispanic (see Table 3). Similarly, 95 percent of the Black alone-or-in-combination population reported as non-Hispanic and about 5 percent reported as Hispanic. However, a much lower proportion (79 percent) of people who reported Black in combination with one or more additional races were non-Hispanic.

Both non-Hispanic Blacks and Hispanic Blacks contributed to the growth of the multiple-race Black population.

Nationwide, the total multiple-race population grew from 6.8 million in 2000 to 9.0 million in 2010 (see Tables 3 and 4). Both non-Hispanic

---

[16] In Census 2000, an error in data processing resulted in an overstatement of the Two or More Races population by about 1 million people (about 15 percent) nationally, which almost entirely affected race combinations involving Some Other Race. Therefore, data users should assess observed changes in the Two or More Races population and race combinations involving Some Other Race between Census 2000 and the 2010 Census with caution. Changes in specific race combinations not involving Some Other Race, such as Black or African American *and* White or Black or African American *and* Asian, generally should be more comparable.

[17] Ennis, S., M. Rios-Vargas, and N. Albert. 2011. *The Hispanic Population: 2010*, U.S. Census Bureau, 2010 Census Briefs, C2010BR-04, available at <www.census.gov/prod/cen2010/briefs /c2010br-04.pdf>.

Table 3.
Black or African American Population by Hispanic or Latino Origin: 2010
(For information on confidentiality protection, nonsampling error, and definitions, see *www.census.gov/prod/cen2010/doc/pl94-171.pdf*)

Race and Hispanic or Latino origin	Alone or in combination			Alone			In combination		
	Number	Percent of total population	Percent of Black or African American population	Number	Percent of total population	Percent of Black or African American population	Number	Percent of total population	Percent of Black or African American population
Total population ...	308,745,538	100.0	(X)	299,736,465	100.0	(X)	9,009,073	100.0	(X)
Black or African American ...	42,020,743	13.6	100.0	38,929,319	13.0	100.0	3,091,424	34.3	100.0
Hispanic or Latino	1,897,218	0.6	4.5	1,243,471	0.4	3.2	653,747	7.3	21.1
Not Hispanic or Latino	40,123,525	13.0	95.5	37,685,848	12.6	96.8	2,437,677	27.1	78.9

(X) Not applicable.

Source: U.S. Census Bureau, *2010 Census Redistricting Data (Public Law 94-171) Summary File,* Tables P1 and P2.

Blacks and Hispanic Blacks contributed to this growth. In 2000, non-Hispanic Blacks accounted for 21 percent of all people who reported multiple races, compared with 27 percent in 2010. Hispanic Blacks accounted for 5 percent of all people who reported multiple races in 2000 and increased to 7 percent in 2010.

Over the last 10 years there has been a large increase in the non-Hispanic Black in combination population who reported Black *and* White (see Table 2). In the 2010 Census, 65 percent of non-Hispanic Blacks who reported multiple races were Black *and* White, compared with 49 percent in 2000. Black *and* American Indian and Alaska Native accounted for 10 percent, and Black *and* White *and* American Indian and Alaska Native, and Black *and* Asian accounted for 7 percent each.

In 2010, among Hispanics who identified as Black and one or more additional races, 38 percent reported Black *and* White, compared with 27 percent in 2000. Black *and* Some Other Race accounted for 35 percent, Black *and* White *and* American Indian and Alaska Native accounted for 8 percent, and Black *and* White *and* Some Other Race accounted for 5 percent.

Table 4.
Black or African American Population by Hispanic or Latino Origin: 2000
(For information on confidentiality protection, nonsampling error, and definitions, see *www.census.gov/prod/cen2000/doc/pl94-171.pdf*)

Race and Hispanic or Latino origin	Alone or in combination			Alone			In combination		
	Number	Percent of total population	Percent of Black or African American population	Number	Percent of total population	Percent of Black or African American population	Number	Percent of total population	Percent of Black or African American population
Total population ..	281,421,906	100.0	(X)	274,595,678	100.0	(X)	6,826,228	100.0	(X)
Black or African American ..	36,419,434	12.9	100.0	34,658,190	12.6	100.0	1,761,244	25.8	100.0
Hispanic or Latino	1,035,683	0.4	2.8	710,353	0.3	2.0	325,330	4.8	18.5
Not Hispanic or Latino	35,383,751	12.6	97.2	33,947,837	12.4	98.0	1,435,914	21.0	81.5

(X) Not applicable.

Source: U.S. Census Bureau, *2000 Census Redistricting Data (Public Law 94-171) Summary File,* Tables PL1 and PL2.

THE GEOGRAPHIC DISTRIBUTION OF THE BLACK POPULATION

The South was the region where Blacks comprised the greatest proportion of the total population.

The South was the region where the Black alone-or-in-combination population comprised the greatest proportion of the total population, at 20 percent (see Table 5).[18] In other regions, the Black alone-or-in-combination population was much smaller in proportion—13 percent in the Northeast, 11 percent in the Midwest, and 6 percent in the West. These results were similar for the Black alone population.

The majority of Blacks in the United States lived in the South.

According to the 2010 Census, of all respondents who reported Black alone-or-in-combination, 55 percent lived in the South, 18 percent in the Midwest, 17 percent in the Northeast, and 10 percent in the West (see Figure 2). This pattern was similar for the Black alone population.

Compared to 2000, the proportions of the Black alone-or-in-combination population for the West stayed about the same, while the proportions increased

[18] The Northeast census region includes Connecticut, Maine, Massachusetts, New Hampshire, New Jersey, New York, Pennsylvania, Rhode Island, and Vermont. The Midwest census region includes Illinois, Indiana, Iowa, Kansas, Michigan, Minnesota, Missouri, Nebraska, North Dakota, Ohio, South Dakota, and Wisconsin. The South census region includes Alabama, Arkansas, Delaware, the District of Columbia, Florida, Georgia, Kentucky, Louisiana, Maryland, Mississippi, North Carolina, Oklahoma, South Carolina, Tennessee, Texas, Virginia, and West Virginia. The West census region includes Alaska, Arizona, California, Colorado, Hawaii, Idaho, Montana, Nevada, New Mexico, Oregon, Utah, Washington, and Wyoming.

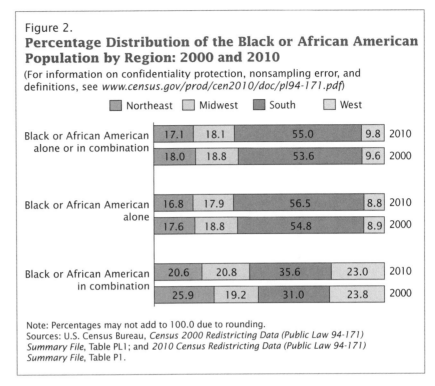

Figure 2.
Percentage Distribution of the Black or African American Population by Region: 2000 and 2010
(For information on confidentiality protection, nonsampling error, and definitions, see *www.census.gov/prod/cen2010/doc/pl94-171.pdf*)

Note: Percentages may not add to 100.0 due to rounding.
Sources: U.S. Census Bureau, *Census 2000 Redistricting Data (Public Law 94-171) Summary File*, Table PL1; and *2010 Census Redistricting Data (Public Law 94-171) Summary File*, Table P1.

in the South and decreased in the Northeast and the Midwest. The proportion of the Black alone population also increased in the South, from 55 percent in 2000 to 57 percent in 2010, whereas the Northeast and the Midwest experienced decreases in their share of the Black alone population.

The multiple-race Black population was more geographically dispersed than the Black alone population.

The Black in combination population had a different regional pattern compared to the Black alone population (see Figure 2). A considerably higher proportion of the multiple-race Black population lived in the West (23 percent), relative to the Black alone population (9 percent). While a large proportion of the multiple-race Black population lived in the South (36 percent), this was much lower than the Black alone population (57 percent).

The Black population grew in every region between 2000 and 2010 with the Black in combination population contributing to this growth, particularly in the South.

The Black alone-or-in-combination population grew in every region between 2000 and 2010, led by 18 percent growth in both the South and the West (see Table 5). The Black alone population also increased in every region, but at a slower rate than the Black alone-or-in-combination population. The Black alone population grew the most in the South, increasing by 16 percent.

The Black in combination population contributed to population growth in every region, particularly the South. In the South, the Black in combination population doubled from 547,000 to 1.1 million, growing 101 percent over the decade. The Midwest also experienced

Table 5.

Black or African American Population for the United States, Regions, and States, and for Puerto Rico: 2000 and 2010

(For information on confidentiality protection, nonsampling error, and definitions, see *www.census.gov/prod/cen2010/doc/pl94-171.pdf*)

Area	Black or African American alone or in combination				Black or African American alone				Black or African American in combination			
	2000	2010	Percent of total population, 2010[1]	Percent change, 2000 to 2010	2000	2010	Percent of total population, 2010[1]	Percent change, 2000 to 2010	2000	2010	Percent of total population, 2010[1]	Percent change, 2000 to 2010
United States	36,419,434	42,020,743	13.6	15.4	34,658,190	38,929,319	12.6	12.3	1,761,244	3,091,424	1.0	75.5
REGION												
Northeast	6,556,909	7,187,488	13.0	9.6	6,099,881	6,550,217	11.8	7.4	457,028	637,271	1.2	39.4
Midwest	6,838,669	7,594,486	11.3	11.1	6,499,733	6,950,869	10.4	6.9	338,936	643,617	1.0	89.9
South	19,528,231	23,105,082	20.2	18.3	18,981,692	22,005,433	19.2	15.9	546,539	1,099,649	1.0	101.2
West	3,495,625	4,133,687	5.7	18.3	3,076,884	3,422,800	4.8	11.2	418,741	710,887	1.0	69.8
STATE												
Alabama	1,168,998	1,281,118	26.8	9.6	1,155,930	1,251,311	26.2	8.3	13,068	29,807	0.6	128.1
Alaska	27,147	33,150	4.7	22.1	21,787	23,263	3.3	6.8	5,360	9,887	1.4	84.5
Arizona	185,599	318,665	5.0	71.7	158,873	259,008	4.1	63.0	26,726	59,657	0.9	123.2
Arkansas	427,152	468,710	16.1	9.7	418,950	449,895	15.4	7.4	8,202	18,815	0.6	129.4
California	2,513,041	2,683,914	7.2	6.8	2,263,882	2,299,072	6.2	1.6	249,159	384,842	1.0	54.5
Colorado	190,717	249,812	5.0	31.0	165,063	201,737	4.0	22.2	25,654	48,075	1.0	87.4
Connecticut	339,078	405,600	11.3	19.6	309,843	362,296	10.1	16.9	29,235	43,304	1.2	48.1
Delaware	157,152	205,923	22.9	31.0	150,666	191,814	21.4	27.3	6,486	14,109	1.6	117.5
District of Columbia	350,455	314,352	52.2	−10.3	343,312	305,125	50.7	−11.1	7,143	9,227	1.5	29.2
Florida	2,471,730	3,200,663	17.0	29.5	2,335,505	2,999,862	16.0	28.4	136,225	200,801	1.1	47.4
Georgia	2,393,425	3,054,098	31.5	27.6	2,349,542	2,950,435	30.5	25.6	43,883	103,663	1.1	136.2
Hawaii	33,343	38,820	2.9	16.4	22,000	21,424	1.6	−2.6	11,340	17,396	1.3	53.4
Idaho	8,127	15,940	1.0	96.1	5,456	9,810	0.6	79.8	2,671	6,130	0.4	129.5
Illinois	1,937,671	1,974,113	15.4	1.9	1,876,875	1,866,414	14.5	−0.6	60,796	107,699	0.8	77.1
Indiana	538,015	654,415	10.1	21.6	510,034	591,397	9.1	16.0	27,981	63,018	1.0	125.2
Iowa	72,512	113,225	3.7	56.1	61,853	89,148	2.9	44.1	10,659	24,077	0.8	125.9
Kansas	170,610	202,149	7.1	18.5	154,198	167,864	5.9	8.9	16,412	34,285	1.2	108.9
Kentucky	311,878	376,213	8.7	20.6	295,994	337,520	7.8	14.0	15,884	38,693	0.9	143.6
Louisiana	1,468,317	1,486,885	32.8	1.3	1,451,944	1,452,396	32.0	−	16,373	34,489	0.8	110.6
Maine	9,553	21,764	1.6	127.8	6,760	15,707	1.2	132.4	2,793	6,057	0.5	116.9
Maryland	1,525,036	1,783,899	30.9	17.0	1,477,411	1,700,298	29.4	15.1	47,625	83,601	1.4	75.5
Massachusetts	398,479	508,413	7.8	27.6	343,454	434,398	6.6	26.5	55,025	74,015	1.1	34.5
Michigan	1,474,613	1,505,514	15.2	2.1	1,412,742	1,400,362	14.2	−0.9	61,871	105,152	1.1	70.0
Minnesota	202,972	327,548	6.2	61.4	171,731	274,412	5.2	59.8	31,241	53,136	1.0	70.1
Mississippi	1,041,708	1,115,801	37.6	7.1	1,033,809	1,098,385	37.0	6.2	7,899	17,416	0.6	120.5
Missouri	655,377	747,474	12.5	14.1	629,391	693,391	11.6	10.2	25,986	54,083	0.9	108.1
Montana	4,441	7,917	0.8	78.3	2,692	4,027	0.4	49.6	1,749	3,890	0.4	122.4
Nebraska	75,833	98,959	5.4	30.5	68,541	82,885	4.5	20.9	7,292	16,074	0.9	120.4
Nevada	150,508	254,452	9.4	69.1	135,477	218,626	8.1	61.4	15,031	35,826	1.3	138.3
New Hampshire	12,218	21,736	1.7	77.9	9,035	15,035	1.1	66.4	3,183	6,701	0.5	110.5
New Jersey	1,211,750	1,300,363	14.8	7.3	1,141,821	1,204,826	13.7	5.5	69,929	95,537	1.1	36.6
New Mexico	42,412	57,040	2.8	34.5	34,343	42,550	2.1	23.9	8,069	14,490	0.7	79.6
New York	3,234,165	3,334,550	17.2	3.1	3,014,385	3,073,800	15.9	2.0	219,780	260,750	1.3	18.6
North Carolina	1,776,283	2,151,456	22.6	21.1	1,737,545	2,048,628	21.5	17.9	38,738	102,828	1.1	165.4
North Dakota	5,372	11,086	1.6	106.4	3,916	7,960	1.2	103.3	1,456	3,126	0.5	114.7
Ohio	1,372,501	1,541,771	13.4	12.3	1,301,307	1,407,681	12.2	8.2	71,194	134,090	1.2	88.3
Oklahoma	284,766	327,621	8.7	15.0	260,968	277,644	7.4	6.4	23,798	49,977	1.3	110.0
Oregon	72,647	98,479	2.6	35.6	55,662	69,206	1.8	24.3	16,985	29,273	0.8	72.3
Pennsylvania	1,289,123	1,507,965	11.9	17.0	1,224,612	1,377,689	10.8	12.5	64,511	130,276	1.0	101.9
Rhode Island	58,051	77,754	7.4	33.9	46,908	60,189	5.7	28.3	11,143	17,565	1.7	57.6
South Carolina	1,200,901	1,332,188	28.8	10.9	1,185,216	1,290,684	27.9	8.9	15,685	41,504	0.9	164.6
South Dakota	6,687	14,705	1.8	119.9	4,685	10,207	1.3	117.9	2,002	4,498	0.6	124.7
Tennessee	953,349	1,107,178	17.4	16.1	932,809	1,057,315	16.7	13.3	20,540	49,863	0.8	142.8
Texas	2,493,057	3,168,469	12.6	27.1	2,404,566	2,979,598	11.8	23.9	88,491	188,871	0.8	113.4
Utah	24,382	43,209	1.6	77.2	17,657	29,287	1.1	65.9	6,725	13,922	0.5	107.0
Vermont	4,492	9,343	1.5	108.0	3,063	6,277	1.0	104.9	1,429	3,066	0.5	114.6
Virginia	1,441,207	1,653,563	20.7	14.7	1,390,293	1,551,399	19.4	11.6	50,914	102,164	1.3	100.7
Washington	238,398	325,004	4.8	36.3	190,267	240,042	3.6	26.2	48,131	84,962	1.3	76.5
West Virginia	62,817	76,945	4.2	22.5	57,232	63,124	3.4	10.3	5,585	13,821	0.7	147.5
Wisconsin	326,506	403,527	7.1	23.6	304,460	359,148	6.3	18.0	22,046	44,379	0.8	101.3
Wyoming	4,863	7,285	1.3	49.8	3,722	4,748	0.8	27.6	1,141	2,537	0.5	122.3
Puerto Rico	416,296	550,259	14.8	32.2	302,933	461,498	12.4	52.3	113,363	88,761	2.4	−21.7

− Percentage rounds to 0.0.

[1] The percent of the total population is calculated by using the total population of all races. The totals for each geography can be found in Table 11, page 18 of the 2010 Census Brief, *Overview of Race and Hispanic Origin: 2010* available at <www.census.gov/prod/cen2010/briefs/c2010br-02.pdf>.

Sources: U.S. Census Bureau, *Census 2000 Redistricting Data (Public Law 94-171) Summary File*, Table PL1; and *2010 Census Redistricting Data (Public Law 94-171) Summary File*, Table P1.

considerable growth in the Black in combination population, increasing 90 percent, followed by increases of 70 percent in the West and 39 percent in the Northeast.

This growth contributed to shifting patterns of the Black in combination population by region. The proportion of the Black in combination population residing in the South increased from 31 percent to 36 percent, and decreased in the Northeast (from 26 percent to 21 percent) (see Figure 2).

The Black population represented over 50 percent of the total population in the District of Columbia and over 25 percent of the total population in six states, all located in the South.

The Black alone-or-in-combination population represented 38 percent of the total population in Mississippi (see Table 5). This was followed by Louisiana (33 percent), Georgia (32 percent), Maryland (31 percent), South Carolina (29 percent), and Alabama (27 percent). These same six states had the highest proportion of the Black alone population and the proportions were similar to the Black alone-or-in-combination population. The Black alone-or-in-combination population represented 52 percent of the total population in the District of Columbia.[19]

The Black alone-or-in-combination population represented less than 3 percent of the total population in 12 states, all located outside of the South. More than half of the states in the West had a Black alone-or-in-combination population of less than 3 percent—Hawaii, New Mexico, and Oregon (about 3 percent each); Utah (about 2 percent); and Wyoming, Idaho, and Montana (about 1 percent each).

---

[19] For this report, the District of Columbia is treated as a state equivalent.

The Black alone-or-in-combination population represented less than 3 percent of the total population in two states in the Midwest—South Dakota and North Dakota (about 2 percent each), and three states in the Northeast—New Hampshire, Maine, (about 2 percent each) and Vermont (1 percent). These same 12 states also had less than 3 percent of the Black alone population and the percentages tended to be slightly lower than the Black alone-or-in-combination population. One additional state (Iowa) had a Black alone population of less than 3 percent, and thus 13 states had Black alone populations of less than 3 percent.

Nearly 60 percent of all people who reported Black lived in ten states.

The ten states with the largest Black alone-or-in-combination populations in 2010 were New York (3.3 million), Florida (3.2 million), Texas (3.2 million), Georgia (3.1 million), California (2.7 million), North Carolina (2.2 million), Illinois (2.0 million), Maryland (1.8 million), Virginia (1.7 million), and Ohio (1.5 million) (see Table 5). Among these states, four experienced substantial growth between 2000 and 2010. The Black alone-or-in-combination population grew by 29 percent in Florida, 28 percent in Georgia, 27 percent in Texas, and 21 percent in North Carolina.

Out of the ten states above, nine of them also had the largest Black alone populations. The state with the tenth largest Black alone population was Louisiana (1.5 million). In a similar fashion to the Black alone-or-in-combination population, the Black alone population also experienced considerable growth in Florida, Georgia, Texas, and North Carolina.

The Black population grew in every state between 2000 and 2010, but declined in the District of Columbia.

Among all states, the states with small Black alone-or-in-combination populations (2 percent or less) in 2010 tended to experience the largest percentage growth. Maine experienced the largest percentage growth in the Black alone-or-in-combination population, increasing by 128 percent between 2000 and 2010. This was followed by South Dakota (120 percent), Vermont (108 percent), North Dakota (106 percent), and Idaho (96 percent).

At the other end of the spectrum, the Black population in the District of Columbia decreased by 10 percent between 2000 and 2010. As discussed earlier, the District of Columbia still had the highest proportion reporting Black among states, with 52 percent in 2010. The same patterns were observed for the Black alone population by state.

The Black in combination population showed even more substantial growth, as it more than doubled in more than half of all states. The states that experienced the most growth were in the South: North Carolina and South Carolina both grew by 165 percent, followed by West Virginia (147 percent), Kentucky (144 percent), and Tennessee (143 percent).

Of the population who identified as Black, people who reported multiple races were more likely to live in California.

Of all respondents who reported as Black alone-or-in-combination, about 8 percent lived in each of these states—New York, Florida, and Texas. Another 7 percent lived in Georgia and 6 percent lived in

Figure 3.
Percentage Distribution of the Black or African American Population by State: 2010

(For information on confidentiality protection, nonsampling error, and definitions, see *www.census.gov/prod/cen2010/doc/pl94-171.pdf*)

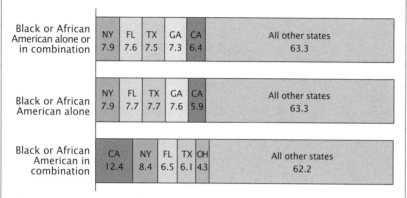

Note: Percentages may not add to 100.0 due to rounding.
Source: U.S. Census Bureau, *2010 Census Redistricting Data (Public Law 94-171) Summary File*, Table P1.

California (see Figure 3). The pattern for the Black alone population was similar, where 8 percent of the Black alone population lived in New York, Florida, Texas, and Georgia and 6 percent lived in California.

The pattern was slightly different for respondents who identified as Black in combination with one or more additional races. Among multiple-race Blacks, 12 percent lived in California, 8 percent in New York, 6 percent lived in both Florida and Texas, and 4 percent in Ohio.

The Black population was highly concentrated in counties in the South.

The Black alone-or-in-combination population was highly concentrated in 2010: 62 percent (1,941 counties) of all counties in the United States had less than 5 percent of the population identified as Black alone-or-in-combination, but in 106 counties, the Black alone-or-in-combination population comprised 50 percent or more of the total county population. All of these counties were located in the South except for the city of St. Louis, MO, which

is considered a county equivalent (see Figure 4). These patterns were similar for the Black alone population.

Concentrations of Blacks outside of the South tended to be in counties located within metropolitan statistical areas. There were 317 counties where the Black alone-or-in-combination population was 25.0 to 49.9 percent of the county population, and only 17 of these counties were not in the South. Of these 17 counties, 15 were in metro areas. This pattern was similar for the Black alone population.

Although the Black alone-or-in-combination population and the Black alone population were not as concentrated in counties in midwestern states, in some metro areas, such as around Chicago, IL, and Detroit, MI, the proportion Black was much higher than the national average of 13 percent. Also, in some metro areas in the West, such as around San Francisco, CA, and Sacramento, CA, the proportion Black was above the national average.

The Black population in the South experienced mixed growth—some counties experienced an increase, while others experienced a decline.

Among the 1,558 counties with a Black alone-or-in-combination population of over 1,000 people, over one-third (536 counties) had an increase of 25 percent or more from 2000 to 2010 (see Figure 5). On the other hand, 100 counties had a decrease of over 10 percent. The Black alone-or-in-combination population in counties located in northeastern states such as Maine and Pennsylvania grew significantly, as well as counties in the South, specifically Florida, which had a number of counties that grew by 25 percent or more.

Large growth in the Black alone-or-in-combination population also occurred in the West and sections of the Midwest. Counties in Arizona, Nevada, California, Oregon, and Washington grew substantially between 2000 and 2010. The Midwest had pockets of high growth in states such as Minnesota, Wisconsin, and Illinois.

The Black alone-or-in-combination population in the South experienced the largest percentage declines between 2000 and 2010. Counties located in southern states such as Texas, Arkansas, Louisiana, Mississippi, Alabama, and Georgia experienced greater declines in the Black alone-or-in-combination population compared to the rest of the nation. The Black alone population had similar results.

The Black in combination population had large concentrations in northeastern states and counties near metro areas in the West, Midwest, and South.

In 2010, large proportions of the Black in combination population were located in counties

Figure 4.
Black or African American Population as a Percent of County Population: 2010
(For information on confidentiality protection, nonsampling error, and definitions, see
www.census.gov/prod/cen2010/doc/pl94-171.pdf)

Black or African American Alone

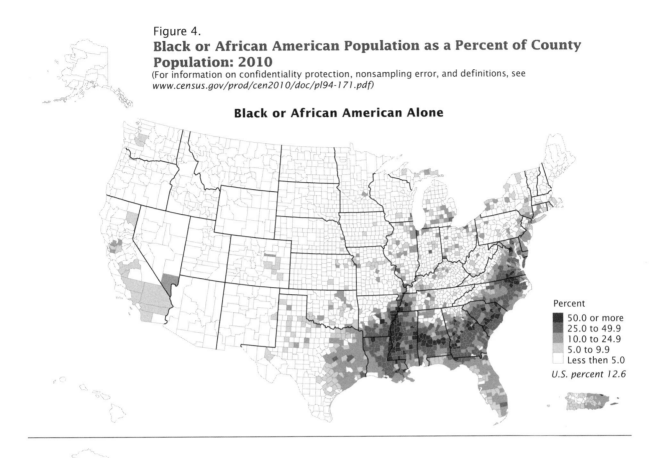

Black or African American Alone or in Combination

Source: U.S. Census Bureau, *2010 Census Redistricting Data (Public Law 94-171) Summary File*, Table P1.

Figure 5.
Percent Change in Black or African American Population: 2000 to 2010

(Counties with a Black or African American population of at least 1,000 are included in the maps. For information on confidentiality protection, nonsampling error, and definitions, see *www.census.gov/prod/cen2010/doc/pl94-171.pdf*)

Black or African American Alone

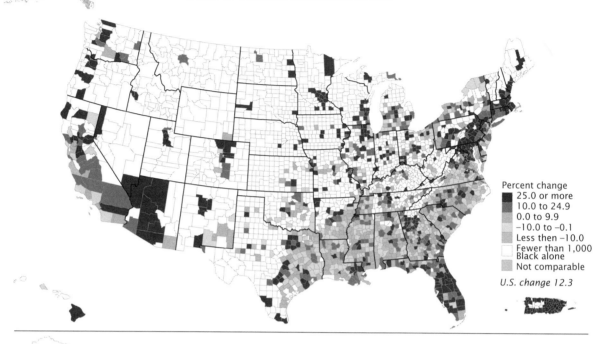

Percent change
- 25.0 or more
- 10.0 to 24.9
- 0.0 to 9.9
- −10.0 to −0.1
- Less then −10.0
- Fewer than 1,000 Black alone
- Not comparable

U.S. change 12.3

Black or African American Alone or in Combination

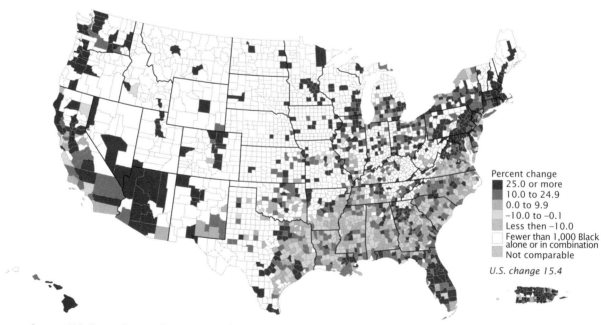

Percent change
- 25.0 or more
- 10.0 to 24.9
- 0.0 to 9.9
- −10.0 to −0.1
- Less then −10.0
- Fewer than 1,000 Black alone or in combination
- Not comparable

U.S. change 15.4

Sources: U.S. Census Bureau, *Census 2000 Redistricting Data (Public Law 94-171) Summary File*, Table PL1; and *2010 Census Redistricting Data (Public Law 94-171) Summary File*, Table P1.

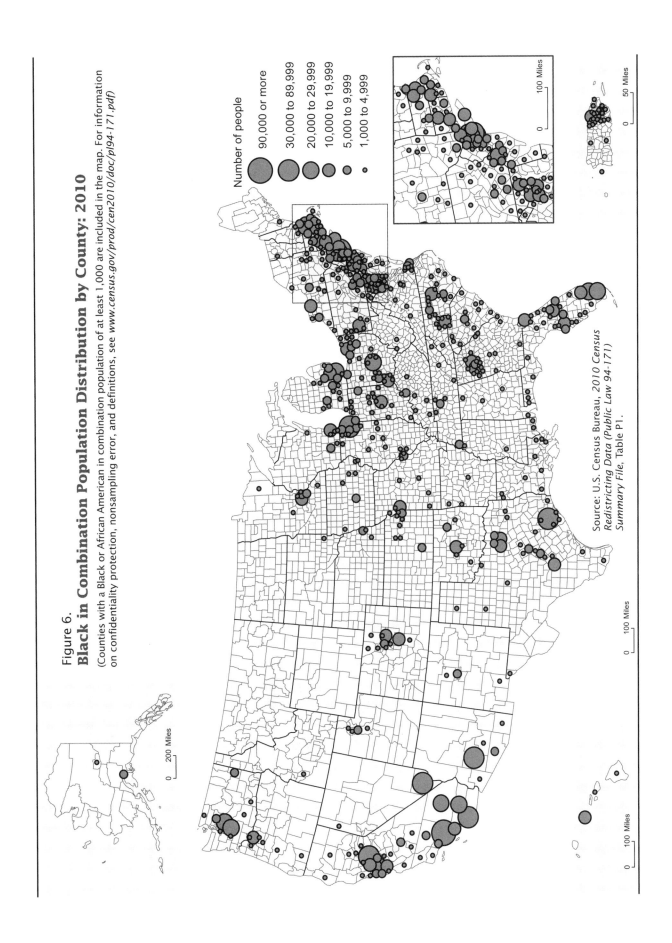

Figure 6.
Black in Combination Population Distribution by County: 2010

(Counties with a Black or African American in combination population of at least 1,000 are included in the map. For information on confidentiality protection, nonsampling error, and definitions, see *www.census.gov/prod/cen2010/doc/pl94-171.pdf*)

Number of people

90,000 or more
30,000 to 89,999
20,000 to 29,999
10,000 to 19,999
5,000 to 9,999
1,000 to 4,999

Source: U.S. Census Bureau, *2010 Census Redistricting Data (Public Law 94-171) Summary File*, Table P1.

Table 6.
Ten Places With the Largest Number of Blacks or African Americans: 2010

(For information on confidentiality protection, nonsampling error, and definitions, see *www.census.gov/prod/cen2010/doc/pl94-171.pdf*)

Place[1]	Total population	Black or African American alone or in combination		Black or African American alone		Black or African American in combination	
		Rank	Number	Rank	Number	Rank	Number
New York, NY.............	8,175,133	1	2,228,145	1	2,088,510	1	139,635
Chicago, IL	2,695,598	2	913,009	2	887,608	3	25,401
Philadelphia, PA..........	1,526,006	3	686,870	3	661,839	4	25,031
Detroit, MI	713,777	4	601,988	4	590,226	13	11,762
Houston, TX.............	2,099,451	5	514,217	5	498,466	8	15,751
Memphis, TN	646,889	6	414,928	6	409,687	58	5,241
Baltimore, MD	620,961	7	403,998	7	395,781	29	8,217
Los Angeles, CA	3,792,621	8	402,448	8	365,118	2	37,330
Washington, DC..........	601,723	9	314,352	9	305,125	22	9,227
Dallas, TX	1,197,816	10	308,087	10	298,993	23	9,094
Columbus, OH...........	787,033	15	237,077	16	220,241	5	16,836
San Diego, CA...........	1,307,402	40	104,374	43	87,949	6	16,425
Phoenix, AZ.............	1,445,632	37	109,544	40	93,608	7	15,936
Indianapolis, IN	829,718	14	240,789	15	226,671	9	14,118
Boston, MA	617,594	21	163,629	23	150,437	10	13,192

[1] Places of 100,000 or more total population. The 2010 Census showed 282 places in the United States with 100,000 or more population. They included 273 incorporated places (including 5 city-county consolidations) and 9 census designated places (CDPs) that were not legally incorporated.

Source: U.S. Census Bureau, *2010 Census Redistricting Data (Public Law 94-171) Summary File*, Table P1.

in northeastern states such as Pennsylvania, New Jersey, New York, and Massachusetts (see Figure 6). The Black in combination population was also concentrated in counties in midwestern states such as Ohio, Michigan, and Indiana, as well as in counties in southern states such as Georgia, North Carolina, and Florida.

Counties near metro areas in the Midwest such as Chicago, IL; Detroit, MI; and Minneapolis, MN, also had large concentrations of the Black in combination population. There were also large concentrations of the Black in combination population in the West in counties near metro areas such as Los Angeles, CA; San Francisco, CA; and Seattle, WA.

The places with the largest Black population were New York and Chicago.

Among the places with populations of 100,000 or more, the 2010 Census showed that New York, NY, had the largest Black

alone-or-in-combination population with 2.2 million, followed by Chicago, IL (913,000) (see Table 6). Three other places had Black alone-or-in-combination populations of over 500,000 people (Philadelphia, PA; Detroit, MI; and Houston, TX).

Five of the ten places with the largest Black alone-or-in-combination populations—Houston, TX; Memphis, TN; Baltimore, MD; Washington, DC; and Dallas, TX—were in the South. These rankings were identical for the Black alone population.

The places with the largest Black in combination populations were New York and Los Angeles.

Among the places with populations of 100,000 or more, New York, NY, had the largest Black in combination population (140,000), followed by Los Angeles, CA (37,000) (see Table 6). Two other places, Chicago, IL, and Philadelphia, PA, had populations over 25,000.

In contrast to the patterns observed for the Black alone-or-in-combination population, only one out of the ten places with the largest Black in combination population was in the South and there was more representation of places in the Midwest and the West.

The place with the greatest proportion Black was Detroit.

Among the places with populations of 100,000 or more, the places with the greatest proportion Black alone-or-in-combination were Detroit, MI (84 percent); followed by Jackson, MS (80 percent); Miami Gardens, FL (78 percent); and Birmingham, AL (74 percent) (see Table 7). Of the top ten places shown, all were majority Black.

Of these places, eight were in the South, and two were in the Midwest, specifically Michigan. These patterns were the same for the Black alone population and the proportions were similar to the Black alone-or-in-combination population.

Table 7.

Ten Places With the Highest Percentage of Blacks or African Americans: 2010

(For information on confidentiality protection, nonsampling error, and definitions, see *www.census.gov/prod/cen2010/doc/pl94-171.pdf*)

Place[1]	Total population	Black or African American alone or in combination		Black or African American alone		Black or African American in combination	
		Rank	Percent of total population	Rank	Percent of total population	Rank	Percent of total population
Detroit, MI	713,777	1	84.3	1	82.7	83	1.6
Jackson, MS	173,514	2	80.1	2	79.4	242	0.7
Miami Gardens, FL	107,167	3	77.9	3	76.3	91	1.6
Birmingham, AL.	212,237	4	74.0	4	73.4	257	0.6
Baltimore, MD	620,961	5	65.1	5	63.7	134	1.3
Memphis, TN	646,889	6	64.1	6	63.3	225	0.8
New Orleans, LA	343,829	7	61.2	7	60.2	184	1.0
Flint, MI	102,434	8	59.5	9	56.6	9	2.9
Montgomery, AL	205,764	9	57.4	8	56.6	231	0.8
Savannah, GA	136,286	10	56.7	10	55.4	139	1.3
Lansing, MI	114,297	69	27.8	78	23.7	1	4.1
Tacoma, WA.	198,397	132	15.0	145	11.2	2	3.8
Killeen, TX	127,921	40	37.9	46	34.1	3	3.8
Syracuse, NY.	145,170	51	33.1	57	29.5	4	3.6
Providence, RI.	178,042	109	19.4	114	16.0	5	3.3
Fairfield, CA.	105,321	111	19.0	118	15.7	6	3.3
Rochester, NY	210,565	29	44.9	33	41.7	7	3.2
Fayetteville, NC	200,564	31	44.8	32	41.9	8	2.9
Vallejo, CA.	115,942	81	24.9	83	22.1	10	2.9

[1] Places of 100,000 or more total population. The 2010 Census showed 282 places in the United States with 100,000 or more population. They included 273 incorporated places (including 5 city-county consolidations) and 9 census designated places (CDPs) that were not legally incorporated.

Source: U.S. Census Bureau, *2010 Census Redistricting Data (Public Law 94-171) Summary File*, Table P1.

The place with the highest proportion of people who identified as multiple-race Black was Lansing, MI.

Among the places with populations of 100,000 or more, the places with the highest proportion of people who identified as Black and one or more other races were Lansing, MI; Tacoma, WA; Killeen, TX; and Syracuse, NY (about 4 percent each) (see Table 7). Of these ten places, three were in the Northeast, three were in the West, two in the Midwest, and two in the South.

Among the 20 largest metropolitan statistical areas, New York-Northern New Jersey-Long Island, NY-NJ-PA, had the highest proportion of the non-Hispanic Black alone population living inside the largest principal city.

The remaining sections discuss geographic patterns for the non-Hispanic Black alone population

and make comparisons to other race and ethnic groups.

Figure 7 shows the proportion of selected race and Hispanic origin groups who lived inside the largest principal city of the 20 largest metro areas in the country versus those who lived outside of that largest principal city.[20] The red bars represent the non-Hispanic Black alone population, the blue bars represent the non-Hispanic White alone population, the green bars represent the Hispanic population, and the orange bars represent other race groups.[21] For example, the red bar denotes the proportion of the

[20] For the remainder of this section, when metro areas are discussed, the report will refer to the largest 20 metropolitan statistical areas.

[21] For this report, the "other" race group refers to the non-Hispanic Asian alone, non-Hispanic American Indian and Alaska Native alone, non-Hispanic Native Hawaiian and Other Pacific Islander alone, and non-Hispanic Some Other Race alone populations, as well as non-Hispanics who reported multiple races.

non-Hispanic Black alone population that lived inside the largest principal city of Boston (46 percent), out of the total non-Hispanic Black alone population in the entire Boston-Cambridge-Quincy, MA-NH metro area.

The top 5 metro areas that had the highest proportion of the non-Hispanic Black alone population living inside their respective largest principal cities were New York-Northern New Jersey-Long Island, NY-NJ-PA (61 percent); Detroit-Warren-Livonia, MI (60 percent); San Diego-Carlsbad-San Marcos, CA (56 percent); Chicago-Joliet-Naperville, IL-IN-WI (54 percent); and Philadelphia-Camden-Wilmington, PA-NJ-DE-MD (53 percent).

The 5 metro areas with the lowest proportion of the non-Hispanic Black alone population living inside their respective largest principal cities were Miami-Fort

Figure 7.
Proportion of Race and Ethnic Groups Living Inside the Largest Principal City of the 20 Largest Metropolitan Statistical Areas: 2010

(For information on confidentiality protection, nonsampling error, and definitions, see *www.census.gov/prod/cen2010/doc/pl94-171.pdf*)

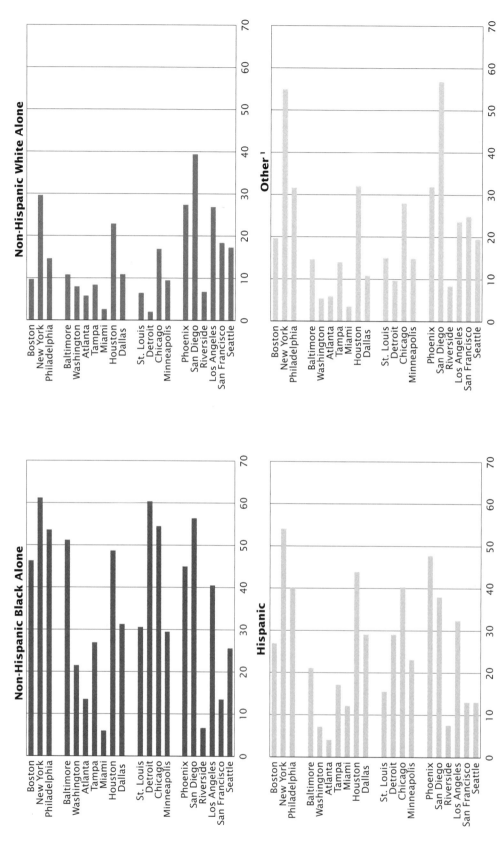

[1] For this figure, the "other" race category refers to the non-Hispanic Asian alone, non-Hispanic American Indian and Alaska Native alone, non-Hispanic Native Hawaiian and Other Pacific Islander alone, and non-Hispanic Some Other Race alone populations, as well as non-Hispanics who reported multiple races.

Note: Principal cities within regions are organized based on proximity to each other. Boston, New York, and Philadelphia are located in the Northeast census region. Baltimore, Washington, Atlanta, Tampa, Miami, Houston, and Dallas are located in the South census region. St. Louis, Detroit, Chicago, and Minneapolis are located in the Midwest census region. Phoenix, San Diego, Riverside, Los Angeles, San Francisco, and Seattle are located in the West census region.

Source: U.S. Census Bureau, 2010 Census special tabulation.

Lauderdale-Pompano Beach, FL (6 percent); Riverside-San Bernardino-Ontario, CA (7 percent); Atlanta-Sandy Springs-Marietta, GA (13 percent); San Francisco-Oakland-Fremont, CA (13 percent); and Washington-Arlington-Alexandria, DC-VA-MD-WV (21 percent).

The proportion of the non-Hispanic Black alone population living inside the largest principal city surpassed 40 percent in all of the northeastern metro areas shown.

Across the northeastern metro areas shown, at least 40 percent of the non-Hispanic Black alone population lived inside their respective largest principal city—New York (61 percent), Philadelphia (53 percent), and Boston (46 percent) (see Figure 7).[22]

In the South, 2 out of the 7 metro areas shown had at least 40 percent of the non-Hispanic Black alone population living inside their respective largest principal city—Baltimore (51 percent) and Houston (49 percent). In the Midwest, this was the case for 2 out of the 4 metro areas shown—Chicago (54 percent) and Detroit (60 percent). In the West, half of the metro areas shown had at least 40 percent of the non-Hispanic Black alone population living inside their largest respective principal city—San Diego (56 percent), Phoenix (45 percent), and Los Angeles (40 percent).

The non-Hispanic Black alone population was more likely to live inside the largest principal cities compared with non-Hispanic White alone, Hispanic, and other race populations.

A higher proportion of the non-Hispanic Black alone population lived inside the largest principal cities in 15 out of the 20 largest metro areas, relative to the non-Hispanic White alone, Hispanic, and other race populations (see Figure 7). This was most pronounced in the metro areas of Detroit-Warren-Livonia, MI, and Baltimore-Towson, MD, where the proportion of the non-Hispanic Black alone population living in the largest principal city surpassed the second largest group, Hispanics, by 30 percentage points.

Metro areas that had a lower proportion of the non-Hispanic Black alone population living inside their largest principal city, relative to the Hispanic and other race group populations, were primarily located in the West—the metro areas of Phoenix-Mesa-Glendale, AZ; Riverside-San Bernardino-Ontario, CA; San Diego-Carlsbad-San Marcos, CA; and San Francisco-Oakland-Fremont, CA. However, the metro area with the lowest proportion was Miami-Fort Lauderdale-Pompano Beach, FL, located in the South.

In the metro areas of Miami-Fort Lauderdale-Pompano Beach, FL, and Phoenix-Mesa-Glendale, AZ, a higher proportion of the Hispanic population lived inside the largest principal cities of Miami and Phoenix, relative to the non-Hispanic Black alone population. In the metro area of Riverside-San Bernardino-Ontario, CA, the non-Hispanic Black alone population had the lowest proportion living

inside the city of Riverside, relative to the other groups shown.

In the metro area of San Diego-Carlsbad-San Marcos, CA, the other race category had a slightly higher proportion living in the city of San Diego relative to the non-Hispanic Black alone population. In the metro area of San Francisco-Oakland-Fremont, CA, both the other race category and the non-Hispanic White alone population had a higher proportion living in the city of San Francisco relative to the non-Hispanic Black alone population.

The proportion of the non-Hispanic Black alone population living inside the largest principal cities within the 20 largest metro areas decreased over the last decade.

Figure 8 shows the percentage-point difference of a race or Hispanic origin group living inside the largest principal city in a metro area, from 2000 to 2010.[23] The red bars represent the non-Hispanic Black alone population, the blue bars represent the non-Hispanic White alone population, the green bars represent the Hispanic population, and the orange bars represent other race groups. For example, in the Boston-Cambridge-Quincy, MA-NH metro area, 57 percent of the non-Hispanic Black alone population lived in the largest principal city, Boston, in 2000. This figure decreased to 46 percent in 2010, representing a decline of 11 percentage points, which is denoted by the red bar.

Across the 20 largest metro areas in the United States, the non-Hispanic Black alone population declined in the largest principal

---

[22] The Philadelphia-Camden-Wilmington, PA-NJ-DE-MD metro area contains counties that are also part of the South region as defined by the U.S. Census Bureau.

[23] Data for the metro areas are based on the 2010 Census boundaries.

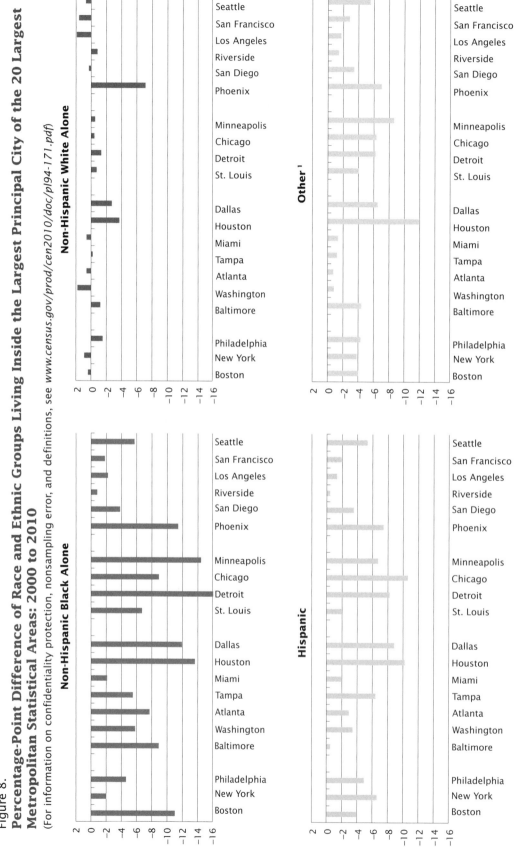

Figure 8.
Percentage-Point Difference of Race and Ethnic Groups Living Inside the Largest Principal City of the 20 Largest Metropolitan Statistical Areas: 2000 to 2010

(For information on confidentiality protection, nonsampling error, and definitions, see *www.census.gov/prod/cen2010/doc/pl94-171.pdf*)

[1] For this figure, the "other" race category refers to the non-Hispanic Asian alone, non-Hispanic American Indian and Alaska Native alone, non-Hispanic Native Hawaiian and Other Pacific Islander alone, and non-Hispanic Some Other Race alone populations, as well as non-Hispanics who reported multiple races.

Note: Principal cities within regions are organized based on proximity to each other. Boston, New York, and Philadelphia are located in the Northeast census region. Baltimore, Washington, Atlanta, Tampa, Miami, Houston, and Dallas are located in the South census region. St. Louis, Detroit, Chicago, and Minneapolis are located in the Midwest census region. Phoenix, San Diego, Riverside, Los Angeles, San Francisco, and Seattle are located in the West census region.

Source: U.S. Census Bureau, 2010 Census special tabulation.

cities and increased outside of these cities from 2000 to 2010. This largely follows the trend of the total population in these metro areas, where the proportion of the total population living inside the largest principal city within a metro area declined in 19 out of the 20 largest metro areas and increased as a proportion outside the largest principal cities from 2000 to 2010. The metro area of Boston-Cambridge-Quincy, MA-NH, was the only metro area that experienced an increase in the proportion of the total population living inside the city of Boston.

The proportion of the non-Hispanic Black alone population in the largest principal cities decreased by at least 10 percentage points in six metro areas from 2000 to 2010, Detroit-Warren-Livonia, MI (16 percentage points); Minneapolis-St. Paul-Bloomington, MN-WI (14 percentage points); Houston-Sugar Land-Baytown, TX (14 percentage points); Dallas-Fort Worth-Arlington, TX (12 percentage points); Phoenix-Mesa-Glendale, AZ (11 percentage points); and Boston-Cambridge-Quincy, MA-NH (11 percentage points).

Among the 20 largest metro areas, the proportion of the non-Hispanic Black alone population living inside the largest principal cities declined by at least 7 percentage points across all midwestern metro areas.

The proportion of the non-Hispanic Black alone population living inside the largest principal cities across midwestern metro areas declined by at least 7 percentage points from 2000 to 2010. The largest change was in the Detroit-Warren-Livonia, MI metro area, where the proportion of the non-Hispanic Black alone population living inside the city of Detroit versus outside

the city decreased by 16 percentage points. This was followed by Minneapolis-St. Paul-Bloomington, MN-WI (14 percentage points); Chicago-Joliet-Naperville, IL-IN-WI (9 percentage points); and St. Louis, MO-IL (7 percentage points).

In the Northeast, the proportion of the non-Hispanic Black alone population living inside the largest principal city declined by at least 7 percentage points in 1 out of the 3 metro areas, Boston-Cambridge-Quincy, MA-NH (11 percentage points). In the South, 4 of the 7 metro areas experienced a decline of at least 7 percentage points— Houston-Sugar Land-Baytown, TX (14 percentage points); Dallas-Fort Worth-Arlington, TX (12 percentage points); Baltimore-Towson, MD (9 percentage points); and Atlanta-Sandy Springs-Marietta, GA (8 percentage points).

The non-Hispanic Black alone population experienced the greatest decline in the proportion living inside the largest principal city for 14 of the 20 largest metro areas.

The proportion of the non-Hispanic Black alone population living inside the largest principal city declined more than the proportion of other race and ethnic groups that also experienced decreases in the largest principal cities in 14 out of the 20 metro areas. In the metro areas of New York-Northern New Jersey-Long Island, NY-NJ-PA; Philadelphia-Camden-Wilmington, PA-NJ-DE-MD; Tampa-St. Petersburg-Clearwater, FL; and Chicago-Joliet-Naperville, IL-IN-WI; the Hispanic population experienced the greatest declines compared to all groups shown. In the metro areas of Riverside-San Bernardino-Ontario, CA, and San Francisco-Oakland-Fremont, CA, the other race category experienced the greatest declines relative to all groups shown.

Although not as sweeping as the decline in the proportion of the non-Hispanic Black alone population living inside the largest principal cities of most major metro areas, the proportion of the Hispanic population and other race group populations living inside the largest principal city also declined in all of the 20 largest metro areas (see Figure 8). On the other hand, in about half of the largest metro areas, the proportion of the non-Hispanic White alone population living inside the largest principal city increased.

SUMMARY

This report provided a portrait of the Black population in the United States and contributes to our understanding of the nation's changing racial and ethnic diversity.

While both the Black alone population and the Black alone-or-in-combination population grew from 2000 to 2010 (by 12 percent and 15 percent, respectively), the Black in combination population experienced the most growth, increasing by 76 percent. Within this population, the Black *and* White population more than doubled.

Additional notable trends were presented in this report. The Black population continued to be concentrated in the South and the proportion increased from 2000 to 2010. Additionally, the Black population that lived outside of the South tended to be more concentrated in metro areas.

Other interesting geographic patterns include, for the largest 20 metro areas, the non-Hispanic Black alone population was more likely to live in a largest principal city relative to the non-Hispanic White alone, Hispanic, and other race group populations in 2010. The non-Hispanic Black alone population also experienced the greatest declines in the proportion living in a largest principal city from 2000 to 2010.

Throughout the decade, the Census Bureau will release additional information on the Black population, including characteristics such as age, sex, and family type, which will provide greater insights into the demographic characteristics of this population at various geographic levels.

ABOUT THE 2010 CENSUS

Why was the 2010 Census conducted?

The U.S. Constitution mandates that a census be taken in the United States every 10 years. This is required in order to determine the number of seats each state is to receive in the U.S. House of Representatives.

Why did the 2010 Census ask the question on race?

The Census Bureau collects data on race to fulfill a variety of legislative and program requirements. Data on race are used in the legislative redistricting process carried out by the states and in monitoring local jurisdictions' compliance with the Voting Rights Act. More broadly, data on race are critical for research that underlies many policy decisions at all levels of government.

How do data from the question on race benefit me, my family, and my community?

All levels of government need information on race to implement and evaluate programs, or enforce laws, such as the Civil Rights Act, Voting Rights Act, Fair Housing Act, Equal Employment Opportunity Act, and the 2010 Census Redistricting Data Program.

Both public and private organizations use race information to find areas where groups may need special services and to plan and implement education, housing, health, and other programs that address these needs. For example, a school system might use this information to design cultural activities that reflect the diversity in their community, or a business could use it to select the mix of merchandise it will sell in a new store. Census information also helps identify areas where residents might need services of particular importance to certain racial groups, such as screening for hypertension or diabetes.

FOR MORE INFORMATION

For more information on race in the United States, visit the Census Bureau's Internet site at <www.census.gov/population /www/socdemo/race/race.html>.

Information on confidentiality protection, nonsampling error, and definitions is available at <www.census.gov/prod/cen2010 /doc/pl94-171.pdf>.

Data on race from the *2010 Census Redistricting Data (Public Law 94-171) Summary File* were released on a state-by-state basis. The 2010 Census redistricting data are available on the Internet at <http://factfinder2 .census.gov/main.html> and on DVD.

For more information on specific race groups in the United States, go to <www.census.gov> and search for "Minority Links." This Web page includes information about the 2010 Census and provides links to reports based on past censuses and surveys focusing on the social and economic characteristics of the Black or African American, American Indian and Alaska Native, Asian, and Native Hawaiian and Other Pacific Islander populations.

Information on other population and housing topics is presented in the 2010 Census Briefs series, located on the Census Bureau's Web site at <www.census.gov/prod /cen2010>. This series presents information about race, Hispanic origin, age, sex, household type, housing tenure, and people who reside in group quarters.

For more information about the 2010 Census, including data products, call the Customer Services Center at 1-800-923-8282. You can also visit the Census Bureau's Question and Answer Center at <ask.census.gov> to submit your questions online.

Black (African-American) History Month: February 2016

To commemorate and celebrate the contributions to our nation made by people of African descent, American historian Carter G. Woodson established Black History Week. The first celebration occurred on Feb. 12, 1926. For many years, the second week of February was set aside for this celebration to coincide with the birthdays of abolitionist/editor Frederick Douglass and Abraham Lincoln. In 1976, as part of the nation's bicentennial, the week was expanded into Black History Month. Each year, U.S. presidents proclaim February as National African-American History Month.

Note: The reference to the black population in this publication is to single-race blacks ("black alone") except in the first section on "Population." In that section the reference is to black alone or in combination with other races; a reference to respondents who said they were one race (black) or more than one race (black plus other races).

Population

45.7 million
The number of blacks, either alone or in combination with one or more other races, on July 1, 2014, up 1.3 percent from July 1, 2013.
Source: 2014 Population Estimates
<http://factfinder.census.gov/bkmk/table/1.0/en/PEP/2014/PEPSR5H?slice=Year~est72014>

74.5 million
The projected black, either alone or in combination, population of the United States (including those of more than one race) for July 1, 2060. On that date, according to the projection, blacks would constitute 17.9 percent of the nation's total population.
Source: 2014 Population Projections, Table 10
<http://www.census.gov/population/projections/data/national/2014/summarytables.html>

3.8 million
The black population in New York, which led all states as of July 1, 2014. Texas had the largest numeric increase since 2013 (88,000). The District of Columbia had the highest percentage of blacks (50.6 percent), followed by Mississippi (38.2 percent).
Source: 2014 Population Estimates
<http://www.census.gov/newsroom/press-releases/2015/cb15-113.html>

1.3 million
Cook County, Ill. (Chicago) had the largest black population of any county in 2014 (1.3 million), and Harris, Texas (Houston) had the largest numeric increase since 2014 (21,000). Holmes, Miss., was the county with the highest percentage of blacks in the nation (82.5 percent).
Source: 2014 Population Estimates
<http://www.census.gov/newsroom/press-releases/2015/cb15-113.html>

Businesses

2.6 million
The number of black-owned firms nationally in 2012, up from 1.9 million or 34.5 percent from 2007.
Source: 2012 Survey of Business Owners-Black or African American Owned Firms: 2012
<http://census.gov/newsroom/press-releases/2015/cb15-209.html>

649,896
The number of African-American/black-owned firms in "other services"— which includes repair and maintenance (automotive, consumer electronics, etc.) and personal/laundry services (hair/nail salons, dry cleaning, pet care) — the largest sector of black-owned businesses. The "other services" sector is followed by health care and social assistance (492,983 black-owned firms); administrative, support, waste management and remediation (294,977); professional, scientific and technical support (206,942); and transportation and warehousing (184,777).
Source: 2012 Survey of Business Owners-Black or African American Owned Firms: 2012
<http://factfinder.census.gov/bkmk/table/1.0/en/SBO/2012/00CSA01/0100000US>

Serving Our Nation

2.2 million
Number of black military veterans in the United States in 2014.
Source: 2014 American Community Survey
<http://factfinder.census.gov/bkmk/table/1.0/en/ACS/14_1YR/C21001B>

Education

84.4%
The percentage of blacks 25 and over with a high school diploma or higher in 2014.
Source: 2014 American Community Survey
<http://factfinder.census.gov/bkmk/table/1.0/en/ACS/14_1YR/S0201//popgroup~004>

19.7%
The percentage of blacks 25 and over who had a bachelor's degree or higher in 2014.
Source: 2014 American Community Survey
<http://factfinder.census.gov/bkmk/table/1.0/en/ACS/14_1YR/S0201//popgroup~004>

1.8 million
Among blacks 25 and over, the number who had an advanced degree in 2014.
Source: 2014 American Community Survey
<http://factfinder.census.gov/bkmk/table/1.0/en/ACS/14_1YR/B15002B>

2.9 million
Number of blacks enrolled in undergraduate college in 2014 compared with 2.8 million in 2009, a 5.3 percent increase.

Source: 2009 and 2014 American Community Survey
<http://factfinder.census.gov/bkmk/table/1.0/en/ACS/14_1YR/B14007B>
<http://factfinder2.census.gov/bkmk/table/1.0/en/ACS/09_1YR/B14007B>

Voting

17.8 million

The number of blacks who voted in the 2012 presidential election. In comparison to the 2008
election, about 1.7 million additional black voters reported going to the polls in 2012.
Source: The Diversifying Electorate — Voting Rates by Race and Hispanic Origin 2012
<http://www.census.gov/prod/2013pubs/p20-568.pdf>

66.2%

Percent of blacks who voted in the 2012 presidential election, higher than the 64.1 percent of
non-Hispanic whites who did so. This marks the first time that blacks have voted at a higher rate
than whites since the Census Bureau started publishing statistics on voting by the eligible citizen
population in 1996.
Source: The Diversifying Electorate — Voting Rates by Race and Hispanic Origin 2012
<http://www.census.gov/prod/2013pubs/p20-568.pdf>

Income, Poverty and Health Insurance

$35,398

The annual median income of black households in 2014, compared with the nation at $53,657.
Source: U.S. Census Bureau, Income and Poverty in the United States: 2014
<http://www.census.gov/content/dam/Census/library/publications/2015/demo/p60-252.pdf>

26.2

Poverty rate in 2014 for blacks, while nationally it was 14.8 percent.
Source: U.S. Census Bureau, Income and Poverty in the United States: 2014
<http://www.census.gov/content/dam/Census/library/publications/2015/demo/p60-252.pdf>

88.2%

Percentage of blacks that were covered by health insurance during all or part of 2014. Nationally,
89.6 percent of all races were covered by health insurance.
Source: U.S. Census Bureau, Health Insurance Coverage in the United States: 2014
<http://www.census.gov/content/dam/Census/library/publications/2015/demo/p60-253.pdf>

Families and Children

61.3%

Among households with a black householder, the percentage that contained a family in 2014.
There were 9.9 million black family households.

Source: 2014 Current Population Survey, Families and Living Arrangements, Table H1
<http://www.census.gov/hhes/families/data/cps2014H.html>

50.0%

Among families with black householders, the percentage that were married couples in 2014.
Source: 2014 Current Population Survey, Families and Living Arrangements, Table H1
<http://www.census.gov/hhes/families/data/cps2014H.html>

1.2 million

Number of black grandparents who lived with their own grandchildren younger than 18 in 2014.
Of this number, 44.0 percent were also responsible for their care.
Source: 2014 American Community Survey
<http://factfinder.census.gov/bkmk/table/1.0/en/ACS/14_1YR/B10051B>

Jobs

28.6%

The percentage of civilian employed blacks 16 and over who worked in management, business, science and arts occupations, while 36.9 percent of the total civilian employed population worked in these occupations.
Source: 2014 American Community Survey
<http://factfinder.census.gov/bkmk/table/1.0/en/ACS/14_1YR/S0201//popgroup~004>
<http://factfinder.census.gov/bkmk/table/1.0/en/ACS/14_1YR/S0201>

The following is a list of observances typically covered by the Census Bureau's *Facts for Features* series:

African-American History Month (February)
Super Bowl
Valentine's Day (Feb. 14)
Women's History Month (March)
Irish-American Heritage Month (March)/
     St. Patrick's Day (March 17)
Earth Day (April 22)
Asian/Pacific American Heritage Month (May)
Older Americans Month (May)
Mother's Day
Hurricane Season Begins (June 1)
Father's Day
The Fourth of July (July 4)
Anniversary of Americans With Disabilities Act (July 26)
Back to School (August)
Labor Day
Grandparents Day
Hispanic Heritage Month (Sept. 15-Oct. 15)
Unmarried and Single Americans Week
Halloween (Oct. 31)
American Indian/Alaska Native Heritage Month (November)
Veterans Day (Nov. 11)
Thanksgiving Day
The Holiday Season (December)

Editor's note: The preceding data were collected from a variety of sources and may be subject to sampling variability and other sources of error. Facts for Features are customarily released about two months before an observance in order to accommodate magazine production timelines.

-X-

Public Information Office
301-763-3030 / pio@census.gov

census.gov
Connect with us on Social media

FURTHER READING

Allen, William Francis, Charles Pickard, Lucy Ware, and Garrison McKim. University of North Carolina at Chapel Hill. Documenting the American South (Project), and University of North Carolina at Chapel Hill. Library. *Slave Songs of the United States*. Chapel Hill: U of North Carolina, 2011. Print.

Allen, Zita. *Black Women Leaders of the Civil Rights Movement*. Danbury, Conn.: Franklin Watts, 1996. Print.

Bates, Beth Tompkins. *Pullman Porters and the Rise of Protest Politics in Black America, 1925-1945*. Chapel Hill: U of North Carolina, 2001. Print.

Boyd, Todd. *African Americans and Popular Culture*. Westport, CT: Praeger, 2008. Print.

Bracks, Lean'tin L. *The Complete Encyclopedia of African American History*. Chalfont, PA: African American Publications, 2014. Print.

Bynum, Thomas L. *NAACP Youth and the Fight for Black Freedom*. Knoxville: U of Tennessee, 2013. Print.

Chalk, Ocania. *Pioneers of Black Sport: The Early Days of the Black Professional Athlete in Baseball, Basketball, Boxing, and Football*. New York: Dodd, Mead, 1975. Print.

Christofferson, Bill. *The Man from Clear Lake Earth Day Founder Senator Gaylord Nelson*. Madison, Wis.: U of Wisconsin, 2004. Print.

Clinton, George, and Ben Greenman. *Brothers Be "yo like George, Ain't That Funkin' Kinda Hard on You?": A Memoir*. New York: Atria, 2014. Print.

Clotfelter, Charles T. *After Brown: The Rise and Retreat of School Desegregation*. Princeton, N.J.: Princeton UP, 2004. Print.

Coleman, J. F B. *Tuskegee to Voorhees: The Booker T. Washington Idea Projected by Elizabeth Evelyn Wright*. [Columbia, S.C.]: [R.L. Bryan], 1922. Print.

Daniels, Douglas Henry. *One O'clock Jump: The Unforgettable History of the Oklahoma City Blue Devils*. Boston: Beacon, 2006. Print.

Danticat, Edwidge. *Create Dangerously: The Immigrant Artist at Work*. New York: Vintage, 2011. Print.

Du, Bois W E B, David W. Blight, and Robert Gooding-Williams. *The Souls of Black Folk*. Boston: Bedford, 1997. Print.

Eldridge, Lawrence Allen. *Chronicles of a Two-front War Civil Rights and Vietnam in the African American Press*. Columbia, MO: U of Missouri, 2011. Print.

Finkelman, Paul. *Encyclopedia of African American History, 1896 to the Present: From the Age of Segregation to the Twenty-first Century*. New York: Oxford UP, 2009. Print.

Gates, Henry Louis,, Evelyn Brooks, Higginbotham, and W.E.B. Du Bois Institute for Afro-American Research. *African American Lives*. New York: Oxford UP, 2004. Print.

Gates, Henry Louis. *Life upon These Shores: Looking at African American History, 1513-2008*. New York: Alfred A. Knopf, 2011. Print.

Gelernter, David Hillel. *1939, the Lost World of the Fair*. New York: Free, 1995. Print.

Goins, Wayne E., and Craig R. McKinney. *A Biography of Charlie Christian, Jazz Guitar's King of Swing*. Lewiston, N.Y.: Edwin Mellen, 2005. Print.

Grant, Alice. *Fashion Magazines from the 1890s to the 1980s: An Account Based on the Holdings of the National Art Library*. [London]: National Art Library, 1988. Print.

Handy, D. Antoinette. *The International Sweethearts of Rhythm*. Metuchen, N.J.: Scarecrow, 1983. Print.

Howard, L. O., United States. Division of Entomology., and United States. Department of Agriculture. *Remedial Work against the Mexican Cotton-boll Weevil*. Washington, D.C.: U.S. Dept. of Agriculture, Division of Entomology, 1898. Print.

Kaplan, Victoria. *Structural Inequality: Black Architects in the United States*. Lanham, Md.: Rowman & Littlefield, 2006. Print.

Kennedy, Randall. *Interracial Intimacies: Sex, Marriage, Identity, and Adoption*. New York: Pantheon, 2003. Print.

Kernodle, Tammy L. *Soul on Soul: The Life and Music of Mary Lou Williams*. Boston: Northeastern UP, 2004. Print.

Kirwin, Bill. *Out of the Shadow: African American Baseball from the Cuban Giants to Jackie Robinson*. Lincoln: U of Nebraska, 2005. Print.

Klarman, Michael J. *Unfinished Business: Racial Equality in American History*. New York: Oxford UP, 2007. Print.

Medina, Tony, Samiya A. Bashir, and Quraysh Ali Lansana. *Role Call: A Generational Anthology of Social and Political Black Art & Literature*. N.p., 2002. Print.

Moye, J. Todd. *Freedom Flyers: The Tuskegee Airmen of World War II*. New York: Oxford UP, 2010. Print. Oxford Oral Ser.

Nelson, H. Viscount, Jr. *Sharecropping, Ghetto, Slum A History of Impoverished Blacks in Twentieth-century America*. N.p.: Xlibris, 2015. Print.

Nieves, Angel David. *"We Gave Our Hearts and Lives to It": African-American Women Reformers, Industrial Education, and the Monuments of Nation-building in the Post-Reconstruction South, 1877-1938*. Ithica, NY: Cornell U, 2001. Print.

Northrup, Cynthia Clark. *The American Economy: A Historical Encyclopedia*. Santa Barbara, Calif.: ABC-CLIO, 2011. Print.

Ogbar, Jeffrey Ogbonna Green. *Hip-hop Revolution: The Culture and Politics of Rap*. Lawrence: U of Kansas, 2007. Print.

Ottley, Roi, and Mark A. Huddle. *Roi Ottley's World War II: The Lost Diary of an African American Journalist*. Lawrence, Kan.: U of Kansas, 2011. Print.

Owens, Jesse, and Paul G. Neimark. *Jesse: The Man Who Outran Hitler*. New York: Ballantine, 1979. Print.

Roll, Jarod Heath. *Road to the Promised Land: Rural Rebellion in the New Cotton South, 1890-1945*. Thesis. Northwestern University, 2006. N.p.: Dissertation Abstracts International, 67-08A, 2006. *WorldCat [OCLC]*. Web.

Schaap, Jeremy. *Triumph: The Untold Story of Jesse Owens and Hitler's Olympics*. Boston: Houghton Mifflin, 2007. Print.

Smith, Jessie Carney,, Millicent Lownes Jackson, and Linda T. Wynn. Westport, CT: Greenwood, 2006. Print.

Snyder, Brad. *A Well-paid Slave: Curt Flood's Fight for Free Agency in Professional Sports*. New York: Viking, 2006. Print.

Stone, A. "Green Wave: The Banatao Brothers Want to Clean up Surfing by Building Boards with Nontoxic Materials." *FORBES* 182.3 (2008): 58-61. Print.

Tischauser, Leslie Vincent. *Jim Crow Laws*. Santa Barbara, CA: Greenwood, 2012. Print. Landmarks of the American Mosaic.

Tussman, Joseph, and United States. Supreme Court. *The Supreme Court on Racial Discrimination*. New York: Oxford UP, 1963. Print.

Warner, Jay. *Just Walkin' in the Rain*. Los Angeles: Renaissance, 2001. Print.

Washington, Booker T. *Teamwork: Dr. Booker T. Washington's Last Sunday Evening Talk to the Teachers and Students, Institute Chapel, October 17, 1915.* [Tuskegee, Ala.]: Tuskeegee Normal and Industrial Institute, 1941. Print.

Washington, Booker T. *Up from Slavery: An Autobiography*. New York: A.L. Burt, 1901. Print.

Wiggins, David Kenneth,, and Patrick B. Miller. *The Unlevel Playing Field: A Documentary History of the African American Experience in Sport*. Urbana: U of Illinois, 2003. Print.

Williams, Chad Louis. *Torchbearers of Democracy: African American Soldiers in the World War I Era*. Chapel Hill: U of North Carolina, 2010. Print.

Zim, Larry, Mel Lerner, and Herbert Rolfes. *The World of Tomorrow: The 1939 New York World's Fair*. New York: Harper & Row, 1988. Print.

INDEX

B

2016 Title List
Visit www.GreyHouse.com for Product Information, Table of Contents, and Sample Pages.

General Reference
An African Biographical Dictionary
America's College Museums
American Environmental Leaders: From Colonial Times to the Present
Encyclopedia of African-American Writing
Encyclopedia of Constitutional Amendments
Encyclopedia of Gun Control & Gun Rights
An Encyclopedia of Human Rights in the United States
Encyclopedia of Invasions & Conquests
Encyclopedia of Prisoners of War & Internment
Encyclopedia of Religion & Law in America
Encyclopedia of Rural America
Encyclopedia of the Continental Congress
Encyclopedia of the United States Cabinet, 1789-2010
Encyclopedia of War Journalism
Encyclopedia of Warrior Peoples & Fighting Groups
The Environmental Debate: A Documentary History
The Evolution Wars: A Guide to the Debates
From Suffrage to the Senate: America's Political Women
Global Terror & Political Risk Assessment
Nations of the World
Political Corruption in America
Privacy Rights in the Digital Era
The Religious Right: A Reference Handbook
Speakers of the House of Representatives, 1789-2009
This is Who We Were: 1880-1900
This is Who We Were: A Companion to the 1940 Census
This is Who We Were: In the 1910s
This is Who We Were: In the 1920s
This is Who We Were: In the 1940s
This is Who We Were: In the 1950s
This is Who We Were: In the 1960s
This is Who We Were: In the 1970s
U.S. Land & Natural Resource Policy
The Value of a Dollar 1600-1865: Colonial Era to the Civil War
The Value of a Dollar: 1860-2014
Working Americans 1770-1869 Vol. IX: Revolutionary War to the Civil War
Working Americans 1880-1999 Vol. I: The Working Class
Working Americans 1880-1999 Vol. II: The Middle Class
Working Americans 1880-1999 Vol. III: The Upper Class
Working Americans 1880-1999 Vol. IV: Their Children
Working Americans 1880-2015 Vol. V: Americans At War
Working Americans 1880-2005 Vol. VI: Women at Work
Working Americans 1880-2006 Vol. VII: Social Movements
Working Americans 1880-2007 Vol. VIII: Immigrants
Working Americans 1880-2009 Vol. X: Sports & Recreation
Working Americans 1880-2010 Vol. XI: Inventors & Entrepreneurs
Working Americans 1880-2011 Vol. XII: Our History through Music
Working Americans 1880-2012 Vol. XIII: Education & Educators
World Cultural Leaders of the 20th & 21st Centuries

Education Information
Charter School Movement
Comparative Guide to American Elementary & Secondary Schools
Complete Learning Disabilities Directory
Educators Resource Directory
Special Education: A Reference Book for Policy and Curriculum Development

Health Information
Comparative Guide to American Hospitals
Complete Directory for Pediatric Disorders
Complete Directory for People with Chronic Illness
Complete Directory for People with Disabilities
Complete Mental Health Directory
Diabetes in America: Analysis of an Epidemic
Directory of Drug & Alcohol Residential Rehab Facilities
Directory of Health Care Group Purchasing Organizations
Directory of Hospital Personnel
HMO/PPO Directory
Medical Device Register
Older Americans Information Directory

Business Information
Complete Television, Radio & Cable Industry Directory
Directory of Business Information Resources
Directory of Mail Order Catalogs
Directory of Venture Capital & Private Equity Firms
Environmental Resource Handbook
Food & Beverage Market Place
Grey House Homeland Security Directory
Grey House Performing Arts Directory
Grey House Safety & Security Directory
Grey House Transportation Security Directory
Hudson's Washington News Media Contacts Directory
New York State Directory
Rauch Market Research Guides
Sports Market Place Directory

Statistics & Demographics
American Tally
America's Top-Rated Cities
America's Top-Rated Smaller Cities
America's Top-Rated Small Towns & Cities
Ancestry & Ethnicity in America
The Asian Databook
Comparative Guide to American Suburbs
The Hispanic Databook
Profiles of America
"Profiles of" Series – State Handbooks
Weather America

Financial Ratings Series
TheStreet Ratings' Guide to Bond & Money Market Mutual Funds
TheStreet Ratings' Guide to Common Stocks
TheStreet Ratings' Guide to Exchange-Traded Funds
TheStreet Ratings' Guide to Stock Mutual Funds
TheStreet Ratings' Ultimate Guided Tour of Stock Investing
Weiss Ratings' Consumer Guides
Weiss Ratings' Guide to Banks
Weiss Ratings' Guide to Credit Unions
Weiss Ratings' Guide to Health Insurers
Weiss Ratings' Guide to Life & Annuity Insurers
Weiss Ratings' Guide to Property & Casualty Insurers

Bowker's Books In Print® Titles
American Book Publishing Record® Annual
American Book Publishing Record® Monthly
Books In Print®
Books In Print® Supplement
Books Out Loud™
Bowker's Complete Video Directory™
Children's Books In Print®
El-Hi Textbooks & Serials In Print®
Forthcoming Books®
Large Print Books & Serials™
Law Books & Serials In Print™
Medical & Health Care Books In Print™
Publishers, Distributors & Wholesalers of the US™
Subject Guide to Books In Print®
Subject Guide to Children's Books In Print®

Canadian General Reference
Associations Canada
Canadian Almanac & Directory
Canadian Environmental Resource Guide
Canadian Parliamentary Guide
Canadian Venture Capital & Private Equity Firms
Financial Post Directory of Directors
Financial Services Canada
Governments Canada
Health Guide Canada
The History of Canada
Libraries Canada
Major Canadian Cities

2016 Title List

Visit www.SalemPress.com for Product Information, Table of Contents, and Sample Pages.

Science, Careers & Mathematics

Ancient Creatures
Applied Science
Applied Science: Engineering & Mathematics
Applied Science: Science & Medicine
Applied Science: Technology
Biomes and Ecosystems
Careers in Building Construction
Careers in Business
Careers in Chemistry
Careers in Communications & Media
Careers in Environment & Conservation
Careers in Healthcare
Careers in Hospitality & Tourism
Careers in Human Services
Careers in Law, Criminal Justice & Emergency Services
Careers in Manufacturing
Careers in Physics
Careers in Sales, Insurance & Real Estate
Careers in Science & Engineering
Careers in Technology Services & Repair
Computer Technology Innovators
Contemporary Biographies in Business
Contemporary Biographies in Chemistry
Contemporary Biographies in Communications & Media
Contemporary Biographies in Environment & Conservation
Contemporary Biographies in Healthcare
Contemporary Biographies in Hospitality & Tourism
Contemporary Biographies in Law & Criminal Justice
Contemporary Biographies in Physics
Earth Science
Earth Science: Earth Materials & Resources
Earth Science: Earth's Surface and History
Earth Science: Physics & Chemistry of the Earth
Earth Science: Weather, Water & Atmosphere
Encyclopedia of Energy
Encyclopedia of Environmental Issues
Encyclopedia of Environmental Issues: Atmosphere and Air Pollution
Encyclopedia of Environmental Issues: Ecology and Ecosystems
Encyclopedia of Environmental Issues: Energy and Energy Use
Encyclopedia of Environmental Issues: Policy and Activism
Encyclopedia of Environmental Issues: Preservation/Wilderness Issues
Encyclopedia of Environmental Issues: Water and Water Pollution
Encyclopedia of Global Resources
Encyclopedia of Global Warming
Encyclopedia of Mathematics & Society
Encyclopedia of Mathematics & Society: Engineering, Tech, Medicine
Encyclopedia of Mathematics & Society: Great Mathematicians
Encyclopedia of Mathematics & Society: Math & Social Sciences
Encyclopedia of Mathematics & Society: Math Development/Concepts
Encyclopedia of Mathematics & Society: Math in Culture & Society
Encyclopedia of Mathematics & Society: Space, Science, Environment
Encyclopedia of the Ancient World
Forensic Science
Geography Basics
Internet Innovators
Inventions and Inventors
Magill's Encyclopedia of Science: Animal Life
Magill's Encyclopedia of Science: Plant life
Notable Natural Disasters
Principles of Astronomy
Principles of Chemistry
Principles of Physics
Science and Scientists
Solar System
Solar System: Great Astronomers
Solar System: Study of the Universe
Solar System: The Inner Planets
Solar System: The Moon and Other Small Bodies
Solar System: The Outer Planets
Solar System: The Sun and Other Stars
World Geography

Literature

American Ethnic Writers
Classics of Science Fiction & Fantasy Literature
Critical Insights: Authors
Critical Insights: Film
Critical Insights: Literary Collection Bundles
Critical Insights: Themes
Critical Insights: Works
Critical Survey of Drama
Critical Survey of Graphic Novels: Heroes & Super Heroes
Critical Survey of Graphic Novels: History, Theme & Technique
Critical Survey of Graphic Novels: Independents/Underground Classics
Critical Survey of Graphic Novels: Manga
Critical Survey of Long Fiction
Critical Survey of Mystery & Detective Fiction
Critical Survey of Mythology and Folklore: Heroes and Heroines
Critical Survey of Mythology and Folklore: Love, Sexuality & Desire
Critical Survey of Mythology and Folklore: World Mythology
Critical Survey of Poetry
Critical Survey of Poetry: American Poets
Critical Survey of Poetry: British, Irish & Commonwealth Poets
Critical Survey of Poetry: Cumulative Index
Critical Survey of Poetry: European Poets
Critical Survey of Poetry: Topical Essays
Critical Survey of Poetry: World Poets
Critical Survey of Shakespeare's Plays
Critical Survey of Shakespeare's Sonnets
Critical Survey of Short Fiction
Critical Survey of Short Fiction: American Writers
Critical Survey of Short Fiction: British, Irish, Commonwealth Writers
Critical Survey of Short Fiction: Cumulative Index
Critical Survey of Short Fiction: European Writers
Critical Survey of Short Fiction: Topical Essays
Critical Survey of Short Fiction: World Writers
Critical Survey of Young Adult Literature
Cyclopedia of Literary Characters
Cyclopedia of Literary Places
Holocaust Literature
Introduction to Literary Context: American Poetry of the 20th Century
Introduction to Literary Context: American Post-Modernist Novels
Introduction to Literary Context: American Short Fiction
Introduction to Literary Context: English Literature
Introduction to Literary Context: Plays
Introduction to Literary Context: World Literature
Magill's Literary Annual 2015
Magill's Survey of American Literature
Magill's Survey of World Literature
Masterplots
Masterplots II: African American Literature
Masterplots II: American Fiction Series
Masterplots II: British & Commonwealth Fiction Series
Masterplots II: Christian Literature
Masterplots II: Drama Series
Masterplots II: Juvenile & Young Adult Literature, Supplement
Masterplots II: Nonfiction Series
Masterplots II: Poetry Series
Masterplots II: Short Story Series
Masterplots II: Women's Literature Series
Notable African American Writers
Notable American Novelists
Notable Playwrights
Notable Poets
Recommended Reading: 600 Classics Reviewed
Short Story Writers

2016 Title List

Visit www.SalemPress.com for Product Information, Table of Contents, and Sample Pages.

History and Social Science

The 2000s in America
50 States
African American History
Agriculture in History
American First Ladies
American Heroes
American Indian Culture
American Indian History
American Indian Tribes
American Presidents
American Villains
America's Historic Sites
Ancient Greece
The Bill of Rights
The Civil Rights Movement
The Cold War
Countries, Peoples & Cultures
Countries, Peoples & Cultures: Central & South America
Countries, Peoples & Cultures: Central, South & Southeast Asia
Countries, Peoples & Cultures: East & South Africa
Countries, Peoples & Cultures: East Asia & the Pacific
Countries, Peoples & Cultures: Eastern Europe
Countries, Peoples & Cultures: Middle East & North Africa
Countries, Peoples & Cultures: North America & the Caribbean
Countries, Peoples & Cultures: West & Central Africa
Countries, Peoples & Cultures: Western Europe
Defining Documents: American Revolution
Defining Documents: Civil Rights
Defining Documents: Civil War
Defining Documents: Emergence of Modern America
Defining Documents: Exploration & Colonial America
Defining Documents: Manifest Destiny
Defining Documents: Postwar 1940s
Defining Documents: Reconstruction
Defining Documents: 1920s
Defining Documents: 1930s
Defining Documents: 1950s
Defining Documents: 1960s
Defining Documents: 1970s
Defining Documents: American West
Defining Documents: Ancient World
Defining Documents: Middle Ages
Defining Documents: Vietnam War
Defining Documents: World War I
Defining Documents: World War II
The Eighties in America
Encyclopedia of American Immigration
Encyclopedia of Flight
Encyclopedia of the Ancient World
Fashion Innovators
The Fifties in America
The Forties in America
Great Athletes
Great Athletes: Baseball
Great Athletes: Basketball
Great Athletes: Boxing & Soccer
Great Athletes: Cumulative Index
Great Athletes: Football
Great Athletes: Golf & Tennis
Great Athletes: Olympics
Great Athletes: Racing & Individual Sports
Great Events from History: 17th Century
Great Events from History: 18th Century
Great Events from History: 19th Century
Great Events from History: 20th Century (1901-1940)
Great Events from History: 20th Century (1941-1970)
Great Events from History: 20th Century (1971-2000)
Great Events from History: Ancient World
Great Events from History: Cumulative Indexes
Great Events from History: Gay, Lesbian, Bisexual, Transgender Events

Great Events from History: Middle Ages
Great Events from History: Modern Scandals
Great Events from History: Renaissance & Early Modern Era
Great Lives from History: 17th Century
Great Lives from History: 18th Century
Great Lives from History: 19th Century
Great Lives from History: 20th Century
Great Lives from History: African Americans
Great Lives from History: American Women
Great Lives from History: Ancient World
Great Lives from History: Asian & Pacific Islander Americans
Great Lives from History: Cumulative Indexes
Great Lives from History: Incredibly Wealthy
Great Lives from History: Inventors & Inventions
Great Lives from History: Jewish Americans
Great Lives from History: Latinos
Great Lives from History: Middle Ages
Great Lives from History: Notorious Lives
Great Lives from History: Renaissance & Early Modern Era
Great Lives from History: Scientists & Science
Historical Encyclopedia of American Business
Issues in U.S. Immigration
Magill's Guide to Military History
Milestone Documents in African American History
Milestone Documents in American History
Milestone Documents in World History
Milestone Documents of American Leaders
Milestone Documents of World Religions
Music Innovators
Musicians & Composers 20th Century
The Nineties in America
The Seventies in America
The Sixties in America
Survey of American Industry and Careers
The Thirties in America
The Twenties in America
United States at War
U.S.A. in Space
U.S. Court Cases
U.S. Government Leaders
U.S. Laws, Acts, and Treaties
U.S. Legal System
U.S. Supreme Court
Weapons and Warfare
World Conflicts: Asia and the Middle East
World Political Yearbook

Health

Addictions & Substance Abuse
Adolescent Health & Wellness
Cancer
Complementary & Alternative Medicine
Genetics & Inherited Conditions
Health Issues
Infectious Diseases & Conditions
Magill's Medical Guide
Psychology & Behavioral Health
Psychology Basics

Grey House Publishing | Salem Press | H.W. Wilson | 4919 Route, 22 PO Box 56, Amenia NY 12501-0056

2016 Title List
Visit www.HWWilsonInPrint.com for Product Information, Table of Contents and Sample Pages

Current Biography
Current Biography Cumulative Index 1946-2013
Current Biography Monthly Magazine
Current Biography Yearbook: 2003
Current Biography Yearbook: 2004
Current Biography Yearbook: 2005
Current Biography Yearbook: 2006
Current Biography Yearbook: 2007
Current Biography Yearbook: 2008
Current Biography Yearbook: 2009
Current Biography Yearbook: 2010
Current Biography Yearbook: 2011
Current Biography Yearbook: 2012
Current Biography Yearbook: 2013
Current Biography Yearbook: 2014
Current Biography Yearbook: 2015

Core Collections
Children's Core Collection
Fiction Core Collection
Graphic Novels Core Collection
Middle & Junior High School Core
Public Library Core Collection: Nonfiction
Senior High Core Collection
Young Adult Fiction Core Collection

The Reference Shelf
Aging in America
American Military Presence Overseas
The Arab Spring
The Brain
The Business of Food
Campaign Trends & Election Law
Conspiracy Theories
The Digital Age
Dinosaurs
Embracing New Paradigms in Education
Faith & Science
Families: Traditional and New Structures
The Future of U.S. Economic Relations: Mexico, Cuba, and Venezuela
Global Climate Change
Graphic Novels and Comic Books
Immigration
Immigration in the U.S.
Internet Safety
Marijuana Reform
The News and its Future
The Paranormal
Politics of the Ocean
Racial Tension in a "Postracial" Age
Reality Television
Representative American Speeches: 2008-2009
Representative American Speeches: 2009-2010
Representative American Speeches: 2010-2011
Representative American Speeches: 2011-2012
Representative American Speeches: 2012-2013
Representative American Speeches: 2013-2014
Representative American Speeches: 2014-2015
Representative American Speeches: 2015-2016
Rethinking Work
Revisiting Gender
Robotics
Russia
Social Networking
Social Services for the Poor
Space Exploration & Development
Sports in America
The Supreme Court
The Transformation of American Cities

U.S. Infrastructure
U.S. National Debate Topic: Surveillance
U.S. National Debate Topic: The Ocean
U.S. National Debate Topic: Transportation Infrastructure
Whistleblowers

Readers' Guide
Abridged Readers' Guide to Periodical Literature
Readers' Guide to Periodical Literature

Indexes
Index to Legal Periodicals & Books
Short Story Index
Book Review Digest

Sears List
Sears List of Subject Headings
Sears: Lista de Encabezamientos de Materia

Facts About Series
Facts About American Immigration
Facts About China
Facts About the 20th Century
Facts About the Presidents
Facts About the World's Languages

Nobel Prize Winners
Nobel Prize Winners: 1901-1986
Nobel Prize Winners: 1987-1991
Nobel Prize Winners: 1992-1996
Nobel Prize Winners: 1997-2001

World Authors
World Authors: 1995-2000
World Authors: 2000-2005

Famous First Facts
Famous First Facts
Famous First Facts About American Politics
Famous First Facts About Sports
Famous First Facts About the Environment
Famous First Facts: International Edition

American Book of Days
The American Book of Days
The International Book of Days

Junior Authors & Illustrators
Eleventh Book of Junior Authors & Illustrations

Monographs
The Barnhart Dictionary of Etymology
Celebrate the World
Guide to the Ancient World
Indexing from A to Z
The Poetry Break
Radical Change: Books for Youth in a Digital Age

Wilson Chronology
Wilson Chronology of Asia and the Pacific
Wilson Chronology of Human Rights
Wilson Chronology of Ideas
Wilson Chronology of the Arts
Wilson Chronology of the World's Religions
Wilson Chronology of Women's Achievements

Grey House Publishing | Salem Press | H.W. Wilson | 4919 Route, 22 PO Box 56, Amenia NY 12501-0056